Collins COBUILD

Key Words for Cambridge English

First

Vocabulary for Cambridge English:
First (FCE) and First for Schools

HarperCollins Publishers
Westerhill Road
Bishopbriggs
Glasgow
G64 2QT

First Edition 2014

Reprint 10 9 8 7 6 5 4 3 2 1 0

© HarperCollins Publishers 2014

ISBN 978-0-00-753599-6

Collins® and COBUILD® are registered
trademarks of HarperCollins Publishers
Limited

www.collinselt.com
www.collinsdictionary.com

A catalogue record for this book is available
from the British Library

Typeset by Davidson Publishing Solutions,
Glasgow

Printed in Great Britain by Clays Ltd,
St Ives plc

Acknowledgements
We would like to thank those authors and
publishers who kindly gave permission for
copyright material to be used in the Collins
Corpus. We would also like to thank Times
Newspapers Ltd for providing valuable data.

EDITORIAL STAFF

Senior editors
Penny Hands
Julie Moore

Project manager
Mary O'Neill

Contributors
Rosalind Combley
Lucy Hollingworth
Laura Wedgeworth

For the publishers
Lucy Cooper
Kerry Ferguson
Sheena Shanks
Lisa Sutherland
Catherine Whitaker
Jennifer Yong

Computing support
Thomas Callan
Agnieszka Urbanowicz
Dave Wark

contents

This book has been created for learners of English who plan to take the *Cambridge English: First* exam (also known as *First Certificate in English* and *FCE*) or *Cambridge English: First for Schools*. It covers the key words and phrases you need to master to get a score that proves you can use everyday written and spoken English for work or study.

The first section of the book contains dictionary-style entries for **key words**. These words regularly appear in the most **common exam topics**, and are clearly labelled by topic area. Vocabulary relating to work and studies has also been included so that you can feel comfortable using English for talking about your school work, your plans for college or university, or preparations for your first job. You will find all the vocabulary you will need when working on writing tasks, such as reports, reviews, and emails.

Each word is illustrated with **examples** of natural English taken from the Collins Corpus and reflects the style of language used in the exam texts. As well as definitions and examples, entries include additional information about **collocations**, as well as **usage notes** to help you put the vocabulary you have learnt into practice.

Words from the same root, for example, *achieve*, *achievement*, *achievable*, are shown together in **Word Family** boxes to help you make these vital **links** between words. By understanding how these words relate to each other, you will be able to vary the way you express your ideas, which will help improve your writing and speaking skills.

There are **synonyms** and **antonyms** at many entries to help you widen your range of vocabulary and create more variety in your writing style. The **Which Word?** boxes help you understand the differences between sets of similar words, so you can be sure that your English is accurate and natural.

After the key words section, you will find a list of **useful phrases**, which provides you with a wide range of phrases that will make your written and spoken English sound natural and fluent.

The last section of the book consists of **word lists** organized by topic area. You can use these lists to help you **revise** sets of vocabulary or when preparing for writing tasks. The words are grouped into **common topics**, such as Media and culture, Hobbies, Sport and activity, and Science and nature.

We hope you enjoy preparing for *Cambridge English: First* and *First for Schools* using this book and that it will help you to not only achieve the score you are aiming for, but equip you for success in the future.

We have used the International Phonetic Alphabet (IPA) to show how the words are pronounced.

IPA Symbols

Vowel Sounds

ɑː	calm, ah
æ	act, mass
aɪ	dive, cry
aɪə	fire, buyer
aʊ	out, down
aʊə	flower, sour
e	met, lend, pen
eɪ	day, weight
eə	bear, where
ɪ	fit, win
iː	feed, me
ɪə	fear, mere
ɒ	lot, spot
əʊ	note, coat
ɔː	claw, maul
ɔɪ	boy, joint
ʊ	could, stood
uː	you, zoo
ʊə	poor, sure
ɜː	burn, learn
ʌ	fund, must
ə	first vowel in about
i	last vowel in happy

Consonant Sounds

b	bed, rub
d	done, red
f	fit, if
g	good, dog
h	hat, horse
j	yellow, you
k	king, pick
l	lip, bill
m	mat, ram
n	not, tin
p	pay, lip
r	run, read
s	soon, bus
t	talk, bet
v	van, love
w	win, wool
z	zoo, buzz
ʃ	ship, wish
ʒ	measure, leisure
ŋ	sing, working
tʃ	cheap, witch
θ	thin, myth
ð	then, bathe
dʒ	joy, bridge

Notes

Primary and secondary stress are shown by marks above and below the line, in front of the stressed syllable. For example, in the word *accommodation*, /əˌkɒməˈdeɪʃən/, the second syllable has secondary stress and the fourth syllable has primary stress.

We do not show pronunciations for compound words (words which are made up of more than one word) if pronunciations for the words that make up the compounds can be found at their entries in other parts of the book. However, these compound words do have stress markers.

Headwords are organized in alphabetical order

Word classes are shown for every meaning of the word

Information boxes help increase your understanding of the word and how to use it

ad|vice /ædˈvaɪs/

UNCOUNTABLE NOUN If you give someone **advice**, you tell them what you think they should do in a particular situation. ○ [+ about] *Don't be afraid to ask for advice about ordering the meal.* ○ [+ on] *Your community officer can give you advice on how to prevent crime in your area.*

▶ COLLOCATIONS:
advice **about/on** *something*
give/offer advice
ask for/seek advice
follow/take *someone's* advice
good/bad advice
expert/legal advice
a **piece of** advice

▶ SYNONYMS: guidance, help

Words from the same root are shown together

> **USAGE**
>
> Note that **advice** is an uncount noun. You can say a **piece of advice** or **some advice**, but you cannot say 'an advice' or 'advices'. ○ *Let me give you a piece of advice; don't trust anyone.*

ad|vise /ædˈvaɪz/ (advises, advising, advised)

VERB If you **advise** someone **to** do something, you tell them what you think they should do. ○ [+ to-inf] *The minister advised him to leave as soon as possible.* ○ [+ against] *I would strongly advise against it.*

Collocations help you put the word into practice

▶ COLLOCATIONS:
advise *someone* **against** *something*
advise *someone* **on** *something*
strongly advise *something*

Labels show common grammatical patterns

> **WORD FAMILY**
>
> | advice | UNCOUNT | ○ *Take my advice and stay away from him!* |
> | advise | VERB | ○ *Doctors advised that he should be transferred to a private room.* |
> | advisor | NOUN | ○ *a careers advisor* ○ *the president and his advisors* |
> | advisable | ADJECTIVE | ○ *It is advisable to book early for city-centre restaurants.* |
> | inadvisable | ADJECTIVE | ○ *He started on a course of action that was highly inadvisable.* |

Word Family boxes help you make links between words from the same root

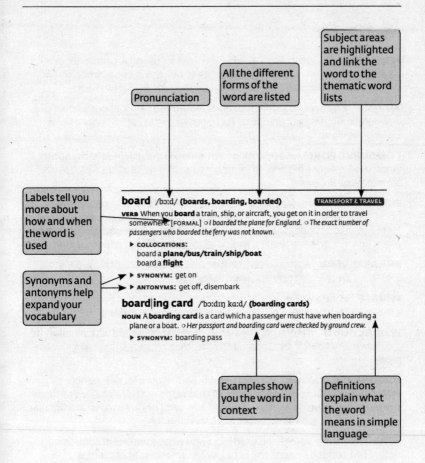

Subject areas are highlighted and link the word to the thematic word lists

All the different forms of the word are listed

Pronunciation

Labels tell you more about how and when the word is used

Synonyms and antonyms help expand your vocabulary

board /bɔːd/ (boards, boarding, boarded)   TRANSPORT & TRAVEL

VERB When you **board** a train, ship, or aircraft, you get on it in order to travel somewhere. [FORMAL] ○ *I boarded the plane for England.* ○ *The exact number of passengers who boarded the ferry was not known.*

▶ **COLLOCATIONS:**
board a **plane/bus/train/ship/boat**
board a **flight**

▶ **SYNONYM:** get on
▶ **ANTONYMS:** get off, disembark

board|ing card /ˈbɔːdɪŋ kɑːd/ (boarding cards)

NOUN A **boarding card** is a card which a passenger must have when boarding a plane or a boat. ○ *Her passport and boarding card were checked by ground crew.*

▶ **SYNONYM:** boarding pass

Examples show you the word in context

Definitions explain what the word means in simple language

Word classes

ADJECTIVE   An adjective is a word that is used for telling you more about a person or thing. You would use an adjective to talk about appearance, colour, size, or other qualities, e.g. *He has been <u>absent</u> from his desk for two weeks*.

ADVERB   An adverb is a word that gives more information about when, how, or where something happens, e.g. *The test can <u>accurately</u> predict what a bigger explosion would do.*

COMBINING FORM   A combining form is a word that is joined with another word, usually with a hyphen, to form compounds, e.g. *We visited my sister and brother-<u>in-law</u> in Germany.*

NOUN   A noun is a word that refers to a person, a thing, or a quality. In this book, the label NOUN is given to all countable nouns. A countable noun is used for talking about things that can be counted, and that have both singular and plural forms, e.g. *When I went for my first <u>interview</u> for this <u>job</u> I arrived extremely early.*

PHRASAL VERB   A phrasal verb consists of a verb and one or more particles, e.g. *Things are changing so fast, it's hard to <u>keep up</u>.*

PHRASE   Phrases are groups of words which are used together and which have a meaning of their own, e.g. *She discovered the problem <u>by accident</u>.*

PLURAL NOUN   A plural noun is always plural, and it is used with plural verbs, e.g. *A woman who witnessed the accident called the <u>emergency services</u> on her mobile phone.*

UNCOUNTABLE NOUN   An uncountable noun is used for talking about things that are not normally counted, or that we do not think of as single items. Uncountable nouns do not have a plural form, and they are used with a singular verb, e.g. *Many schools do not have enough sports <u>equipment</u>.*

VERB   A verb is a word that is used for saying what someone or something does, or what happens to them, or to give information about them, e.g. *I <u>exercise</u> regularly, so I <u>have</u> lots of energy.*

Other grammatical terms

ANTONYM   An antonym is a word that means the opposite of another word, e.g. *present* is an antonym of *absent*.

COLLOCATION   A collocation is a word that is often used with another word, e.g. *cause* is used with 'an accident', whereas *make* is not.

SYNONYM   A synonym is a word that means the same as another word, e.g. *humorous* is a synonym of *amusing*.

Key words
A-Z

Aa

---

abil|ity /əˈbɪlɪti/ (abilities) PERSONALITY

NOUN Your **ability to** do something is the fact that you can do it. ○ *a student's academic ability* ○ *The public never had faith in his ability to handle the job.* ○ *Intelligence tests measure the ability of people to do well in intelligence tests.*

▶ **COLLOCATIONS:**
the ability **of** *someone to do something*
have the ability *to do something*
show/demonstrate/lack ability
leadership/language/athletic ability
technical/academic ability
natural/great ability

▶ **SYNONYMS:** capability, skill

▶ **ANTONYM:** inability

> **WORD FAMILY**
>
> | ability | **NOUN** | ○ *the human ability to communicate using language* |
> | **be able to** | **PHRASE** | ○ *I was never able to play any sports.* |

---

abol|ish /əˈbɒlɪʃ/ (abolishes, abolishing, abolished) HISTORY

VERB If someone in authority **abolishes** a system or practice, they formally put an end to it. ○ *The government abolished the death penalty for murder in 1965.*

▶ **COLLOCATIONS:**
abolish **the death penalty/slavery/the monarchy/a system**
the government abolishes *something*

▶ **SYNONYMS:** eliminate, end

> **WORD FAMILY**
>
> | abolish | **VERB** | ○ *Parliament voted to abolish fox-hunting.* |
> | abolition | **UNCOUNT** | ○ *the abolition of slavery* |

---

ab|sent /ˈæbsənt/ EDUCATION

ADJECTIVE If someone or something is **absent from** a place or situation where they should be or where they usually are, they are not there. ○ *Several children*

a

were absent on test day. ○ [+ from] He has been absent from his desk for two weeks.

▶ **ANTONYM:** present

> | WORD FAMILY | | |
> | --- | --- | --- |
> | **absent** | **ADJECTIVE** | ○ He is frequently absent or late for work. |
> | **absence** | **NOUN** | ○ repeated absences from school ○ The letters had arrived in my absence. |

ab|sorb /əb'zɔːb/ (absorbs, absorbing, absorbed) `SCIENCE & NATURE`

VERB If something **absorbs** a liquid, gas, or other substance, it soaks it up or takes it in. ○ Plants absorb carbon dioxide from the air and moisture from the soil. ○ [+ into] Refined sugars are absorbed into the bloodstream very quickly.

▶ **SYNONYM:** soak up

> | WORD FAMILY | | |
> | --- | --- | --- |
> | **absorb** | **VERB** | ○ Add extra water if the water is absorbed too quickly. |
> | **absorbent** | **ADJECTIVE** | ○ The towels are highly absorbent. |
> | **absorption** | **UNCOUNT** | ○ the absorption of iron from food |

ab|stract /'æbstrækt/ `MEDIA & CULTURE`

ADJECTIVE **Abstract** art makes use of shapes and patterns rather than showing people or things. ○ a modern abstract painting ○ His work seems inspired by boldly coloured geometric and abstract patterns.

▶ **COLLOCATIONS:**
abstract **art**
an **abstract** painting/design/pattern
an abstract **painter/artist**

▶ **ANTONYM:** figurative

aca|dem|ic /ˌækə'demɪk/ `EDUCATION`

ADJECTIVE **Academic** is used to describe things that relate to the work done in schools, colleges, and universities, especially work which involves studying and reasoning rather than practical or technical skills. ○ I was terrible at school and left with few academic qualifications. ○ Their academic standards are high.

▶ **COLLOCATIONS:**
the academic **year**
academic **ability/achievement/standards**
academic **study/research/work/staff**
an academic **subject/qualification**

> **WORD FAMILY**
>
> | | | |
> |---|---|---|
> | academic | **ADJECTIVE** | ○ *The Department has an academic staff of thirty-four.* |
> | academic | **NOUN** | ○ *a panel of leading academics* |
> | academically | **ADVERB** | ○ *He is academically gifted.* |
> | academy | **NOUN** | ○ *the Royal Academy of Music* |
> | academia | **UNCOUNT** | ○ *links between industry and academia* |

ac|ces|so|ries /æk'sesəriz/   CLOTHES & APPEARANCE

NOUN Accessories are articles such as belts and scarves which you wear or carry but which are not part of your main clothing. ○ *It sells clothing and outdoor accessories.*

▶ **COLLOCATIONS:**
fashion accessories
hair accessories

ac|ci|dent /'æksɪdənt/ (accidents)   HEALTH

1 **NOUN** An **accident** happens when a vehicle hits a person, an object, or another vehicle, causing injury or damage. ○ *She was involved in a serious car accident last week.* ○ *Six passengers were killed in the accident.*

2 **NOUN** If someone has an **accident**, something unpleasant happens to them that was not intended, sometimes causing injury or death. ○ *5,000 people die every year because of accidents in the home.* ○ *The police say the killing of the young man was an accident.*

→ see Useful Phrases **by accident**

▶ **COLLOCATIONS:**
in an accident
have/cause an accident
prevent/avoid/report an accident
an accident **happens/occurs**
a **fatal/tragic/freak** accident
a **serious/bad/terrible** accident
a **car/road/traffic** accident

ac|ci|den|tal /ˌæksɪ'dentəl/

ADJECTIVE An **accidental** event happens by chance or as the result of an accident, and is not deliberately intended. ○ *The fire was accidental.* ○ *The jury returned a verdict of accidental death.*

▶ **COLLOCATIONS:**
accidental **death/damage/injury**
purely accidental

▶ **ANTONYM:** deliberate

a

ac|com|mo|da|tion /əˌkɒməˈdeɪʃən/ TRANSPORT & TRAVEL
(accommodations)

UNCOUNTABLE NOUN **Accommodation** is used to refer to buildings or rooms where people live or stay. [BRIT] ○ Prices start at £2,095 per person, including flights and hotel accommodation. ○ The university offers all first-year students on-campus accommodation.

▶ **COLLOCATIONS:**
hotel/B&B/holiday/self-catering accommodation
student/rented accommodation
temporary/emergency accommodation
include/provide/offer accommodation
find/book/arrange accommodation

> **USAGE**
>
> In British English, **accommodation** is an uncountable noun, but in American English, you can use **accommodations**. ○ Rates are higher for deluxe accommodations.

ac|count|ant /əˈkaʊntənt/ **(accountants)** WORK

NOUN An **accountant** is a person whose job is to keep financial accounts. ○ You can hire an accountant to take care of your finances. ○ a newly qualified accountant ○ a retired accountant

WORD FAMILY		
accountant	NOUN	○ Accountants advise clients about tax.
accountancy	UNCOUNT	○ She is now at college studying accountancy.

ac|cu|rate /ˈækjʊrət/

ADJECTIVE Something that is **accurate** is correct to a detailed level. ○ Police say this is an accurate description of the killer. ○ This is an accurate way of monitoring the amount of carbon dioxide in the air.

▶ **COLLOCATIONS:**
an accurate **description/diagnosis/measurement/prediction**
accurate **information/figures**

reasonably/fairly accurate
remarkably/astonishingly accurate
historically/factually/scientifically accurate

▶ SYNONYM: precise

▶ ANTONYM: inaccurate

WORD FAMILY		
accurate	ADJECTIVE	○ Quartz watches are very accurate.
accurately	ADVERB	○ The test can accurately predict what a bigger explosion would do.
accuracy	UNCOUNT	○ the accuracy of the story
inaccurate	ADJECTIVE	○ The reports are totally inaccurate.
innacurately	ADVERB	○ Some people believe, inaccurately, that the disease is curable.
inaccuracy	NOUN	○ There are many inaccuracies in her article.

---

ac|cuse /əˈkjuːz/ (accuses, accusing, accused)   BELIEFS & OPINIONS

VERB If you **accuse** someone **of** doing something wrong or dishonest, you say or tell them that you believe that they did it. ○ [+ of] He accused her of having an affair. ○ [+ of] Her assistant was accused of theft and fraud by the police.

▶ COLLOCATIONS:
accuse someone **of** something
falsely/wrongly/unfairly accuse someone
openly accuse someone

WORD FAMILY		
accuse	VERB	○ They falsely accused him of stealing $26 million.
accusation	NOUN	○ She denied the accusation that she was being dishonest.

---

ache /eɪk/ (aches, aching, ached)   HEALTH

VERB If you **ache** or a part of your body **aches**, you feel a steady, fairly strong pain. ○ Her head was throbbing and she ached all over. ○ [v-ing] They soothed their aching feet in the sea.

▶ COLLOCATION: your **head/muscles/leg/joints** ache

▶ SYNONYM: hurt

---

achieve /əˈtʃiːv/ (achieves, achieving, achieved)

VERB If you **achieve** a particular aim or effect, you succeed in doing it or causing it to happen, usually after a lot of effort. ○ Achieving our goals makes us feel good. ○ We have achieved what we set out to do.

a

▶ **COLLOCATIONS:**
achieve a **result/goal/objective/target**
achieve **success**
achieve a **level/standard**
successfully achieve *something*
easily achieve *something*

▶ **SYNONYM:** accomplish

achieve|ment /əˈtʃiːvmənt/ (achievements)

NOUN An **achievement** is something which someone has succeeded in doing, especially after a lot of effort. ○ *Winning the event was a great achievement* ○ *The Conference will be a celebration of women's achievements.*

▶ **COLLOCATIONS:**
a **great/remarkable/outstanding** achievement
a **major/big/significant** achievement
a **sporting/academic** achievement
celebrate/recognize an achievement

▶ **SYNONYM:** accomplishment

WORD FAMILY		
achieve	**VERB**	○ *Singer Lauryn Hill went on to achieve massive solo success.*
achievement	**NOUN**	○ *Academic achievement is not the only measure of success.*
achiever	**NOUN**	○ *Both children were high achievers at school.*
achievable	**ADJECTIVE**	○ *Start with smaller, easily achievable goals.*
unachievable	**ADJECTIVE**	○ *Have ministers set themselves an unachievable target?*

ac|tion film/movie /ˈækʃən fɪlm, ˈækʃən muːvi/ MEDIA & CULTURE
(action films/movies)

NOUN An **action film** or **action movie** is a film in which a lot of dangerous and exciting things happen. ○ *Bruce Willis starred in the Die Hard action films.*

ac|tor /ˈæktə/ (actors) MEDIA & CULTURE

NOUN An **actor** is someone whose job is acting in plays or films. ○ *His father was an actor in the Cantonese Opera Company.* ○ *You have to be a very good actor to play that part.*

▶ **COLLOCATIONS:**
an actor **in** *something*
an actor **plays** *someone*
an actor **stars/appears in** *something*
an actor **performs/auditions/rehearses**
be/become an actor

a **lead/supporting** actor
a **good/talented/fine** actor
a **famous/well-known** actor
an **unemployed/out-of-work/struggling** actor

USAGE

Note that many women who act prefer to be called **actors** rather than **actresses**. ○ *She wants to be an actor when she grows up.*

WORD FAMILY

actor	NOUN	○ *William Shatner is the actor who played Captain Kirk in Star Trek.*
actress	NOUN	○ *Kate Winslet is a very talented actress.*
act	VERB	○ *Every time I see her act I am filled with admiration.*
acting	NOUN	○ *superb acting* ○ *her acting career*

---

ad|min|is|tra|tion /ædˌmɪnɪˈstreɪʃən/ `WORK`

UNCOUNTABLE NOUN **Administration** is the range of activities connected with organizing and supervising the way that an organization functions. **Admin** is also used in informal and spoken English. ○ *Too much time is spent on administration.* ○ *business administration* ○ *an administration fee*

WORD FAMILY

administration	UNCOUNT	○ *His role lay in the day-to-day administration of the company.*
admin assistant	NOUN	○ *He works as an admin assistant in a clothing company.*
administrative	ADJECTIVE	○ *administrative costs* ○ *administrative tasks* ○ *an administrative error*

---

ad|mire /ədˈmaɪə/ (admires, admiring, admired)

VERB If you **admire** someone or something, you like and respect them very much. ○ *He admired the way she had coped with life.* ○ *[+ for] All those who knew him will admire him for his work.*

▶ **COLLOCATIONS:**
admire *someone/something* **for** *something*
secretly admire *someone/something*
greatly/hugely admire *someone/something*
admire *someone/something* **enormously**

▶ **SYNONYMS:** respect, look up to

a

---

ad|mit /æd'mɪt/ (admits, admitting, admitted)

VERB If you **admit** that something bad, unpleasant, or embarrassing is true, you agree, often unwillingly, that it is true. ○ [+ *that*] *I admit that I sometimes make mistakes.* ○ [+ *to*] *Up to two thirds of 14 to 16 year olds admit to buying drink illegally.* ○ [+ v-ing] *I'd be ashamed to admit feeling jealous.* ○ *None of these people will admit responsibility for their actions.*

▶ **COLLOCATIONS:**
admit **to** something
readily/freely/grudgingly admit something
openly/privately/publicly admit something
admit **guilt/responsibility/involvement**
admit a **mistake/error**
admit the **truth**

▶ **SYNONYM:** confess

▶ **ANTONYM:** deny

---

ado|les|cent /ˌædə'lesənt/ 　　　　　PEOPLE

ADJECTIVE **Adolescent** is used to describe young people who are no longer children but who have not yet become adults. It also refers to their behaviour. ○ *Adolescent boys should have an adult in whom they can confide.* ○ *his adolescent years* ○ *adolescent rebellion*

▶ **SYNONYM:** teenage

---

adult /'ædʌlt, AM ə'dʌlt/ (adults) 　　　　　PEOPLE

NOUN An **adult** is a mature, fully developed person. An adult has reached the age when they are legally responsible for their actions. ○ *Children under 14 must be accompanied by an adult.* ○ *Becoming a father signified that he was now an adult.*

▶ **COLLOCATIONS:**
a **young/responsible** adult
an adult **male/female/son/child**

adult **literacy/education**
someone's adult **life**
adult **supervision**

▶ **SYNONYM:** grown-up

▶ **ANTONYM:** child

WORD FAMILY		
adult	**NOUN**	○ *You are supposed to be a responsible adult.*
adult	**ADJECTIVE**	○ *I've lived most of my adult life in London.*
adulthood	**UNCOUNT**	○ *Many children reach adulthood with no fillings in their teeth.*

---

ad|van|tage /æd'vɑːntɪdʒ, -'væn-/ **(advantages)** `BELIEFS & OPINIONS`

NOUN An **advantage** is a way in which one thing is better than another. ○ [+ *of*] *The great advantage of this system is that it's safe.* ○ [+ *over*] *This custom-built kitchen has many advantages over a standard one.*

→ see Useful Phrases **take advantage of something**

▶ **COLLOCATIONS:**
the advantage **of** *something*
an advantage **over** *something*
have/be an advantage
a **distinct/added/obvious** advantage
a **slight/great/huge** advantage
a **psychological/tactical/territorial/technological** advantage

▶ **SYNONYM:** benefit

▶ **ANTONYM:** disadvantage

WORD FAMILY		
advantage	**NOUN**	○ *The great advantage of home-grown oranges is their magnificent flavour.*
advantageous	**ADJECTIVE**	○ *The new system is advantageous to the workers.*
disadvantage	**NOUN**	○ *Every job has its disadvantages.*

---

ad|ver|tise|ment /æd'vɜːtɪsmənt, AM ˌædvə'taɪz-/ `MEDIA & CULTURE`
(advertisements)

NOUN An **advertisement** is an announcement in a newspaper, on television, or on a poster that tells people about a product, event, or job vacancy. **Advert** is also used in informal and spoken English. ○ *They placed an advertisement in the local paper.* ○ *an advertisement for cigarettes* ○ *job advertisements*

▶ **COLLOCATIONS:**
an advertisement **for** *something*
an advertisement **in** *something*

put/place an advertisement *somewhere*
an advertisement **appears** *somewhere*
a **full-page/half-page** advertisement
a **television/newspaper/cinema** advertisement

▶ **SYNONYM:** advert

ad|ver|tis|ing /ˈædvətaɪzɪŋ/

UNCOUNTABLE NOUN Advertising is the activity of creating advertisements and making sure people see them. ○ *I work in advertising.* ○ *a ban on tobacco advertising* ○ *an advertising agency*

▶ **COLLOCATIONS:**
television/Internet/print advertising
tobacco/cigarette advertising
an advertising **campaign/agency/hoarding/executive**

WORD FAMILY		
advertisement	NOUN	○ *Job advertisements appear in the national press.*
advert	NOUN	○ *job adverts* ○ *an advert for dog food*
advertise	VERB	○ *We advertised for staff in a local newspaper.*
advertising	UNCOUNT	○ *The benefits of Internet advertising may be exaggerated.*

ad|vice /ædˈvaɪs/

UNCOUNTABLE NOUN If you give someone **advice**, you tell them what you think they should do in a particular situation. ○ [+ *about*] *Don't be afraid to ask for advice about ordering the meal.* ○ [+ *on*] *Your community officer can give you advice on how to prevent crime in your area.*

▶ **COLLOCATIONS:**
advice **about/on** *something*
give/offer advice
ask for/seek advice
follow/take *someone's* advice
good/bad advice
expert/legal advice
a **piece of** advice

▶ **SYNONYMS:** guidance, help

USAGE
Note that **advice** is an uncount noun. You can say a **piece of advice** or **some advice**, but you cannot say 'an advice' or 'advices'. ○ *Let me give you a piece of advice; don't trust anyone.*

ad|vise /æd'vaɪz/ (advises, advising, advised)

VERB If you **advise** someone **to** do something, you tell them what you think they should do. ○ [+ to-inf] *The minister advised him to leave as soon as possible.* ○ [+ *against*] *I would strongly advise against it.*

▶ **COLLOCATIONS:**
advise *someone* **against** *something*
advise *someone* **on** *something*
strongly advise *something*

WORD FAMILY		
advice	**UNCOUNT**	○ *Take my advice and stay away from him!*
advise	**VERB**	○ *Doctors advised that he should be transferred to a private room.*
advisor	**NOUN**	○ *a careers advisor* ○ *the president and his advisors*
advisable	**ADJECTIVE**	○ *It is advisable to book early for city-centre restaurants.*
inadvisable	**ADJECTIVE**	○ *He started on a course of action that was highly inadvisable.*

af|ford /ə'fɔːd/   `MONEY` `SHOPPING`

VERB If you **cannot afford** something, you do not have enough money to pay for it. ○ *My parents can't even afford a new refrigerator.* ○ [+ to-inf] *We couldn't afford to buy a new rug.* ○ *Although I could probably afford a car, I prefer to take the bus.*

▶ **COLLOCATIONS:**
can't/couldn't afford *something*
can/could afford *something*
afford to **pay for/buy** *something*

afraid /ə'freɪd/

ADJECTIVE If you are **afraid of** someone or **afraid to** do something, you are frightened because you think that something very unpleasant is going to happen to you. ○ [+ *of*] *I was afraid of the other boys.* ○ [+ to-inf] *I'm still afraid to sleep in my own bedroom.*

→ see also **fear**

▶ **COLLOCATIONS:**
afraid **of** *someone/something*
be/feel afraid

▶ **SYNONYMS:** frightened, scared

agen|cy /'eɪdʒənsi/ (agencies)   `WORK`

NOUN An **agency** is a business which provides a service on behalf of other businesses. ○ *They hired a babysitter through an agency.* ○ *a successful advertising agency*

▶ COLLOCATIONS:
an **advertising** agency
a **job/employment** agency
a **travel/estate** agency
a **dating** agency

---

ag|gres|sive /ə'grɛsɪv/ PERSONALITY

ADJECTIVE An **aggressive** person or animal has a quality of anger and determination that makes them ready to attack other people. ○ *Some children are much more aggressive than others.* ○ *aggressive behaviour* ○ *aggressive driving*

> **WORD FAMILY**
>
> | | | |
> |---|---|---|
> | **aggressive** | **ADJECTIVE** | ○ *These fish are very aggressive.* |
> | **aggressively** | **ADVERB** | ○ *The dog was barking more aggressively now.* |
> | **aggression** | **UNCOUNT** | ○ *Aggression is not a male-only trait.* |

---

air con|di|tion|ing /'eə kən,dɪʃənɪŋ/ HOME

UNCOUNTABLE NOUN **Air conditioning** is a method of providing buildings and vehicles with cool dry air. ○ *She's having air-conditioning installed in her apartment.* ○ *the air-conditioning system in the museum* ○ *an air-conditioning unit*

---

al|bum /'ælbəm/ (albums) MEDIA & CULTURE

NOUN An **album** is a collection of songs on a CD or record or in a file that is available to download from the Internet. ○ *This new single is taken from their latest album.* ○ *Chris likes music and has a large collection of albums.*

▶ COLLOCATIONS:
produce/release an album
someone's **first/debut/latest/new** album
a **live/solo** album

---

al|co|hol /'ælkəhɒl, AM -hɔːl/ HEALTH

UNCOUNTABLE NOUN Drinks that can make people drunk, such as beer, wine, and whisky, can be referred to as **alcohol**. ○ *Do either of you smoke cigarettes or drink alcohol?* ○ *No alcohol is allowed on the premises.*

▶ COLLOCATIONS:
drink/consume alcohol
serve/sell alcohol
abuse alcohol
alcohol **abuse/addiction/misuse**
someone's alcohol **intake**

> **WORD FAMILY**
>
> | alcohol | **UNCOUNT** | ○ Some Indian restaurants do not serve alcohol. |
> | alcoholic | **ADJECTIVE** | ○ Wine is by far the most popular alcoholic drink amongst the Portuguese. |

---

alike /ə'laɪk/

CLOTHES & APPEARANCE

1 ADJECTIVE If two or more people or things are **alike**, they are similar. ○ We looked very alike. ○ No two fingerprints were alike.

▶ **SYNONYM:** the same

▶ **ANTONYM:** different

2 ADVERB If two or more people think **alike**, they have similar opinions. If two or more people dress **alike**, they wear similar clothes. ○ They assume that all men and women think alike.

▶ **COLLOCATION:**
   look/sound alike

---

al|ter|na|tive /ɔːl'tɜːnətɪv/ (alternatives)

1 NOUN If one thing is an **alternative to** another, the first can be found, used, or done instead of the second. ○ [+ to] Rugs are a cheaper alternative to carpet. ○ [+ to] New ways to treat arthritis may provide an alternative to painkillers.

▶ **COLLOCATIONS:**
   an alternative **to** something
   offer/provide/suggest/find an alternative
   a **viable/credible/realistic** alternative
   a **cheap/healthy/safe** alternative

2 ADJECTIVE An **alternative** plan or offer is different from the one that you already have, and can be done or used instead. ○ There were alternative methods of travel available. ○ They had a right to seek alternative employment.

▶ **COLLOCATIONS:**
   an alternative **method/route/explanation/source**
   alternative **arrangements**

▶ **SYNONYMS:** other, different, alternate

> **WORD FAMILY**
>
> | alternative | **NOUN** | ○ Supermarkets offer own-brand alternatives to manufacturers' brands. |
> | alternative | **ADJECTIVE** | ○ We may need to make alternative arrangements. |
> | alternatively | **ADVERB** | ○ It takes 8 hours to drive there. Alternatively, you can fly. |

a

amazed /əˈmeɪzd/

ADJECTIVE If you are **amazed** by something, you are very surprised by it. ○ [+ by] *Most of the cast was amazed by the play's success.* ○ [+ at] *Aren't you amazed at what they've done?* ○ [+ to-inf] *I was amazed to learn she was still writing her stories.*

▶ **COLLOCATIONS:**
 amazed **at/by** something
 look/seem/sound amazed
 totally/absolutely amazed

▶ **SYNONYM:** astonished

amaz|ing /əˈmeɪzɪŋ/

ADJECTIVE You say that something is **amazing** when it is very surprising and makes you feel pleasure, approval, or wonder. ○ [+ what/how] *It's amazing what she can remember.* ○ *This movie has some of the most amazing stunts you will ever see.* ○ *a really amazing experience*

▶ **COLLOCATIONS:**
 an amazing **story/experience/feeling**
 an amazing **achievement/ability/success**
 an amazing **person/woman/man**
 look amazing
 just/pretty/quite amazing
 absolutely/truly/really amazing
 amazing **to see/to watch/to think**

▶ **SYNONYM:** astonishing

WORD FAMILY		
amazed	ADJECTIVE	○ She is amazed that people still risk travelling without insurance.
amazing	ADJECTIVE	○ It's the most amazing thing to watch.
amazingly	ADVERB	○ She was an amazingly good cook.
amaze	VERB	○ He amazed us by his knowledge of Welsh history.
amazement	UNCOUNT	○ Both men stared at her in amazement.

am|bi|tious /æmˈbɪʃəs/

PERSONALITY   WORK

ADJECTIVE Someone who is **ambitious** has a strong desire to be successful, rich, or powerful. ○ *He's a very ambitious boy who wants to play football at the highest level.* ○ *an ambitious young journalist*

▶ **ANTONYM:** unambitious

WORD FAMILY		
ambitious	ADJECTIVE	○ Karen has proved an energetic and ambitious worker.
ambitiously	ADVERB	○ He ambitiously attempted to sail around the world.
ambition	NOUN	○ His real ambition is to be a writer.
unambitious	ADJECTIVE	○ When I was a teenager I was lazy and unambitious.

an|ces|tor /ˈænsestə/ (ancestors)

HISTORY PEOPLE

NOUN Your **ancestors** are the people from whom you are descended. ○ *Our daily lives are very different from those of our ancestors.* ○ *He could trace his ancestors back seven hundred years.*

▶ **ANTONYM:** descendant

an|cient /ˈeɪnʃənt/

HISTORY

1 ADJECTIVE **Ancient** means belonging to the distant past, especially to the period in history before the end of the Roman Empire. ○ *Heraclitus was an ancient Greek philosopher.* ○ *In Ancient Rome, those in high office wore purple robes.*

2 ADJECTIVE **Ancient** means very old, or having existed for a long time. ○ *We visited ancient Buddhist monuments.* ○ *ancient woodland* ○ *ancient Jewish tradition*

▶ **COLLOCATIONS:**
   an ancient **Greek/Chinese/Egyptian** *thing/place*
   an ancient **city/site/monument/temple**
   an ancient **tradition/culture/people**
   ancient **history**
   the ancient **world**

▶ **ANTONYMS:** modern, contemporary

an|gry /ˈæŋgri/ (angrier, angriest)

ADJECTIVE When you are **angry**, you feel strong dislike or impatience about something. ○ *[+ with] Are you angry with me for some reason?* ○ *[+ about] I was angry about the rumours.* ○ *an angry mob*

▶ **COLLOCATIONS:**
   angry **at/with** *someone*
   angry **about** *something*
   visibly angry
   justifiably/understandably angry
   feel/sound/look angry
   get/become/grow angry

▶ **SYNONYM:** mad

▶ **ANTONYMS:** content, calm

an|ger /ˈæŋgə/

UNCOUNTABLE NOUN **Anger** is the strong emotion that you feel when you think that someone has behaved in an unfair, cruel, or unacceptable way. ○ *He cried with anger and frustration.* ○ *[+ at] Ellen felt both despair and anger at her mother.* ○ *[+ about] widespread public anger about tax cuts for the rich*

▶ **COLLOCATIONS:**
   anger **at** *someone/something*
   anger **over/about** *something*
   show/express anger

a

cause/provoke anger
public/widespread/growing anger

▶ SYNONYMS: rage, fury

---

an|nounce /əˈnaʊns/   MEDIA & CULTURE
(announces, announcing, announced)

VERB If you **announce** something, you tell people about it publicly or officially.
○ [+ that] *He will announce tonight that he is resigning from office.* ○ *She was planning to announce her engagement to Peter.*

▶ SYNONYMS: make public, reveal

WORD FAMILY		
announce	VERB	○ It was announced that the groups have agreed to a cease-fire.
annoucement	NOUN	○ I have an announcement to make.
announcer	NOUN	○ The radio announcer said it was nine o'clock.

---

an|noy /əˈnɔɪ/ **(annoys, annoying, annoyed)**

VERB If someone or something **annoys** you, it makes you fairly angry and impatient. ○ [+ that] *It annoyed me that I didn't have time to do more reading.*
○ [+ to-inf] *It just annoyed me to hear him going on.*

▶ SYNONYM: irritate

an|noyed /əˈnɔɪd/

ADJECTIVE If you are **annoyed**, you are fairly angry about something. ○ [+ at] *Eleanor was annoyed at having to wait so long.* ○ [+ with] *If you wake up in the middle of the night, don't get annoyed with yourself.*

▶ COLLOCATIONS:
annoyed **at/about/by** something
annoyed **with** someone
look/sound/feel/seem annoyed
become/get annoyed
very/really/slightly/quite annoyed
clearly/visibly annoyed

▶ SYNONYM: irritated

an|noy|ing /əˈnɔɪɪŋ/

ADJECTIVE Someone or something that is **annoying** makes you feel fairly angry and impatient. ○ *It's very annoying when this happens.* ○ *He has this annoying habit of finishing your sentences.*

▶ COLLOCATIONS:
find something annoying
an annoying **habit/delay/cough**

an annoying **child**
extremely/really annoying

▶ SYNONYM: irritating

WORD FAMILY		
annoy	VERB	○ *Try making a note of the things which annoy you.*
annoyed	ADJECTIVE	○ *She looked annoyed with herself.*
annoying	ADJECTIVE	○ *You must have found my attitude annoying.*
annoyance	UNCOUNT	○ *To her annoyance, the stranger did not go away.*

---

an|nual /ˈænjʊəl/

1 ADJECTIVE **Annual** events happen once every year. ○ *There is an annual festival of regional food.* ○ *our annual holiday* ○ *an annual meeting*

▶ SYNONYM: yearly

2 ADJECTIVE **Annual** quantities or rates relate to a period of one year. ○ *The annual fee is £40.* ○ *The company has annual sales of about $80 million.*

▶ SYNONYM: yearly

WORD FAMILY		
annual	ADJECTIVE	○ *We hope to make the concert an annual event.*
annually	ADVERB	○ *Interest will be paid annually.*

---

anti|bi|ot|ic /ˌæntibaɪˈɒtɪk/ (antibiotics)   `HEALTH`

NOUN **Antibiotics** are medical drugs used to kill bacteria and treat infections. ○ *Your doctor may prescribe a course of antibiotics.* ○ *She was on antibiotics for an eye infection.*

▶ COLLOCATIONS:
 a **course of** antibiotics
 be on/take antibiotics
 prescribe/give antibiotics

---

an|tique /ænˈtiːk/ (antiques)

NOUN An **antique** is an old object such as a piece of china or furniture which is valuable because it is beautiful or rare. ○ *He started collecting antiques as a hobby.* ○ *I'd found it in a local antiques shop.* ○ *antique silver jewellery*

▶ COLLOCATIONS:
 an antiques **shop/fair/market**
 an antiques **dealer/expert/collector**
 sell/buy/collect antiques

anx|ious /ˈæŋkʃəs/

1 **ADJECTIVE** If you are **anxious to** do something or **anxious that** something
should happen, you very much want to do it or very much want it to happen.
○ [+ to-inf] *Everyone was anxious to know what had happened.* ○ [+ that] *He is anxious
that there should be no delay.*

▶ **COLLOCATIONS:**
anxious **for** something
anxious to **hear/know/see** something
anxious to **avoid** something

▶ **SYNONYMS:** eager, keen

2 **ADJECTIVE** If you are **anxious**, you are nervous or worried about something.
○ [+ about] *Many young people are anxious about the future and whether they will find
jobs.* ○ *A friend of mine is a very anxious person.*

▶ **COLLOCATIONS:**
anxious **about** something
become/get/feel/seem anxious

▶ **SYNONYM:** nervous

anxi|ety /æŋˈzaɪɪti/

UNCOUNTABLE NOUN **Anxiety** is a feeling of nervousness or worry. ○ *Changing
classes can cause great anxiety for students.* ○ [+ about] *Anxiety about work or school is
one of the main causes of sleeplessness.*

▶ **COLLOCATIONS:**
anxiety **about** something
cause anxiety
reduce/increase anxiety
great anxiety

▶ **SYNONYM:** worry

apart|ment /əˈpɑːtmənt/ (apartments)   `HOME`

NOUN An **apartment** is a set of rooms for living in, usually on one floor of a large
building. [mainly AM; in BRIT, use **flat**] ○ *Christina has her own apartment.* ○ *a tiny
apartment* ○ *bleak cities of concrete apartment blocks*

▶ **COLLOCATIONS:**
an apartment **building/block/complex**
a **one-bedroom/two-bedroom** etc. apartment
a **luxury** apartment

apolo|gize /əˈpɒlədʒaɪz/ (apologizes, apologizing, apologized)
[in BRIT, also use **apologise**]

VERB When you **apologize to** someone, you say that you are sorry that you
have hurt them or caused trouble for them. ○ [+ for] *He publicly apologized for his*

remarks. ○ [+ to] *He apologized to the people who had been affected.* ○ *Costello later apologized, saying she had made an honest mistake.*

▶ COLLOCATIONS:
apologize **for** something
apologize **to** someone
publicly apologize
apologize **profusely**

apol|ogy /əˈpɒlədʒi/ (apologies)

NOUN An **apology** is something that you say or write in order to tell someone that you are sorry that you have hurt them or caused trouble for them. ○ *I didn't get an apology.* ○ *We received a letter of apology.* ○ *He made a public apology for the team's performance.*

▶ COLLOCATIONS:
an apology **from** someone
make/offer an apology
get/receive an apology
demand an apology
accept an apology
a **public/formal/written** apology
a **full** apology
a **letter of** apology

WORD FAMILY		
apologize	VERB	○ *Mrs Wabash apologized profusely for all the trouble she had caused.*
apology	NOUN	○ *She demanded an apology from the editor of the newspaper for using her private photographs.*
apologetic	ADJECTIVE	○ *The manager was very apologetic and offered to refund our money.*
apologetically	ADVERB	○ *'I went too far,' he said apologetically.*

ap|peal /əˈpiːl/ (appeals, appealing, appealed) `MEDIA & CULTURE`

VERB If you **appeal to** someone **to** do something, you make a serious and urgent request to them. ○ [+ to] *The Prime Minister appealed to young people to use their vote.* ○ [+ for] *Police are appealing for information from anyone who saw the attack.*

▶ COLLOCATIONS:
appeal **to** someone
appeal **for** something
appeal for **help/information/calm**
appeal for **witnesses**

▶ SYNONYM: call

a

ap|pear|ance /əˈpɪərəns/ [MEDIA & CULTURE] [CLOTHES & APPEARANCE]
(appearances)

1 NOUN When someone makes an **appearance** at a public event or in a broadcast, they take part in it. ○ *It was the president's second public appearance to date.* ○ *The actor continued to make brief stage appearances until he was almost 90.*

▶ **COLLOCATIONS:**
make an appearance
a **public** appearance
a **brief** appearance
a **television/stage/screen** appearance
a **guest** appearance

2 UNCOUNTABLE NOUN Someone's or something's **appearance** is the way that they look. ○ *She used to be so careful about her appearance.* ○ *He had the appearance of a college student.* ○ *creams that improve the appearance of your skin*

▶ **COLLOCATIONS:**
physical appearance
change *your* appearance
give/have the appearance **of** *something*

WORD FAMILY		
appear	**VERB**	○ *Student leaders appeared on television to ask for calm.*
appearance	**NOUN**	○ *Timberlake was making a guest appearance on the show to promote his new album.*

ap|ply /əˈplaɪ/ **(applies, applying, applied)** [WORK]

VERB If you **apply for** something such as a job or membership of an organization, you write a letter or fill in a form in order to ask formally for it. ○ *[+ for] I am continuing to apply for jobs.* ○ *[+ to-inf] They may apply to join the organization.*

▶ **COLLOCATIONS:**
apply **for** a **job**
apply **for** a **licence/visa/permit/passport**
apply **for** a **grant/loan**
apply **for membership**
apply for **asylum/citizenship**

ap|pli|ca|tion /ˌæplɪˈkeɪʃən/ **(applications)** [WORK] [COMMUNICATIONS]

1 NOUN An **application for** something such as a job or membership of an organization is a formal written request for it. ○ *[+ for] His application for membership of the organisation was rejected.* ○ *[+ to-inf] Turkey's application to join the European Community*

▶ **COLLOCATIONS:**
make/submit an application
receive an application

reject/accept an application
a **job** application
a **visa/asylum/passport** application
a **grant/loan** application
an application **form**

2 **NOUN** In computing, an **application** is a piece of software designed to carry out a particular task. **App** is also used, especially to talk about software for mobile phones. ○ *The first time you use some applications there is an option to take a tour around the software.* ○ *Mobile applications already on the market can keep track of your fat intake.*

▶ **COLLOCATIONS:**
a **software/computer** application
a **web/Internet** application
a **wireless/mobile/desktop** application
use/run/download an application

▶ **SYNONYM:** software

WORD FAMILY		
apply	**VERB**	○ *To enter India you will need to apply for a standard tourist visa.*
application	**NOUN**	○ *Applications should be submitted as early as possible.*
applicant	**NOUN**	○ *Many studies have shown that job applicants are sometimes less than truthful when doing personality tests.*
applicable	**ADJECTIVE**	○ *The discount is not applicable to promotional fares.*

---

ap|pro|pri|ate /əˈprəʊpriət/

ADJECTIVE Something that is **appropriate** is suitable or acceptable for a particular situation. ○ [+ to-inf] *I thought it would be appropriate to take Miss Rondel a small gift.* ○ [+ for/to] *Dress neatly in an outfit appropriate to the job.* ○ *The teacher can then take appropriate action.*

▶ **COLLOCATIONS:**
appropriate **for/to** *something*
the appropriate **time/level/place**
an appropriate **action/response/way**
entirely appropriate

▶ **SYNONYMS:** correct, suitable, acceptable, relevant

▶ **ANTONYMS:** inappropriate, improper, incorrect

a

<table>
<tr><td colspan="3">WORD FAMILY</td></tr>
<tr><td>appropriate</td><td>ADJECTIVE</td><td>○ The club says the ride is appropriate for all ages.</td></tr>
<tr><td>appropriately</td><td>ADVERB</td><td>○ I was dressed appropriately for the weather.</td></tr>
<tr><td>inappropriate</td><td>ADJECTIVE</td><td>○ The product is offensive and totally inappropriate for children.</td></tr>
<tr><td>inappropriately</td><td>ADVERB</td><td>○ Our stay at the inappropriately named 'Paradise Hotel' was extremely unpleasant.</td></tr>
</table>

ap|prove /ə'pruːv/

BELIEFS & OPINIONS

(approves, approving, approved)

VERB If you **approve of** an action, event, or suggestion, you like it or are pleased about it. ○ [+ of] Not everyone approves of the festival. ○ You don't approve, do you?

▶ **COLLOCATION:** approve **of** someone/something

▶ **ANTONYM:** disapprove

<table>
<tr><td colspan="3">WORD FAMILY</td></tr>
<tr><td>approve</td><td>VERB</td><td>○ Her parents didn't approve of the marriage.</td></tr>
<tr><td>approval</td><td>NOUN</td><td>○ It's always good to get the approval of other writers.</td></tr>
<tr><td>approving</td><td>ADJECTIVE</td><td>○ Helen gave me an approving nod.</td></tr>
<tr><td>disapprove</td><td>VERB</td><td>○ I loved him even though my parents and friends disapproved of the relationship.</td></tr>
</table>

ap|proxi|mate /ə'prɒksɪmət/

ADJECTIVE An **approximate** number, time, or position is close to the correct number, time, or position, but is not exact. ○ The approximate cost varies from around £150 to £250. ○ The times are approximate only.

▶ **ANTONYMS:** exact, precise

ap|proxi|mate|ly /ə'prɒksɪmətli/

ADVERB If something is **approximately** a particular number, time, or position, it is close to that number, time, or position, but is not exact. ○ The journey time is approximately 25 minutes. ○ Approximately $150 million is to be spent on improvements.

▶ **SYNONYMS:** about, roughly

▶ **ANTONYMS:** exactly, precisely

<table>
<tr><td colspan="3">WORD FAMILY</td></tr>
<tr><td>approximate</td><td>ADJECTIVE</td><td>○ All print sizes are approximate.</td></tr>
<tr><td>approximate</td><td>VERB</td><td>○ By about 6 weeks of age, most babies begin to show something approximating a day/night sleeping pattern.</td></tr>
<tr><td>approximately</td><td>ADVERB</td><td>○ They've spent approximately £200.</td></tr>
<tr><td>approximation</td><td>NOUN</td><td>○ This figure is only an approximation.</td></tr>
</table>

ar|chae|ol|ogy /ɑːkɪˈɒlədʒi/ also **archeology** `HISTORY`

UNCOUNTABLE NOUN **Archaeology** is the study of the societies and peoples of the past by examining the remains of their buildings, tools, and other objects. ○ *Elizabeth is studying archaeology at Cambridge University.* ○ *an archaeology student*

WORD FAMILY		
archaeology	UNCOUNT	○ *Archaeology has confirmed the existence of a Roman cemetery on this site.*
archaeological	ADJECTIVE	○ *one of the region's most important archaeological sites*
archaeologist	NOUN	○ *The archaeologists found a house built around 300 BC.*

archi|tect /ˈɑːkɪtekt/ **(architects)** `WORK`

1 NOUN An **architect** is a person who designs buildings. ○ *He wanted to become an architect.* ○ *The town has several buildings designed by distinguished Chicago architects such as Frank Lloyd Wright.*

2 NOUN You can use **architect** to refer to a person who plans large projects such as landscaping or railways. ○ *Merrick Denton-Thompson, the landscape architect for Hampshire county council* ○ [+ of] *Paul Andreu, chief architect of French railways*

archi|tec|ture /ˈɑːkɪtektʃə/ `PLACES`

UNCOUNTABLE NOUN **Architecture** is the art of planning, designing, and constructing buildings. ○ *He studied classical architecture and design in Rome.* ○ *an architecture student*

WORD FAMILY		
architect	NOUN	○ *The architect had already been employed to prepare plans for the new school.*
architecture	UNCOUNT	○ *He was very interested in architecture.*
architectural	ADJECTIVE	○ *Italy's architectural heritage*
architecturally	ADVERB	○ *The old city centre is architecturally rich.*

area /ˈeəriə/ **(areas)** `PLACES`

NOUN An **area** is a particular part of a town, a country, a region, or the world. ○ *60 years ago half the French population still lived in rural areas.* ○ *urban areas with social and economic problems* ○ [+ of] *one of the wealthier areas of the city*

▶ **COLLOCATIONS:**
an area **of** somewhere
the area **near/around** somewhere
a **rural/urban/residential/industrial** area

▶ **SYNONYMS:** district, place, region

a

ar|gu|ment /ˈɑːgjʊmənt/ (arguments) BELIEFS & OPINIONS

NOUN An **argument** is a statement or set of statements that you use in order to try to convince people that your opinion about something is correct. ○ [+ for] *There's a strong argument for lowering the price.* ○ [+ against] *Teachers have put forward their arguments against the proposals.* ○ [+ that] *There is an argument that companies have a responsibility to act that way.*

▸ **COLLOCATIONS:**
an argument **for/against** something
an argument **in favour of** something
put forward/present an argument
a **strong/persuasive/convincing** argument

WORD FAMILY		
argue	VERB	○ His lawyers are arguing that he is unfit to stand trial.
argument	NOUN	○ The book provides a convincing argument for change.

ar|rest /əˈrest/ (arrests, arresting, arrested) CRIME

VERB If the police **arrest** you, they take charge of you and take you to a police station, because they believe you may have committed a crime. ○ *Police arrested five young men in connection with one of the attacks.* ○ *The police say seven people were arrested for minor offences.*

▸ **COLLOCATIONS:**
be arrested **for** something
be arrested **in connection with** something
be arrested **on suspicion of** a crime

ar|ri|vals /əˈraɪvəlz/ TRANSPORT & TRAVEL

UNCOUNTABLE NOUN **Arrivals** is the place at an airport where people who have just got off a plane come to. ○ *Clare and James were standing by their bags outside arrivals.* ○ *Security guards were patrolling arrivals.*

→ see also **departures**

ar|ti|cle /ˈɑːtɪkəl/ (articles) MEDIA & CULTURE

NOUN An **article** is a piece of writing that is published in a newspaper or magazine. ○ *a newspaper article* ○ *a travel article* ○ *She has written various articles on solar energy.*

▸ **COLLOCATIONS:**
an article **on/about** something
an article **in** a newspaper/magazine
a **newspaper/magazine** article
write/read/publish an article

art|ist /'ɑːtɪst/ (artists)　　　　MEDIA & CULTURE

NOUN An **artist** is someone who draws or paints pictures or creates sculptures as a job or a hobby. ○ *Each poster is signed by the artist.* ○ *I'm not a good artist.*

ar|tis|tic /ɑː'tɪstɪk/

ADJECTIVE **Artistic** means relating to art or artists. ○ *Her artistic talent was soon recognized.* ○ *the campaign for artistic freedom* ○ *their 1,300 year old artistic traditions*

WORD FAMILY		
art	UNCOUNT	○ She has been exhibiting her paintings in local art exhibitions.
artist	NOUN	○ This sale of paintings by Japanese artists will include 'Meeting the Dawn', by Hishida Shunso.
artistic	ADJECTIVE	○ The style expressed their mood and artistic ideas.
artistically	ADVERB	○ Artistically, the photographs are stunning.

ashamed /ə'ʃeɪmd/

1 **ADJECTIVE** If someone is **ashamed**, they feel embarrassed or guilty because of something they do or they have done, or because of their appearance. ○ [+ of] *I felt incredibly ashamed of myself for getting so angry.* ○ [+ that] *She was ashamed that she looked so shabby.*

▶ **ANTONYM:** proud

2 **ADJECTIVE** If you are **ashamed of** someone, you feel embarrassed to be connected with them, often because of their appearance or because you disapprove of something they have done. ○ [+ of] *I've never told this to anyone, but I was terribly ashamed of my mum.* ○ *She wasn't ashamed of Ludovico or her marriage.*

▶ **COLLOCATIONS:**
ashamed **of** someone/something
feel ashamed
deeply/bitterly ashamed

▶ **ANTONYM:** proud

as|sign|ment /ə'saɪnmənt/ (assignments)　　　　EDUCATION

NOUN An **assignment** is a task or piece of work that you are given to do, especially as part of your job or studies. ○ *The assessment for the course involves written assignments and practical tests.* ○ *A student who fails any assignment will normally be required to redo it.*

▶ **COLLOCATIONS:**
a **written** assignment
complete an assignment
give/set someone an assignment

▶ **SYNONYM:** task

a

WORD FAMILY		
assign	**VERB**	○ *When teachers assign homework, students usually feel an obligation to do it.*
assignment	**NOUN**	○ *The candidate must complete at least four assignments successfully.*

as|sis|tant /əˈsɪstənt/ (assistants) WORK

1 NOUN Someone's **assistant** is a person who helps them in their work. ○ *Kalan called his assistant, Hashim, to take over while he went out.* ○ *The salesman had been accompanied to the meeting by an assistant.*

▶ **COLLOCATIONS:**
   a **personal /administrative** assistant
   a **care/research** assistant
   a **teaching/classroom** assistant
   a **kitchen/nursery/library** assistant

▶ **SYNONYM:** aide

2 NOUN An **assistant** is a person who works in a shop selling things to customers. ○ *The assistant took the book and checked the price on the back cover.* ○ *She got a job as a sales assistant selling handbags.*

▶ **SYNONYMS:** shop assistant, sales assistant

as|trono|my /əˈstrɒnəmi/ SCIENCE & NATURE

UNCOUNTABLE NOUN Astronomy is the scientific study of the stars, planets, and other natural objects in space. ○ *He was very interested in astronomy and he used to lecture on the stars.*

WORD FAMILY		
astronomy	**UNCOUNT**	○ *I have become interested in astronomy, so I want to buy a telescope.*
astronomer	**NOUN**	○ *When astronomers discover a new star, there are special procedures for registering it.*
astronomical	**ADJECTIVE**	○ *the British Astronomical Association*

ath|lete /ˈæθliːt/ (athletes) SPORT & ACTIVITY

NOUN An **athlete** is a person who does a sport, especially athletics, or track and field events. ○ *Over 140 Australian athletes are competing in this year's event.* ○ *All professional athletes have a coach.*

▶ **COLLOCATIONS:**
   a **professional** athlete
   a **top/great** athlete
   an **Olympic** athlete

ath|let|ics /æθ'letɪks/

UNCOUNTABLE NOUN **Athletics** refers to track and field sports such as running, the high jump, and the javelin. [mainly BRIT] ○ *Arlene was a member of the Northern Ireland athletics team.* ○ *A six lane running track makes it one of Britain's top venues for indoor athletics.*

▶ **COLLOCATIONS:**
  an athletics **event/competition**
  an athletics **coach**
  an athletics **team/club**
  athletics **facilities**
  an athletics **stadium/track**

WORD FAMILY		
athlete	NOUN	○ He is an Olympic athlete who has won gold medals in Beijing and London.
athletics	UNCOUNT	○ She was training for an athletics event.
athletic	ADJECTIVE	○ athletic ability
athletically	ADVERB	○ McIntosh is the most athletically gifted player.

at|mos|phere /'ætməsfɪə/

UNCOUNTABLE NOUN The **atmosphere** of a place is the general impression that you get of it. ○ *Young people will enjoy the relaxed atmosphere and beachfront setting of Club San Miguel.* ○ *[+ of] There's still an atmosphere of great hostility and tension in the city.*

▶ **COLLOCATIONS:**
  an atmosphere **of** something
  a **friendly/relaxed/informal** atmosphere
  a **tense** atmosphere
  create an atmosphere

WORD FAMILY		
atmosphere	UNCOUNT	○ The entertainments team create a fantastic atmosphere, with live music.
atmospheric	ADJECTIVE	○ an atmospheric photograph of a winter landscape

at|tack /ə'tæk/ (attacks, attacking, attacked)

VERB To **attack** a person or place means to try to hurt or damage them using physical violence. ○ *Fifty civilians in Masawa were killed when government planes attacked the town.* ○ *He bundled the old lady into her hallway and brutally attacked her.*

▶ **COLLOCATIONS:**
  attack *someone/something* **with** *something*
  attack *someone/something* with a **knife/bomb/bottle**
  viciously/brutally attack *someone*

▶ **ANTONYM:** defend

a

at|tend /ə'tend/ (attends, attending, attended)   EDUCATION

1 **VERB** If you **attend** a meeting or other event, you are present at it. ○ *She attended evening classes in Italian.* ○ *The party was attended by 1,400 guests from around the world.*

▶ COLLOCATIONS:
   attend a **meeting/conference/class**
   attend a **service/event/ceremony**
   attend a **party/funeral/concert**

2 **VERB** If you **attend** an institution such as a school, college, or church, you go there regularly. ○ *My brother and I attend different schools.* ○ *They attended college together at the University of Pennsylvania.*

▶ COLLOCATIONS:
   attend **school/college/university**
   attend **church**
   attend **regularly**

▶ SYNONYM: go to

> **WORD FAMILY**
>
> | attend | **VERB** | ○ *Thousands of people attended the funeral.* |
> | **attendance** | **UNCOUNT** | ○ *Reducing truancy and improving school attendance is critical.* |

at|ten|tion /ə'tenʃən/

1 **UNCOUNTABLE NOUN** If you give someone or something your **attention**, you look at it, listen to it, or think about it carefully. ○ *You have my undivided attention.* ○ *More than ever before, the food industry is paying attention to young consumers.* ○ *young children with short attention spans*

▶ COLLOCATIONS:
   give/turn your attention **to** *someone/something*
   focus your attention **on** *someone/something*
   pay attention **to** *something*
   draw *someone's* attention **to** *something*
   bring *something* **to** *someone's* attention
   get/attract *someone's* attention
   undivided/full attention
   close/careful/special attention
   attention **span**

2 **UNCOUNTABLE NOUN** **Attention** is great interest that is shown in someone or something, particularly by the public. ○ *His work was starting to attract international attention.* ○ *The player has been plagued with injuries, and unwanted media attention.*

▶ COLLOCATIONS:
   attract/receive attention
   focus attention **on** *something/someone*

public/media attention
national/international attention
great/considerable attention
unwanted attention

at|trac|tion /əˈtrækʃən/ (attractions) `PLACES`

NOUN An **attraction** is something that people can go to for interest or enjoyment, for example a famous building. ○ *The walled city is an important tourist attraction.* ○ *More than 3.8 million people visit the attraction each year.*

▸ **COLLOCATIONS:**
a **tourist/visitor** attraction
the **top/star** attraction
a **popular** attraction
visit an attraction

at|trac|tive /əˈtræktɪv/ `CLOTHES & APPEARANCE`

1 **ADJECTIVE** A person who is **attractive** is pleasant to look at. ○ *She's a very attractive young woman.* ○ *He is physically attractive but his personality is a turn-off.*

▸ **COLLOCATIONS:**
physically/sexually attractive
find *someone* attractive

▸ **SYNONYM:** good-looking

▸ **ANTONYMS:** unattractive, ugly

2 **ADJECTIVE** Something that is **attractive** has a pleasant appearance or sound. ○ *The flat was small but attractive.* ○ *They had gone to a lot of trouble to make the town attractive and had some lovely flower displays.*

▸ **COLLOCATIONS:**
look attractive
make *something* attractive

▸ **ANTONYMS:** unattractive, ugly

WORD FAMILY		
attract	**VERB**	○ *The course attracts students from all over the country.*
attraction	**NOUN**	○ *One of Tanzania's top attractions is the Serengeti National Park.*
attractive	**ADJECTIVE**	○ *The house stands in attractive gardens.*
attractively	**ADVERB**	○ *All the hotel's rooms are clean and attractively decorated.*
attractiveness	**UNCOUNT**	○ *The forest will enhance the attractiveness of the region.*
unattractive	**ADJECTIVE**	○ *I found him physically unattractive.*

audi|ence /ˈɔːdiəns/ (audiences)   MEDIA & CULTURE

NOUN The **audience** at a play, concert, film, or public meeting is the group of people watching or listening to it. ○ *He was speaking to an audience of students.* ○ *The concert attracted a large audience.* ○ *He asked all the college students in the audience to stand up.*

▶ **COLLOCATIONS:**
an audience **of** *people*
in the audience
in front of an audience
attract an audience
entertain/address an audience
a **large** audience
a **young/older** audience
an audience **member**

author /ˈɔːθə/ (authors)   MEDIA & CULTURE

NOUN The **author of** a piece of writing is the person who wrote it. ○ [+ of] *The author of the report was a professional psychologist.* ○ *a best-selling crime author*

▶ **SYNONYM:** writer

auto|mat|ic /ˌɔːtəˈmætɪk/

1 ADJECTIVE An **automatic** machine or device is one which has controls that enable it to perform a task without needing to be constantly operated by a person. **Automatic** methods and processes involve the use of such machines. ○ *Modern trains have automatic doors.* ○ *The car has an automatic temperature control.*

2 ADJECTIVE An **automatic** action is one that you do without thinking about it. ○ *His response was automatic.* ○ *All of the automatic body functions, even breathing, are affected.*

WORD FAMILY		
automatic	**ADJECTIVE**	○ *Soldiers armed with automatic weapons were posted at the gates.*
automatically	**ADVERB**	○ *She put her hand up to her face, almost automatically.*

avail|able /əˈveɪləbəl/   SHOPPING

ADJECTIVE If something you want or need is **available**, you can find it or obtain it. ○ [+ for] *There are three small boats available for hire.* ○ *Both snacks and light meals are readily available in Turkey.* ○ *documents available on the Internet*

▶ **COLLOCATIONS:**
available **for** *something*
available **to** *someone*
readily/widely/freely available
currently available

▶ **ANTONYM:** unavailable

WORD FAMILY		
available	**ADJECTIVE**	○ This was the only option available to them.
availability	**UNCOUNT**	○ The easy availability of junk food is contributing to the problem of obesity.
unavailable	**ADJECTIVE**	○ The book is currently unavailable in English.

award /əˈwɔːd/ (awards)　　MEDIA & CULTURE

NOUN An **award** is a prize or certificate that a person is given for doing something well. ○ [+ for] He won the award for best actor. ○ She presented a bravery award to schoolgirl Caroline Tucker.

▶ **COLLOCATIONS:**
an award **for** something
win/receive an award
present an award
a **special/prestigious** award
an award **winner**
an award **ceremony**

aware of /əˈweə əv, STRONG ɒv, AM ʌv/

1 ADJECTIVE If you are **aware of** something, you know about it. ○ Smokers are well aware of the dangers to their own health. ○ He should have been aware of what his junior officers were doing.

▶ **ANTONYM:** unaware

2 ADJECTIVE If you are **aware of** something, you realize that it is present or is happening because you hear it, see it, smell it, or feel it. ○ He was vaguely aware of someone behind him. ○ She became acutely aware of the noise of the city.

▶ **COLLOCATIONS:**
well/fully/acutely/keenly aware of something
vaguely/dimly aware of something
painfully aware of something
become aware of something
be made aware of something

▶ **SYNONYM:** conscious

▶ **ANTONYM:** unaware

WORD FAMILY		
aware of	**ADJECTIVE**	○ He was painfully aware of the way he looked.
awareness	**UNCOUNT**	○ There has been an increasing awareness that many people are affected by crime.
unaware of	**ADJECTIVE**	○ Many young people are unaware of the dangers of drugs.

Bb

back|ground /ˈbækgraʊnd/ (backgrounds) PEOPLE

1 NOUN Your **background** is the kind of family you come from and the kind of education you have had. It can also refer to such things as your social and racial origins, your financial status, or the type of work experience that you have. ○ *She came from a working-class background.* ○ *His background was in engineering.*

▸ **COLLOCATIONS:**
   someone's **ethnic/social/educational** background
   someone's **cultural/religious** background
   someone's **family** background
   a **poor/disadvantaged** background
   a **privileged** background
   come from/have a ... background

2 NOUN You can use **background** to refer to the things in a picture or scene that are less noticeable or important than the main things or people in it. ○ *The figures were standing on grass and in the background were trees.* ○ *Paint the background tones lighter and the colours cooler.*

▸ **COLLOCATION: in** the background

▸ **ANTONYM:** foreground

back|pack|ing /ˈbækpækɪŋ/ TRANSPORT & TRAVEL

UNCOUNTABLE NOUN If you go **backpacking**, you go travelling with a bag that you carry on your back. ○ *We were going backpacking in Corfu.* ○ *Scott had been on a backpacking holiday in the Sierra Nevada mountains.*

WORD FAMILY		
backpack	NOUN	○ *Children marched by carrying pink backpacks.*
backpack	VERB	○ *Duncan recently backpacked around China with his family.*
backpacking	UNCOUNT	○ *a six-month backpacking trip*
backpacker	NOUN	○ *The hostel is popular with backpackers.*

ba|con /ˈbeɪkən/ FOOD & DRINK

UNCOUNTABLE NOUN **Bacon** is salted or smoked meat which comes from the back or sides of a pig. ○ *bacon and eggs* ○ *He helped himself to one of the bacon sandwiches.*

bad|min|ton /'bædmɪntən/ SPORT & ACTIVITY

UNCOUNTABLE NOUN Badminton is a game played by two or four players on a rectangular court with a high net across the middle. The players try to score points by hitting a small object called a shuttlecock across the net using a racket. ○ *Students were playing badminton.* ○ *a game of badminton*

▶ **COLLOCATIONS:**
play badminton
a badminton **player/court/racket**

bake /beɪk/ (bakes, baking, baked) FOOD & DRINK

1 VERB If you **bake**, you spend some time preparing and mixing together ingredients to make bread, cakes, pies, or other food which is cooked in the oven. ○ *I love to bake.*

2 VERB When a cake or bread **bakes** or when you **bake** it, it cooks in the oven without any extra liquid or fat. ○ *Bake the cake for 35 to 50 minutes.* ○ *The batter rises as it bakes.*

▶ **COLLOCATIONS:**
bake **bread/cookies/biscuits**
bake a **cake**
freshly baked

WORD FAMILY		
bake	VERB	○ freshly baked bread
baking	UNCOUNT	○ On a Thursday she used to do all the baking.
baker	NOUN	○ His father was a baker.
bakery	NOUN	○ Bread is available either from supermarkets or from a bakery.

bald /bɔːld/ (balder, baldest) CLOTHES & APPEARANCE

ADJECTIVE Someone who is **bald** has little or no hair on the top of their head. ○ *He is going bald.* ○ *The man's bald head was beaded with sweat.*

▶ **COLLOCATIONS:**
go bald
a bald **head**
a bald **patch/spot**
a bald **man**
completely/nearly bald

band /bænd/ (bands) MEDIA & CULTURE

NOUN A **band** is a small group of musicians who play popular music such as jazz, rock, or pop. ○ *He was a drummer in a rock band.* ○ *A band was playing and the floor was full of people dancing.*

b

► **COLLOCATIONS:**
play in a band
form/join a band
a band **plays/performs**
a **rock/jazz/pop** band
a **boy** band
a **live** band

---

bang /bæŋ/ (bangs, banging, banged)

1 NOUN A **bang** is a sudden loud noise such as the noise of an explosion. ○ *I heard four or five loud bangs.* ○ *She slammed the door with a bang.*

► **COLLOCATIONS:**
hear a bang
go bang
with a bang
a **loud** bang

2 VERB If something **bangs**, it makes a sudden loud noise, once or several times. ○ *The door banged shut behind them.*

---

bar|becue /ˈbɑːbɪkjuː/ (barbecues)　　　[SOCIAL LIFE]
[in AM, also use **barbeque**, **Bar-B-Q**]

NOUN If someone has a **barbecue**, they cook and eat food outside. ○ *On these fine evenings we usually have a barbecue.* ○ *He went to a barbecue at his girlfriend's house.*

► **COLLOCATIONS:**
have a barbecue
go to a barbecue
a **family** barbecue

---

bare /beə/　　　[CLOTHES & APPEARANCE]

ADJECTIVE If a part of your body is **bare**, it is not covered by any clothing. ○ *She was wearing only a thin robe and her feet were bare.* ○ *She had bare arms and a bare neck.*

► **COLLOCATION:** bare **feet/legs/arms**

► **SYNONYM:** naked

► **ANTONYM:** clothed

---

bar|gain /ˈbɑːgɪn/ (bargains)　　　[SHOPPING]

NOUN Something that is a **bargain** is good value for money, usually because it has been sold at a lower price than normal. ○ *At this price the phone is a bargain.* ○ *good-quality shoes at bargain prices* ○ *bargain hunters queuing for the sales*

► **COLLOCATIONS:**
get/find a bargain
a bargain **price**
a bargain **hunter**
bargain **hunting**

base|ball /ˈbeɪsbɔːl/ SPORT & ACTIVITY

UNCOUNTABLE NOUN In America, **baseball** is a game played by two teams of nine players. Each player from one team hits a ball with a bat and then tries to run around three bases and get to the home base before the other team can get the ball back. ○ *Like most young Americans, he played baseball.* ○ *a professional baseball player*

▶ **COLLOCATIONS:**
   play baseball
   a baseball **game**
   a baseball **team/player/fan**
   a baseball **bat**
   a baseball **field/stadium**

ba|sin /ˈbeɪsən/ (basins) HOME

NOUN A **basin**, or **washbasin**, is a large bowl, usually with taps for hot and cold water, for washing your hands and face. ○ *Fill the basin with warm water.* ○ *a cast-iron bath with a matching basin and WC*

bas|ket /ˈbɑːskɪt, ˈbæs-/ (baskets) SHOPPING

1 NOUN A **basket** is a container that is used for carrying or storing objects, for example things you are buying in a shop. Baskets are made from thin strips of materials such as straw, plastic, or wire woven together. ○ *He piled bread rolls and fresh milk into a wire shopping basket.* ○ *She carried a basket full of groceries.*

▶ **COLLOCATIONS:**
   a **shopping** basket
   a **wire/wicker** basket
   a **laundry/washing** basket
   a **picnic** basket

2 NOUN A **basket** is the place on a website where you put things that you plan to buy. ○ *You can save items in your basket for later and then think about whether you really need them.* ○ *Click on the item to put it in your basket.*

basket|ball /ˈbɑːskɪtbɔːl, ˈbæs-/ SPORT & ACTIVITY

UNCOUNTABLE NOUN **Basketball** is a game in which two teams of five players each try to score goals by throwing a large ball through a circular net fixed to a metal ring at each end of the court. ○ *My hobbies are playing basketball and football.* ○ *At school he was in the basketball team.*

▶ **COLLOCATIONS:**
   play basketball
   a basketball **game**
   a basketball **team/player/coach**
   a basketball **court**

b

bat /bæt/ (bats) SPORT & ACTIVITY

NOUN A **bat** is a specially shaped piece of wood that is used for hitting the ball in baseball, softball, cricket, rounders, or table tennis. ○ *a baseball bat* ○ *a cricket bat* ○ *The injury affected his ability to swing the bat.*

bat|tle /'bætəl/ (battles) HISTORY

NOUN A **battle** is a violent fight between groups of people, especially one between military forces during a war. ○ *the victory of King William III at the Battle of the Boyne* ○ *Gun battles broke out right the way through the area.* ○ *men who die in battle*

▶ **COLLOCATIONS:**
fight a battle
win/lose a battle
a battle **breaks out/erupts**
a **fierce/bloody** battle
a **gun** battle

beach /biːtʃ/ (beaches) SCIENCE & NATURE TRANSPORT & TRAVEL

NOUN A **beach** is an area of sand or stones beside the sea. ○ *I just want to lie on the beach in the sun.* ○ *a beautiful sandy beach* ○ *the Thai beach resort of Phuket*

▶ **COLLOCATIONS:**
on the beach
go to the beach
a **sandy/rocky/pebble** beach
a beach **holiday**
a beach **resort**
a beach **house/hut**

▶ **SYNONYM:** seashore

bed|room /'bedruːm/ (bedrooms) HOME

NOUN A **bedroom** is a room used for sleeping in. ○ *a two-bedroom apartment* ○ *bedroom furniture* ○ *The master bedroom overlooked Central Park.*

▶ **COLLOCATIONS:**
in the bedroom
the **main/master** bedroom
a **spare/guest** bedroom

beef /biːf/ FOOD & DRINK

UNCOUNTABLE NOUN **Beef** is the meat of a cow, bull, or ox. ○ *roast beef* ○ *beef stew* ○ *The large Hindu population does not generally eat beef.*

▶ **COLLOCATIONS:**
eat beef
roast beef
ground/minced beef
beef **products**

be|have /bɪˈheɪv/ (behaves, behaving, behaved)

1 **VERB** The way that you **behave** is the way that you do and say things, and the things that you do and say. ○ *He'd behaved badly.* ○ *Jo-Beth's behaving really strangely.*

▶ **COLLOCATIONS:**
behave **badly**
behave **well/properly/responsibly**
behave **strangely/normally**

▶ **SYNONYM:** act

2 **VERB** If you **behave** or **behave yourself**, you act in the way that people think is correct and proper. ○ *You have to behave.* ○ *They were expected to behave themselves.*

▶ **SYNONYM:** be good

be|hav|iour /bɪˈheɪvjə/ [in AM, use **behavior**]

UNCOUNTABLE NOUN People's or animals' **behaviour** is the way that they behave. ○ *Make sure that good behaviour is rewarded.* ○ *If someone is hurt, then normal human behaviour is for others to comfort them.*

▶ **COLLOCATIONS:**
good behaviour
bad/anti-social/unacceptable behaviour
aggressive/violent behaviour
normal behaviour
bizarre/erratic behaviour
human behaviour

▶ **SYNONYM:** conduct

WORD FAMILY		
behave	**VERB**	○ *Most parents like to know that their children will behave well when in a restaurant.*
behaviour	**UNCOUNT**	○ *You will have to be very firm in dealing with the bad behaviour.*
behavioural	**ADJECTIVE**	○ *behavioural problems*

be|lief /bɪˈliːf/ (beliefs)   BELIEFS & OPINIONS

1 **NOUN** **Belief** is a feeling of certainty that something exists, is true, or is good. ○ [+ in] *One billion people throughout the world are Muslims, united by belief in one god.* ○ [+ in] *a strong belief in life after death* ○ [+ that] *There is a widespread belief that the elections will change little.*

→ see Useful Phrases **beyond belief**

2 **PLURAL NOUN** Your religious or political **beliefs** are your opinions on religious or political matters. ○ *He refuses to compete on Sundays because of his religious beliefs.* ○ *Many of us had opposing political beliefs.*

▶ **COLLOCATIONS:**
belief **in** something
religious/political beliefs
strong/firm beliefs
a **widespread/popular/common** belief
have/hold a belief

▶ **SYNONYM:** principles

be|lieve /bɪ'liːv/ (believes, believing, believed)

1 VERB If you **believe** that something is true, you think that it is true, but you are not sure. ○ [+ that] *They believed he could help them.* ○ [+ that] *She firmly believes that the best way to learn a language is to travel to the country in which it is spoken.*

▶ **SYNONYM:** think

2 VERB If you **believe in** a way of life or an idea, you are in favour of it because you think it is good or right. ○ [+ in] *He believed passionately in human rights.* ○ [+ in] *people who believe in freedom and justice*

▶ **COLLOCATIONS:**
believe **in** something
firmly/strongly/honestly believe something

WORD FAMILY		
belief	NOUN	○ *Bill grew up with the belief that he could never be as good as his father.*
believe	VERB	○ *He believed strongly that the country should remain as one nation.*
believable	ADJECTIVE	○ *believable evidence*
unbelievable	ADJECTIVE	○ *a weird and unbelievable story*

belt /belt/ (belts)

CLOTHES & APPEARANCE

NOUN A **belt** is a strip of leather or cloth that you fasten round your waist. ○ *He wore a belt with a large brass buckle.* ○ *a black leather belt*

ben|efit /'benɪfɪt/ (benefits)

NOUN The **benefit of** something is the help that you get from it or the advantage that results from it. ○ [+ of] *The health benefits of giving up smoking are enormous.* ○ *For maximum benefit, use your treatment every day.*

▶ **COLLOCATIONS:**
the benefits **of** something
get/see/enjoy the benefit of something
great/significant benefits
a **potential** benefit
health/economic/financial benefits

▶ **SYNONYM:** advantage

WORD FAMILY

benefit	NOUN	○ You will also be getting the benefit of being out of doors.
benefit	VERB	○ a variety of government programmes benefiting children
beneficial	ADJECTIVE	○ A moderate amount of exercise is beneficial.

bi|og|ra|phy /baɪˈɒgrəfi/ (biographies) `MEDIA & CULTURE`

NOUN A **biography** of someone is an account of their life, written by someone else. ○ [+ of] He has written a biography of Paul McCartney.

▶ COLLOCATIONS:
a biography **of** someone
write/read/publish a biography
an **official** biography

bi|ol|ogy /baɪˈɒlədʒi/ `SCIENCE & NATURE`

UNCOUNTABLE NOUN **Biology** is the science which is concerned with the study of living things. ○ Andy studied biology at university. ○ a biology lesson ○ biology books

▶ COLLOCATIONS:
study/teach biology
a biology **teacher/professor/student**
a biology **class/lesson/course**

WORD FAMILY

biology	UNCOUNT	○ She's training to be a biology teacher.
biologist	NOUN	○ We interviewed a team of biologists studying the fruit fly.
biological	ADJECTIVE	○ biological processes, such as ageing
biologically	ADVERB	○ Much of our behaviour is biologically determined.

blame /bleɪm/ (blames, blaming, blamed) `BELIEFS & OPINIONS`

VERB If you **blame** a person or thing **for** something bad, you believe or say that they are responsible for it or that they caused it. ○ It's easy to blame the parents of teenagers when things go wrong. ○ [+ for] Pollution has been blamed for the problem. ○ [+ on] Six deaths were blamed on the weather.

▶ COLLOCATIONS:
blame someone **for** something
blame something **on** someone/something

blis|ter /ˈblɪstə/ (blisters) `HEALTH`

NOUN A **blister** is a painful swelling on the surface of your skin. Blisters contain a clear liquid and are usually caused by heat or by something repeatedly rubbing your skin. ○ *New shoes can rub and cause blisters.* ○ *I wore these boots for the first time yesterday and got blisters.*

▸ COLLOCATIONS:
   get a blister
   cause a blister

---

block /blɒk/ (blocks) `PLACES`

NOUN A **block** of flats or offices is a large building containing them. ○ [+ *of*] *He lives in a 20-storey block of flats on Westferry Road.* ○ *The company's headquarters are on the fourth floor of a smart new office block.*

▸ COLLOCATIONS:
   a block **of** *something*
   a block **of** flats
   an **apartment/office** block
   a **tower** block

---

blow /bləʊ/ (blows, blowing, blew, blown) `SCIENCE & NATURE`

VERB When a wind or breeze **blows**, the air moves. ○ *A cold wind blew at the top of the hill.* ○ *We woke to find a gale blowing outside.*

▸ COLLOCATION: a **wind/breeze/gale** blows

---

board /bɔːd/ (boards, boarding, boarded) `TRANSPORT & TRAVEL`

VERB When you **board** a train, ship, or aircraft, you get on it in order to travel somewhere. [FORMAL] ○ *I boarded the plane for England.* ○ *The exact number of passengers who boarded the ferry was not known.*

▸ COLLOCATIONS:
   board a **plane/bus/train/ship/boat**
   board a **flight**

▸ SYNONYM: get on

▸ ANTONYMS: get off, disembark

---

board|ing card /ˈbɔːdɪŋ kɑːd/ (boarding cards)

NOUN A **boarding card** is a card which a passenger must have when boarding a plane or a boat. ○ *Her passport and boarding card were checked by ground crew.*

▸ SYNONYM: boarding pass

---

boil /bɔɪl/ (boils, boiling, boiled) `FOOD & DRINK`

1 **VERB** When a hot liquid **boils** or when you **boil** it, bubbles appear in it and it starts to change into steam or vapour. ○ *Boil the water in the saucepan and add the sage.* ○ *a saucepan of boiling water* ○ *Marianne put the kettle on to boil.*

2 **VERB** When you **boil** food, or when it **boils**, it is cooked in boiling water. ○ *Boil the chick peas, add garlic and lemon juice.* ○ *boiled eggs and toast*

book /bʊk/ (books, booking, booked) `TRANSPORT & TRAVEL`

VERB When you **book** something such as a hotel room or a ticket, you arrange to have it or use it at a particular time. ○ *Stephanie booked a room at the Hotel Castex in Marais.* ○ *It's fairly simple to book cinema tickets online.*

▶ **COLLOCATIONS:**
book a **flight/ticket/hotel**
book a **holiday/trip**
book a **room/table/seat**
book **accommodation**
a booking **fee**
book **online**

▶ **SYNONYM:** reserve

book in or book into

PHRASAL VERB When you **book into** a hotel or when you **book in**, you officially state that you have arrived to stay there, usually by signing your name in a register. [BRIT; in AM, use **check in**, **check into**] ○ *He was happy to book into the Royal Pavilion Hotel.* ○ *They have booked in for four nights.*

▶ **SYNONYMS:** check in, check into

▶ **ANTONYMS:** check out, check out of

boots /buːts/ (boots) `CLOTHES & APPEARANCE` `SPORT & ACTIVITY`

1 PLURAL NOUN **Boots** are shoes that cover your whole foot and the lower part of your leg. ○ *She was wearing knee-high black boots.* ○ *He reached down and pulled off his boots.*

2 PLURAL NOUN **Boots** are strong, heavy shoes which may cover your ankle and which have thick soles. You wear them to protect your feet, for example when you are walking or taking part in sport. ○ *his first pair of football boots* ○ *Wear comfortable walking boots.*

▶ **COLLOCATIONS:**
a **pair of** boots
wear boots
put on/pull on boots
take off/pull off boots
football boots
walking/hiking boots
leather/suede/rubber boots
high-heeled boots

bored /bɔːd/

ADJECTIVE If you are **bored**, you feel tired and impatient because you have lost interest in something or because you have nothing to do. ○ [+ *with/of*] *After a while Jan got bored of the programme and I watched on my own.* ○ *Can't think what to do with bored children on a Sunday afternoon?*

b

▶ COLLOCATIONS:
bored **with/of** something
get/become/grow bored
look bored
a bored **child/teenager/housewife**

▶ ANTONYM: interested

bor|ing /ˈbɔːrɪŋ/

ADJECTIVE Someone or something **boring** is so dull and uninteresting that they make people tired and impatient. ○ *I work long hours at a boring job.* ○ *I realise my life is quite boring and ordinary compared to his.*

▶ COLLOCATIONS:
get/become boring
find someone/something boring
a boring **job/life/game/place**
a boring **person**

▶ SYNONYMS: dull, tedious

▶ ANTONYM: interesting

WORD FAMILY		
boring	ADJECTIVE	○ I found the subject pretty boring when I was younger.
bored	ADJECTIVE	○ There were also groups of teenagers standing around looking bored.
bore	VERB	○ Adrina was easily bored and the seemingly endless journey offered little entertainment.
boredom	UNCOUNT	○ I started taking photographs as a way to relieve boredom.

brace|let /ˈbreɪslɪt/ (bracelets)   CLOTHES & APPEARANCE

NOUN A **bracelet** is a chain or band, usually made of metal, which you wear around your wrist as jewellery. ○ *She wore a large gold bracelet.*

▶ COLLOCATIONS:
wear a bracelet
a **gold/silver/diamond** bracelet

brand /brænd/ (brands)   SHOPPING

NOUN A **brand** of a product is the version of it that is made by one particular manufacturer. ○ [+ of] *I know what brand of toothpaste he uses.* ○ *I bought one of the leading brands.* ○ *a supermarket's own brand*

▶ COLLOCATIONS:
a brand **of** something
a **global/leading/top** brand
a **new** brand

launch a brand
buy a brand

▶ SYNONYM: make

---

brand-new /ˌbrændˈnjuː, AM '-nuː/   `SHOPPING`   **b**

ADJECTIVE A **brand-new** object is completely new. ○ *Yesterday he went off to buy himself a brand-new car.* ○ *a brand-new house*

---

break down /breɪk ˈdaʊn/ (breaks down,   `TRANSPORT & TRAVEL`
breaking down, broke down, broken down)

PHRASAL VERB If a machine or a vehicle **breaks down**, it stops working. ○ *Their car broke down.* ○ *The central heating at work had broken down.*

---

breathe /briːð/ (breathes, breathing, breathed)

VERB When people or animals **breathe**, they take air into their lungs and let it out again. ○ *He stood there breathing deeply and evenly.* ○ *No American should have to drive out of town to breathe clean air.*

▶ COLLOCATIONS:
breathe **deeply/heavily/hard/slowly**
barely/hardly breathe

WORD FAMILY		
breathe	VERB	○ She was hugging him so tightly he could barely breathe.
breathing	UNCOUNT	○ Her breathing became slow and heavy.
breath	NOUN	○ He took a deep breath and began to climb the stairs.
breathless	ADJECTIVE	○ Jahdo stopped running, too breathless to do anything.

---

breeze /briːz/ (breezes)   `SCIENCE & NATURE`

NOUN A **breeze** is a gentle wind. ○ *a cool summer breeze* ○ *A stiff breeze blew off the ocean.* ○ *She let the sea breeze ruffle through her hair.*

▶ COLLOCATIONS:
a **cool/cooling/warm** breeze
a **light/gentle/slight** breeze
a **stiff/strong** breeze
a **summer/sea** breeze
an **evening/night/morning/afternoon** breeze
a breeze **blows**

WORD FAMILY		
breeze	NOUN	○ He slept outside to get the cool evening breeze.
breezy	ADJECTIVE	○ Take care on bright, breezy days, as you could get sunburnt even if you feel cool.

b

bride /braɪd/ (brides)   `SOCIAL LIFE`

NOUN A **bride** is a woman who is getting married or who has just got married.
  ○ *The bride wore a white dress.* ○ *Now the bride and groom will cut the cake.*

→ see also **groom**

bril|liant /ˈbrɪliənt/

1 ADJECTIVE A **brilliant** person, idea, or performance is extremely clever or skilful.
  ○ *He was a brilliant musician.* ○ *It was a brilliant performance by Williams.* ○ *What a brilliant idea!*

▶ **COLLOCATIONS:**
    a brilliant **idea**
    a brilliant **performance/display**
    a brilliant **student/player/scientist**

2 ADJECTIVE You can say that something is **brilliant** when you are very pleased about it or think that it is very good. [mainly BRIT, INFORMAL, SPOKEN]
  ○ *My sister's given me this brilliant book.* ○ *He said his trip was absolutely brilliant.*

▶ **SYNONYMS:** great, fantastic

▶ **ANTONYM:** awful

WORD FAMILY		
brilliant	ADJECTIVE	○ *So what's this brilliant idea of yours?*
brilliantly	ADVERB	○ *The strategy worked brilliantly.*
brilliance	UNCOUNT	○ *He was a deeply serious musician who had shown his brilliance very early.*

bring up /brɪŋ ˈʌp/ (brings up, bringing up, brought up)   `PEOPLE`

PHRASAL VERB When someone **brings up** a child, they look after it until it is an adult.
  ○ *His grandmother and his father brought him up.* ○ *He was brought up in England.*

▶ **SYNONYM:** raise

browse /braʊz/ (browses, browsing, browsed)   `COMMUNICATIONS`

VERB If you **browse** on a computer, you search for information, especially on the Internet. ○ *Students were browsing websites rather than working.* ○ *People now use mobile phones to browse the Internet.*

▶ **COLLOCATIONS:**
    browse the **Internet**
    browse a **website**

budg|et /ˈbʌdʒɪt/ (budgets)   `MONEY`

NOUN Your **budget** is the amount of money that you have available to spend. The **budget** for something is the amount of money that a person, organization, or country has available to spend on it. ○ *A holiday is still one of the costliest items* *in any family budget.* ○ *Someone had furnished the place on a tight budget.* ○ [+ for] *This year's budget for education probably won't be much higher.*

▶ **COLLOCATIONS:**
the budget **for** something
a **tight/low/modest** budget
a **big/huge** budget
the **total/overall** budget
cut/increase a budget
keep to/keep within a budget

---

build|er /ˈbɪldə/ (builders) WORK

NOUN A **builder** is a person whose job is to build or repair houses and other buildings. ○ *The builders have finished the roof.* ○ *In rural areas, it can be harder to find builders.*

> **WORD FAMILY**
> | build | VERB | ○ *The house was built in the early 19th century.* |
> |---|---|---|
> | building | NOUN | ○ *They were on the upper floor of the building.* |
> | builder | NOUN | ○ *His father was a builder.* |

---

burg|er /ˈbɜːgə/ (burgers) FOOD & DRINK

NOUN A **burger** is a flat round mass of minced meat or vegetables, which is fried and often eaten in a bread roll. ○ *burger and chips* ○ *vegetable burgers*

▶ **COLLOCATION:** a **chicken/beef/lamb/vegetable** burger

---

bur|gla|ry /ˈbɜːgləri/ (burglaries) CRIME

NOUN If someone commits a **burglary**, they enter a building by force and steal things. ○ *An 11-year-old boy committed a burglary.* ○ *He's been arrested for burglary.*

▶ **COLLOCATIONS:**
commit a burglary
be **arrested for** burglary
an **attempted** burglary
a burglary **suspect/victim**

bur|glar /ˈbɜːglə/ (burglars)

NOUN A **burglar** is a thief who enters a house or other building by force. ○ *Burglars broke into their home.* ○ *The burglars stole her two wedding rings from her bedside table as she slept.*

→ see note at **thief**

▶ **COLLOCATIONS:**
a burglar **breaks into** somewhere
a burglar **steals** something
catch/confront a burglar

bus /bʌs/ (buses)

`TRANSPORT & TRAVEL`

NOUN A **bus** is a large motor vehicle which carries passengers from one place to another. ○ *He missed his last bus home.* ○ *They had to travel everywhere by bus.*

▸ COLLOCATIONS:
  by bus
  get/catch/take the bus
  get on/board a bus
  get off a bus
  miss the bus
  a **school** bus
  a bus **driver/passenger**
  a bus **stop/station**
  a bus **ride/trip**
  a bus **service/route**
  a bus **fare**

but|ter /ˈbʌtə/

`FOOD & DRINK`

UNCOUNTABLE NOUN **Butter** is a soft yellow substance made from cream. You spread it on bread or use it in cooking. ○ *bread and butter* ○ *Pour the melted butter into a large mixing bowl.*

▸ COLLOCATIONS:
  unsalted/salted butter
  melt butter

but|ton /ˈbʌtən/ (buttons)

`CLOTHES & APPEARANCE`

NOUN **Buttons** are small hard objects sewn on to shirts, coats, or other pieces of clothing. You fasten the clothing by pushing the buttons through holes called buttonholes. ○ *a coat with brass buttons*

Cc

cake /keɪk/ (cakes)

FOOD & DRINK

NOUN A **cake** is a sweet food made by baking a mixture of flour, eggs, sugar, and fat in an oven. ○ *Would you like a piece of chocolate cake?* ○ *Mum asked me to ice his birthday cake.*

▶ **COLLOCATIONS:**
   bake/make a cake
   decorate/ice a cake
   a **piece/slice** of cake
   a **chocolate/lemon** cake
   a **birthday/wedding** cake
   a **homemade** cake
   a cake **recipe/decoration**

call back /kɔːl ˈbæk/
(calls back, calling back, called back)

COMMUNICATIONS

PHRASAL VERB If you **call** someone **back**, you telephone them again or in return for a telephone call that they have made to you. ○ *If we're not around she'll take a message and we'll call you back.* ○ *If you want further advice, you can call back and speak to the same adviser.*

▶ **SYNONYM:** ring back

call cen|tre /ˈkɔːl sentə/ (call centres)

WORK   COMMUNICATIONS

[in AM, use **call center**]

NOUN A **call centre** is an office where people work answering or making telephone calls for a particular company. ○ *In the United States, call centres handle a billion calls per year.* ○ *Working in a call centre does not suit everyone.*

call for /ˈkɔːl fə, STRONG ˌfɔː/
(calls for, calling for, called for)

SOCIAL LIFE

PHRASAL VERB If you **call for** someone, you go to the building where they are, so that you can both go somewhere. ○ *I'll call for you after lunch.*

call off /kɔːl ˈɒf/ (calls off, calling off, called off)

PHRASAL VERB If you **call off** an event that has been planned, you cancel it. ○ *He has called off the trip.* ○ *The union threatened a strike but called it off at the last minute.*

▶ **SYNONYM:** cancel

calm down /kɑːm ˈdaʊn/ (calms down, calming down, calmed down)

PHRASAL VERB If you **calm down**, or if someone **calms** you **down**, you become less angry, upset, or excited. ○ *Calm down for a minute and listen to me.* ○ *You always calmed me down when I was nervous.*

calo|rie /ˈkæləri/ (calories)　　FOOD & DRINK　HEALTH

NOUN **Calories** are units used to measure the energy value of food. People who are on diets try to eat food that does not contain many calories. ○ *Cream cakes do have quite a lot of calories.* ○ *Sport is the most effective way to burn calories.* ○ *reduce your calorie intake*

▶ COLLOCATIONS:
   eat/consume calories
   burn calories
   count calories
   calorie **intake**

camp|ing /ˈkæmpɪŋ/　　TRANSPORT & TRAVEL

UNCOUNTABLE NOUN **Camping** is the activity of staying in a tent or caravan for a short time. ○ *We have gone camping at the lake a few times.* ○ *a camping trip*

▶ COLLOCATIONS:
   go camping
   camping **gear/equipment**
   a camping **stove**

camp|site /ˈkæmpsaɪt/ (campsites)

NOUN A **campsite** is a place where people who are on holiday can stay in tents. ○ *The first night was spent at a beautiful campsite on the shore of Lake Onega.*

▶ SYNONYM: camping site

cam|pus /ˈkæmpəs/ (campuses)　　EDUCATION

NOUN A **campus** is an area of land that contains the main buildings of a university or college. ○ *The students' union building is in the centre of the university campus.* ○ *Cars are not allowed on campus.*

▶ COLLOCATIONS:
   on/off campus
   a **university/college** campus

can|di|date /ˈkændɪdeɪt/ (candidates)　　WORK

NOUN A **candidate** is someone who is being considered for a job which he or she has applied for. ○ [+ for] *There were six candidates for the job.* ○ *We all spoke to them and John emerged as the best candidate.*

▶ COLLOCATION: a candidate **for** something

cap /kæp/ (caps)

CLOTHES & APPEARANCE

NOUN A **cap** is a soft, flat hat with a curved part at the front which is called a peak.
○ *a dark-blue baseball cap*

▸ **COLLOCATIONS:**
wear a cap
a **baseball/flat/peaked** cap

ca|pable /ˈkeɪpəbəl/

PERSONALITY

1 ADJECTIVE If a person or thing is **capable of** doing something, they have the ability to do it. ○ [+ of] *Please don't fuss. I'm perfectly capable of looking after myself.*
○ [+ of] *Today's sportbikes are capable of truly astonishing speeds.*

▸ **COLLOCATIONS:**
capable **of** *something*
perfectly/fully/quite capable
physically capable

▸ **ANTONYM:** incapable

2 ADJECTIVE Someone who is **capable** has the skill or qualities necessary to do a particular thing well, or is able to do most things well. ○ *She's a very capable speaker.* ○ *We have assembled a highly capable team for this project.*

▸ **COLLOCATIONS:**
extremely/highly capable
a capable **person/manager/leader**

▸ **SYNONYMS:** competent, able, talented

▸ **ANTONYMS:** incapable, incompetent

WORD FAMILY		
capable	ADJECTIVE	○ She was physically capable of running for just over 30 minutes.
capably	ADVERB	○ He will do the job capably.
capability	UNCOUNT	○ The software has the capability to translate 26 different languages.
incapable	ADJECTIVE	○ He seemed to be completely incapable of understanding how I felt.

cards /kɑːdz/

FREE TIME

PLURAL NOUN **Cards** are thin pieces of cardboard with numbers or pictures printed on them which are used to play various games. ○ *I taught Rachel how to play cards.*
○ *a pack of cards*

▸ **SYNONYM:** playing cards

ca|reer /kəˈrɪə/ (careers)

WORK

NOUN A **career** is your job or profession, or the part of your life that you spend

C

working. ○ *During his career, he wrote more than fifty plays.* ○ *[+ as] She is now concentrating on a career as a fashion designer.* ○ *We can give you careers advice, if you need it.*

▶ **COLLOCATIONS:**
during someone's career
a career **as** something
a career **in** something
have/build/start/choose a career
change careers
ruin/end/wreck someone's career
a **successful/good/promising** career
a **long/short** career
an **acting/political/modelling/musical** career
careers **advice/guidance**
a career **path/move/choice**
a career **change/break**

---

car park /ˈkɑː pɑːk/ (car parks) PLACES

NOUN A **car park** is an area or building where people can leave their cars. ○ *I parked the car in an underground car park.* ○ *the airport car park* ○ *a multi-storey car park*

---

car|riage /ˈkærɪdʒ/ (carriages) TRANSPORT & TRAVEL

NOUN A **carriage** is one of the separate, long sections of a train that carries passengers. ○ *She got on the train and found a seat in one of the crowded carriages.* ○ *the first-class carriage* ○ *the rear carriage*

---

car|ry out /ˌkæri ˈaʊt/ (carries out, carrying out, carried out)

PHRASAL VERB If you **carry out** a threat, task, or instruction, you do it or act according to it. ○ *Women were paid less for carrying out the same work.* ○ *They believe the attacks were carried out by nationalists.* ○ *The surgeon will carry out the operation under general anaesthetic.*

▶ **COLLOCATIONS:**
carry out a **study/test/survey/search**
carry out **research**
carry out **work/repairs/checks**
carry out an **operation**
carry out an **investigation/inspection/examination**
carry out a **bombing/attack/raid**

▶ **SYNONYM:** perform

---

car|toon /kɑːˈtuːn/ (cartoons) MEDIA & CULTURE

1 NOUN A **cartoon** is a humorous drawing or series of drawings in a newspaper or magazine. ○ *His cartoons appeared in nearly all national newspapers.* ○ *the cartoon character, Charlie Brown* ○ *a cartoon strip*

2 NOUN A **cartoon** is a film in which all the characters and scenes are drawn rather than being real people or objects. ○ *The children were in the playroom watching cartoons.* ○ *Saturday morning cartoons on TV* ○ *a cartoon series*

▶ SYNONYM: animation

---

cash /kæʃ/ SHOPPING MONEY

UNCOUNTABLE NOUN **Cash** is money, especially in the form of notes and coins. ○ *I prefer to pay cash.* ○ *two thousand pounds in cash* ○ *a financial services company with plenty of cash*

▶ COLLOCATIONS:
in cash
pay cash
withdraw/deposit cash
spend/raise/need cash
spare/extra cash

▶ SYNONYM: money

---

cast /kɑːst, kæst/ **(casts)** MEDIA & CULTURE

NOUN The **cast** of a play or film is all the people who act in it. ○ *The show is very amusing and the cast are very good.* ○ *All of the original cast have been reunited for this play.* ○ [+ *of*] *the cast of ER*

▶ COLLOCATIONS:
cast **of** something
the **supporting/original** cast
an **all-star** cast

---

cas|ual /ˈkæʒʊəl/ CLOTHES & APPEARANCE

ADJECTIVE **Casual** clothes are ones that you normally wear at home or on holiday, and not on formal occasions. ○ *I bought some casual clothes for the weekend.* ○ *casual wear* ○ *casual trousers*

▶ ANTONYM: formal

WORD FAMILY		
casual	**ADJECTIVE**	○ *You should wear loose casual clothing when meditating.*
casually	**ADVERB**	○ *They were smartly but casually dressed.*

---

cata|logue /ˈkætəlɒg/ **(catalogues)**
[in AM, usually use **catalog**] SHOPPING

NOUN A **catalogue** is a list of the things that you can buy from a particular company. ○ *The catalogue contains a whole range of unusual gifts.* ○ *an online catalogue* ○ *a glossy catalogue*

▶ SYNONYM: brochure

ca|ter|ing /ˈkeɪtərɪŋ/ `WORK`

▶ **UNCOUNTABLE NOUN Catering** is the work of providing food and drink for a large number of people, for example at weddings and parties. ○ [+ for] *He recently did the catering for a presidential reception.* ○ *His catering business made him a millionaire at 41.*

▶ **COLLOCATIONS:**
catering **for** something
a catering **business/manager/assistant**
catering **staff/equipment/facilities**
airline/hotel/hospital/school catering
do/provide/organize/arrange the catering

▶ **SYNONYM:** cooking

WORD FAMILY		
cater	**VERB**	○ *The hotel restaurant can cater for 200 guests.*
catering	**UNCOUNT**	○ *School catering is not always very good.*
caterer	**NOUN**	○ *The caterers were laying out the tables for lunch.*

ce|leb|rity /sɪˈlebrɪti/ (celebrities) `MEDIA & CULTURE`

NOUN A **celebrity** is someone who is famous, especially in areas of entertainment such as films, music, writing, or sport. ○ *At the age of 30, he suddenly became a celebrity.* ○ *A-list celebrities are very rich and globally famous.*

▶ **COLLOCATIONS:**
be/become a celebrity
a **well-known/minor/instant** celebrity
an **A-list/B-list** celebrity
a **TV** celebrity
a celebrity **chef/host/guest**
celebrity **status**
celebrity **gossip**

▶ **SYNONYM:** star

cen|tu|ry /ˈsentʃəri/ (centuries) `HISTORY`

1 NOUN A **century** is a period of a hundred years that is used when stating a date. For example, the 19th century was the period from 1801 to 1900. ○ *The novel is set in the late eighteenth century.* ○ *a 17th-century merchant's house* ○ *the early twenty-first century*

▶ **COLLOCATIONS:**
in a century
the **thirteenth/eighteenth/twenty-first** etc. century

2 NOUN A **century** is any period of a hundred years. ○ *The drought there is the worst in a century.* ○ *The first settlers arrived here centuries ago.*

cer|emo|ny /ˈserɪməni, AM -məʊni/ (ceremonies) `SOCIAL LIFE`

NOUN A **ceremony** is a formal event such as a wedding. ○ *The wedding ceremony was a private affair, attended only by close family.* ○ *Today's award ceremony took place at the British Embassy in Tokyo.*

▶ **COLLOCATIONS:**
   an opening/closing **ceremony**
   a **wedding/award/graduation** ceremony
   a **private** ceremony
   attend/watch a ceremony
   hold a ceremony
   conduct/perform a ceremony

chal|lenge /ˈtʃælɪndʒ/ (challenges)

NOUN A **challenge** is something new and difficult that requires great effort and determination. ○ *Winning our next game will be a big challenge.* ○ *The new government's first challenge is the economy.*

▶ **COLLOCATIONS:**
   be/present a challenge
   face/meet a challenge
   enjoy a challenge
   rise to the challenge
   a **big/new/real/tough** challenge
   a challenge **faces/confronts** someone

chal|leng|ing /ˈtʃælɪndʒɪŋ/

ADJECTIVE A **challenging** task or job requires great effort and determination. ○ *Mike found a challenging job as a computer programmer.* ○ *The expedition was both mentally and physically challenging.*

▶ **COLLOCATIONS:**
   a challenging **job/course**
   challenging **work**
   intellectually/technically/mentally/physically challenging

▶ **SYNONYMS:** demanding, difficult

▶ **ANTONYMS:** undemanding, easy

change /tʃeɪndʒ/ `CLOTHES & APPEARANCE`
(changes, changing, changed)

VERB When you **change** your clothes or **change**, you take some or all of your clothes off and put on different ones. ○ *Ben had changed his shirt.* ○ *I've got to get changed first.* ○ *[+ into] I changed into joggers and a hoodie.*

▶ **COLLOCATIONS:**
   change **into** something
   change **out of** something
   get changed

C

chan|nel /'tʃænəl/ (channels)   MEDIA & CULTURE

NOUN A **channel** is a television station. ○ *Do you mind if I switch channels?* ○ *It is the only serious current affairs programme on either channel.*

▸ COLLOCATIONS:
on a channel
switch/change channels
a **digital/satellite/cable** channel
a **news/movie/entertainment** channel

▸ SYNONYMS: station, side

char|ac|ter /'kærɪktə/ (characters)   MEDIA & CULTURE

NOUN The **characters** in a film, book, or play are the people that it is about.
○ *The central character of the film is played by Tom Cruise.* ○ *The author has made the characters really believable.*

▸ COLLOCATIONS:
the **central/main** character
a **fictional/minor** character
a **believable/interesting** character
cartoon characters
play/create/feature a character
character **development**

char|ac|ter|is|tic /ˌkærɪktə'rɪstɪk/ (characteristics)   PERSONALITY

NOUN The **characteristics** of a person or thing are the qualities or features that belong to them and make them recognizable. ○ [+ *of*] *Genes determine the characteristics of every living thing.* ○ *She inherited some of her mother's physical characteristics.*

▸ COLLOCATIONS:
characteristic **of** *someone/something*
have/show/share a characteristic
lack a characteristic
physical characteristics
different/distinguishing characteristics
an **important/basic** characteristic

▸ SYNONYMS: feature, trait

WORD FAMILY		
characteristic	NOUN	○ *These new drugs share the same basic characteristics.*
characteristically	ADVERB	○ *Rose was characteristically early for their meeting.*
uncharacteristic	ADJECTIVE	○ *It was uncharacteristic of her father to disappear like this.*

char|ity /ˈtʃærɪti/ (charities)

1 **NOUN** A **charity** is an organization which raises money in order to help people who are ill, disabled, or very poor. ○ *He raises a lot of money for a cancer charity.* ○ [+ for] *a charity for road traffic victims* ○ *an Aids charity*

2 **UNCOUNTABLE NOUN** If you give money **to charity**, you give it to one or more of these organizations. If you do something **for charity**, you do it in order to raise money for one or more of these organizations. ○ *I regularly give money to charity.* ○ *Graham will be raising money for charity.* ○ *a charity event*

▶ **COLLOCATIONS:**
a charity **for** someone
give something **to** charity
do something **for** charity
a charity **supports/helps** someone
a **local/small** charity
a **large/international** charity
a **cancer/conservation/homelessness** charity
charity **work**
a charity **shop**
a charity **match/concert/dinner**

WORD FAMILY		
charity	NOUN	○ *The charity helps homeless people find somewhere to live.*
charitable	ADJECTIVE	○ *Charitable organizations welcome help from volunteers.*

chart /tʃɑːt/ (charts)　　　MEDIA & CULTURE

NOUN The **charts** is the official list that shows which popular songs have sold the most copies each week. ○ *Their album went straight to number one in the charts.* ○ *Her fans wonder why she isn't at the top of the charts.*

▶ **COLLOCATIONS:**
in the charts
number one/two/twenty-five etc. in the charts
be at/reach the top of the charts
move up/down the charts
the **album/singles** charts
the **pop/music** charts
chart **success**
a chart **hit**

checked /tʃekt/　　　CLOTHES & APPEARANCE

ADJECTIVE Something that is **checked** has a pattern of small squares, usually of two colours. ○ *He was wearing blue jeans and a checked shirt.* ○ *Burberry's famous checked pattern* ○ *a blue and green checked fabric*

▶ **SYNONYM:** check

C

check in /tʃek 'ɪn/ TRANSPORT & TRAVEL
(checks in, checking in, checked in)

1 **PHRASAL VERB** When you **check in** or **check into** a hotel, you arrive and go through the necessary procedures before you stay there. ○ *I'll call the hotel. I'll tell them we'll check in later.* ○ *We checked into our hotel just after 5.*

> ▶ **ANTONYM:** check out

2 **PHRASAL VERB** When you **check in** at an airport, you arrive and show your ticket before going on a flight. ○ [+ at] *He checked in at Amsterdam's Schiphol airport for a flight to Manchester.*

> ▶ **COLLOCATIONS:**
> check in **at** *a hotel/airport*
> check in **for** *a flight*

check|out /ˈtʃekaʊt/ (checkouts) also **check-out** SHOPPING

NOUN In a supermarket, the **checkout** is the place where you pay for things you are buying. ○ *We were queuing at the checkout in Aldi.* ○ *They're advertising for checkout staff.*

> ▶ **COLLOCATIONS:**
> **at** the checkout
> a **supermarket** checkout
> the **express/self-service** checkout
> a checkout **counter/queue**
> a checkout **operator/assistant**
> checkout **staff**

check out /tʃek 'aʊt/ TRANSPORT & TRAVEL
(checks out, checking out, checked out)

PHRASAL VERB When you **check out of** a hotel where you have been staying, you pay the bill and leave. ○ [+ of] *They packed their bags and checked out of the hotel.* ○ *I was disappointed to miss Brian, who had just checked out.*

> ▶ **ANTONYM:** check in

cheer|ful /ˈtʃɪəfʊl/ PERSONALITY

ADJECTIVE Someone who is **cheerful** is happy and shows this in their behaviour. ○ *They are both very cheerful in spite of all the problems.* ○ [+ about] *Jack sounded quite cheerful about the idea.*

> ▶ **COLLOCATIONS:**
> cheerful **about** *something*
> **very/quite** cheerful
> **remarkably/surprisingly** cheerful
> **look/feel/sound/seem** cheerful
> **keep/stay** cheerful
> a cheerful **man/woman/girl/boy/child**
> a cheerful **voice/face/smile**

▶ SYNONYM: happy

▶ ANTONYMS: miserable, depressed

cheer up /tʃɪə ˈʌp/

PHRASAL VERB When you **cheer up** or when something **cheers** you **up**, you stop feeling depressed and you become more cheerful. ○ I couldn't think of anything to say to cheer him up. ○ I wrote that song just to cheer myself up. ○ Cheer up, it's not the end of the world!

WORD FAMILY		
cheerful	ADJECTIVE	○ She was making an effort to look cheerful.
cheerfully	ADVERB	○ She greeted him cheerfully.
cheerfulness	UNCOUNT	○ He faced his illness with great courage and cheerfulness.
cheer up	PHRASAL VERB	○ He cheered up when he saw his girlfriend arrive.

chef /ʃef/ (chefs)

WORK

NOUN A **chef** is a cook in a restaurant or hotel. ○ He trained as a chef in London. ○ The restaurant is recruiting a new head chef.

→ see note at **cook**

▶ COLLOCATIONS:
  be/become a chef
  train as a chef
  a **head/trainee** chef
  a **TV/celebrity** chef
  a **hotel/restaurant** chef

▶ SYNONYM: cook

chem|is|try /ˈkemɪstri/

SCIENCE & NATURE

UNCOUNTABLE NOUN **Chemistry** is the scientific study of the structure of substances and of the way that they react with other substances. ○ She went to university to study chemistry. ○ The chemistry experiment involved running an electric current through water to produce hydrogen and oxygen.

▶ COLLOCATIONS:
  study/teach chemistry
  a chemistry **teacher/professor/student**
  a chemistry **experiment**
  a chemistry **test/exam**
  a chemistry **class/lesson**
  a chemistry **lab/textbook**
  the chemistry **department**

c

> **WORD FAMILY**
>
> | **chemistry** | **UNCOUNT** | ○ *Once he caused an explosion in a chemistry lesson.* |
> | **chemical** | **ADJECTIVE** | ○ *chemical reactions* ○ *the chemical composition of blood* |
> | **chemically** | **ADVERB** | ○ *chemically treated foods* ○ *chemically similar substances* |
> | **chemist** | **NOUN** | ○ *Hoffman was a chemist working for Bayer Pharmaceuticals.* |

---

chess /tʃes/ `FREE TIME`

UNCOUNTABLE NOUN Chess is a game for two people, played on a chessboard. Each player has 16 pieces, including a king. Your aim is to move your pieces so that your opponent's king cannot escape being taken. ○ *Do you play chess?* ○ *He leaned forward to study the remaining chess pieces on the board.*

▶ COLLOCATIONS:
  play chess
  a chess **player**
  a chess **set/piece/board**
  a chess **game/match**
  a chess **tournament/championship**
  a chess **club**

---

child|ish /'tʃaɪldɪʃ/ `PEOPLE`

ADJECTIVE If you describe someone, especially an adult, as **childish**, you disapprove of them because they behave in an immature way. ○ *Don't be so childish.* ○ *It was childish of me to try to frighten you away.*

▶ COLLOCATIONS:
  childish **of** someone
  seem/sound childish
  childish **behaviour**
  a childish **attitude**
  very/rather childish

▶ SYNONYM: immature

---

choir /kwaɪə/ (choirs) `MEDIA & CULTURE`

NOUN A **choir** is a group of people who sing together, for example in a church or school. ○ *He has been singing in his church choir since he was six.* ○ *They should be encouraged to join the school choir.*

▶ COLLOCATIONS:
  in a choir
  join/form/lead a choir
  a choir **sings/performs** something
  a **church/school** choir

a **gospel/youth** choir
a choir **boy/girl**
a choir **member/singer**
choir **practice**

WORD FAMILY		
choir	NOUN	○ *All the choir members are former coal miners.*
choral	ADJECTIVE	○ *She has always had a love of choral music.*

---

chop /tʃɒp/ (chops, chopping, chopped) `FOOD & DRINK`

1 VERB If you **chop** something, you cut it into pieces with strong downward movements of a knife. ○ [+ into] *Chop the butter into small pieces.* ○ [+ up] *Chop up three firm tomatoes.* ○ [+ off] *He cut down one of the coconuts and expertly chopped off the top.* ○ *finely chopped herbs*

▶ COLLOCATIONS:
chop something **into** something
chop something **up**
chop something **off**
chop something **finely/roughly/coarsely**

▶ SYNONYM: cut

2 NOUN A **chop** is a small piece of meat cut from the ribs of a sheep or pig. ○ *Cook the chops on the grill for two minutes.* ○ *lamb chops marinated in rosemary, garlic and lemon*

▶ COLLOCATIONS:
cook/serve/eat chops
a **lamb/pork** chop
a **thick** chop

---

chores /tʃɔːz/ `HOME`

PLURAL NOUN **Chores** are tasks such as cleaning, washing, and ironing that have to be done regularly at home. ○ *Saturday is the day for doing chores.* ○ *My husband and I both go out to work so we share the household chores.*

▶ COLLOCATIONS:
do chores
share the chores
finish your chores
household chores
daily/routine chores

▶ SYNONYM: jobs

---

church /tʃɜːtʃ/ (churches) `PLACES`

NOUN A **church** is a building in which Christians worship. You usually refer to this place as **church** when you are talking about the time that people spend there.

◦ *I didn't see you in church on Sunday.* ◦ *They had seen each other at church several times.* ◦ *In some church services, there are a lot of hymns and prayers.*

▶ **COLLOCATIONS:**
at/in church
go to church
a **Catholic/Protestant/Baptist** church
a church **service**
a church **wedding/school/choir**
a church **hall/tower/door**
church **bells**
church **leaders**

---

cin|ema /ˈsɪnɪmɑː/ **(cinemas)** MEDIA & CULTURE

1 NOUN A **cinema** is a place where people go to watch films for entertainment. [mainly BRIT; in AM, usually use **movie theater**, **movie house**] ◦ *The country has relatively few cinemas.* ◦ *The director said he didn't want everyone leaving the cinema feeling sad.*

▶ **COLLOCATIONS:**
a **multi-screen/drive-in** cinema
a cinema **ticket/seat**
a cinema **complex/chain**
a cinema **audience**

2 NOUN You can talk about **the cinema** when you are talking about seeing a film in a cinema. [mainly BRIT; in AM, usually use **the movies**] ◦ *I can't remember the last time we went to the cinema.* ◦ *They decided to spend an evening at the cinema.*

▶ **COLLOCATIONS:**
at the cinema
go to the cinema

---

city /ˈsɪti/ **(cities)** PLACES

NOUN A **city** is a large town. ◦ *I was brought up in a big city.* ◦ *The company has offices in almost every capital city in Europe.* ◦ *[+ of] the city of Bologna*

▶ **COLLOCATIONS:**
in a city
the city **of** *something*
a **capital** city
a **big/major** city
a **historic/industrial** city
a **university/port/border** city
the city **centre**
city **streets**

---

civ|il /ˈsɪvəl/ SOCIAL LIFE

ADJECTIVE You use **civil** to describe things that are connected with the state rather

than with a religion. ○ *They were married on August 9 in a civil ceremony in Venice.*
○ *Jewish civil and religious law*

▶ **ANTONYM:** religious

---

civi|li|za|tion /ˌsɪvɪlaɪˈzeɪʃən/ (civilizations)
[in BRIT, also use **civilisation**]

HISTORY

NOUN A **civilization** is a human society with its own social organization and
culture. ○ *Western civilization was in grave danger.* ○ *the ancient civilizations of
Central and Latin America* ○ *one of the world's earliest civilisations*

▶ **COLLOCATIONS:**
Western/European civilization
an **ancient/modern** civilization
a **great** civilization
early civilizations

WORD FAMILY		
civilize	**VERB**	○ *They went to Africa to try to civilise the natives.*
civilized	**ADJECTIVE**	○ *I believed that in civilized countries, torture had ended long ago.*
civilization	**NOUN**	○ *The exhibition explores the history and culture of the world's great civilizations.*

---

claim /kleɪm/ (claims, claiming, claimed)

BELIEFS & OPINIONS

VERB If you say that someone **claims that** something is true, you mean they say
that it is true but you are not sure whether or not they are telling the truth.
○ [+ to-inf] *The man claimed to be a journalist.* ○ [+ that] *He claimed that it was all
a conspiracy against him.* ○ *He claims a 70 to 80 per cent success rate.*

▶ **SYNONYM:** maintain

---

clas|si|cal /ˈklæsɪkəl/

ADJECTIVE **Classical** music is music that is considered to be serious and of lasting
value. ○ *I prefer listening to classical music.* ○ *Radio rarely broadcasts classical
concerts.*

▶ **COLLOCATIONS:**
classical **music**
a classical **concert**
a classical **musician/composer/guitarist**
classical **guitar/piano**

▶ **ANTONYMS:** pop, modern

---

class|mate /ˈklɑːsmeɪt, ˈklæs-/ (classmates)

PEOPLE **EDUCATION**

NOUN Your **classmates** are students who are in the same class as you at school or college. ○ *His classmates teased him about his father.* ○ *According to former classmates, she was a very hard worker.*

---

clean|er /'kliːnə/ (cleaners)

NOUN A **cleaner** is someone who is employed to clean the rooms and furniture inside a building. ○ *She got a job as a cleaner working three hours a night.* ○ *an office cleaner* ○ *a team of hospital cleaners*

WORD FAMILY		
clean	**VERB**	○ *It took ages to clean the marks off the bath.*
clean	**ADJECTIVE**	○ *Kitchen floors are not easy to keep clean.*
cleaning	**UNCOUNT**	○ *I do the cleaning myself.*
cleaner	**NOUN**	○ *His mother worked as a cleaner for a wealthy family.*

---

click /klɪk/ (clicks, clicking, clicked)

VERB If you **click on** an area of a computer screen, you point the cursor at that area and press one of the buttons on the mouse in order to make something happen. ○ *For more information, click here.* ○ [+ on] *I clicked on a link and recent reviews of the production came up.*

▶ **COLLOCATIONS:**
click **on** *something*
click (on) a **link/icon/attachment/file**
click a **mouse/button**

---

cliff /klɪf/ (cliffs)

NOUN A **cliff** is a high area of land with a very steep side, especially one next to the sea. ○ *The car rolled over the edge of a cliff.* ○ *The road winds down between high cliffs.*

▶ **COLLOCATIONS:**
climb/scale a cliff
a **high/steep/sheer** cliff
a **limestone/granite/chalk** cliff
a cliff **face/edge/top**
a cliff **path**

---

cli|mate /'klaɪmət/ (climates)

NOUN The **climate** of a place is the general weather conditions that are typical of it. ○ *Cyprus has a hot and humid climate.* ○ *Pollution is affecting the climate in many cities.* ○ [+ of] *the tropical climate of South India*

▶ **COLLOCATIONS:**
the climate **of** *somewhere*
have a climate
change/affect the climate
a **warm/hot/tropical** climate
a **cool/cold/mild** climate

a climate **system**
a climate **conference**
a climate **expert**
climate **research**

WORD FAMILY		
climate	NOUN	○ *People in cold climates need their energies for survival.*
climatic	ADJECTIVE	○ *Climatic conditions were quite different in the Stone Age.*

'cli|mate change

UNCOUNTABLE NOUN Climate change is a gradual change in the earth's climate caused by high levels of carbon dioxide and other gases in the atmosphere.
○ *Sea levels are rising due to climate change.* ○ *Scientists found a link between carbon dioxide and climate change.*

→ see also **global warming**

climb|ing /ˈklaɪmɪŋ/ SPORT & ACTIVITY

UNCOUNTABLE NOUN Climbing is the activity of climbing rocks or mountains. ○ *We went climbing in the Alps.* ○ *dangerous activities such as rock climbing and parachuting*

WORD FAMILY		
climb	VERB	○ *His favourite pastime is climbing mountains.*
climbing	UNCOUNT	○ *She likes sports of every kind, from chess to mountain climbing.*
climber	NOUN	○ *Three climbers were killed on the Scottish hills.*

cloudy /ˈklaʊdi/ (cloudier, cloudiest) SCIENCE & NATURE

ADJECTIVE If it is **cloudy**, there are a lot of clouds in the sky. ○ *He lay on his back staring at the cloudy sky.* ○ *Even on cloudy days you can get sunburnt.*

▶ **COLLOCATIONS:**
a cloudy **sky**
cloudy **weather**
a cloudy **day/night/morning/afternoon**
cloudy **weather/conditions**
partly/mostly cloudy
become/turn cloudy

▶ **ANTONYMS:** cloudless, clear, fine

WORD FAMILY		
cloud	NOUN	○ *Dark clouds formed overhead.*
cloudy	ADJECTIVE	○ *Some days it is cloudy and raining.*
cloudless	ADJECTIVE	○ *There was no wind and the sky was cloudless.*

c

club /klʌb/ (clubs)

SPORT & ACTIVITY

1 **NOUN** A **club** is an organization of people interested in a particular activity who usually meet regularly. ○ *I used to be in the school chess club.* ○ *She decided to join the local tennis club.*

▶ **COLLOCATIONS:**
  in a club
  join/leave a club
  run/lead a club
  a **sports** club
  a **chess/drama** club
  a **youth** club
  a **local** club
  a club **member/chairman/secretary**

2 **NOUN** A **club** is a team which competes in sporting competitions. ○ *Which football club do you support?* ○ *the New York Yankees baseball club* ○ *Bath rugby club*

▶ **SYNONYM:** team

3 **NOUN** A **club** is a place where people go late in the evening to drink and dance. ○ *It's a big dance hit in the clubs.* ○ *Younger staff prefer the London club scene.*

▶ **SYNONYM:** nightclub

club|bing /'klʌbɪŋ/

UNCOUNTABLE NOUN **Clubbing** is the activity of going to nightclubs. ○ *We used to go clubbing nearly every Saturday.* ○ *After a weekend of clubbing, we were all very tired.*

coast /kəʊst/ (coasts)

SCIENCE & NATURE

NOUN The **coast** is an area of land that is next to the sea. ○ *[+ of] the west coast of Scotland* ○ *Campsites are usually situated along the coast, close to beaches.* ○ *the Caribbean coast*

▶ **COLLOCATIONS:**
  the coast **of** *somewhere*
  along the coast
  the **north/south/west/east** coast
  the **African/Australian/French** etc. coast
  a coast **road**
  the coast **guard**

WORD FAMILY		
coast	NOUN	○ *There are several hotels along the north coast of the island.*
coastal	ADJECTIVE	○ *Local radio stations serving coastal areas often broadcast forecasts for yachtsmen.*
coastline	NOUN	○ *This is some of the most exposed coastline in the world.*

coat /kəʊt/ (coats)   CLOTHES & APPEARANCE

NOUN A **coat** is a piece of clothing with long sleeves which you wear over your other clothes when you go outside. ○ *She was wearing a thick brown coat.* ○ *He turned off the television, put on his coat and walked out.*

▶ COLLOCATIONS:
  put on/take off a coat
  wear a coat
  hang up a coat
  a **long/heavy/thick/warm** coat
  a **fur/leather/wool** coat
  a **winter** coat
  a coat **pocket/sleeve/button**
  a coat **hook/cupboard/rack**

coin /kɔɪn/ (coins)   TRANSPORT & TRAVEL

NOUN A **coin** is a small piece of metal which is used as money. ○ *The ticket machines only accept coins.* ○ *Do you have change for a pound coin?*

▶ COLLOCATIONS:
  take/accept coins
  a **pound/50 pence/10p** coin
  a **euro/dollar** coin

cold /kəʊld/ (colds)   HEALTH

NOUN If you have a **cold**, you have a mild, very common illness which makes you sneeze a lot and gives you a sore throat or a cough. ○ *I had a pretty bad cold.* ○ *Take those wet clothes off or you'll catch a cold.*

▶ COLLOCATIONS:
  catch/get a cold
  have a cold
  a **bad/slight** cold
  a **head** cold

col|league /ˈkɒliːg/ (colleagues)   PEOPLE

NOUN Your **colleagues** are the people you work with, especially in a professional job. ○ *He invited some work colleagues to dinner.* ○ *Most of his male colleagues hated him.*

▶ COLLOCATIONS:
  a **former/old** colleague
  a **male/female** colleague
  a **work/business** colleague

▶ SYNONYM: workmate

col|lec|tion /kəˈlekʃən/ (collections) `MEDIA & CULTURE`

NOUN A **collection of** things is a group of similar things that have been collected, usually over a period of time. ○ [+ of] *The Art Gallery of Ontario has the world's largest collection of sculptures by Henry Moore.* ○ *a contemporary art collection* ○ *one of the best museum collections in the world*

▶ **COLLOCATIONS:**
a collection **of** something
a **large/vast/small** collection
a **private** collection
a **record/art/music** collection
a **museum** collection

col|our|ful /ˈkʌləfʊl/ [in AM, use **colorful**]

ADJECTIVE Something that is **colourful** has bright colours or a lot of different colours. ○ *I love the colourful clothes she wears.* ○ *colourful flowers* ○ *a colourful display of fruit and vegetables*

▶ **SYNONYM:** bright

▶ **ANTONYMS:** bland, colourless, dull

WORD FAMILY		
colour	**NOUN**	○ *What colour is the car?*
colour	**VERB**	○ *Many women begin colouring their hair in their mid-30s.*
colourful	**ADJECTIVE**	○ *The dancers wore bells on their colourful costumes.*
colourless	**ADJECTIVE**	○ *He filled a glass with a colourless liquid.*

com|bine /kəmˈbaɪn/ (combines, combining, combined)

VERB If you **combine** two or more things or if they **combine**, they exist or join together. ○ [+ with] *Combine the flour with 3 tablespoons of water to make a paste.* ○ [+ to-inf] *Disease and starvation combine to kill thousands.* ○ [+ into] *David was given the job of combining the data from 19 studies into one giant study.*

▶ **COLLOCATIONS:**
combine something **with** something
combine something **into** something
combine two things **together**

▶ **SYNONYMS:** mix, join

▶ **ANTONYMS:** divide, separate

com|bi|na|tion /ˌkɒmbɪˈneɪʃən/ (combinations)

NOUN A **combination of** things is a mixture of them. ○ *A boiled egg and a glass of orange juice is a good combination.* ○ [+ of] *a fantastic combination of colours* ○ [+ of] *the combination of science and art*

▶ **COLLOCATIONS:**
combination **of** *something* **and** *something*
a **different/new/unique** combination
a **good/perfect** combination
the **right** combination
a **dangerous/lethal/deadly** combination
a **rare/unusual** combination

come across /ˌkʌm əˈkrɒs, ᴀᴍ əˈkrɔːs/ (comes across, coming across, came across)

PHRASAL VERB If you **come across** something or someone, you find them or meet them by chance. ○ *I came across a group of children playing.* ○ *We like to identify and celebrate women's success whenever we come across it.*

▶ **SYNONYM:** find

com|edy /ˈkɒmədi/ (comedies)　　[MEDIA & CULTURE]

1 **UNCOUNTABLE NOUN** **Comedy** consists of types of entertainment that are intended to make people laugh. ○ *When I tried doing comedy, no-one laughed.* ○ *It's a TV comedy series.*

▶ **COLLOCATIONS:**
do comedy
stand-up comedy
a comedy **series/show/drama**
a comedy **club**
a comedy **routine/act**
a comedy **actor**

2 **NOUN** A **comedy** is a play, film, or television programme that is intended to make people laugh. ○ *My favourite films are love stories or romantic comedies.* ○ *This new comedy centres on a suburban housewife.*

▶ **COLLOCATIONS:**
a **new/good/classic** comedy
a **romantic/black** comedy

▶ **ANTONYM:** tragedy

WORD FAMILY		
comedy	UNCOUNT	○ When did you first start doing stand-up comedy?
comedian	NOUN	○ Comedians like to make jokes about anything.

come up with /ˌkʌm ˈʌp wɪθ/ (comes up with, coming up with, came up with)

PHRASAL VERB If you **come up with** a plan or idea, you think of it and suggest it. ○ *We couldn't come up with an answer.* ○ *She has come up with some really clever designs.* ○ *So far, they haven't come up with anything new.*

▶ COLLOCATIONS:
come up with a **suggestion/idea/theory**
come up with a **solution/answer**
come up with a **story/excuse**
come up with a **concept/design**

com|mer|cial /kəˈmɜːʃəl/ `WORK`

1 ADJECTIVE **Commercial** means relating to the buying and selling of goods.
○ *Docklands was once a major centre of industrial and commercial activity.* ○ *Attacks were reported on police, vehicles and commercial premises.*

▶ COLLOCATIONS:
a commercial **development/building**
commercial **premises**
commercial **use/purposes**
commercial **activities/services**

2 ADJECTIVE **Commercial** activities, organizations and products are concerned with making a profit. ○ *The company has become more commercial over the past decade.* ○ *The airline will restart commercial flights next month.*

▶ COLLOCATIONS:
a commercial **company/bank**
a commercial **activity/product**
a commerical **flight/aircraft**
commercial **success**

WORD FAMILY		
commerce	UNCOUNT	○ *They made their wealth from industry and commerce.*
commercial	ADJECTIVE	○ *Whether the project will be a commercial success is still uncertain.*
commercially	ADVERB	○ *The fruit trees are grown commercially in Queensland.*
commercialize	VERB	○ *The company develops and commercializes medical devices.*

com|mu|ni|ca|tion skills `WORK` `PERSONALITY`
/kəˌmjuːnɪˈkeɪʃən ˌskɪlz/

PLURAL NOUN If someone has good **communication skills**, they are able to communicate well with people. ○ *She has excellent written and verbal communication skills.* ○ *Working at the front desk requires communication skills.*

▶ COLLOCATIONS:
good/excellent/strong communication skills
poor communication skills
oral/verbal/written communication skills
have/require communication skills
develop/improve *your* communication skills

com|mu|nity /kəˈmjuːnɪti/ (communities) `PEOPLE`

UNCOUNTABLE NOUN **The community** is all the people who live in a particular area or place. ○ *He's well liked by people in the community.* ○ *The event was supported by the local community.*

▶ **COLLOCATIONS:**
  in the community
  the **local** community
  help/serve the community
  divide/involve/represent the community
  community **leaders/groups/workers**
  a community **centre**
  community **spirit/relations**

▶ **SYNONYMS:** neighbourhood, public

com|mute /kəˈmjuːt/ `TRANSPORT & TRAVEL` `WORK`
(commutes, commuting, commuted)

VERB If you **commute**, you travel a long distance every day between your home and your place of work. ○ [+ to/from] *Mike commutes to London every day.* ○ [+ between] *McLaren began commuting between Paris and London.*

WORD FAMILY		
commute	**VERB**	○ *He spends two hours a day commuting to work.*
commute	**NOUN**	○ *the daily commute to work* ○ *a fifty-minute commute*
commuter	**NOUN**	○ *The number of commuters to London has dropped by 100,000.*

com|pe|ti|tion /ˌkɒmpɪˈtɪʃən/ (competitions) `SPORT & ACTIVITY`

NOUN A **competition** is an event in which many people take part in order to find out who is best at a particular activity. ○ *You must be over 18 to enter the competition.* ○ *The council has organised a series of events and competitions for school children in the area.*

▶ **COLLOCATIONS:**
  win/enter/hold a competition
  a **national/international** competition
  a **major** competition
  a **club/cup/team** competition
  a **knockout** competition
  a **football/talent/dance/singing** competition

▶ **SYNONYM:** contest

com|peti|tive /kəmˈpetɪtɪv/ PERSONALITY

ADJECTIVE A **competitive** person is eager to be more successful than other people. ○ *I'm a very competitive person and I was determined not be beaten.* ○ *He has always been ambitious and fiercely competitive.*

▶ COLLOCATIONS:
  very/fiercely/pretty/really competitive
  a competitive **nature/spirit**

WORD FAMILY		
compete	VERB	○ *Eight entrants competed for prizes totalling $1000.*
competition	NOUN	○ *a drawing competition* ○ *a talent competition*
competitor	NOUN	○ *The competitors are given a brief before the race.*
competitive	ADJECTIVE	○ *I'm a very competitive person. I like to be the best.*
competitively	ADVERB	○ *I have been skiing competitively for five years.*
uncompetitive	ADJECTIVE	○ *Yoga is totally uncompetitive.*

com|plain /kəmˈpleɪn/ (complains, complaining, complained)

VERB If you **complain about** a situation, you say that you are not satisfied with it. ○ [+ about] *The neighbours complained about the noise.* ○ [+ that] *They complained that their questions were never answered.*

▶ COLLOCATIONS:
  complain **about** something
  complain **to** someone
  complain **bitterly/constantly**
  complain **publicly**

com|plaint /kəmˈpleɪnt/ (complaints)

NOUN A **complaint** is a statement in which you say that you are not happy with a situation. ○ [+ about] *There have been a lot of complaints about the service in this restaurant.* ○ *Some people made formal complaints to the police.*

▶ COLLOCATIONS:
  a complaint **about** something
  a complaint **to/from** someone
  a complaint **against** someone
  make a complaint
  receive/investigate a complaint
  a **formal/official** complaint

com|pos|er /kəmˈpəʊzə/ (composers) MEDIA & CULTURE

NOUN A **composer** is a person who writes music, especially classical music. ○ *Mozart and Beethoven are my favourite classical composers.*

> **WORD FAMILY**
>
> | **compose** | **VERB** | ○ *The album includes eleven songs composed by lead singer, Gary Barlow.* |
> | **composer** | **NOUN** | ○ *His brother Charles was a violinist and composer.* |

com|pul|so|ry /kəmˈpʌlsəri/ EDUCATION

ADJECTIVE If something is **compulsory**, you must do it or accept it, because it is the law or because someone in a position of authority says you must. ○ [+ *for*] *Education was compulsory for all children between the ages of 5 and 16.* ○ *English is a compulsory subject in secondary school.*

▶ **COLLOCATIONS:**
  compulsory **for** *someone*
  a compulsory **subject/course**
  compulsory **education/schooling**
  a compulsory **requirement**
  make *something* compulsory
  become compulsory

▶ **ANTONYMS:** optional, voluntary

con|cen|trate /ˈkɒnsəntreɪt/ (concentrates, concentrating, concentrated)

VERB If you **concentrate on** something, you give all your attention to it. ○ [+ *on*] *I was finding it hard to concentrate on my studies.* ○ *You need to find a place where you can sit and concentrate.*

▶ **COLLOCATIONS:**
  concentrate **on** *something*
  concentrate **mainly/solely/exclusively** on *something*
  concentrate **hard**

con|cen|tra|tion /ˌkɒnsənˈtreɪʃən/

UNCOUNTABLE NOUN Concentration on something involves giving all your attention to it. ○ *Neil kept interrupting, breaking my concentration.* ○ *Here are some tips on how you can maintain concentration during a 3-hour exam.*

▶ **COLLOCATIONS:**
  intense concentration
  good/poor concentration
  lose concentration
  improve concentration
  maintain concentration
  break *someone's* concentration

con|cerned /kən'sɜːnd/

ADJECTIVE If you are **concerned about** something, it worries you. ○ [+ *about*] *Many people are concerned about environmental pollutants entering our food chain.* ○ [+ *for*] *They were concerned for their daughter's safety.*

▶ COLLOCATIONS:
   concerned **about/for** *someone/something*
   become/feel/seem/sound concerned
   deeply/seriously/gravely concerned
   genuinely concerned

con|cert /'kɒnsət/ (concerts)   MEDIA & CULTURE

NOUN A **concert** is a performance of music. ○ *I've been to a few live rock concerts.* ○ [+ *of*] *a short concert of piano music* ○ *a new concert hall*

▶ COLLOCATIONS:
   a concert **of** *something*
   a concert **by** *someone*
   go to a concert
   play in/perform in a concert
   a **pop/rock/classical/jazz** concert
   a **live** concert
   a concert **hall/venue**

con|fer|ence /'kɒnfrəns/ (conferences)

NOUN A **conference** is a meeting, often lasting a few days, which is organized on a particular subject or to bring together people who have a common interest. ○ *The conference was attended by scientists from around the world.* ○ [+ *on*] *a conference on education* ○ [+ *for*] *a conference for teachers*

▶ COLLOCATIONS:
   a conference **on** *something*
   a conference **for** *someone*
   be **at** a conference
   attend a conference
   hold/host a conference
   organize a conference
   speak at a conference
   an **international/national** conference
   an **annual** conference
   a conference **centre/room**
   conference **facilities**

con|fi|dent /'kɒnfɪdənt/

1 **ADJECTIVE** If you are **confident** about something, you are certain that it will happen in the way you want it to. ○ [+ *about*] *Students who are successful in school are usually confident about their future.* ○ [+ *of*] *The team is confident of success.*

▶ **COLLOCATIONS:**
confident **of** something
confident of **success/victory**
confident **about** something
become/remain/seem/sound confident
fairly/reasonably confident
extremely/supremely confident
increasingly confident
quietly confident

▶ **ANTONYM:** sceptical

2 **ADJECTIVE** If a person or their manner is **confident**, they feel sure about their own abilities, qualities, or ideas. ○ *I am not a very confident person.* ○ *He smiled at her and hoped he looked more confident than he felt.*

▶ **COLLOCATION: feel/look/seem/sound** confident

▶ **SYNONYM:** self-assured

WORD FAMILY		
confident	**ADJECTIVE**	○ *Kate seemed to be quietly confident about the exam.*
		○ *I tried to look confident even though I was terrified.*
confidently	**ADVERB**	○ *She walked confidently across the hall.*
confidence	**UNCOUNT**	○ *If you can regularly reach small goals, it will boost your confidence.*

---

con|ges|tion /kən'dʒestʃən/ 　　　TRANSPORT & TRAVEL　 　PLACES

UNCOUNTABLE NOUN If there is **congestion** in a place, the place is extremely crowded and blocked with traffic or people. ○ *The report addresses the problems of traffic congestion in big cities.* ○ *A new road is being built to relieve congestion in the town.*

▶ **COLLOCATIONS:**
reduce/relieve/ease congestion
cause/increase congestion
traffic/road congestion
heavy congestion

---

con|gratu|late /kən'grætʃʊleɪt/ 　　　SOCIAL LIFE
(congratulates, congratulating, congratulated)

VERB If you **congratulate** someone, you tell them that you are pleased about their success or happiness. ○ *He congratulated some students on their outstanding academic performance.* ○ *She congratulated this year's winners of the award.*

▶ **COLLOCATIONS:**
congratulate someone **on** something
warmly/heartily congratulate someone
publicly congratulate someone

con|gratu|la|tions /kənˌgrætʃʊˈleɪʃənz/

PLURAL NOUN You say '**Congratulations**' to someone in order to tell them that you are pleased about their success or happiness. [SPOKEN] ○ [+ on] *Congratulations on your exam results!* ○ [+ to] *Congratulations to the winners!*

▶ COLLOCATIONS:
   congratulations **on** *something*
   congratulations **to** *someone*

---

con|ser|va|tion /ˌkɒnsəˈveɪʃən/   SCIENCE & NATURE

1 UNCOUNTABLE NOUN **Conservation** is the practice of protecting the environment. ○ *We are involved in tree-planting and other conservation projects.* ○ *conservation groups working to protect the environment* ○ *The organization spreads awareness about environmental conservation around the world.*

▶ COLLOCATIONS:
   the conservation **of** *something*
   the conservation of **wildlife/forests/birds/the environment**
   a conservation **project/programme**
   conservation **work**
   a conservation **group/organization**
   wildlife/nature/forest conservation
   environmental/marine conservation

2 UNCOUNTABLE NOUN The **conservation** of a supply of something is the careful use of it so that it lasts for a long time. ○ [+ of] *Recycling waste encourages the conservation of natural resources.* ○ *Voluntary water conservation may help safeguard our water supply.* ○ *projects aimed at promoting energy conservation*

▶ COLLOCATIONS:
   the conservation **of** *something*
   the conservation of **resources/energy/water**
   energy/water conservation
   encourage/promote conservation

WORD FAMILY		
conserve	VERB	○ *We need to conserve precious water resources.*
conservation	UNCOUNT	○ *the conservation and protection of land*
conservationist	NOUN	○ *Conservationists say that the tiger population is in danger.*

---

con|serva|tive /kənˈsɜːvətɪv/   BELIEFS & OPINIONS

ADJECTIVE Someone who is **conservative** or has **conservative** ideas is unwilling to accept changes and new ideas. ○ *People tend to be more aggressive when they're young and more conservative as they get older.* ○ *My parents have very conservative views.*

▶ **COLLOCATIONS:**
  a conservative **view/approach**
  extremely/very/rather conservative

▶ **SYNONYMS:** traditionalist, conventional

▶ **ANTONYM:** radical

---

con|sid|er|ate /kənˈsɪdərət/ `PERSONALITY`

ADJECTIVE Someone who is **considerate** pays attention to the needs, wishes, or feelings of other people. ○ *I think he's the most considerate person I've ever known.* ○ *[+ of] It's important to try and be considerate of other people.*

▶ **COLLOCATION:** considerate **of** *someone/something*

▶ **ANTONYM:** inconsiderate

WORD FAMILY		
consider	**VERB**	○ *You have to consider the feelings of those around you.*
considerate	**ADJECTIVE**	○ *We try to be considerate of our neighbours.*
considerately	**ADVERB**	○ *He treats everyone fairly and considerately.*
inconsiderate	**ADJECTIVE**	○ *It was inconsiderate of her not to tell you she was coming.*
consideration	**UNCOUNT**	○ *Show consideration for your flatmates.*

---

con|sist of /kənˈsɪst əv, STRONG ɒv, AM ʌv/ (consists of, consisting of, consisted of)

PHRASAL VERB Something that **consists of** particular things or people is formed from them. ○ *Their meals consist mainly of fish.* ○ *Each team consisted of three people.*

▶ **COLLOCATIONS:**
  consist **mainly/largely/mostly/primarily** of *someone/something*
  consist **entirely/solely** of *someone/something*
  usually/generally/typically consist of *someone/something*

▶ **SYNONYM:** be made up of

---

con|struc|tion /kənˈstrʌkʃən/ `WORK`

UNCOUNTABLE NOUN **Construction** is the work of building things such as houses, factories, roads, and bridges. **Construction** is also the industry that carries out this work. ○ *The company finally began construction of the railway in 2012.* ○ *The power station is still under construction.* ○ *Connor wants a job in construction.*

▶ **COLLOCATIONS:**
  construction **of** *something*
  under construction
  work in construction
  begin/start the construction of *something*

> **complete** the construction of *something*
> the construction **industry**
> a construction **company/worker**
> a construction **site/project**
> construction **work/jobs**

▶ **SYNONYM:** building

▶ **ANTONYM:** demolition

WORD FAMILY		
construct	**VERB**	○ *Builders are constructing houses beside the golf course.*
construction	**UNCOUNT**	○ *Construction workers have already started work on the site.*

---

con|sum|er /kən'sjuːmə, AM -'suː-/ **(consumers)**   `SHOPPING`

NOUN A **consumer** is a person who buys things or uses services. ○ *Consumers want to know where a product has come from.* ○ *The aim of the agency is to protect consumers from dangerous products.*

▶ **COLLOCATIONS:**
  protect consumers
  mislead consumers
  the **average** consumer
  Japanese/European/American etc. consumers
  consumer **choice**
  a consumer **group/watchdog**

WORD FAMILY		
consume	**VERB**	○ *He does not consume animal products at all.*
consumer	**NOUN**	○ *Consumers were misled by the banks.*
consumption	**UNCOUNT**	○ *The car's design reduces fuel consumption by half.*
consumerism	**UNCOUNT**	○ *The past few decades have seen the growth of consumerism.*

---

con|tent /kən'tent/

1 ADJECTIVE If you are **content with** something, you are willing to accept it, rather than wanting something more or something better. ○ [+ to-inf] *Some people are quite content to stay in their home town all their life.* ○ [+ with] *He was not content with his situation, and decided to do something about it.*

▶ **COLLOCATIONS:**
  content **with** *something*
  quite/perfectly content

2 ADJECTIVE If you are **content**, you are happy or satisfied. ○ *Maria appeared to be completely content.*

WORD FAMILY

content	**ADJECTIVE**	○ She's perfectly content with the way she looks.
		○ I'm very content and happy with what I'm doing.
contented	**ADJECTIVE**	○ Richard was a contented and happy baby.
contentment	**UNCOUNT**	○ A feeling of contentment swept over me.

C

con|veni|ent /kən'viːniənt/   SHOPPING

1 ADJECTIVE If a way of doing something is **convenient**, it is easy or very useful.
○ A debit card is the most convenient way to pay. ○ [+ to-inf] It's more convenient to eat in the canteen.

▶ **ANTONYM:** inconvenient

2 ADJECTIVE A **convenient** time to meet someone is a time when you are free to do it. ○ [+ for] Would this evening be convenient for you? ○ We'll try to arrange a mutually convenient time and place for an interview.

▶ **COLLOCATIONS:**
convenient **for** someone
a convenient **time**
mutually convenient

▶ **ANTONYM:** inconvenient

WORD FAMILY

convenient	**ADJECTIVE**	○ What is the most convenient time to visit?
conveniently	**ADVERB**	○ The body spray slips conveniently into your sports bag.
convenience	**UNCOUNT**	○ the convenience of a fast non-stop flight
inconvenient	**ADJECTIVE**	○ I know it's inconvenient, but I have to see you now.
inconveniently	**ADVERB**	○ The office was inconveniently located miles across town.
inconvenience	**UNCOUNT**	○ We apologize for any inconvenience caused during the repairs.

cook /kʊk/ (cooks, cooking, cooked)   FOOD & DRINK

1 VERB When you **cook** a meal, you prepare food for eating by heating it. ○ I have to go and cook the dinner. ○ We'll cook them a nice Italian meal.

▶ **SYNONYMS:** make, prepare

2 VERB When you **cook** food, or when food **cooks**, it is heated until it is ready to be eaten. ○ They gave us basic instructions on how to cook a turkey. ○ Let the vegetables cook gently for about 10 minutes. ○ Drain the pasta as soon as it is cooked.

▶ **COLLOCATIONS:**
cook a **meal**
cook **dinner/lunch**

cook *something* **gently**
freshly cooked
cook *something* **thoroughly**

▶ **SYNONYM:** heat up

3 **NOUN** A **cook** is a person whose job is to prepare and cook food, especially in someone's home or in an institution. ○ *a school cook*

4 **NOUN** If you say that someone is a good **cook**, you mean they are good at preparing and cooking food. ○ *My boyfriend is a great cook.*

▶ **COLLOCATIONS:**
a **good/great/excellent** cook
a **keen** cook

cook|er /ˈkʊkə/ (cookers)

NOUN A **cooker** is a large metal device for cooking food using gas or electricity. A cooker usually consists of a grill, an oven, and some gas or electric rings. [BRIT] ○ *a gas cooker* ○ *an electric cooker*

> **WHICH WORD: cook, cooker, or chef?**
>
> You use **cook** to talk about a person who cooks food, either at home or as a job. ○ *Sam is a keen cook.* ○ *She retired from her job as a school cook.*
>
> You use **chef** to talk about someone whose job is to cook food in a restaurant or a hotel, etc., especially high quality food. ○ *a head chef in a top New York restaurant*
>
> A **cooker** is the piece of equipment you use to cook food. A **cooker** often includes an **oven** for baking bread and roasting meat, and a **hob**, for pans. ○ *The kitchen has a gas cooker, fridge and dishwasher.*

> **WORD FAMILY**
>
> | cook | **VERB** | ○ They advise you to only eat meat that has been cooked thoroughly. |
> |---|---|---|
> | cook | **NOUN** | ○ I got a job as a cook in a company canteen. |
> | cooking | **UNCOUNT** | ○ Her hobbies include music, dancing, sport and cooking. |
> | cooked | **ADJECTIVE** | ○ Are raw vegetables better for you than cooked ones? |
> | cooker | **NOUN** | ○ We bought a TV, a fridge and a cooker. |

cool /kuːl/ (cooler, coolest) [SCIENCE & NATURE] [CLOTHES & APPEARANCE]

1 **ADJECTIVE** Something that is **cool** has a temperature that is low but not very low. ○ *It's nice when you get a current of cool air.* ○ *The drinks are kept cool in refrigerators.*

▶ **COLLOCATIONS:**
cool **water/air**
a cool **breeze/wind**
keep *something* cool

▶ **ANTONYM:** warm

2 **ADJECTIVE** If it is **cool**, or if a place is **cool**, the temperature of the air is low but not very low. ○ *Thank goodness it's cool in here.* ○ *Store medicines in a cool, dry place.* ○ *a cool November evening*

→ see note at **mild**

▶ **COLLOCATIONS:**
  a cool **place**
  cool **weather**
  a cool **evening/night/day**

▶ **ANTONYM:** warm

3 **ADJECTIVE** Clothing that is **cool** is made of thin material so that you do not become too hot in hot weather. ○ *In warm weather, you should wear clothing that is cool and comfortable.* ○ *long, cool cotton or linen trousers*

▶ **ANTONYM:** warm

---

cope with /ˈkəʊp wɪθ/ (copes with, coping with, coped with)

VERB If you **cope with** a problem or task, you deal with it successfully. ○ *The website offers useful tips for students struggling to cope with exam stress.* ○ *Most children cope well with the social and emotional demands of school.*

▶ **COLLOCATIONS:**
  cope **well/admirably/successfully** with *something*
  have difficulty/have trouble coping with *something*

▶ **SYNONYM:** manage

---

cost /kɒst, AM kɔːst/ (costs, costing, cost)   MONEY

VERB If something **costs** a particular amount of money, you can buy, do, or make it for that amount. ○ *This course is limited to 12 people and costs £50.* ○ *It cost me $500 to travel to Denver.*

▶ **COLLOCATIONS:**
  cost **£10/$500**, etc.
  cost **a lot/a fortune**
  not cost **much**
  cost **more/less**

---

cost of liv|ing /ˌkɔːst əv ˈlɪvɪŋ/   MONEY

NOUN The **cost of living** is the average amount of money that people in a particular place need in order to be able to afford basic food, housing, and clothing. ○ *the high cost of living in London*

→ see also **standard of living**

▶ **COLLOCATIONS:**
  the cost of living **in** *a place*
  the **high/low/rising** cost of living
  a **rise/increase in** the cost of living

cos|tume /'kɒstjuːm, ᴀᴍ -tuːm/ (costumes)   `MEDIA & CULTURE`

NOUN An actor's or performer's **costume** is the set of clothes they wear while they are performing. ○ *She wore a silver sequinned costume.* ○ *In all, she has eight costume changes.*

▶ **COLLOCATIONS:**
wear a costume
make/design a costume
a costume **designer**
a costume **change**

cot|tage /'kɒtɪdʒ/ (cottages)   `HOME`

NOUN A **cottage** is a small house, usually in the country. ○ *My parents used to have a cottage in Scotland.* ○ *They live in an old cottage in a traditional English village.*

▶ **COLLOCATIONS:**
a **small/little/tiny** cottage
an **old** cottage
a **thatched** cottage
a **country** cottage
a **holiday** cottage
a **one-bedroom/two-bedroom** cottage

cot|ton /'kɒtən/   `CLOTHES & APPEARANCE`

UNCOUNTABLE NOUN **Cotton** is a type of cloth made from the soft fibres of a plant called a 'cotton plant'. ○ *a cotton shirt* ○ *white cotton sheets*

country|side /'kʌntrisaɪd/   `SCIENCE & NATURE`

UNCOUNTABLE NOUN The **countryside** is land that is away from towns and cities. ○ *I've always enjoyed family holidays in the countryside.* ○ *We love the English countryside.* ○ *The views of the surrounding countryside from the top of the hill are amazing.*

→ see note at **nature**

▶ **COLLOCATIONS:**
in the countryside
the **surrounding** countryside
beautiful/unspoilt countryside
open/rolling countryside
the **English/French,** etc. countryside

cou|ple /'kʌpəl/ (couples)   `PEOPLE`

NOUN A **couple** is two people who are married, living together, or having a sexual relationship. ○ *The couple have no children.* ○ *a young married couple* ○ *Most couples meet via work, friends or colleagues.*

▶ **COLLOCATIONS:**
a **married/unmarried** couple
a **young/elderly/middle-aged** couple
a **gay/same-sex** couple
a **childless** couple
a couple **meets**
a couple **marries**
a couple **splits up/divorces**

---

course /kɔːs/ (courses)

`EDUCATION`

NOUN A **course** is a series of lessons or lectures on a particular subject. ○ [+ in] She had done a course in Spanish. ○ The colleges run courses that are readily accessible to overseas candidates.

→ see Useful Phrases **take a course/subject**

▶ **COLLOCATIONS:**
a course **in/on** something
do/take a course
enrol on a course
run/offer a course
change courses
a **degree/diploma/postgraduate** course
a **university/college** course
a **training** course
a **management/computer** course
a **language/English** course
a course **includes** something

---

cous|in /ˈkʌzən/ (cousins)

`PEOPLE`

NOUN Your **cousin** is the child of your uncle or aunt. ○ My cousin Mark helped me. ○ We are cousins.

---

crash /kræʃ/ (crashes, crashing, crashed)

1 VERB If something **crashes** somewhere, it moves and hits something else violently, making a loud noise. ○ The walls above us crashed down, filling the cellar with dust. ○ He jumped off a trampoline and crashed through a basement window.

2 NOUN A **crash** is a sudden, loud noise. ○ Two people in the flat recalled hearing a loud crash about 1.30 a.m.

---

crawl /krɔːl/ (crawls, crawling, crawled)

VERB When you **crawl**, you move forward on your hands and knees. ○ Her baby girl was just learning to crawl. ○ I slowly began to crawl towards the door.

c

cream /kriːm/ FOOD & DRINK

UNCOUNTABLE NOUN **Cream** is a thick yellowish-white liquid taken from milk. You can use it in cooking or put it on fruit or desserts. ○ *strawberries and cream* ○ *Vienna coffee is served with whipped cream.*

cre|ate /kriˈeɪt/ **(creates, creating, created)**

1 VERB To **create** something means to cause it to happen or exist. ○ *I didn't want to create any problems.* ○ *Something must be done to create more jobs.* ○ *Mirrors on the walls create an impression of light.*

▶ **COLLOCATIONS:**
create **jobs**
create **problems/tension**
create a **chance/opportunity**
create a **situation**
create an **atmosphere/environment**
create an **impression/effect**

▶ **SYNONYM:** produce

▶ **ANTONYM:** destroy

2 VERB When someone **creates** a new product or process, they invent it or design it. ○ *It is really great for a young producer to create a show like this.* ○ *The software industry should create products that are easier to use.*

crea|tive /kriˈeɪtɪv/ WORK PERSONALITY

ADJECTIVE A **creative** person has the ability to invent and develop original ideas, especially in the arts. ○ *Like so many creative people, he was never satisfied.* ○ *Until then, no one had recognized her creative talents.*

WORD FAMILY		
create	**VERB**	○ *Creating a good atmosphere in the classroom helps to produce good results.*
creation	**UNCOUNT**	○ *the creation of a £500m technology park*
creative	**ADJECTIVE**	○ *He was full of creative ideas.*
creatively	**ADVERB**	○ *Encourage children to think creatively.*

cred|it card /ˈkredɪt kɑːd/ **(credit cards)** MONEY

NOUN A **credit card** is a plastic card that you use to buy things now and pay for them later. ○ *All the major hotels accept credit cards.* ○ *Have your credit card details ready, and just tell us the items you require.*

▶ **COLLOCATIONS:**
pay by credit card
take/accept credit cards
a credit card **number**

credit card **details**
a credit card **bill**
a credit card **company**
credit card **fraud**

---

crime /kraɪm/ (crimes)

NOUN A **crime** is an illegal action or activity for which a person can be punished by law. ○ *About a third of the crimes were committed by girls under 17.* ○ *Police officers want to prevent and solve crime – that is their job.* ○ *rising crime rates*

▶ **COLLOCATIONS:**
  commit a crime
  investigate a crime
  solve a crime
  fight/tackle crime
  a **violent/serious** crime
  an **unsolved** crime
  organized crime
  a **gun/sex/car** crime
  computer/cyber/Internet crime
  street crime
  crime **prevention**
  the crime **rate**
  a crime **scene**

crimi|nal /ˈkrɪmɪnəl/ (criminals)

NOUN A **criminal** is a person who regularly commits crimes. ○ *Thousands of criminals are caught every year using DNA technology.* ○ *a convicted criminal with a two-year prison record* ○ *Police are looking for a dangerous criminal.*

▶ **COLLOCATIONS:**
  a **violent/dangerous** criminal
  a **convicted** criminal
  a **suspected/wanted** criminal
  catch a criminal

WORD FAMILY		
crime	NOUN	○ It is mainly the job of the police to tackle crime.
criminal	NOUN	○ The prison houses some of the country's most violent criminals.
criminal	ADJECTIVE	○ He faces various criminal charges.
criminally	ADVERB	○ Some members of staff were judged to have been criminally negligent.

crisps /krɪsps/

FOOD & DRINK

PLURAL NOUN **Crisps** are very thin slices of fried potato that are eaten cold as a snack. [BRIT; in AM, use **chips** or **potato chips**] ○ *a packet of crisps* ○ *cheese and onion crisps*

crit|ic /ˈkrɪtɪk/ **(critics)**

MEDIA & CULTURE

NOUN A **critic** is a person who writes about and expresses opinions about things such as books, films, music, or art. ○ *Mather was film critic on the Daily Telegraph for many years.* ○ *The New York critics had praised her performance.*

▶ **COLLOCATIONS:**
a **film/art/music/theatre** critic
a **literary** critic
a **TV/restaurant** critic

▶ **SYNONYM:** reviewer

criti|cal /ˈkrɪtɪkəl/

BELIEFS & OPINIONS

ADJECTIVE To be **critical of** someone or something means to criticize them. ○ [+ of] *His report is highly critical of the trial judge.* ○ *She is also critical of the decision to broadcast the programme.* ○ *a highly critical report on school meals*

▶ **COLLOCATIONS:**
critical **of** *someone/something*
highly critical
openly critical
a critical **report**
a critical **comment/remark**

WORD FAMILY		
critic	**NOUN**	○ *He's described by critics as Hollywood's next great leading man.*
criticize	**VERB**	○ *Federal boarding schools have been criticized for providing substandard education.*
critical	**ADJECTIVE**	○ *His departure from the club came after critical comments from teammates.*
critically	**ADVERB**	○ *She spoke critically of Lara.*
criticism	**NOUN**	○ *He has been facing strong criticism over his comments on immigration.*

cross /krɒs, AM krɔːs/ **(crosser, crossest)**

ADJECTIVE Someone who is **cross** is rather angry or irritated. ○ [+ with] *I'm terribly cross with him.* ○ [+ about] *She was cross about the last-minute change of plan.*

▶ **COLLOCATIONS:**
cross **about** *something*
cross **with** *someone*

▶ **SYNONYMS:** annoyed, irritated, angry

cross|roads /ˈkrɒsrəʊdz, AM ˈkrɔːs-/ (crossroads) `PLACES`

NOUN A **crossroads** is a place where two roads meet and cross each other. ○ *Turn right at the first crossroads.*

▶ **COLLOCATION: at** the crossroads

cross|word /ˈkrɒswɜːd, AM ˈkrɔːs-/ (crosswords) `FREE TIME`

NOUN A **crossword** or **crossword puzzle** is a word game in which you write the answers to clues in rows and columns of white squares that cross each other. ○ *He passed the time by doing crosswords.* ○ *a book of crossword puzzles*

▶ **COLLOCATIONS:**
  do a crossword
  a crossword **clue**

crowd /kraʊd/ (crowds) `PLACES`

NOUN A **crowd** is a large group of people who have gathered together. ○ *A huge crowd gathered in the square.* ○ *[+ of] Crowds of people were on the streets doing their Christmas shopping.*

▶ **COLLOCATIONS:**
  a crowd **of** *people*
  in a crowd
  a **large/big/huge/small** crowd
  an **angry/enthusiastic** crowd
  a crowd **gathers**
  a crowd **disperses**
  something **attracts** a crowd
  a crowd **cheers/chants/boos**

crowd|ed /ˈkraʊdɪd/

1 ADJECTIVE If a place is **crowded**, it is full of people. ○ *We pushed our way through the crowded streets.* ○ *The café was getting crowded.* ○ *[+ with] The old town square was crowded with people.*

▶ **COLLOCATIONS:**
  crowded **with** *people*
  get crowded
  a crowded **street**
  a crowded **bus/train**
  a crowded **restaurant/bar/room**

2 ADJECTIVE If a place is **crowded**, a lot of people live there. ○ *a crowded city of 5 million people* ○ *Their houses were crowded and filthy.*

cul|ture /ˈkʌltʃə/ (cultures) `MEDIA & CULTURE`

1 UNCOUNTABLE NOUN **Culture** consists of activities such as music, literature, art and philosophy. ○ *Movies are part of our popular culture.* ○ *We went to Rome for some culture.*

▶ **COLLOCATIONS:**
popular/ancient/modern culture
American/Western/European etc. culture

2 NOUN A **culture** is a particular society, especially considered in relation to its beliefs, way of life, or art. ○ *people from different cultures* ○ *I was brought up in a culture where the elderly are respected.*

WORD FAMILY		
culture	**NOUN**	○ Yul worked to improve his English and absorb American culture.
cultural	**ADJECTIVE**	○ There are major cultural differences between the two countries.
culturally	**ADVERB**	○ Here, it is not culturally acceptable to ask someone how much they earn.

cu|ri|ous /ˈkjʊəriəs/

ADJECTIVE If you are **curious about** something, you are interested in it and want to know more about it. ○ *Children are naturally curious.* ○ [+ to-inf] *I was curious to know who he was.* ○ [+ about] *By the age of two, children are curious about everything.*

▶ **COLLOCATIONS:**
curious **about** *something*
a curious **look/glance**
curious to **know/find out/see** *something*

▶ **SYNONYM:** inquisitive

WORD FAMILY		
curious	**ADJECTIVE**	○ Aren't you curious to know who he is?
curiously	**ADVERB**	○ 'How did you get that scar on your face?' Beth asked curiously.
curiosity	**UNCOUNT**	○ A good teacher can arouse our curiosity and encourage a desire to learn more.

curly /ˈkɜːli/ (curlier, curliest) `CLOTHES & APPEARANCE`

ADJECTIVE **Curly** hair is full of curves and circles called curls. ○ *I've got naturally curly hair.* ○ *His hair is dark and curly.*

▶ **SYNONYM:** wavy

▶ **ANTONYM:** straight

WORD FAMILY		
curl	**NOUN**	○ She has an attractive face and a mass of blonde curls.
curl	**VERB**	○ How can you curl your hair without causing heat damage?
curly	**ADJECTIVE**	○ a short woman with brown curly hair

cur|rent /ˈkʌrənt, AM ˈkɜːr-/

ADJECTIVE **Current** means happening, being used, or being done at the present time. ○ *The current situation is very different from that in 2008.* ○ *She has been in her current job for three months.*

cur|rent af|fairs /ˌkʌrənt əˈfeəz, AM ˌkɜːr-/ MEDIA & CULTURE

PLURAL NOUN **Current affairs** are political events and problems in society which are discussed in newspapers and on television and radio. ○ *I'm interested in political ideas and in current affairs in general.* ○ *a current affairs programme*

WORD FAMILY		
current	ADJECTIVE	○ My current job gives me time to work on my art.
currently	ADVERB	○ Sharmishta is currently studying law at the London School of Economics.
current affairs	PLURAL NOUN	○ Some of my friends take no interest in politics and current affairs.

cut down (on) /kʌt ˈdaʊn/ HEALTH
(cuts down, cutting down, cut down)

PHRASAL VERB If you **cut down** or **cut down on** something, you use or do less of it. ○ *He needs to cut down on coffee and eat a more balanced diet.* ○ *Sugar is hard to give up; try to cut down gradually.*

▶ **COLLOCATIONS:**
cut down on **coffee/chocolate/fatty foods/sugar/junk food/salt**
cut down on **cigarettes/alcohol**
cut down on **waste/paperwork/accidents/mistakes**
cut down **gradually/slowly**

cut off /kʌt ˈɒf/ **(cuts off, cutting off, cut off)**

PHRASAL VERB If you get **cut off** when you are on the telephone, the line is suddenly disconnected and you can no longer speak to the other person. ○ *I called her back and managed to speak to her, but then we got cut off.*

▶ **SYNONYM:** disconnect

cut out /kʌt ˈaʊt/ **(cuts out, cutting out, cut out)** HEALTH

PHRASAL VERB If you **cut out** a particular type of food, you stop eating it, usually because it is bad for you. ○ *He's trying to lose weight by cutting out junk food.*

▶ **SYNONYM:** eliminate

cy|cle /ˈsaɪkəl/ **(cycles, cycling, cycled)** SPORT & ACTIVITY

VERB If you **cycle**, you ride a bicycle. ○ *I cycle to college every day.* ○ *Britain could save £4.6 billion a year in road transport costs if more people cycled.*

WORD FAMILY		
cycle	VERB	○ At 12, he was cycling 10 miles a day to school and back.
cycling	UNCOUNT	○ We went cycling for a week in Holland.
cyclist	NOUN	○ Cyclists should use bike lanes where possible.

Dd

dai|ly /ˈdeɪli/

1 **ADJECTIVE** A **daily** activity or event happens every day. ○ *There are daily flights from Manchester to Munich.*

2 **ADVERB** If something happens **daily**, it happens every day. ○ *The Visitor Centre is open daily from 8.30 a.m. to 4.30 p.m.*

dam|age /ˈdæmɪdʒ/ **(damages, damaging, damaged)**

1 **VERB** To **damage** something means to break it, spoil it physically, or stop it from working properly. ○ *The sun can damage your skin.* ○ *The building was severely damaged by fire.*

  ▶ COLLOCATIONS:
    damage a **car/building/home/house**
    damage the **environment**
    seriously/severely/extensively damage *something*
    permanently/irreparably damage *something*
    slightly damage *something*

  ▶ SYNONYM: harm

2 **UNCOUNTABLE NOUN Damage** is physical harm that is caused to something. ○ [+ *to*] *The blast caused extensive damage to the house.* ○ *Motorists are doing irreparable damage to the earth's environment.*

  ▶ COLLOCATIONS:
    damage **to** *something*
    damage **from** *something*
    do/cause damage
    suffer damage
    assess/repair the damage
    serious/severe/extensive damage
    permanent/irreparable/long-term damage
    minor damage
    environmental damage
    brain/liver damage
    fire/water/flood damage

  ▶ SYNONYM: harm

> **WORD FAMILY**
>
> | | | |
> |---|---|---|
> | **damage** | **VERB** | ○ *Hepatitis B can permanently damage the liver.* |
> | **damage** | **UNCOUNT** | ○ *There was some minor fire damage in the living room.* |
> | **damaged** | **ADJECTIVE** | ○ *Police warned the public to stay away from damaged buildings.* |
> | **damaging** | **ADJECTIVE** | ○ *Stress can have damaging effects on both mind and body.* |

dark /dɑːk/ (darker, darkest)   CLOTHES & APPEARANCE

1 **ADJECTIVE** When you use **dark** to describe a colour, you are referring to a shade of that colour which is close to black, or seems to have some black in it. ○ *Elaine was wearing a dark blue dress.* ○ *The carpet is dark green.*

▶ **COLLOCATION:** dark **blue/green/brown/red/grey**

▶ **ANTONYMS:** light, pale

2 **ADJECTIVE** If someone has **dark** hair, eyes, or skin, they have brown or black hair, eyes, or skin. ○ *She's got dark, curly hair.* ○ *Leo listened, his dark eyes wide with concern.*

da|ta /ˈdeɪtə/   SCIENCE & NATURE

1 **UNCOUNTABLE NOUN** You can refer to information as **data**, especially when it is in the form of facts or statistics that you can analyse. ○ *The study was based on data from 2,100 women.* ○ *The data shows that people who eat margarine are more likely to develop heart disease.*

▶ **COLLOCATIONS:**
data **from** *something*
collect/gather/compile data
analyse data
data **shows/suggests/indicates** *something*
economic/scientific data

▶ **SYNONYMS:** facts, figures, information, statistics

2 **UNCOUNTABLE NOUN** **Data** is information that can be stored and used by a computer program. ○ *You can store huge amounts of data on a CD-ROM.* ○ *Computers divide data into chunks, or packets.*

▶ **COLLOCATIONS:**
store/process data
transmit/send data

> **USAGE**
>
> In American English, **data** is usually a plural noun. In technical or formal British English, **data** is also sometimes a plural noun. ○ *The data were collected and analysed.*
>
> In more general British English contexts, **data** is an uncountable noun. ○ *The data suggests that most people prefer the new system.*

day off /deɪ ˈɒf/ (days off)
WORK FREE TIME

NOUN A **day off** is a day when you do not go to work or school. ○ *I'm taking the day off to go to my sister's wedding.* ○ *Do you get many days off?* ○ *On his days off he worked on his music.*

▶ **COLLOCATIONS:**
on a day off
have/take/get a day off

dead|line /ˈdedlaɪn/ (deadlines)
EDUCATION

NOUN A **deadline** is a time or date before which a particular task must be finished. ○ [+ for] *The deadline for applications is April 1.* ○ *Students are missing coursework deadlines due to the amount of paid work they are forced to do.*

▶ **COLLOCATIONS:**
the deadline **for** something
meet/miss a deadline
set/impose a deadline
extend a deadline
a **tight** deadline
a **payment/work/essay** deadline

debt /det/ (debts)
MONEY

1 NOUN A **debt** is a sum of money that you owe someone. ○ *Three years later, he is still paying off his debts.* ○ *Student debts often prevent graduates saving for a home or pension.*

▶ **COLLOCATIONS:**
pay off/repay a debt
reduce/cut a debt
run up/have a debt
an **outstanding/unpaid** debt
a **huge/crippling** debt
mounting/rising debts
a **student/government** debt

2 UNCOUNTABLE NOUN Debt is the state of owing money. ○ *He was already deeply in debt.* ○ *How can I earn enough money to get out of debt?*

▶ **COLLOCATIONS:**
in debt
get into/get out of debt
be **deeply/heavily** in debt

dec|ade /ˈdekeɪd/ (decades)

NOUN A **decade** is a period of ten years, especially one that begins with a year ending in 0, for example 1980 to 1989. ○ *I was born in the last decade of the twentieth century.* ○ *The tiger population has declined dramatically in recent decades.* ○ *His singing career spanned six decades.*

d

▶ **COLLOCATIONS:**
in/during a decade
the **past/last/previous** decade
the **next/coming** decade
recent decades
something **spans** *x* decades

---

de|clare /dɪˈkleə/ (declares, declaring, declared)   BELIEFS & OPINIONS

VERB If you **declare** that something is true, you say that it is true in a firm, deliberate way. You can also **declare** an attitude or intention. [WRITTEN]
○ [+ that] *The prime minister declared that he would not resign.* ○ *'I'm absolutely delighted with the results,' she declared.* ○ *He declared his intention to become the best golfer in the world.*

▶ **SYNONYM:** announce

---

deco|rate /ˈdekəreɪt/ (decorates, decorating, decorated)   HOME

VERB If you **decorate** a room or building, you put paint or wallpaper on the walls.
○ *Most of the rooms need decorating.* ○ *I had the flat decorated quickly so that Philippa could move in.*

▶ **COLLOCATIONS:**
have *something* decorated
need decorating
beautifully/tastefully decorated
newly decorated

deco|ra|tion /ˌdekəˈreɪʃən/ (decorations)

1 UNCOUNTABLE NOUN The **decoration** of a room is its furniture, wallpaper, and ornaments. ○ *Everybody has their own ideas on home decoration.* ○ *The decoration and furnishings have to be practical enough for a family home.*

▶ **SYNONYM:** decor

2 NOUN Decorations are features that are added to something in order to make it look more attractive. ○ *The only wall decorations are candles and a single mirror.* ○ *The Christmas tree was covered in colourful decorations.*

WORD FAMILY		
decorate	**VERB**	○ All the rooms are beautifully decorated.
decorating	**NOUN**	○ I did all the decorating myself.
decoration	**NOUN**	○ With its simple decoration, the main bedroom is a peaceful haven.
decorator	**NOUN**	○ Good decorators clear up thoroughly at the end of the job.

de|gree /dɪˈɡriː/ (degrees)

EDUCATION

NOUN A **degree** at a university or college is a course of study that you take there, or the qualification that you get when you have passed the course. ○ *He took a master's degree in economics at Yale.* ○ *an engineering degree* ○ *the first year of a degree course*

▶ **COLLOCATIONS:**
a degree **in** *something*
do/take a degree
have/get/need a degree
a **good** degree
a **law/science/business/history**, etc. degree
a **masters/postgraduate/honours** degree
a degree **course/ceremony/certificate**

de|light|ed /dɪˈlaɪtɪd/

ADJECTIVE If you are **delighted**, you are extremely pleased and excited about something. ○ [+ to-inf] *I know Frank will be delighted to see you.* ○ [+ with] *He said that he was delighted with the public response.*

▶ **COLLOCATIONS:**
delighted **with** *something*
delighted **about** *something*
absolutely/really delighted
clearly/obviously delighted
be/feel delighted
seem/look/sound delighted

▶ **SYNONYM:** thrilled

▶ **ANTONYM:** disappointed

de|mand /dɪˈmɑːnd, -ˈmænd/
(demands, demanding, demanded)

BELIEFS & OPINIONS

VERB If you **demand** something, you ask for it in a very forceful way. ○ *They demanded an explanation.* ○ [+ that] *We demanded that a police officer arrest them.* ○ [+ to-inf] *The hijackers are demanding to speak to representatives of both governments.*

▶ **COLLOCATIONS:**
demand *something* **from** *someone*
demand **money/action/change**
demand an **apology/explanation/answer**

▶ **SYNONYM:** insist on

de|mand|ing /dɪˈmɑːndɪŋ, -ˈmænd-/

ADJECTIVE A **demanding** job or task requires a lot of your time, energy, or attention. ○ *He couldn't cope with his demanding job any more.* ○ *People nowadays do less physically demanding work.*

► COLLOCATIONS:
a demanding **job/task/course**
demanding **work**
very/extremely demanding
physically demanding

► ANTONYM: easy

---

den|im /'denɪm/ CLOTHES & APPEARANCE

UNCOUNTABLE NOUN Denim is a thick cotton cloth, usually blue, which is used to make clothes. Jeans are made from denim. ○ *He was dressed from head to toe in denim.* ○ *a blue denim jacket* ○ *faded denim jeans*

► COLLOCATIONS:
in denim
a denim **jacket/shirt/skirt**
denim **jeans**
wear denim

---

den|tist /'dentɪst/ (dentists) WORK HEALTH

NOUN A **dentist** is a person who is qualified to examine and treat people's teeth. ○ *She's at the dentist's having a filling.* ○ *Visit your dentist twice a year for a check-up.*

► COLLOCATIONS:
at the dentist's
go to/visit/see the dentist
a dentist's **chair/appointment/surgery**

---

deny /dɪ'naɪ/ (denies, denying, denied) BELIEFS & OPINIONS

VERB When you **deny** something, you say that it is not true. ○ [+ v-ing] *They all denied having seen her.* ○ [+ that] *The government denied that anyone had died during the war.*

► COLLOCATIONS:
deny a **charge/allegation/accusation**
deny **knowledge of/responsibility for** something
deny a **rumour**
strongly/strenuously deny something
categorically/flatly deny something
angrily deny something

► ANTONYM: admit

WORD FAMILY		
deny	**VERB**	○ *She denied both accusations.*
denial	**UNCOUNT**	○ *No one believed his denial.*

de|part|ment /dɪ'pɑːtmənt/ (departments) [EDUCATION] [WORK]

NOUN A **department** is one of the parts of a large business, shop or organization such as a university. ○ *She runs the English department at a school in London.* ○ *[+ of] the U.S. Department of Health, Education and Welfare* ○ *He now works in the sales department.*

▸ **COLLOCATIONS:**
the department **of** something
run/head a department
create/join/leave a department
a **government/university** department
the **engineering/English/science** department
the **human resources/marketing/finance** department

▸ **SYNONYMS:** division, section

de|par|tures /dɪ'pɑːtʃəz/ [TRANSPORT & TRAVEL]

PLURAL NOUN Departures is the area of an airport where people go before getting on an aircraft. ○ *We took the lift up to departures.*

→ see also **arrivals**

▸ **COLLOCATIONS:**
the departures **lounge/hall**
the departures **board**

WORD FAMILY		
depart	**VERB**	○ *Our flight departs from Heathrow airport.*
departure	**UNCOUNT**	○ *His departure was delayed by more than an hour.*
departures	**PLURAL NOUN**	○ *The departures board said our flight would leave in 20 minutes.*

de|pressed /dɪ'prest/ [HEALTH]

ADJECTIVE If you are **depressed**, you are sad, and you feel that you cannot enjoy anything because your situation is difficult and unpleasant. ○ *He seemed depressed when he heard the news.* ○ *[+ about] She's been very depressed and upset about this whole situation.*

▸ **COLLOCATIONS:**
depressed **about** something
become/get depressed
feel depressed
look/seem/sound depressed
very/severely/really depressed
clinically depressed

▸ **SYNONYMS:** unhappy, sad, miserable

▸ **ANTONYM:** cheerful

de|press|ing /dɪˈpresɪŋ/

ADJECTIVE Something that is **depressing** makes you feel sad and disappointed. ○ *The hospital was a very depressing place to be.* ○ *I want to go on holiday in February because it's a dismal, depressing month.*

▶ **COLLOCATIONS:**
very/pretty/deeply depressing
depressing **news**
a depressing **thought/experience/sight**
a depressing **place/picture**
a depressing **day**

▶ **SYNONYMS:** miserable, sad

de|pres|sion /dɪˈpreʃən/

UNCOUNTABLE NOUN Depression is a mental state in which someone feels unhappy and has no energy or enthusiasm. ○ *Mr Thomas was suffering from depression.* ○ *I slid into a depression after my friend died.*

▶ **COLLOCATIONS:**
suffer from/have/develop depression
treat/fight depression
cause depression
fall/slide into a depression
severe/deep/mild depression
clinical depression
post-natal depression

---

de|scribe /dɪˈskraɪb/
(describes, describing, described)

`MEDIA & CULTURE`

VERB If you **describe** someone or something, you say what they are like or what happened. ○ [+ what] *We asked her to describe what she did in her spare time.* ○ *This poem describes their life together.* ○ [+ as] *He was described as a man addicted to fame.*

▶ **COLLOCATIONS:**
describe *someone/something* **as** *something*
describe **what/where/why/how**
accurately/briefly describe *something*
describe *something* **in detail**

WORD FAMILY		
describe	**VERB**	○ *She described how she had been sent to hospital.*
description	**NOUN**	○ *Each disc has a brief description of the music on it.*
descriptive	**ADJECTIVE**	○ *Write a short descriptive piece about a place you know well.*

des|ert /ˈdezət/ (deserts)

SCIENCE & NATURE

NOUN A **desert** is a large area of land, usually in a hot region, which has almost no water, rain, trees, or plants. ○ *Las Vegas was built in the desert.* ○ *the Sahara Desert* ○ *the burning desert sun*

▶ COLLOCATIONS:
in the desert
the **Iraqi/Australian/African** desert
desert **sand/sun/heat**
a desert **town/region/landscape**
desert **conditions**

des|ti|na|tion /ˌdestɪˈneɪʃən/ (destinations)

TRANSPORT & TRAVEL

NOUN A person's or place's **destination** is the place where they are going. ○ *His preferred holiday destination is Hawaii.* ○ *Only half of the emergency supplies have reached their destination.*

▶ COLLOCATIONS:
reach a destination
something's **final/likely/intended** destination
an **unknown** destination
a **tourist/holiday/travel** destination

de|stroy /dɪˈstrɔɪ/ (destroys, destroying, destroyed)

VERB To **destroy** something means to cause so much damage to it that it is completely ruined or does not exist any more. ○ *The building was completely destroyed in the explosion.* ○ *He totally destroyed my confidence.*

▶ COLLOCATIONS:
destroy a **house/building/city**
destroy **life/evidence/crops**
destroy a **document**
completely/totally/utterly destroy *something*
partially destroy *something*
almost/nearly/virtually destroy *something*

▶ SYNONYM: ruin

▶ ANTONYMS: build, create, repair

WORD FAMILY		
destroy	**VERB**	○ *His decision to leave almost destroyed his life.*
destruction	**UNCOUNT**	○ *The bombing resulted in the destruction of many homes.*
destructive	**ADJECTIVE**	○ *Guilt can be very destructive.*
destructively	**ADVERB**	○ *What makes people behave destructively?*

de|tec|tive /dɪˈtektɪv/ (detectives) `CRIME`

NOUN A **detective** is someone whose job is to discover the facts about a crime or other situation. ○ *She hired a private detective to help her find her daughter.*
○ *Detectives are appealing for witnesses who may have seen anything suspicious.*

▶ COLLOCATIONS:
a **private/undercover** detective
a **young/female/former** detective
a **police/store** detective
detective **work**
a detective **story/novel/series**

de|vel|op /dɪˈveləp/ (develops, developing, developed)

VERB When something **develops**, it grows or changes over a period of time and usually becomes more advanced, complete, or severe. ○ *As children develop, they learn a lot of important things.* ○ [+ into] *The rain did not develop into a real storm.*
○ [+ from] *Most of these settlements developed from agricultural centres.*

▶ COLLOCATIONS:
develop **into** *something*
develop **from** *something*
develop **quickly/slowly/normally**
fully develop

de|vel|oped /dɪˈveləpt/ `PLACES`

ADJECTIVE **Developed** countries have changed from being poor agricultural countries to rich industrial countries. ○ *The major causes of death in the developed countries are heart disease and cancer.* ○ *The industrial revolution was spreading to the less developed world.*

▶ COLLOCATIONS:
developed **countries/nations**
the developed **world**
more/less developed

de|vel|op|ing /dɪˈveləpɪŋ/

ADJECTIVE If you talk about **developing** countries or the **developing** world, you mean the countries or the parts of the world that are poor and have few industries. ○ *The developing countries still face many problems.* ○ *In the developing world, cigarette consumption is increasing.*

▶ COLLOCATIONS:
developing **countries/nations**
the developing **world**

de|vel|op|ment /dɪˈveləpmənt/

1 UNCOUNTABLE NOUN **Development** is the gradual growth or formation of something. ○ *The child's language development may be delayed.* ○ [+ of] *Hands-on experience is essential for the development of skills.*

▶ COLLOCATIONS:
development **of** *something*
professional/personal development
technological development
career development
language/child development
staff/player development

2 **UNCOUNTABLE NOUN Development** is the growth of something such as a business or an industry. ○ *Education is central to a country's economic development.* ○ [+ of] *What are your plans for the development of your company?*

▶ COLLOCATIONS:
development **of** *something*
economic/industrial development
business development

WORD FAMILY		
develop	VERB	○ *It's hard to say how the market will develop.*
development	UNCOUNT	○ *The company spends a lot of money on staff development.*
developed	ADJECTIVE	○ *The population of the more developed nations has remained about the same.*
developing	ADJECTIVE	○ *Society has an impact on the developing child.*
developmental	ADJECTIVE	○ *a child with developmental problems* ○ *the final developmental stage of adult life*

---

dia|ry /ˈdaɪəri/ (diaries)   `MEDIA & CULTURE`

NOUN A **diary** is a book which has a separate space for each day of the year. You use a diary to write down things you plan to do, or to record what happens in your life day by day. ○ *Hold on a moment, I'll just check my diary.* ○ *I didn't even know she kept a diary.* ○ *He turned to his most recent diary entries.*

▶ COLLOCATIONS:
keep/write a diary
read *someone's* diary
a **secret/private/personal** diary
a **daily/weekly** diary
a **desk/pocket** diary
an **online** diary
a diary **entry**

---

diet /ˈdaɪət/ (diets, dieting, dieted)   `HEALTH` `FOOD & DRINK`

1 **NOUN** Your **diet** is the type and range of food that you regularly eat. ○ *It's never too late to improve your diet.* ○ *a healthy diet rich in fruit and vegetables* ○ *Poor diet will eventually damage your health.*

d

▶ COLLOCATIONS:
a **balanced/healthy/good** diet
a **poor** diet
a **vegetarian/vegan** diet
a **high-fat/low-fat** diet
eat/have a diet
improve your diet

2 NOUN If you are on a **diet**, you eat special kinds of food or you eat less food than usual because you are trying to improve your health or lose weight. ○ *Have you been on a diet? You've lost a lot of weight.* ○ *[+ of] He was put on a diet of milky food.* ○ *a special diet for children with high cholesterol*

▶ COLLOCATIONS:
a diet **of** something
go on a diet
put someone **on** a diet
a **strict/special** diet
a **crash** diet
a **low-calorie/high-fibre** diet
diet **pills/supplements**
a diet **drink**

3 VERB If you **are dieting**, you eat special kinds of food or you eat less food than usual because you are trying to lose weight. ○ *Most of us have dieted at some time in our lives.*

---

din|ing room /ˈdaɪnɪŋ ruːm/ (dining rooms) HOME
also **dining-room**

NOUN The **dining room** is the room in a house where people have their meals, or a room in a hotel where meals are served. ○ *We were having dinner in the dining room.*

▶ COLLOCATIONS:
in the dining room
a **kitchen-**dining room
a **hotel** dining room

---

di|no|saur /ˈdaɪnəsɔː/ (dinosaurs) HISTORY

NOUN **Dinosaurs** were large reptiles that lived in prehistoric times. ○ *How did the dinosaurs die out?* ○ *dinosaur bones* ○ *a dinosaur egg*

---

di|rec|tor /daɪˈrektə, dɪr-/ (directors) MEDIA & CULTURE

NOUN The **director** of a play, film, or television programme is the person who decides how it will appear on stage or screen, and who tells the actors and technical staff what to do. ○ *'A Bronx Tale' was De Niro's first film as director.* ○ *[+ of] the director of the Austin Powers films, Jay Roach* ○ *He received a nomination for 'best director'.*

WORD FAMILY		
director	**NOUN**	○ The play's director is Dmitry Semakin.
direct	**VERB**	○ Andrew acted in, and directed, this film.

dis|ap|point|ed /ˌdɪsəˈpɔɪntɪd/

ADJECTIVE If you are **disappointed**, you are rather sad because something has not happened or because something is not as good as you had hoped. ○ [+ that] I was disappointed that he was not there. ○ [+ with] You won't be disappointed with this film – it's brilliant. ○ [+ to-inf] I was disappointed to see there were no women in the competition.

▸ COLLOCATIONS:
   disappointed **with/in** someone/something
   disappointed **about** something
   be/feel disappointed
   look/seem/sound disappointed
   very/bitterly/extremely disappointed
   slightly/a little disappointed

▸ SYNONYMS: fed up, unhappy

dis|ap|point|ing /ˌdɪsəˈpɔɪntɪŋ/

ADJECTIVE Something that is **disappointing** is not as good or as large as you hoped it would be. ○ [+ to-inf] It was disappointing to lose the game in this way. ○ [+ for] It must have been disappointing for you to find nothing there.

▸ COLLOCATIONS:
   disappointing **for** someone
   very/really/extremely disappointing
   slightly/a little disappointing
   a disappointing **result/performance/start**
   disappointing **news**

WORD FAMILY		
disappoint	**VERB**	○ I hate to disappoint you, but I'm afraid I can't make it to your party.
disappointment	**UNCOUNT**	○ Book your ticket early to avoid disappointment.
disappointed	**ADJECTIVE**	○ I'm surprised and disappointed in you.
disappointing	**ADJECTIVE**	○ This is very disappointing news indeed.
disappointingly	**ADVERB**	○ Progress is disappointingly slow.

dis|ap|prove /ˌdɪsəˈpruːv/   BELIEFS & OPINIONS
(disapproves, disapproving, disapproved)

VERB If you **disapprove of** something or someone, you feel or show that you do not like them or do not approve of them. ○ [+ of] *Most people disapprove of the use of violence.* ○ [+ of] *Her mother disapproved of her working in a bar.*

▶ COLLOCATIONS:
disapprove **of** *someone/something*
strongly disapprove
clearly disapprove

▶ ANTONYM: approve

WORD FAMILY		
disapprove	VERB	○ *Her father made it clear that he disapproved.*
disapproval	UNCOUNT	○ *Try to avoid showing disapproval.*
disapproving	ADJECTIVE	○ *Janet gave him a disapproving look.*
disapprovingly	ADVERB	○ *Antonio looked at me disapprovingly.*

dis|ci|pline /ˈdɪsɪplɪn/

PERSONALITY EDUCATION

1 **UNCOUNTABLE NOUN** Discipline is the practice of making people obey rules or standards of behaviour, and punishing them when they do not. ○ *He believes that children need strict discipline.* ○ *discipline problems in the classroom* ○ *the need to improve school discipline*

▶ COLLOCATIONS:
impose/enforce/improve discipline
need discipline
discipline **problems**
a **lack of** discipline
strict/good/poor discipline
school/classroom discipline

2 **UNCOUNTABLE NOUN** Discipline is the quality of being able to behave and work in a controlled way which involves obeying particular rules or standards. ○ *I don't have the discipline to just sit down and write.* ○ *People fail because they lack the discipline to organize themselves.*

▶ COLLOCATIONS:
have/show discipline
lack discipline
instill/teach/learn discipline
good/great/poor discipline

▶ SYNONYM: self-control

WORD FAMILY		
discipline	UNCOUNT	○ *The discipline imposed by his father was very strict.*
discipline	VERB	○ *The workman was disciplined by his company but not dismissed.*
disciplined	ADJECTIVE	○ *She is very disciplined and hard-working.*
disciplinary	ADJECTIVE	○ *No disciplinary action was taken.*

dis|count /ˈdɪskaʊnt/ (discounts)

SHOPPING

NOUN A **discount** is a reduction in the usual price of something. ○ *They are often available at a discount.* ○ *Full-time staff get a 20 per cent discount.*

▶ **COLLOCATIONS:**
at a discount
a discount **of** something
get a discount
discount **prices**
a discount **store**

▶ **SYNONYM:** reduction

dis|cour|age /dɪsˈkʌrɪdʒ, AM -ˈkɜːr-/ (discourages, discouraging, discouraged)

VERB If someone or something **discourages** you, they cause you to lose your enthusiasm for something. ○ *It may be difficult to do at first. Don't let this discourage you.*

▶ **SYNONYM:** dishearten

▶ **ANTONYM:** encourage

WORD FAMILY		
discourage	**VERB**	○ *Even the terrible weather did not discourage them.*
discouraged	**ADJECTIVE**	○ *She was determined not to be too discouraged.*
discouraging	**ADJECTIVE**	○ *Today's news is rather discouraging for the economy.*

dis|cov|ery /dɪsˈkʌvəri/ (discoveries)

SCIENCE & NATURE HISTORY

1 NOUN If someone makes a **discovery**, they become aware of something that they did not know about before. ○ *I made a remarkable discovery.* ○ [+ that] *The discovery that he has a sister shocked us all.*

2 NOUN If someone makes a **discovery**, they are the first person to find or become aware of something that no one knew about before. ○ *In that year, two momentous discoveries were made.* ○ [+ of] *the discovery of the ozone hole over the South Pole*

▶ **COLLOCATIONS:**
the discovery **of** something
make a discovery
a **new/recent** disovery
a **great/important/exciting** discovery
a **surprising/remarkable** discovery
a **scientific** discovery

WORD FAMILY		
discover	**VERB**	○ *She discovered that they had escaped.*
discovery	**NOUN**	○ *I was tidying my room when I made a surprising discovery.*

dis|play /dɪsˈpleɪ/ (displays, displaying, displayed) `MEDIA & CULTURE`

1 **VERB** When a computer **displays** information, it shows the information on a screen. ○ *The departures board displays up-to-date flight information.* ○ *[+ on] My name and address were displayed on the screen.*

▶ **COLLOCATIONS:**
   display something **on** something
   display an **image**
   display **text**

▶ **SYNONYMS:** show, present

2 **NOUN** A **display** is an arrangement of things that have been put in a particular place, so that people can see them easily. ○ *[+ of] You are invited to display of final-year work* ○ *Most of the work on display was fantastic*

▶ **COLLOCATIONS:**
   a display **of** something
   on display
   a **public** display
   a **large/permanent/interactive** display
   a **window/museum** display
   a display **case/cabinet**

▶ **SYNONYMS:** exhibition, presentation

3 **NOUN** A **display** is a public performance or other event which is intended to entertain people. ○ *[+ of] There were some spectacular displays of gymnastics.* ○ *a firework display*

---

dis|pose of /dɪsˈpəʊz əv, STRONG ɒv, AM ʌv/ `SCIENCE & NATURE`
(disposes of, disposing of, disposed of)

PHRASAL VERB If you **dispose of** something that you no longer want or need, you throw it away. ○ *What is the safest way of disposing of chemical waste?* ○ *Do not dispose of engine oil down a drain.*

▶ **SYNONYMS:** get rid of, throw away

dis|pos|able /dɪsˈpəʊzəbəl/

ADJECTIVE A **disposable** product is designed to be thrown away after it has been used. ○ *He shaved himself with a disposable razor.* ○ *disposable nappies* ○ *a disposable camera*

WORD FAMILY		
dispose of	PHRASAL VERB	○ *Matthew quickly disposed of the evidence.*
disposal	UNCOUNT	○ *the disposal of radioactive waste* ○ *a bomb disposal expert*
disposable	ADJECTIVE	○ *The nurse was wearing disposable gloves.*

dis|ser|ta|tion /ˌdɪsəˈteɪʃən/ (dissertations) `EDUCATION`

NOUN A **dissertation** is a long formal piece of writing on a particular subject, especially for a university degree. ○ [+ on] *He is currently writing a dissertation on the American Civil War.* ○ *You have to submit a dissertation of 20,000 words.*

▶ **COLLOCATIONS:**
a dissertation **on** something
write/finish/submit a dissertation

▶ **SYNONYMS:** essay, paper

dis|tance /ˈdɪstəns/ (distances) `TRANSPORT & TRAVEL`

NOUN The **distance between** two points or places is the amount of space between them. ○ [+ from] *He was standing a short distance from the house.* ○ [+ between] *the distance between the island and the nearby shore* ○ *within walking distance*

▶ **COLLOCATIONS:**
the distance **between** somewhere **and** somewhere
the distance **from** somewhere
a **long/short/equal** distance
a **safe** distance
walking distance

WORD FAMILY		
distance	**NOUN**	○ *Make sure you are a safe distance away from the fire.*
distant	**ADJECTIVE**	○ *creatures on a distant planet* ○ *distant lands*

dis|tinc|tive /dɪˈstɪŋktɪv/ `MEDIA & CULTURE`

ADJECTIVE Something that is **distinctive** has special qualities that make it easily recognizable. ○ *His voice was very distinctive.* ○ *Both authors have their own distinctive styles.*

▶ **COLLOCATIONS:**
very/highly/quite distinctive
a distinctive **style/flavour/sound**
a distinctive **feature/quality/character**
a distinctive **pattern/shape/design**

▶ **SYNONYMS:** recognizable, special

WORD FAMILY		
distinctive	**ADJECTIVE**	○ *the distinctive smell of chlorine* ○ *a distinctive blue and yellow flag*
distinctively	**ADVERB**	○ *It has a strong, distinctively tangy flavour.*
distinctiveness	**UNCOUNT**	○ *The problem with this product is that it lacks distinctiveness.*

dis|trict /ˈdɪstrɪkt/ **(districts)**

`PLACES`

NOUN A **district** is a particular area of a town or country. ○ *I drove around the business district.* ○ *It is a poor district on the outskirts of town.*

▶ **COLLOCATIONS:**
the **business/shopping** district
the **financial/historic/commercial** district
the **central/local** district
a **poor/wealthy** district

▶ **SYNONYMS:** area, neighbourhood

div|ing /ˈdaɪvɪŋ/

`SPORT & ACTIVITY`

1 UNCOUNTABLE NOUN Diving is the sport or activity of going under the surface of the sea or a lake, using special breathing equipment. ○ *You can go diving in the coral reef.* ○ *equipment and accessories for diving*

▶ **COLLOCATIONS:**
go diving
a diving **instructor/course/suit**
diving **gear/equipment**
scuba/deep-sea diving

2 UNCOUNTABLE NOUN Diving is the sport of jumping head first into water with your arms straight above your head. ○ *High diving is one of the scariest sports I have ever tried.* ○ *In diving, the aim is to cause the smallest splash possible.*

▶ **COLLOCATIONS:**
high diving
synchronized diving
a diving **board**

WORD FAMILY		
dive	**VERB**	○ *She was standing by a pool, about to dive in.*
diving	**UNCOUNT**	○ *I've been scuba diving in the Maldives.*
diver	**NOUN**	○ *Divers found the wreck just off the west coast of the island.*

docu|men|tary /ˌdɒkjəˈmentri/ **(documentaries)** `MEDIA & CULTURE`

NOUN A **documentary** is a television or radio programme, or a film, which provides factual information about a particular subject. ○ *[+ about] A TV company wants to make a documentary about him.* ○ *[+ on] a TV documentary on homelessness* ○ *the subject of a recent documentary*

▶ **COLLOCATIONS:**
a documentary **on/about** something
watch/see a documentary
make/produce a documentary
show/broadcast a documentary

a **good/fascinating** documentary
a **controversial** documentary
a **new/recent** documentary
a **television/radio** documentary
a **nature/history/music** documentary

---

do|mes|tic /dəˈmestɪk/ PLACES

ADJECTIVE Domestic activities and situations happen or exist within one particular country. ○ *John took a domestic flight to Madrid.* ○ *Sales in the domestic market increased by 1%.*

▶ **COLLOCATIONS:**
a domestic **flight**
domestic **politics**
the domestic **market/economy**
domestic **demand/sales**

▶ **SYNONYMS:** internal, home

▶ **ANTONYMS:** foreign, international

---

domi|nate /ˈdɒmɪneɪt/ (dominates, dominating, dominated)

VERB To **dominate** a situation means to be the most powerful or important person or thing in it. ○ *Our team totally dominated the game.* ○ *Events in the Middle East dominated the news.*

▶ **COLLOCATIONS:**
dominate a **game/race**
dominate the **world**
dominate **politics/sport**
dominate the **news**
still dominate *something*
totally/completely dominate *something*

WORD FAMILY		
dominate	VERB	○ *The book is expected to dominate the best-seller lists.*
dominant	ADJECTIVE	○ *She was a dominant figure in the French film industry.*
dominance	UNCOUNT	○ *the growing dominance of the English language* ○ *the Democrats' political dominance*
domination	UNCOUNT	○ *the team's total domination of Spanish football* ○ *the domination of the market by a small number of organizations*

---

do|nate /dəʊˈneɪt/ (donates, donating, donated) MONEY

VERB If you **donate** something **to** a charity or other organization, you give it to them. ○ [+ to] *He frequently donates large sums of money to charity.* ○ *Others donated secondhand clothes.*

▶ **COLLOCATIONS:**
donate *something* **to** *someone/something*
donate **money/food/clothes**

WORD FAMILY		
donate	VERB	○ *The silver trophy was donated by a local businessman.*
donation	NOUN	○ *She made a £500,000 donation to the charity last year.*
donor	NOUN	○ *Foreign donors provided millions of dollars to the tsunami victims.*

do up /duː ˈʌp/ (does up, doing up, did up, done up) HOME

PHRASAL VERB If you **do up** an old building, you decorate and repair it so that it is in a better condition. [BRIT] ○ *We decided to do up the house ourselves.* ○ *Nicholas has bought a barn in Provence and is spending August doing it up.*

do with|out /duː wɪˈðaʊt/ MONEY
(does without, doing without, did without, done without)

PHRASAL VERB If you **do without** something, you manage or survive in spite of not having it. ○ *More than 100,000 people had to do without electricity.* ○ *We didn't have any sugar, so we had to do without.*

dra|ma /ˈdrɑːmə/ (dramas) MEDIA & CULTURE

NOUN A **drama** is a serious play for the theatre, television, or radio. ○ *He acts in radio dramas.* ○ *I decided I wanted to be a lawyer after I watched a courtroom drama on TV.*

▶ **COLLOCATIONS:**
watch/see a drama
make/produce a drama
a **new/good** drama
a **political/medical/legal** drama
a **courtroom/hospital** drama
a **costume** drama
a **TV/radio** drama

draw /drɔː/ (draws, drawing, drew, drawn) MEDIA & CULTURE

VERB When you **draw**, or when you **draw** something, you use a pencil or pen to produce a picture, pattern, or diagram. ○ *He starts a painting by drawing shapes.* ○ *She would sit there drawing for hours.*

▶ **SYNONYM:** sketch

draw|ing /ˈdrɔːɪŋ/ (drawings)

NOUN A **drawing** is a picture made with a pencil or pen. ○ [+ of] She did a drawing of me. ○ You won't always have time for detailed drawings.

▶ **COLLOCATIONS:**
a drawing **of** something/someone
do a drawing
a **detailed/simple** drawing
a **line/colour/pencil** drawing

▶ **SYNONYM:** sketch

---

dress /dres/
(dresses, dressing, dressed)

`CLOTHES & APPEARANCE` `SOCIAL LIFE`

1 NOUN A **dress** is a piece of clothing worn by a woman or girl. It covers her body and part of her legs. ○ She was wearing a black dress. ○ Designer wedding dresses are very expensive.

▶ **COLLOCATIONS:**
put on/wear a dress
make/design a dress
buy/borrow a dress
a **black/white/floral** dress
a **short/long/tight** dress
a **strapless** dress
a **beautiful/pretty** dress
a **wedding/party/summer** dress
a **silk/cotton/lace** dress
a **designer** dress

2 VERB If someone **dresses** in a particular way, they wear clothes of a particular style or colour. ○ [+ in] She used to dress in jeans. ○ He prefers to dress casually.

▶ **COLLOCATIONS:**
dress **in** something
dress **well**
dress **casually/smartly**
dress **formally/informally**
dress **appropriately**

dressed /dresd/

1 ADJECTIVE If you are **dressed**, you are wearing clothes rather than being naked or wearing your night clothes. If you **get dressed**, you put on your clothes. ○ He went into his bedroom to get dressed. ○ He was fully dressed, including shoes.

▶ **COLLOCATIONS:**
get dressed
fully dressed

2 ADJECTIVE If you are **dressed** in a particular way, you are wearing clothes of a particular colour or kind. ○ Make sure you are smartly dressed when you go for an interview. ○ [+ in] a thin woman dressed in black ○ a tall, elegantly dressed man

d

▶ **COLLOCATIONS:**
dressed **in** *something*
well dressed
casually dressed
smartly/neatly/immaculately dressed
beautifully/elegantly dressed
badly dressed

dress|ing room /ˈdresɪŋ ruːm, rʊm/ MEDIA & CULTURE
(dressing rooms)

NOUN A **dressing room** is a room in a theatre where performers can dress and get ready for their performance. ○ *The dancers were still in their dressing room.*

WORD FAMILY		
dress	NOUN	○ *I put on a summer dress and sandals.*
dress	VERB	○ *Everyone dressed formally for dinner.*
dressed	ADJECTIVE	○ *She is always beautifully dressed.*
undressed	ADJECTIVE	○ *He went into the bathroom and got undressed.*
dressing room	NOUN	○ *Her bedroom looks like a Broadway dressing room.*

drive /draɪv/ **(drives)** FREE TIME   HOME

1 NOUN A **drive** is a journey in a car or other vehicle. ○ *Shall we go for a drive?* ○ *It was a long drive back to the city.*

▶ **COLLOCATIONS:**
go for a drive
a **long/short** drive
a **two-hour/10-minute**, etc. drive

2 NOUN A **drive** is a wide piece of hard ground, or sometimes a private road, that leads from the road to a person's house. ○ *Two large cars were parked on the front drive.*

▶ **COLLOCATIONS:**
on the drive
the **front** drive

▶ **SYNONYM:** driveway

driv|er /ˈdraɪvə/ **(drivers)** TRANSPORT & TRAVEL

NOUN The **driver** of a vehicle is the person who is driving it. ○ *The driver got out of his van.* ○ *a taxi driver* ○ *lorry drivers*

drop /drɒp/ **(drops, dropping, dropped)** SCIENCE & NATURE

VERB If the temperature **drops**, it quickly becomes less. ○ [+ *to*] *Temperatures can drop to freezing at night.*

drought /draʊt/ (droughts)

SCIENCE & NATURE

NOUN A **drought** is a long period of time when no rain falls. ○ *Spain was suffering a severe drought.* ○ *The drought has wiped out large areas of crops.*

▶ COLLOCATIONS:
suffer/experience a drought
cause a drought
a **severe/bad/long** drought
drought **conditions**

drug /drʌg/ (drugs)

HEALTH

1 NOUN A **drug** is a chemical that is given to people in order to treat or prevent an illness or disease. ○ *If you want to stop taking the drug, you have to do so slowly.* ○ *Trials are carried out to check that the drug is safe.*

▶ COLLOCATIONS:
be on/take a drug
prescribe/give a drug
test a drug
a **safe/effective/expensive** drug
a drug **company**
drug **treatment/testing**

2 NOUN **Drugs** are substances that some people take because of their pleasant effects, but which are usually illegal. ○ *His mother was on drugs.* ○ *She was sure Leo was taking drugs.* ○ *the problem of drug abuse*

▶ COLLOCATIONS:
be on/take/use drugs
hard drugs
a **dangerous/illegal** drug
drug **use/abuse**
a drug **problem**
a drug **dealer/trafficker**
a drug **addict/user**

dry /draɪ/ (drier, dryer, driest)

SCIENCE & NATURE

1 ADJECTIVE If something is **dry**, there is no water or moisture on it or in it. ○ *Clean the metal with a soft dry cloth.* ○ *Pat it dry with a soft towel.*

▶ COLLOCATION: **completely/barely/almost** dry

▶ ANTONYMS: wet, damp

2 ADJECTIVE If the weather or a period of time is **dry**, there is no rain, or there is much less rain than average. ○ *Weeks of dry weather have made the grass yellow.* ○ *This spring has been unusually dry.*

▶ COLLOCATIONS:
quite/relatively/mainly dry
dry **weather/conditions**

a dry **spell/summer/day**
the dry **season**

▶ ANTONYM: wet

---

dust /dʌst/   SCIENCE & NATURE

UNCOUNTABLE NOUN Dust is very small dry particles of earth or sand. ○ *I could see a thick layer of dust on the stairs.* ○ *He reversed the car in a cloud of dust.*

▶ COLLOCATIONS:
a **cloud of** dust
fine/thick dust
coal/chalk dust
dust **particles**

WORD FAMILY		
dust	**UNCOUNT**	○ *The classroom smelled of chalk dust.*
dusty	**ADJECTIVE**	○ *She took a book from a dusty shelf.*

DVD /ˌdiː viː ˈdiː/ **(DVDs)**   FREE TIME

NOUN A **DVD** is a disc on which a film or music is recorded. ○ *I like watching DVDs with friends.* ○ *The film has just been released on DVD.*

▶ COLLOCATIONS:
on DVD
watch/buy/play a DVD
a **new/special/free** DVD
a DVD **player/recorder**
a DVD **collection**

---

dy|nam|ic /daɪˈnæmɪk/   PERSONALITY

ADJECTIVE A **dynamic** person is full of energy. ○ *She is an incredibly dynamic woman.* ○ *He seemed a dynamic and energetic leader.*

WORD FAMILY		
dynamic	**ADJECTIVE**	○ *Marcus was handsome, dynamic and ambitious.*
dynamically	**ADVERB**	○ *He is dynamically attractive to the opposite sex.*

Ee

earn /ɜːn/ (earns, earning, earned)

MONEY WORK

VERB If you **earn** money, you receive money in return for work that you do.
○ *She earns £27,000 a year.* ○ *Soon, I'll be able to get a job and earn some money.*
○ *What a lovely way to earn a living.*

▶ COLLOCATIONS:
earn **money**
earn a **living**
earn **more/less/a little/enough**

> **WHICH WORD: earn or win?**
>
> Use **earn** to talk about getting money in return for work. ○ *The workers were earning as little as a dollar a day.*
>
> Use **win** to talk about getting a prize, or being first in a race or competition. ○ *Jodie Foster won the Best Actress award.* ○ *We did well to win the game.*

ear|rings /'ɪərɪŋz/ (earrings)

CLOTHES & APPEARANCE

PLURAL NOUN **Earrings** are pieces of jewellery that you attach to your ears.
○ *She wore several earrings in each ear.*

▶ COLLOCATIONS:
wear earrings
a **pair of** earrings
diamond/gold/pearl earrings
big/dangly earrings

earth /ɜːθ/

SCIENCE & NATURE

NOUN The **Earth** is the planet on which we live. ○ *The moon orbits the Earth about once each month.* ○ *a fault in the Earth's crust* ○ *planet earth*

earth|quake /'ɜːθkweɪk/ (earthquakes)

NOUN An **earthquake** is a sudden shaking of the ground caused by movement of the Earth's crust. ○ *An earthquake caused the roof of the school to collapse.*
○ *Somehow they survived the dreadful earthquake.*

▶ COLLOCATIONS:
cause/trigger an earthquake

survive an earthquake
an earthquake **hits/strikes**
an earthquake **kills/destroys/devastates** *someone/something*
a **powerful/major/massive** earthquake
a **small** earthquake
an earthquake **victim/survivor**
earthquake **damage**

---

easy-going /ˌiːziˈgəʊɪŋ/ `PERSONALITY`

ADJECTIVE If you describe someone as **easy-going**, you mean that they are not easily annoyed, worried, or upset. ○ *He is easy-going and good-natured.* ○ *People around here have a very easy-going attitude to life.*

▶ COLLOCATIONS:
an easy-going **manner/personality/nature/attitude**
an easy-going **person/guy**

---

ecol|ogy /ɪˈkɒlədʒi/ `SCIENCE & NATURE`

UNCOUNTABLE NOUN Ecology is the study of the relationships between plants, animals, people, and their environment, and the balances between these relationships. ○ *a senior lecturer in ecology*

▶ COLLOCATIONS:
an ecology **professor/expert/graduate**
study/teach ecology

WORD FAMILY		
ecology	UNCOUNT	○ He went to York University to study ecology.
ecologist	NOUN	○ Ecologists warn that the loss of the hippos could have serious consequences for the park.
ecological	ADJECTIVE	○ There could be an ecological disaster if this practice continues.
ecologically	ADVERB	○ There are more ecologically sound ways of disposing of waste.

---

econo|my /ɪˈkɒnəmi/ **(economies)** `MONEY`

NOUN An **economy** is the system according to which the money, industry, and trade of a country or region are organized. A country's **economy** is the wealth that it gets from business and industry. ○ *The Japanese economy grew at a rate of 10 per cent a year.* ○ *The local economy relies on travel.*

▶ COLLOCATIONS:
a **strong/booming** economy
a **weak** economy
the **global/world/local/national** economy
the **American/Japanese**, etc. economy

boost/stimulate an economy
an economy **grows**
an economy **picks up/recovers**
an economy **slows/shrinks**

eco|nom|ic /ˌiːkəˈnɒmɪk, ˌek-/

ADJECTIVE **Economic** means concerned with the organization of the money, industry, and trade of a country, region, or society. ○ *Poland has undergone some radical economic reforms.* ○ *The pace of economic growth is picking up.* ○ *The impact of the economic crisis was immense.*

▶ **COLLOCATIONS:**
economic **growth/recovery**
an economic **crisis/downturn**
the economic **situation/climate**
economic **reforms**
economic **policy**

eco|nomi|cal /ˌiːkəˈnɒmɪkəl, ˌek-/

ADJECTIVE Something that is **economical** does not require a lot of money to operate. ○ *They plan to trade in their car for something smaller and more economical.* ○ [+ to-inf] *It is more economical to wait until the dishwasher is full before switching it on.* ○ [+ on] *The car is very economical on fuel.*

WHICH WORD: economic or economical?

You use **economic** to describe things that relate to a country's economy. ○ *The economic situation had become much worse.*

You use **economical** to describe products, machines, and methods that are not expensive to use and do not waste resources. ○ *These new dishwashers are efficient, economical and great time-savers.*

WORD FAMILY

economy	NOUN	○ The economy has recovered a little over the past 18 months.
economics	UNCOUNT	○ Liam has a degree in economics.
economist	NOUN	○ Leading economists are calling for a reform of the banking system.
economic	ADJECTIVE	○ the beginnings of an economic recovery
economical	ADJECTIVE	○ The engine is very economical.
economically	ADVERB	○ Services could be operated more efficiently and economically.
economize	VERB	○ Another way of economizing is to save seeds from plants in your garden.
uneconomic	ADJECTIVE	○ The government is closing uneconomic factories.

edi|tor /'edɪtə/ (editors)

MEDIA & CULTURE

1 **NOUN** An **editor** is the person who is in charge of a newspaper or magazine and who decides what will be published in each edition of it. ○ [+ of] *She started out as an editor of a teen magazine.* ○ *Eventually, I'd like to be a newspaper editor.*

▶ COLLOCATIONS:
   the editor **of** *something*
   a **newspaper/magazine** editor

2 **NOUN** An **editor** is a journalist who is responsible for a particular section of a newspaper or magazine. ○ *She's the fashion editor of 'Company' magazine.*

▶ COLLOCATION: a **political/fashion/business** editor

3 **NOUN** An **editor** is a person who checks and corrects texts before they are published. ○ *Even the best writers need a good editor.* ○ *a book editor*

WORD FAMILY		
edit	**VERB**	○ *He moved to Berlin to edit a music magazine.*
editor	**NOUN**	○ *Newspaper editors must be held responsible for what they publish.*
editorial	**ADJECTIVE**	○ *journalists and editorial staff*

edu|ca|tion /ˌedʒʊ'keɪʃən/ (educations)

EDUCATION

1 **NOUN** **Education** involves teaching or learning various subjects, usually at a school or college. ○ *The government has cut funding for education.* ○ *The education system in Scotland is quite different from that in England.* ○ *Every child should get the chance to have a really good education.*

▶ COLLOCATIONS:
   have/get/receive an education
   provide education
   the education **system**
   a **good/poor** education
   basic education
   full-time education
   compulsory education

2 **UNCOUNTABLE NOUN** **Education** of a particular kind involves teaching the public about a particular issue. ○ *There should be better health education in schools.*

▶ COLLOCATION: **health/sex/drugs** education

WORD FAMILY		
educate	**VERB**	○ *Mary was educated at Cambridge University and in Switzerland.*
educated	**ADJECTIVE**	○ *He is highly educated and has a top-class degree.*
education	**NOUN**	○ *My parents wanted me to have an English education.*
educational	**ADJECTIVE**	○ *Educational opportunities are opening up for people with learning difficulties.*

ef|fect /ɪ'fekt/ (effects)

NOUN The **effect of** one thing **on** another is the change that the first thing causes in the second thing. ○ [+ on] *This illness can have a devastating effect on your life.* ○ [+ of] *Remember, you may not feel the effects of the sun at the time.* ○ *the long-term effects of bullying*

▶ **COLLOCATIONS:**
the effect **of** something
an effect **on** someone/something
have an effect
produce an effect
see/feel the effect
an **adverse/negative/harmful** effect
a **positive** effect
the **desired** effect
a **dramatic/profound/significant** effect
a **long-term** effect
a **knock-on** effect

USAGE

Note that the verb **affect** is connected with the noun **effect**. You can say that something **affects** you. ○ *Noise affects different people in different ways.*

You can also say that something has an **effect** on you. ○ *The study looked at the effect that noise has on people in factories.*

WORD FAMILY

| effect | NOUN | ○ *Studies show that smiling and laughing have a positive effect on health.* |
| affect | VERB | ○ *The new law will mainly affect young people.* |

---

ef|fec|tive /ɪ'fektɪv/

ADJECTIVE Something that is **effective** works well and produces the results that were intended. ○ *The city needs a more effective public transport system.* ○ [+ in] *This type of policing seems to be more effective in preventing crime.* ○ [+ against] *Antibiotics are not effective against viruses.*

▶ **COLLOCATIONS:**
effective **against** something
effective **in** doing something
highly effective
prove effective
an effective **way/method/means**
an effective **strategy/system**
an effective **treatment/drug**

▶ **ANTONYM:** ineffective

e

ef|fi|cient /ɪˈfɪʃənt/   WORK

ADJECTIVE If something or someone is **efficient**, they are able to do tasks successfully, without wasting time or energy. ○ We aim to ensure the most efficient use of resources. ○ New technology brings highly efficient methods of production. ○ Lighting is now more energy efficient.

▶ COLLOCATIONS:
  highly efficient
  efficient **use of** something
  an efficient **way/method/manner**
  make something efficient
  fuel/energy efficient

▶ ANTONYM: inefficient

WORD FAMILY		
efficient	ADJECTIVE	○ The first step is to make the system more efficient.
efficiently	ADVERB	○ I work very efficiently and am decisive, and accurate in my judgement.
efficiency	UNCOUNT	○ He runs the school with great efficiency.
inefficient	ADJECTIVE	○ The current system is inefficient and very expensive.

egg /eg/ (eggs)   SCIENCE & NATURE   FOOD & DRINK

1 NOUN An **egg** is an oval object that is produced by a female bird and which contains a baby bird. Other animals such as reptiles and fish also lay eggs. ○ The eggs hatch after a week or ten days. ○ The hen laid four eggs on consecutive days.

▶ COLLOCATIONS:
  lay an egg
  an egg **hatches**

2 NOUN In many countries, **eggs** often means hen's eggs, eaten as food. ○ bacon and eggs ○ I ordered more coffee and some scrambled eggs.

▶ COLLOCATIONS:
  a **fried/boiled/hard-boiled/poached** egg
  scrambled eggs
  free-range eggs
  beat an egg
  an egg **yolk/white**

el|der|ly /ˈeldəli/

`PEOPLE`

ADJECTIVE You use **elderly** as a polite way of saying that someone is old. ○ An elderly couple were in front of me in the queue. ○ Many of those affected by the changes are elderly.

> **WHICH WORD: old** or **elderly**?
>
> You use **old** to describe people who are not young, or things that are not new. ○ One old man was swimming slowly up and down the pool. ○ We live in an old house.
>
> You use **elderly** as a polite way of describing people who are not young. ○ An elderly woman was waiting for the bus.
>
> You can also say **the elderly** to talk about old people as a group. ○ The disease is more common in the elderly.

elec|tri|cian /ɪlekˈtrɪʃən, ˈiːlek-/ (electricians)

`WORK`

NOUN An **electrician** is a person whose job is to install and repair electrical equipment. ○ Mains lighting should be installed by a qualified electrician.

> **WORD FAMILY**
>
> | | | |
> |---|---|---|
> | **electrician** | **NOUN** | ○ I'm training to become an electrician. |
> | **electricity** | **UNCOUNT** | ○ About 40% of the world's electricity is generated using coal. |
> | **electrical** | **ADJECTIVE** | ○ The fire broke out because of an electrical fault. |
> | **electric** | **ADJECTIVE** | ○ The log cabins are fully equipped with electric light and hot running water. |

em|bar|rassed /ɪmˈbærəst/

ADJECTIVE A person who is **embarrassed** feels shy, ashamed, or guilty about something. ○ He looked a bit embarrassed. ○ an embarrassed silence ○ My mum won't try anything on in a communal changing room. She gets too embarrassed.

▶ **COLLOCATIONS:**
  look/feel embarrassed
  get embarrassed
  slightly/a little embarrassed
  very/deeply embarrassed

▶ **SYNONYM:** awkward

em|bar|rass|ing /ɪmˈbærəsɪŋ/

ADJECTIVE Something that is **embarrassing** makes you feel shy or ashamed. ○ That was an embarrassing situation! ○ [+ to-inf] It's embarrassing to find that you've forgotten your wallet. ○ [+ for] The whole thing was incredibly embarrassing for the girl's parents.

▶ COLLOCATIONS:
embarrassing **for** *someone*
an embarrassing **moment/situation/incident**
an embarrassing **question**
an embarrassing **defeat**
an embarrassing **problem/mistake**
highly/slightly embarrassing

▶ SYNONYMS: uncomfortable, awkward

WORD FAMILY		
embarrass	VERB	○ He didn't want to embarrass his son.
embarrassed	ADJECTIVE	○ Ella was deeply embarrassed when she realised what she'd said.
embarrassing	ADJECTIVE	○ I've got a rather embarrassing problem.
embarrassment	UNCOUNT	○ I could feel my cheeks burning with embarrassment.

---

emer|gen|cy ser|vices /ɪˈmɜːdʒənsi ˌsɜːvɪsɪz/   WORK

PLURAL NOUN The **emergency services** are the public organizations whose job is to take quick action to deal with emergencies when they occur, especially the fire brigade, the police, and the ambulance service. ○ *A woman who witnessed the accident called emergency services on her mobile phone.* ○ *The man might have survived if the emergency services had arrived sooner.*

---

emis|sions /ɪˈmɪʃənz/   SCIENCE & NATURE

PLURAL NOUN **Emissions** are gases or radiation that are released into the atmosphere. ○ *Carbon dioxide emissions are thought to be a principle cause of global warming.* ○ *The aim is to cut harmful greenhouse gas emissions, caused by burning fossil fuels.*

▶ COLLOCATIONS:
reduce/cut/limit emissions
produce emissions
harmful/toxic emissions
low/high emissions
greenhouse gas/carbon dioxide emissions
exhaust/vehicle emissions

WORD FAMILY		
emit	VERB	○ The device measures the radiation emitted by mobile phones.
emissions	PLURAL NOUN	○ a small engine with low emissions
emission	UNCOUNT	○ There are limits on the emission of sulphur dioxide.

emo|tion /ɪˈməʊʃən/ (emotions)

NOUN An **emotion** is a feeling such as happiness, love, fear, anger, or hatred, which can be caused by the situation that you are in or the people you are with. ○ *Her voice trembled with emotion.* ○ *Her face showed no emotion.* ○ *It was a day of mixed emotions for me.*

▸ **COLLOCATIONS:**
  show/express your emotions
  feel/have/experience emotions
  strong/powerful emotions
  mixed /different emotions
  a **negative** emotion

▸ **SYNONYM:** feeling

WORD FAMILY		
emotion	**NOUN**	○ She has strong emotions on the subject.
emotional	**ADJECTIVE**	○ I still get very emotional when I talk about it.
		○ a strong emotional reaction
emotionally	**ADVERB**	○ It affected me emotionally and physically.

em|pha|size /ˈemfəsaɪz/
BELIEFS & OPINIONS
(emphasizes, emphasizing, emphasized) [in BRIT, also use **emphasise**]

VERB To **emphasize** something means to indicate that it is particularly important or true, or to draw special attention to it. ○ [+ that] *He emphasized that most young people never use drugs.* ○ *My parents always emphasized the importance of education.*

▸ **COLLOCATIONS:**
  emphasize **the importance of** something
  emphasize **the need for** something
  emphasize a **point**
  repeatedly/strongly emphasize

▸ **SYNONYM:** highlight

WORD FAMILY		
emphasize	**VERB**	○ I always try to emphasize the positive aspects of a situation.
emphasis	**NOUN**	○ Too much emphasis is placed on material wealth.
emphatic	**ADJECTIVE**	○ His response was an emphatic 'yes'.

em|ploy /ɪmˈplɔɪ/ (employs, employing, employed)
WORK

VERB If a person or company **employs** you, they pay you to work for them. ○ *The company employs 18 staff.* ○ *More than 3,000 local workers are employed in the tourism industry.*

▶ COLLOCATIONS:
be employed **by** *someone*
be employed by a **company/firm/organization**
be employed **in** *something*
be employed in an **industry**
be employed in **teaching/engineering/agriculture**, etc.
employ **staff/workers**
employ **people/men/women**

em|ployee /ɪmˈplɔɪiː/ (employees)

NOUN An **employee** is a person who is paid to work for an organization or for another person. ○ *Hamilton is a former government employee.* ○ *[+ of] He began his career as an employee of the First National Bank* ○ *Several employees resigned when they heard the news.*

▶ COLLOCATIONS:
an employee **of** *something*
a **full-time/part-time** employee
a **former** employee
a **young/senior** employee
a **government** employee
a **company/school/bank** etc. employee
employee **benefits**

WORD FAMILY		
employ	VERB	○ At one point, the company had 150,000 employees in the UK.
employee	NOUN	○ the replacement of older staff with younger employees
employer	NOUN	○ Many employers are keen to attract young people into the industry.
employed	ADJECTIVE	○ At 26, I abandoned my employed life and began to travel widely.
unemployed	ADJECTIVE	○ This is a region where half of all young adults are unemployed.
employment	UNCOUNT	○ It was a bad time to be looking for employment.
unemployment	UNCOUNT	○ There has been a dramatic increase in youth unemployment.

en|cour|age /ɪnˈkʌrɪdʒ, AM -ˈkɜːr-/ (encourages, encouraging, encouraged)

VERB If you **encourage** someone, you give them confidence by telling them that what they are doing is good and saying that they should continue to do it. ○ *When things aren't going well, he encourages me, telling me not to give up.* ○ *The programme is aimed at helping and encouraging students who struggle with reading.*

▶ SYNONYM: discourage

encourage	**VERB**	○ Parents should encourage any child who shows special interest in music.
encouraging	**ADJECTIVE**	○ He was very encouraging when I told him about my plans.
encouragement	**UNCOUNT**	○ Most of us need some form of encouragement at certain points in our lives.

en|dan|gered /ɪnˈdeɪndʒəd/ SCIENCE & NATURE

ADJECTIVE An **endangered** animal or plant may soon become extinct (= no longer exist in the world). ○ We found out about endangered species such as the lynx and wolf. ○ The brown pelican has been on the endangered list since 1972.

▶ COLLOCATIONS:
an endangered **species**
an endangered **animal/bird/plant**
endangered **wildlife**

WORD FAMILY

| endanger | **VERB** | ○ Their senseless behaviour endangered the lives of hundreds of rail passengers. |
| endangered | **ADJECTIVE** | ○ Don't buy products made from endangered animals. |

end|ing /ˈendɪŋ/ (endings) MEDIA & CULTURE

NOUN You can refer to the last part of a book, story, play, or film as the **ending**, especially when you are considering the way that the story ends. ○ The film has a happy ending. ○ Pocahontas – the first Disney movie with a sad ending

▶ COLLOCATIONS:
a **happy** ending
a **sad/tragic/unhappy** ending
a **good/bad** ending

end up /end ˈʌp/ (ends up, ending up, ended up)

PHRASAL VERB If you **end up** doing something or **end up** in a particular state, you do that thing or get into that state even though you did not originally intend to. ○ We ended up taking a cab home around eleven. ○ I wonder if Jessica will end up an artist like her mother.

▶ SYNONYM: finish up

en|er|gy /ˈenədʒi/ SPORT & ACTIVITY SCIENCE & NATURE

1 UNCOUNTABLE NOUN Energy is the ability and strength to do active physical things and the feeling that you are full of physical power and life. ○ He's saving his energy for next week's race. ○ Too much sugary food can affect your energy levels.

▶ COLLOCATIONS:
save/conserve energy
use/expend energy
waste energy
energy **levels**

2 **UNCOUNTABLE NOUN Energy** is determination and enthusiasm about doing things. ○ *At 74 years old, my gran's energy and looks are amazing.* ○ *You need to have drive and energy to be successful in your chosen career.*

3 **UNCOUNTABLE NOUN Energy** is the power from sources such as electricity and coal that makes machines work or provides heat. ○ *It's quite easy to improve the energy efficiency of your home.* ○ *Renewable energy sources for producing electricity, such as wind, water and the sun are currently in use.* ○ *programmes for recycling waste and conserving energy*

▶ COLLOCATIONS:
save/conserve energy
generate/produce energy
use energy
waste energy
renewable energy
nuclear/solar/wind energy
energy **efficient/efficiency**
an energy **source**
an energy **company**
the energy **industry**
an energy **supply**
energy **use/consumption**
energy **prices**
an energy **bill**
an energy **crisis**

en|er|get|ic /ˌenəˈdʒetɪk/   PERSONALITY

ADJECTIVE If you are **energetic** in what you do, you have a lot of enthusiasm and determination. ○ *The restaurant is run by energetic young owners.* ○ *Rob was very energetic, very committed and dedicated.*

WORD FAMILY		
energy	**UNCOUNT**	○ *New houses are more energy efficient than old ones.*
energetic	**ADJECTIVE**	○ *They are looking for young, energetic reporters to join the team.*
energetically	**ADVERB**	○ *He worked energetically for peace in his country.*

en|gi|neer /ˌendʒɪˈnɪə/ (engineers)   WORK   SCIENCE & NATURE

1 **NOUN** An **engineer** is a person who uses scientific knowledge to design, construct, and maintain engines and machines or structures such as roads, railways, and bridges. ○ *He became a skilled engineer.*

▶ COLLOCATIONS:
   become an engineer
   an engineer **designs/works on/develops** something

2 NOUN An **engineer** is a person who repairs mechanical or electrical devices.
   ○ They sent an engineer to fix the disk drive.

en|gi|neer|ing /ˌendʒɪˈnɪərɪŋ/

UNCOUNTABLE NOUN **Engineering** is the work involved in designing and constructing engines and machinery, or structures such as roads and bridges. **Engineering** is also the subject studied by people who want to do this work.
   ○ The company is involved in the design and engineering of spacecraft. ○ graduates with a degree in engineering ○ He went to Edinburgh University to study engineering.

▶ COLLOCATIONS:
   study engineering
   engineering **work**
   an engineering **job**
   an engineering **company/firm**
   an engineering **project**
   an engineering **student/degree**

WORD FAMILY		
engineer	NOUN	○ He was one of the Japanese engineers who designed the railway.
engineer	VERB	○ Porsche took a minimum of six years to design and engineer a new car.
engineering	UNCOUNT	○ The Channel Tunnel was one of the biggest engineering projects of its time.

en|ter /ˈentə/
(enters, entering, entered)

SHOPPING COMMUNICATIONS

VERB To **enter** information **into** a computer means to record it there, for example by typing it on a keyboard. ○ [+ into] Every patient's details are entered into a computer. ○ Please enter your username and password.

▶ COLLOCATIONS:
   enter something **into** something
   enter **information/data/details/text**
   enter a **code/username/password**

en|ter|tain /ˌentəˈteɪn/
(entertains, entertaining, entertained)

MEDIA & CULTURE

VERB If a performer, performance, or activity **entertains** you, it amuses you, interests you, or gives you pleasure. ○ The website provides games and ideas to entertain children during the holidays. ○ They were entertained by top singers, dancers and celebrities.

en|ter|tain|ing /ˌentəˈteɪnɪŋ/

ADJECTIVE An **entertaining** performer, performance, or activity amuses you, interests you, or gives you pleasure. ○ *That was a really entertaining film.* ○ *Some lecturers can be highly entertaining.*

▶ **COLLOCATION: highly/hugely** entertaining

en|ter|tain|ment /ˌentəˈteɪnmənt/

UNCOUNTABLE NOUN Entertainment consists of performances of plays and films, and activities such as reading and watching television, that give people pleasure. ○ *Free live entertainment is provided in the cafe most Saturdays.* ○ *Competition for a job in the entertainment industry is fierce.*

▶ **COLLOCATIONS:**
  provide/offer entertainment
  enjoy entertainment
  live entertainment
  light/family entertainment
  home/in-flight entertainment
  the entertainment **industry**

WORD FAMILY		
entertain	VERB	○ *Bands entertained the crowd throughout the day.*
entertainment	UNCOUNT	○ *There has been a drive to turn football matches into family entertainment*
entertaining	ADJECTIVE	○ *The sport needs to be more entertaining.*
entertainer	NOUN	○ *He was a leading singer and entertainer for over thirty years.*

en|thu|si|as|tic /ɪnˌθjuːziˈæstɪk, AM -ˌθuː-/ `PERSONALITY`

ADJECTIVE If you are **enthusiastic about** something, you show or say how much you like or enjoy it. ○ [+ *about*] *Tom was very enthusiastic about the place.* ○ *He was performing in front of an enthusiastic crowd of about 3,000.*

▶ **COLLOCATIONS:**
  enthusiastic **about** something
  an enthusiastic **crowd/audience**
  enthusiastic **supporters/fans**
  an enthusiastic **response/welcome/reception**
  enthusiastic **applause**
  seem/sound/get enthusiastic
  wildly enthusiastic

▶ **SYNONYM:** excited

WORD FAMILY		
enthusiastic	ADJECTIVE	○ She had received a wildly enthusiastic response from the audience.
enthusiastically	ADVERB	○ The announcement was greeted enthusiastically.
enthusiasm	UNCOUNT	○ Young people showed enthusiasm for the scheme.
unenthusiastic	ADJECTIVE	○ He sounded distinctly unenthusiastic.

en|vi|ron|ment /ɪnˈvaɪərənmənt/ (environments) SCIENCE & NATURE

UNCOUNTABLE NOUN The environment is the natural world of land, sea, air, plants, and animals. ○ These chemical substances can damage the environment and people's health. ○ The report focuses on ways to reduce poverty and protect the environment.

▶ **COLLOCATIONS:**
protect the environment
damage/harm/pollute/threaten the environment
affect the environment

en|vi|ron|men|tal /ɪnˌvaɪərənˈmentəl/

ADJECTIVE Environmental means concerned with the protection of the environment. ○ It's important to minimize the environmental damage that new roads cause. ○ Environmental groups plan to stage public protests during the conference.

▶ **COLLOCATIONS:**
environmental **issues/problems**
environmental **protection**
environmental **damage/impact**
an environmental **disaster**
an environmental **group/activist**
an environmental **policy/law**

en|vi|ron|men|tal|ly friend|ly /ɪnˌvaɪərənˈmentəli ˈfrendli/

ADJECTIVE An environmentally friendly product or method does not harm the environment. ○ Cycling is the only real environmentally friendly form of travel. ○ environmentally friendly farming techniques ○ the high price of environmentally friendly goods

epi|sode /ˈepɪsəʊd/ (episodes) MEDIA & CULTURE

NOUN An episode of a television series is one of the separate parts in which it is broadcast. ○ [+ of] The final episode of 'Big Brother' will be shown next Sunday.

▶ **COLLOCATIONS:**
an episode **of** something
watch an episode
show/broadcast/air an episode

▶ **SYNONYM:** instalment

equip|ment /ɪˈkwɪpmənt/

SCIENCE & NATURE

UNCOUNTABLE NOUN Equipment consists of the things that are used for a particular purpose, for example a hobby or job. ○ *Many schools do not have enough sports equipment.* ○ *Scientists are using increasingly sophisticated equipment.*

▶ **COLLOCATIONS:**
a **piece of** equipment
instal/use equipment
computer/sports/camera equipment
safety equipment
electronic/electrical equipment
special/sophisticated/high-tech equipment

▶ **SYNONYMS:** gear, accessories

> **USAGE**
>
> Remember that **equipment** is an uncountable noun so you do not talk about 'equipments' or 'an equipment'. ○ *The company supplies schools with computer equipment.*
>
> You can talk about **a piece of equipment**. ○ *The most important piece of equipment you'll need is a helmet.*

er|ror /ˈerə/ (errors)

NOUN An **error** is something you have done which is considered to be incorrect or wrong, or which should not have been done. ○ [+ *in*] *Unfortunately, they made several errors in their calculations.* ○ *Ninety per cent of car accidents are due to human error.*

▶ **COLLOCATIONS:**
make an error
correct an error
a **serious/grave/fatal** error
a **glaring** error
a **costly/expensive** error
a **spelling** error
a **computer** error
human error
an error **of judgment**

▶ **SYNONYM:** mistake

event /ɪˈvent/ (events)

MEDIA & CULTURE

NOUN An **event** is a planned and organized occasion, for example a social gathering or a sports match. ○ *Wimbledon is one of Britain's major sporting events.* ○ *See our website for our programme of lectures and social events.* ○ *We hold a series of special events throughout the summer.*

▶ COLLOCATIONS:
attend an event
hold/host/organize an event
an event **takes place**
a **sporting/socal/charity** event
a **big/major/special** event
an **annual** event

▶ SYNONYM: occasion

---

evi|dence /ˈevɪdəns/ HISTORY CRIME e

1 **UNCOUNTABLE NOUN Evidence** is something that causes you to believe that something is true or has really happened. ○ [+ of] *Tests showed no evidence of brain damage.* ○ [+ for] *There is now clear evidence for changes in the world's climate.* ○ [+ that] *Is there any evidence that the meeting actually took place?*

▶ COLLOCATIONS:
evidence **of/for** *something*
provide/offer evidence
new/further evidence
strong/good/clear/compelling evidence
hard/firm/concrete evidence
scientific/medical evidence

2 **UNCOUNTABLE NOUN Evidence** is the information that is used in a court of law to try to prove something. Evidence is obtained from documents, objects, or witnesses. ○ [+ against] *The evidence against him was purely circumstantial.* ○ *After hearing the evidence, the judge ordered the defendants to pay £8,000 in compensation.*

▶ COLLOCATIONS:
evidence **against** *someone*
circumstantial evidence
gather evidence
hear evidence
forensic/DNA/fingerprint evidence
new/fresh evidence
sufficient/insufficient evidence

---

ex|cit|ed /ɪkˈsaɪtɪd/

ADJECTIVE If you are **excited**, you are so happy that you cannot relax, especially because you are thinking about something pleasant that is going to happen to you. ○ [+ about] *I'm very excited about the possibility of playing for the team.* ○ *It's my dad's 50th birthday tomorrow and we are all getting excited.*

▶ COLLOCATIONS:
excited **about** *something*
get excited

ex|cit|ing /ɪkˈsaɪtɪŋ/

ADJECTIVE If something is **exciting**, it makes you feel very happy or enthusiastic. ○ *The race itself is very exciting.* ○ *It was a very exciting time for both of us.*

▶ COLLOCATIONS:
an exciting **time/day/year**
an exciting **prospect/opportunity/experience/challenge**
exciting **news**
an exciting **game/event**

WORD FAMILY		
excited	ADJECTIVE	○ *He was like an excited child when he heard the news.*
excitedly	ADVERB	○ *'You're coming?' he said excitedly. 'That's fantastic!'*
exciting	ADJECTIVE	○ *I have some very exciting news for you that you won't believe!*
excitingly	ADVERB	○ *He is an excitingly original writer.*
excite	VERB	○ *I'm moving abroad soon, and the idea really excites me.*
excitement	UNCOUNT	○ *A buzz of excitement ran through the crowd.*

ex|er|cise /ˈeksəsaɪz/
(exercises, exercising, exercised)

`SPORT & ACTIVITY`

1 VERB When you **exercise**, you move your body energetically in order to get fit and remain healthy. ○ *I exercise regularly, so I have lots of energy.* ○ *She doesn't exercise as much as she should.*

▶ COLLOCATIONS:
exercise **regularly/often**
not exercise **much/enough**

▶ SYNONYM: work out

2 UNCOUNTABLE NOUN Exercise is the activity of moving your body energetically in order to get fit and remain healthy. ○ *We can tackle the problem of obesity by getting children to do more exercise.* ○ *Cycling is very good exercise.*

▶ COLLOCATIONS:
do/take/get exercise
regular exercise
good exercise
vigorous/strenuous/aerobic exercise
gentle/moderate exercise
an exercise **regime/programme/routine**
an exercise **class**

ex|hi|bi|tion /ˌeksɪˈbɪʃən/ (exhibitions)

`MEDIA & CULTURE`

NOUN An **exhibition** is a public event at which pictures, sculptures, or other objects of interest are displayed, for example at a museum or art gallery.

○ [+ of] *There's an exhibition of expressionist art at the City Museum.* ○ *This exhibition features a wide range of Matisse's work.*

▶ **COLLOCATIONS:**
an exhibition **of** something
an **art/photographic** exhibition
have/hold an exhibition
see/visit an exhibition
an exhibition **includes/features/shows** something
a **permanent/temporary** exhibition
an exhibition **space**

WORD FAMILY		
exhibit	**VERB**	○ *The gallery has been designed to exhibit contemporary art and sculpture.*
exhibit	**NOUN**	○ *There are barriers to stop people touching the exhibits.*
exhibition	**NOUN**	○ *The exhibition is being held at the Black Art Gallery in Brixton.*
exhibitor	**NOUN**	○ *This year's show includes work from 78 exhibitors from the United States and Europe.*

ex|ist /ɪgˈzɪst/ (exists, existing, existed)

VERB If something **exists**, it is present in the world as a real thing. ○ *These problems have existed for many years.* ○ *None of the bird species on the islands exist on the mainland.*

ex|ist|ence /ɪgˈzɪstəns/

UNCOUNTABLE NOUN The **existence** of something is the fact that it is present in the world as a real thing. ○ [+ of] *His work led to the idea of the existence of other galaxies.* ○ *The company has been in existence for more than half a century.* ○ *Global warming is threatening the existence of polar bears.*

▶ **COLLOCATIONS:**
the existence **of** something
in existence
reveal/confirm/prove the existence of something
threaten the existence of something

WORD FAMILY		
exist	**VERB**	○ *Sadly, racism still exists.*
existing	**ADJECTIVE**	○ *The new system will be a vast improvement on the existing exam structure.*
existence	**UNCOUNT**	○ *They have evidence that might prove the existence of life on other planets.*

ex|pect /ɪkˈspekt/ (expects, expecting, expected) `MEDIA & CULTURE`

1 VERB If you **expect** something **to** happen, you believe that it will happen.
○ [+ to-inf] *I still expect to be there, but I might be late.* ○ *The team is widely expected to win.* ○ *We expect a gradual improvement in weather conditions.* ○ [+ that] *I expect that his next film will be even more popular.*

▶ COLLOCATIONS:
still expect *something*
fully expect *something*
be **widely** expected

2 VERB If you **are expecting** something or someone, you believe that they will be delivered to you or come to you soon, often because this has been arranged earlier. ○ *I am expecting several important letters but nothing has arrived.* ○ *I wasn't expecting a visitor.*

→ see Useful Phrases **expecting a baby**

▶ COLLOCATIONS:
be expecting a **letter/parcel/call**
be expecting a **visitor**

WHICH WORD: expect or **wait for**?

You use **expect** *someone* or *something* when you think that the person or thing is going to arrive or that the thing is going to happen. ○ *We are expecting rain.* ○ *We weren't expecting you so soon.*

You use **wait for** *someone* or *something* when you stay in the same place until the person or thing arrives or until the thing happens. ○ *I waited for a taxi outside the hotel.* ○ *Nancy was waiting for him at the gate.*

WORD FAMILY

expect	VERB	○ *We both fully expected to be in the same class.*
expectation	NOUN	○ *People's expectations of marriage have changed.*

---

ex|peri|ence /ɪkˈspɪəriəns/ `WORK`

UNCOUNTABLE NOUN Experience is knowledge or skill that you have gained because you have done a particular job or activity for a long time. ○ *Josephine is trying to get some teaching experience.* ○ *Relevant work experience, such as your current or last position, should appear on the first page of your CV.* ○ *No previous experience of this type of work is necessary.*

▶ COLLOCATIONS:
have experience
get/gain experience
lack experience
no/little/limited experience
previous experience
relevant experience

work experience
teaching/management/business experience

▶ **ANTONYM:** inexperience

WORD FAMILY		
experience	UNCOUNT	○ Graham gained experience at the Europa Hotel, where he was head chef.
experience	VERB	○ For the first time in my life I experienced real fear.
experienced	ADJECTIVE	○ Ross is an experienced pilot.
inexperienced	ADJECTIVE	○ Most of the candidates were young and inexperienced.

ex|peri|ment /ɪkˈsperɪmənt/ (experiments) SCIENCE & NATURE

NOUN An **experiment** is a scientific test that is done in order to discover what happens to something in particular conditions. ○ The astronauts are conducting an experiment to learn more about weightlessness. ○ We did an experiment in the science lab today. ○ [+ on] It would be wrong to perform experiments like these on humans.

▶ COLLOCATIONS:
an experiment **on** someone/something
carry out/conduct/perform/do an experiment
design an experiment
an experiment **shows/proves** something
a **scientific** experiment
a **science/chemistry/physics** experiment

ex|pert /ˈekspɜːt/ (experts) SCIENCE & NATURE

NOUN An **expert** is a person who is very skilled at doing something or who knows a lot about a particular subject. ○ [+ on] He's one of Britain's leading experts on education. ○ Health experts predict a steep rise in the number of people needing care. ○ [+ in] I'm not an expert in this area, but it seems to me that those figures are wrong.

▶ COLLOCATIONS:
an expert **on/in** something
a **leading/top** expert
a **legal/medical/forensic** expert
a **security/health/computer** expert
an **independent** expert
expert **advice/knowledge/opinion**

▶ SYNONYM: specialist

WORD FAMILY		
expert	NOUN	○ You should, perhaps, think of getting some expert advice from a careers officer.
expertly	ADVERB	○ The four men worked quickly and expertly.
expertise	UNCOUNT	○ The job requires a high level of expertise.

ex|press /ɪkˈspres/
MEDIA & CULTURE

(expresses, expressing, expressed)

VERB When you **express** an idea or feeling, or **express yourself**, you show what you think or feel. ○ *The report expresses concern that children are not getting enough exercise.* ○ *Parents have expressed outrage at the injustice of the decision.* ○ *Children may find it easier to express themselves in a letter than in a formal essay.*

▶ **COLLOCATIONS:**
   privately express *something*
   publicly/openly express *something*

WORD FAMILY		
express	**VERB**	○ *Doubts were expressed about Robert's honesty.*
expression	**NOUN**	○ *'I hope you understand,' he said, with an expression of concern on his face.*
expressive	**ADJECTIVE**	○ *Her eyes are warm and expressive.*
expressively	**ADVERB**	○ *Michael sang expressively, and with great passion.*

extraor|di|nary /ɪkˈstrɔːdənri, AM -neri/

ADJECTIVE If you describe something or someone as **extraordinary**, you mean that they have some extremely good or special quality. ○ *The task requires extraordinary patience and endurance.* ○ *Taylor is an extraordinary musician.*

▶ **SYNONYMS:** exceptional, remarkable, amazing

WORD FAMILY		
extraordinary	**ADJECTIVE**	○ *We've made extraordinary progress in terms of communications.*
extraordinarily	**ADVERB**	○ *She's extraordinarily disciplined.*

Ff

fa|cil|ities /fəˈsɪlɪtiz/

PLURAL NOUN **Facilities** are buildings, equipment, or services that are provided for a particular purpose. ○ *Many hotels offer leisure facilities such as a swimming pool or gym.* ○ *[+ for] We need better education facilities for children with special needs.*

▶ **COLLOCATIONS:**
facilities **for** someone/something
provide/offer facilities
use facilities
improve/upgrade facilities
good/excellent facilities
modern/state-of-the-art facilities
sports/recreational/leisure facilities

fact /fækt/ (facts)

NOUN **Facts** are pieces of information that can be discovered. ○ *At dinner, we learned a few more facts about each other.* ○ *It's an easy-to-read book with interesting facts and figures about the different peoples of Africa.*

▶ **COLLOCATIONS:**
facts **about** someone/something
establish/find the facts
learn a fact
facts **and figures**

fac|tual /ˈfæktʃʊəl/

ADJECTIVE Something that is **factual** is concerned with facts or contains facts, rather than giving theories or personal interpretations. ○ *The article contained several factual errors.* ○ *How much of the story is historically factual?*

▶ **COLLOCATIONS:**
factual **information/evidence**
a factual **account**
a factual **error**
purely/strictly factual
historically factual

> | WORD FAMILY | | |
> | --- | --- | --- |
> | fact | **NOUN** | ○ *I think we need to establish the facts first.* |
> | factual | **ADJECTIVE** | ○ *Keep factual information clearly separate from opinions and judgments.* |
> | factually | **ADVERB** | ○ *A number of statements in his talk were factually wrong.* |

fac|tor /ˈfæktə/ (factors, factoring, factored)

NOUN A **factor** is one of the things that affects an event, decision, or situation.
○ [+ in] *Physical activity is an important factor in maintaining fitness.* ○ *There may be genetic factors that cause some people to develop the disease.*

▶ COLLOCATIONS:
a factor **in** something
a **crucial/key/major/important** factor
a **contributing** factor
environmental/economic/genetic factors

fac|ul|ty /ˈfækəlti/ (faculties)   EDUCATION

NOUN A **faculty** is a group of related departments in some universities, or the people who work in them. [BRIT] ○ [+ of] *the Faculty of Social and Political Sciences* ○ *the dean of the medical faculty*

▶ COLLOCATIONS:
the faculty **of** something
the **arts/history/English** faculty
the **law/business/economics** faculty
the **science/engineering/medical** faculty

fair /feə/ (fairer, fairest)   CLOTHES & APPEARANCE

1 **ADJECTIVE** Someone who is **fair**, or who has **fair** hair, has light-coloured hair.
○ *Both children look like Rachel, but they are much fairer than her.* ○ *A tall, fair-haired man stood at the door.*

2 **ADJECTIVE** **Fair** skin is pale and usually burns easily. ○ *It's important to protect fair skin from the sun.* ○ *The disease is more common in fair-skinned people.*

fall out (with someone) /fɔːl ˈaʊt/   SOCIAL LIFE
(falls out, falling out, fell out, fallen out)

PHRASAL VERB If you **fall out** with someone, you have an argument and stop being friendly with them. You can also say that two people **fall out**. ○ *She fell out with her sister over a boyfriend.* ○ *Mum and I used to fall out a lot.*

fa|mous /'feɪməs/

PLACES

ADJECTIVE Someone or something that is **famous** is very well known. ○ *John Constable: England's most famous landscape artist.* ○ *[+ for] Switzerland is famous for its cheese.* ○ *Henley later became famous for his poems.*

▶ **COLLOCATIONS:**
famous **for** *something*
become famous
make *someone/something* **famous**
internationally famous

▶ **SYNONYM:** renowned

▶ **ANTONYMS:** obscure, unknown

WORD FAMILY		
fame	**UNCOUNT**	○ He later achieved fame as a novelist.
famous	**ADJECTIVE**	○ The railway line was made famous by the film 'The Railway Children'.
famously	**ADVERB**	○ We went to St Vaast, a famously beautiful seaside town.

fan /fæn/ (fans)

MEDIA & CULTURE

NOUN If you are a **fan** of a famous person or a sport, you like them a lot and are very interested in them. ○ *If you're a Billy Crystal fan, you'll love this movie.* ○ *[+ of] I'm a great fan of reggae.*

▶ **COLLOCATIONS:**
a fan **of** *someone/something*
a **big/huge/great** fan of *someone/something*
a **sports** fan
a **football/hockey/golf** fan
a **music/film/jazz** fan

fan|tas|tic /fæn'tæstɪk/

ADJECTIVE If you say that something or someone is **fantastic**, you think they are very good or you like them a lot. ○ *The organizers had done a fantastic job.* ○ *She looked absolutely fantastic.*

▶ **COLLOCATIONS:**
absolutely fantastic
look/feel/sound fantastic

▶ **SYNONYM:** great

WORD FAMILY		
fantastic	**ADJECTIVE**	○ I've had a fantastic time in London.
fantastically	**ADVERB**	○ He was fantastically successful.
fantasy	**NOUN**	○ Swimming with dolphins is one of my favourite fantasies.

fare /feə/ (fares)

TRANSPORT & TRAVEL

NOUN A **fare** is the money that you pay for a journey that you make, for example, in a bus, train, or taxi. ○ *He could barely afford the rail fare.* ○ *The price includes air fares and hotel accommodation.*

▶ **COLLOCATIONS:**
pay a fare
increase/raise the fare
a **low/cheap** fare
a **single/one-way/return** fare
a **bus/taxi/air/train/rail** fare
a fare **increase**

fas|ci|nat|ing /ˈfæsɪneɪtɪŋ/

ADJECTIVE If you describe something as **fascinating**, you find it very interesting and attractive. ○ *Madagascar is the most fascinating place I have ever been to.* ○ *I found the course absolutely fascinating.*

▶ **SYNONYM:** compelling

▶ **ANTONYM:** boring

WORD FAMILY		
fascinating	**ADJECTIVE**	○ *The book provides a fascinating insight into the British way of life.*
fascinated	**ADJECTIVE**	○ *I was really fascinated by his story.*
fascinate	**VERB**	○ *The celebrity lifestyle tends to fascinate people.*
fascination	**UNCOUNT**	○ *He developed a morbid fascination with knives.*

fash|ion /ˈfæʃən/

MEDIA & CULTURE   CLOTHES & APPEARANCE

1 **UNCOUNTABLE NOUN Fashion** refers to activities or business that involve styles of clothing and appearance. ○ *She works in the fashion industry.* ○ *'Vogue' was different from any other fashion magazine.*

▶ **COLLOCATIONS:**
the fashion **industry/world**
a fashion **designer/photographer**
a fashion **model**
a fashion **show/magazine**

2 **UNCOUNTABLE NOUN** If something is **in fashion**, it is popular and approved of at a particular time. If it is **out of fashion**, it is not popular or approved of. ○ *That sort of house is back in fashion.* ○ *Marriage seems to be going out of fashion.*

WORD FAMILY		
fashion	**UNCOUNT**	○ *Fashion models are usually thin and tall.*
fashionable	**ADJECTIVE**	○ *Baseball caps were fashionable at the time.*
fashionably	**ADVERB**	○ *fashionably dressed women*
unfashionable	**ADJECTIVE**	○ *He was wearing unfashionable black glasses.*

fast food /ˌfɑːst ˈfuːd, ˌfæst/ `FOOD & DRINK` `HEALTH`

UNCOUNTABLE NOUN **Fast food** is hot food, such as hamburgers and chips that is served quickly after you order it. ○ *James works at a fast food restaurant.* ○ *Most of the time we just ate snacks and fast food.*

▸ **COLLOCATIONS:**
  eat fast food
  a fast food **restaurant/chain**
  the fast food **industry**
  a fast food **diet**

fat /fæt/ `HEALTH` `FOOD & DRINK`

UNCOUNTABLE NOUN **Fat** is a substance contained in foods such as meat, cheese, and butter which forms an energy store in your body. ○ *An easy way to cut the amount of fat in your diet is to avoid eating red meat.* ○ *low-fat yoghurts* ○ *a high-fat diet*

fat|ten|ing /ˈfætənɪŋ/

ADJECTIVE Food that is **fattening** is considered to make people fat easily. ○ *Some foods are more fattening than others.* ○ *I don't eat chocolate any more - it's too fattening.*

WORD FAMILY		
fat	**UNCOUNT**	○ *Doctors are telling us to eat less fat.*
fatty	**ADJECTIVE**	○ *fatty foods* ○ *fatty meat such as sausages*
fattening	**ADJECTIVE**	○ *Fruit and vegetables are not fattening.*

fear /fɪə/

UNCOUNTABLE NOUN **Fear** is the unpleasant feeling you have when you think that you are in danger. ○ *She was sitting on the floor shivering with fear.* ○ [+ of] *Fear of the dark is very common in children.*

→ see also **afraid**

▸ **COLLOCATIONS:**
  fear **of** something
  fear **about/over** something
  with fear
  face/overcome your fear
  live in fear
  hide your fear
  great/real/deep fear
  widespread/public fear
  constant fear
  irrational fear

> **WORD FAMILY**
>
> | | | |
> |---|---|---|
> | **fear** | **UNCOUNT** | ○ How can I overcome my fear of spiders? |
> | **fear** | **VERB** | ○ She feared she had pneumonia. |
> | **fearful** | **ADJECTIVE** | ○ Bankers were fearful of a world banking crisis. |

---

fed up /ˌfed ˈʌp/

ADJECTIVE Someone who is **fed up** is bored or annoyed. ○ [+ with] He had become fed up with city life. ○ [+ of] I got fed up of asking for my money back.

> ▶ **COLLOCATIONS:**
> fed up **with** someone/something
> fed up **of** doing something
> **get** fed up
> **so/absolutely** fed up

---

fe|male /ˈfiːmeɪl/ `PEOPLE`

ADJECTIVE Someone who is **female** is a woman or a girl. ○ Most of his friends are female. ○ a female singer ○ female employees

→ see also **male**

femi|nine /ˈfemɪnɪn/ `CLOTHES & APPEARANCE`

ADJECTIVE **Feminine** means typical of, or suitable for, women. ○ She has a very feminine style of dressing. ○ feminine clothes ○ a feminine look

---

fence /fens/ (fences) `HOME`

NOUN A **fence** is a barrier made of wood or wire supported by posts. ○ The garden is surrounded by a high fence. ○ Would you like me to put up a new fence for you?

> ▶ **COLLOCATIONS:**
> **put up/build** a fence
> a **high** fence
> a **wooden/electric** fence
> a **garden** fence
> a fence **post**

---

fer|ry /ˈferi/ (ferries) `TRANSPORT & TRAVEL`

NOUN A **ferry** is a boat that carries passengers or vehicles across a river or narrow stretch of sea. ○ They crossed the river by ferry. ○ I was on my way home on the overnight ferry.

> ▶ **COLLOCATIONS:**
> **by** ferry
> **on** a ferry
> **take/catch** a ferry
> **get on/board** a ferry

a **car/passenger** ferry
the **overnight** ferry
a ferry **terminal/port**
a ferry **crossing/ride**

▸ **SYNONYMS:** ship, boat

---

fes|ti|val /ˈfestɪvəl/ (festivals)　　`SOCIAL LIFE`　`MEDIA & CULTURE`

1 NOUN A **festival** is an organized series of performances or cultural events.
○ *Thousands of people go to the annual music festival in Glastonbury.* ○ *the Edinburgh Film Festival*

▸ **COLLOCATIONS:**
go to a festival
hold/organize a festival
a **music/rock/film/art** festival
a **big/free/outdoor** festival
an **annual/international** festival
a **literary/cultural** festival

2 NOUN A **festival** is a day or period when people have a holiday and celebrate some special event, often a religious event. ○ *The dates of all the religious festivals are on the calendar.* ○ [+ *of*] *the Hindu festival of Diwali*

▸ **COLLOCATIONS:**
the festival **of** *something*
celebrate a festival
a **religious** festival
a **Jewish/Christian/Muslim/Hindu** festival

---

fi|an|cé /fiˈɒnseɪ, AM ˌfiːɑːnˈseɪ/ (fiancés)　　`PEOPLE`

NOUN A woman's **fiancé** is the man to whom she is engaged to be married. ○ *This is Fiona, and this is Danny, her fiancé.*

> **USAGE**
>
> Use the female form **fiancée** to refer to a woman who a man is going to marry. ○ *He took his fiancée, Laura, to meet his parents.*

---

fic|tion /ˈfɪkʃən/　　`MEDIA & CULTURE`

UNCOUNTABLE NOUN **Fiction** refers to books and stories about imaginary people and events. ○ *I like reading fiction.* ○ *Diana is a writer of historical fiction.*

▸ **COLLOCATIONS:**
read/write/publish fiction
science fiction
crime fiction
historical/romantic fiction
a fiction **writer/book/story**

▶ **ANTONYM:** non-fiction

> **WORD FAMILY**
>
> | fiction | **UNCOUNT** | ○ He's writing a science fiction book. |
> | ficitional | **ADJECTIVE** | ○ Ulverton is a fictional village in Sussex. |
> | non-fiction | **UNCOUNT** | ○ He likes reading non-fiction, especially self-improvement books. |

fi|nance /ˈfaɪnæns, fɪˈnæns/ MONEY WORK

UNCOUNTABLE NOUN Finance is the activity of managing money. ○ He wants to work in international finance. ○ The finance department of a company is sometimes referred to as 'accounts'.

▶ **COLLOCATIONS:**
work in finance
international finance
the finance **department**
a finance **director/minister**

fi|nan|cial /faɪˈnænʃəl, fɪ-/

ADJECTIVE Financial means relating to or involving money. ○ She told him about the financial problems she was having. ○ How can I improve my financial situation?

▶ **COLLOCATIONS:**
financial **problems/difficulties**
someone's financial **situation/position**
a financial **adviser**
a financial **crisis**

▶ **SYNONYM:** monetary

> **WORD FAMILY**
>
> | finance | **UNCOUNT** | ○ the world of finance ○ Canada's Minister of Finance |
> | financial | **ADJECTIVE** | ○ He's been having some financial difficulties. |
> | financially | **ADVERB** | ○ I would like to be more financially independent. |

find|ings /ˈfaɪndɪŋz/ SCIENCE & NATURE

PLURAL NOUN Someone's **findings** are the information they get as the result of doing research. ○ Several interesting findings resulted from the study. ○ The committee reported its findings yesterday.

▶ **COLLOCATIONS:**
findings **on/about** something
new/preliminary/key findings
surprising/interesting/important findings
publish/report/present your findings

▶ **SYNONYM:** results

fine /faɪn/ (fines, fining, fined)   `CRIME`

1 **NOUN** A **fine** is a punishment in which a person is ordered to pay a sum of money. ○ *They had no money to pay the fine.* ○ [+ for] *She got a £300 fine for speeding.*

> ▶ **COLLOCATIONS:**
> a fine **for** something
> **pay** a fine
> **get/receive** a fine
> **give/impose/issue** a fine
> a **big/hefty/heavy** fine
> a **small** fine
> a **maximum** fine
> an **on-the-spot** fine
> a **parking** fine

2 **VERB** If someone **is fined**, they are punished by being ordered to pay a sum of money. ○ *She was fined £300 and banned from driving for one month.* ○ *The school fines pupils who break the rules.*

---

fire|fighter /ˈfaɪəfaɪtə/ (firefighters)   `WORK`

NOUN A **firefighter** is a person whose job is to put out fires. ○ *Firefighters were unable to control the flames.*

> ▶ **SYNONYM:** fireman

---

fit /fɪt/   `CLOTHES & APPEARANCE` `HEALTH` `SPORT & ACTIVITY`
(fits, fitting, fitted, fitter, fittest)

1 **VERB** If clothes **fit** someone, they are the right size and shape to go onto the person's body. ○ *The clothes were made to fit a child.* ○ *She has to go to the men's department to find trousers that fit.*

> ▶ **COLLOCATIONS:**
> fit **well/perfectly/snugly**
> **just** fit

2 **ADJECTIVE** Someone who is **fit** is healthy and physically strong. ○ *As you get fitter, you can run further.* ○ *People who are physically fit are less likely to get ill.*

> ▶ **COLLOCATIONS:**
> **physically** fit
> **very/really/reasonably** fit
> **get/keep/stay** fit
> **feel/look** fit

> ▶ **ANTONYM:** unfit

WORD FAMILY		
fit	**ADJECTIVE**	○ *She is very fit and healthy.*
fitness	**UNCOUNT**	○ *Squash is good for all-round fitness.*

f

flat|mate /ˈflætmeɪt/ (flatmates) `PEOPLE`

NOUN Someone's **flatmate** is a person who shares a flat with them. [BRIT; in AM, use **roommate**] ○ *His flatmate had already left for work.* ○ *George and I are flatmates.*

flex|ible /ˈfleksɪbəl/ `WORK`

ADJECTIVE Something or someone that is **flexible** is able to change easily to new conditions and circumstances. ○ *Flexible working hours appeal to parents with children.* ○ [+ about] *They are flexible about the date of the meeting.* ○ *flexible study arrangements*

▶ COLLOCATIONS:
   flexible **about** *something*
   flexible **working**
   flexible **hours**
   a flexible **arrangement/approach/system**
   very/pretty/fairly flexible

▶ SYNONYM: adaptable

WORD FAMILY		
flexible	ADJECTIVE	○ *For certain situations, flexible arrangements are difficult.*
flexibly	ADVERB	○ *Many companies allow their employees to work flexibly.*
flexibility	UNCOUNT	○ *The flexibility of distance learning suits people with jobs and families.*
inflexible	ADJECTIVE	○ *Workers insisted the new system was too inflexible.*

flood /flʌd/ (floods, flooding, flooded) `SCIENCE & NATURE`

1 **NOUN** If there is a **flood**, a large amount of water covers an area that is usually dry. ○ *Over a hundred people were killed in the floods.* ○ *A typhoon hit the Philippines, causing devastating floods.*

▶ COLLOCATIONS:
   in a flood
   cause/prevent a flood
   a **bad/big/devastating** flood
   a **sudden** flood
   a **flash** flood
   flood **water/damage/defences**

2 **VERB** If something such as a river **floods** an area, or if an area **floods**, it becomes covered with water. ○ *The Chicago River flooded the city's underground tunnel system.* ○ *The kitchen flooded.*

flood|ing /ˈflʌdɪŋ/

UNCOUNTABLE NOUN If **flooding** occurs, an area of land that is usually dry is covered with water, for example after heavy rain. ○ *Heavy monsoon rains caused widespread flooding.* ○ [+ of] *A rise in the sea level would result in the flooding of some coastal areas.*

▶ **COLLOCATIONS:**
flooding **of** *something*
cause/prevent flooding
severe/bad/widespread flooding

WORD FAMILY		
flood	**NOUN**	○ *The area is at risk from flash floods.*
flood	**VERB**	○ *Extreme weather flooded many homes.*
flooded	**ADJECTIVE**	○ *flooded land* ○ *a flooded basement*
flooding	**UNCOUNT**	○ *The flooding is the worst this century.*

---

floor /flɔː/ (floors)   HOME

NOUN A **floor** of a building is all the rooms that are on a particular level. ○ [+ of] *It is on the fifth floor of the hospital.* ○ *He slept in a room on the ground floor.*

▶ **COLLOCATIONS:**
a floor **of** *something*
on a floor
the **ground** floor
the **first/second/third**, etc. floor
the **top/next/same** floor

> **WHICH WORD: floor or storey?**
>
> You use **floor** to refer to one of the levels of a building. ○ *Her bedroom is on the first floor.* ○ *We took the lift to the top floor.*
>
> You use **storey** to say how many levels there are in a building. ○ *The tower was twenty storeys high.* ○ *a three-storey house*

---

flour /flaʊə/   FOOD & DRINK

UNCOUNTABLE NOUN **Flour** is a white or brown powder that is made by grinding grain. It is used to make bread, cakes, and pastry. ○ *Sift the flour and salt into a mixing bowl.* ○ *225 grams of self-raising flour*

▶ **COLLOCATIONS:**
sift/add flour
white/wholemeal flour
plain/self-raising flour

flow /fləʊ/ (flows, flowing, flowed)

SCIENCE & NATURE

VERB If a liquid, gas, or electrical current **flows** somewhere, it moves there steadily and continuously. ○ [+ out] *The water flows out through a narrow tube.* ○ [+ into] *The current flows into an electric motor that drives the wheels.* ○ [+ from] *Blood was flowing freely from a wound in his head.*

▶ COLLOCATIONS:
flow **in/out**
flow **back/away**
flow **from** something
flow **down/through/over/up** something
flow **freely/smoothly**

flow|er /flaʊə/ (flowers)

SCIENCE & NATURE

1 NOUN A **flower** is the brightly coloured part of a plant which grows at the end of a stem. ○ *Each plant had flowers of a different colour.* ○ *large, purplish-blue flowers*

▶ COLLOCATIONS:
dried/fresh flowers
white/small/bright/delicate flowers

2 NOUN Flowers are small plants that are grown for their flowers as opposed to trees, shrubs, and vegetables. ○ *I've been planting flowers all afternoon.* ○ *a bunch of flowers*

▶ COLLOCATIONS:
grow/plant flowers
buy/arrange/pick flowers
wild flowers
spring/summer flowers
a flower **arrangement/shop/show**
a flower **bed/garden/border**

flu /fluː/

HEALTH

UNCOUNTABLE NOUN Flu is an illness caused by a virus. The symptoms are like those of a cold but more serious. ○ *I got flu.* ○ *He had the flu.* ○ *the bird flu virus*

▶ COLLOCATIONS:
have/get/catch flu
bad/severe/mild flu
bird/swine flu
a flu **vaccine/jab**
the flu **virus/bug**
a flu **outbreak/epidemic/case**
flu **symptoms**

flu|ent /ˈfluːənt/

COMMUNICATIONS

ADJECTIVE Someone who is **fluent in** a particular language can speak the language easily and correctly. ○ [+ in] *She is fluent in three languages.* ○ *He speaks fluent Russian.*

▶ **COLLOCATIONS:**
fluent **in** *something*
completely fluent
fluent **French/German/English**, etc.
become fluent

WORD FAMILY		
fluent	ADJECTIVE	○ *She has become more fluent in English.*
fluently	ADVERB	○ *He speaks three languages fluently.*
fluency	UNCOUNT	○ *Translators need fluency in at least one foreign language.*

fog /fɒg/

SCIENCE & NATURE

UNCOUNTABLE NOUN When there is **fog**, there are tiny drops of water in the air which form a thick cloud and make it difficult to see things. ○ *The crash happened in thick fog.* ○ *There was freezing fog and rain.*

▶ **COLLOCATIONS:**
in fog
thick/heavy/white fog
morning/freezing fog
fog **lifts/descends**

WORD FAMILY		
fog	UNCOUNT	○ *By ten o'clock, the fog had lifted.*
foggy	ADJECTIVE	○ *a foggy night* ○ *foggy conditions*

folk /fəʊk/

MEDIA & CULTURE

ADJECTIVE **Folk** music is music that is traditional or typical of a particular community or nation. ○ *I love Irish folk music.* ○ *He plays in a folk band.*

▶ **COLLOCATIONS:**
folk **music**
a folk **band/group**
a folk **song/singer/festival**

foot|ball /ˈfʊtbɔːl/

SPORT & ACTIVITY

UNCOUNTABLE NOUN Football is a game played by two teams of eleven players who try to score by kicking or heading a ball into their opponent's goal. [BRIT; in AM, use **soccer**] ○ *Several boys were still out playing football.* ○ *Arsenal Football Club* ○ *Italian football fans*

▶ COLLOCATIONS:
  play/watch/love football
  a football **team/club**
  a football **player/coach/manager**
  a football **fan/supporter/hooligan**
  a football **match/game**
  a football **field/pitch**
  a football **ground/stadium**
  a football **shirt**

▶ SYNONYM: soccer

for|est /ˈfɒrɪst, AM ˈfɔːr-/ (forests)

SCIENCE & NATURE

NOUN A **forest** is a large area where trees grow close together. ○ *Parts of the forest are very dense.* ○ *A dry climate means a greater risk of forest fires.*

▶ COLLOCATIONS:
  a **dense/thick** forest
  a **dark/deep/large** forest
  the **rain** forest
  a forest **fire/trail**

▶ SYNONYM: wood

fort|night /ˈfɔːtnaɪt/ (fortnights)

NOUN A **fortnight** is a period of two weeks. [mainly BRIT] ○ *I hope to be back in a fortnight.* ○ *She left a fortnight ago.* ○ *[+ of] There will be a fortnight of intensive training before the season starts.*

▶ COLLOCATIONS:
  in a fortnight
  for a fortnight
  a fortnight **of** something
  a fortnight **ago/before/away**
  a fortnight **earlier/later**
  the **last/past/previous** fortnight
  the **next** fortnight
  spend a fortnight somewhere
  take/last a fortnight

▶ SYNONYM: two weeks

for|tu|nate /ˈfɔːtʃʊnɪt/

ADJECTIVE If you say that someone or something is **fortunate**, you mean that they are lucky. ○ [+ to-inf] *He was extremely fortunate to survive.* ○ [+ in] *Central London is fortunate in having so many open spaces.* ○ [+ that] *It was fortunate that the water was shallow.*

▶ **COLLOCATIONS:**
 fortunate **in** *something*
 very/extremely/really fortunate
 pretty/quite fortunate
 more/less fortunate
 a fortunate **position/situation**

▶ **SYNONYM:** lucky

▶ **ANTONYM:** unfortunate

for|tu|nate|ly /ˈfɔːtʃʊnətli/

ADVERB Fortunately is used to introduce or indicate a statement about an event or situation that is good. ○ *A bomb hit the building but fortunately no one was hurt.* ○ [+ for] *Fortunately for me, my friend saw what happened.*

▶ **SYNONYM:** luckily

▶ **ANTONYM:** unfortunately

WORD FAMILY		
fortunate	**ADJECTIVE**	○ *She is in the fortunate position of having plenty of choice.*
fortunately	**ADVERB**	○ *Fortunately, the weather was quite warm.*
unfortunate	**ADJECTIVE**	○ *He is one of those unfortunate people who put on weight very easily.*
unfortunately	**ADVERB**	○ *Unfortunately, I failed my geography exam.*

for|tune /ˈfɔːtʃuːn/ (fortunes)

MONEY

NOUN A fortune is a very large amount of money. ○ *We had to eat out all the time. It cost a fortune.* ○ *He made a fortune selling luxury yachts.*

▶ **COLLOCATIONS:**
 make/earn a fortune
 cost a fortune
 spend/pay a fortune
 save a fortune

fos|sil fuel /ˌfɒsəl ˈfjuːəl/ (fossil fuels)

`SCIENCE & NATURE`

NOUN **Fossil fuels** are fuels such as coal, oil, and natural gas. ○ *The main source of greenhouse gases is the burning of fossil fuels.*

freez|er /ˈfriːzə/ (freezers)

`HOME`

NOUN A **freezer** is a fridge in which the temperature is kept below freezing point so you can store food inside it for long periods. ○ *I took the ice cream out of the freezer.* ○ *a fridge-freezer*

WORD FAMILY		
freeze	**VERB**	○ *Garlic doesn't freeze well.*
freezer	**NOUN**	○ *I usually keep some sausages in the freezer.*
frozen	**ADJECTIVE**	○ *Frozen fish is a very healthy convenience food.*

friend /frend/ (friends)

`SOCIAL LIFE`

NOUN A **friend** is someone who you know well and like, but who is not related to you. ○ *I had a long talk with my best friend.* ○ *Don't worry; you'll soon make new friends.* ○ *[+ of] She never was a close friend of mine.*

→ see Useful Phrases **make friends**

▶ **COLLOCATIONS:**
a friend **of** *someone's*
a **good/close/old** friend
your **best** friend
a **family/childhood** friend
make/become friends

friend|ly /ˈfrendli/ (friendlier, friendliest)

`PERSONALITY`

ADJECTIVE If someone is **friendly**, they behave in a pleasant, kind way, and like to be with other people. ○ *[+ to] She's always very friendly to me.* ○ *Robert has a friendly relationship with his customers.*

▶ **COLLOCATIONS:**
friendly **to** *someone*
a friendly **face/smile**
a friendly **relationship**
a friendly **atmosphere/place**

WORD FAMILY		
friend	**NOUN**	○ *We became good friends.*
friendly	**ADJECTIVE**	○ *He had a pleasant, friendly face.*
friendliness	**UNCOUNT**	○ *She loves the friendliness of the Irish people.*
unfriendly	**ADJECTIVE**	○ *The staff in the café are slow and unfriendly.*
friendship	**UNCOUNT**	○ *The two boys developed a close friendship.*

fright|en /ˈfraɪtən/ (frightens, frightening, frightened)

VERB If something or someone **frightens** you, they cause you to suddenly feel afraid or anxious. ○ *Sudden loud noises frighten her.* ○ [+ away] *The boats frighten away the fish.*

▶ **COLLOCATIONS:**
frighten *someone* **away/off**
frighten *someone* **into** *something*

▶ **SYNONYM:** scare

fright|ened /ˈfraɪtənd/

ADJECTIVE If you are **frightened**, you are anxious or afraid, often because of something that has just happened or that you think may happen. ○ [+ of] *She was frightened of flying.* ○ [+ to-inf] *Miriam was too frightened to tell her family what had happened.*

▶ **COLLOCATIONS:**
frightened **of** *something*
very/so/really/quite frightened
a **little/bit** frightened
be/feel frightened
get/become frightened
look/seem/sound frightened

▶ **SYNONYM:** scared

fright|en|ing /ˈfraɪtənɪŋ/

ADJECTIVE If something is **frightening**, it makes you feel afraid or anxious.
○ *Having an asthma attack can be very frightening.* ○ [+ to-inf] *It is frightening to think that a terrorist attack could happen here.*

▶ **COLLOCATIONS:**
very/quite/so/really frightening
a **little/bit** frightening
a frightening **experience/situation**
a frightening **thought/prospect**

▶ **SYNONYMS:** alarming, scary

frost /frɒst, AM frɔːst/   `SCIENCE & NATURE`

UNCOUNTABLE NOUN When there is **frost**, the temperature outside falls below freezing point and the ground becomes covered in ice crystals. ○ *Severe frost was forecast last night.* ○ *plants suffering from frost damage*

WORD FAMILY		
frost	**UNCOUNT**	○ *Some crops can't survive frost.*
frosty	**ADJECTIVE**	○ *sharp, frosty nights* ○ *the frosty pavement*

fro|zen /ˈfrəʊzən/

SCIENCE & NATURE

ADJECTIVE If the ground is **frozen** it has become hard because the weather is very cold. ○ *It was bitterly cold and the ground was frozen.*

WORD FAMILY

freeze	**VERB**	○ *Water freezes when the temperature drops below 0°C.*
freezing	**ADJECTIVE**	○ *You must be freezing.*
frozen	**ADJECTIVE**	○ *They went skating on a frozen lake.*

---

fruit /fruːt/

FOOD & DRINK

UNCOUNTABLE NOUN Fruit is something that grows on a tree or bush and that contains seeds or a stone covered by flesh. ○ *Fresh fruit and vegetables provide vitamins.* ○ *Try to eat at least one piece of fruit a day.*

▶ **COLLOCATIONS:**
   fresh/canned fruit
   a **piece of** fruit

fry /fraɪ/ (fries, frying, fried)

FOOD & DRINK

VERB When you **fry** food, you cook it in a pan that contains hot fat or oil. ○ *Fry the breadcrumbs until golden brown.* ○ [+ in] *The fish can be grilled or fried in vegetable oil.*

▶ **COLLOCATIONS:**
   fry *something* **in** *something*
   deep fry *something*
   fried **food**
   a fried **egg**
   fried **onions/fish/chicken**

fry|ing pan /ˈfraɪɪŋ ˌpæn/ (frying pans)

FOOD & DRINK

NOUN A **frying pan** is a flat metal pan with a long handle, in which you fry food. ○ *Heat the oil in a frying pan.*

fuel /ˈfjuːəl/

SCIENCE & NATURE   TRANSPORT & TRAVEL

UNCOUNTABLE NOUN Fuel is a substance such as coal, oil, or petrol that is burned to provide heat or power. ○ [+ for] *They needed some more fuel for the car.* ○ *the fuel necessary to heat their homes* ○ *research into cleaner fuel*

▶ **COLLOCATIONS:**
   fuel **for** *something*
   use/burn fuel
   fossil/nuclear/solid fuel
   clean/cheap fuel
   motor/aircraft fuel
   a fuel **shortage**
   a fuel **pump/tank**

fun /fʌn/

ADJECTIVE If something is **fun**, you enjoy doing it. If someone is **fun**, you enjoy their company. [INFORMAL] ○ *It should be a fun evening.* ○ *Now comes the fun part – the food.* ○ [+ to-inf] *Tom is good fun to be around.*

→ see Useful Phrases **make fun of someone/something**

▶ COLLOCATIONS:
should be/ought to be fun
good/great fun
fun **stuff**
a fun **time**
the fun **part**

▶ SYNONYM: entertaining

▶ ANTONYM: boring

> **WHICH WORD: fun** or **funny**?
>
> **Fun** is used to describe someone who is good to be with or an activity that is enjoyable to do. ○ *Liz is great fun to be with.* ○ *They all thought canoeing was great fun.*
>
> **Funny** is used to describe someone or something that makes you laugh. ○ *Jim Carrey is a very funny man.* ○ *She told a really funny joke.*

fun|ny /ˈfʌni/ (funnier, funniest)   `PERSONALITY`

ADJECTIVE Someone or something that is **funny** is amusing and likely to make you smile or laugh. ○ *We all thought he was hysterically funny.* ○ *I didn't find that joke very funny.*

→ see note at **fun**

▶ COLLOCATIONS:
very/really/hysterically funny
a funny **story/joke**
a funny **film/show**
find *something* **funny**

▶ SYNONYMS: amusing, comical

> **WORD FAMILY**
>
> | funny | **ADJECTIVE** | ○ *I'll tell you a funny story.* |
> | funnily | **ADVERB** | ○ *Funnily enough, I have exactly the same problem.* |

fu|ri|ous /ˈfjʊəriəs/

ADJECTIVE Someone who is **furious** is extremely angry. ○ [+ at/with] *He is furious at the way he has been treated.* ○ [+ that] *I am furious that it has taken so long to uncover what really happened.*

▶ COLLOCATIONS:
furious **with/at** someone/something
furious **about** something
absolutely furious
a furious **row/reaction**
get/become furious
look/feel/sound furious

▶ SYNONYMS: mad, livid

WORD FAMILY		
fury	UNCOUNT	○ He became red-faced with fury.
furious	ADJECTIVE	○ I was absolutely furious about it all.
furiously	ADVERB	○ He slammed the door furiously behind him.

Gg

---

gal‖lery /ˈɡæləri/ (galleries) PLACES

NOUN A **gallery** is a place that has permanent exhibitions of works of art in it.
○ *We used to go to art galleries together.* ○ *the National Portrait Gallery*

▶ **COLLOCATIONS:**
an **art** gallery
a **portrait/photo/picture** gallery
a **new/small/large/national** gallery
go to/visit a gallery

---

gap year /ˈɡæp jɪə/ (gap years) EDUCATION

NOUN A **gap year** is a period of time during which a student takes a break from studying after they have finished school and before they start college or university. [BRIT] ○ *I went around the world in my gap year.* ○ *He is planning to take a gap year before going to university.*

▶ **COLLOCATIONS:**
in/during someone's gap year
take/be on/have a gap year

---

gar‖age /ˈɡærɑːʒ, -rɪdʒ, ᴀᴍ ɡəˈrɑːʒ/ (garages) HOME

1 **NOUN** A **garage** is a building in which you keep a car. A garage is often built next to or as part of a house. ○ *I put the car in the garage.* ○ *Outside there is a double garage and a large garden.*

▶ **COLLOCATIONS:**
in the garage
a **double/single** garage
the garage **door/roof/floor**
a garage **sale**

2 **NOUN** A **garage** is a place where you can have your car repaired, buy fuel for your car, or buy cars. ○ *I take the car to the local garage for a service every six months.* ○ *The garage mechanic said the car would be easy to fix.*

▶ **COLLOCATIONS:**
a **local/independent** garage
a **repair** garage
a garage **mechanic/attendant/owner**
a garage **forecourt**

gate /geɪt/ **(gates)**   `HOME` `TRANSPORT & TRAVEL`

1 **NOUN** A **gate** is a structure like a door which is used at the entrance to a field, a garden, or the grounds of a building. ○ *He opened the gate and walked towards the house.* ○ *A few parents were already waiting at the school gates.*

▶ **COLLOCATIONS:**
   open/close a gate
   an **open** gate
   the **front/main/back/side** gate
   a **wooden/iron/metal** gate
   a **big/high/wide/electronic** gate
   a **garden** gate
   the **school/factory/prison** gates

2 **NOUN** In an airport, a **gate** is a place where passengers leave the airport and get on their aeroplane. ○ *Passengers with hand luggage can go straight to the departure gate.* ○ *Flight 666 is now boarding at gate 13.*

▶ **COLLOCATIONS:**
   at a gate
   a **departure** gate
   gate **two/five/twelve**, etc.

gaze /geɪz/ **(gazes, gazing, gazed)**

VERB If you **gaze at** someone or something, you look steadily at them for a long time. ○ [+ at] *She stood gazing at herself in the mirror.* ○ [+ into] *He was just gazing into the distance.* ○ [+ through] *The children gazed longingly through the toy shop window.*

▶ **COLLOCATIONS:**
   gaze **at** something
   gaze **out of/through** something
   gaze **into** something
   gaze **longingly/lovingly/intently**

▶ **SYNONYM:** stare

gen|era|tion /ˌdʒenəˈreɪʃən/ **(generations)**   `PEOPLE`

NOUN A **generation** consists of all the people in a group or country who are of a similar age. ○ [+ of] *My grandmother's generation of women made all their own clothes.* ○ *The younger generation must carry on these traditions.*

▶ **COLLOCATIONS:**
   a generation **of** something
   the **younger/older** generation
   a **new/future/different** generation
   a generation **gap**

gen|er|ous /ˈdʒenərəs/ `PERSONALITY`

1 **ADJECTIVE** A **generous** person gives more of something, especially money, than is usual or expected. ○ [+ with] *David is generous with his time and money.* ○ [+ of] *It was very generous of him to fly us over here.*

▶ **COLLOCATIONS:**
generous **with** *something*
generous **of** *someone*
very/so/incredibly generous
a generous **offer/donation/gift**

▶ **ANTONYM:** mean

2 **ADJECTIVE** A **generous** person is friendly, helpful, and willing to see the good qualities in someone or something. ○ [+ of] *It was very generous of her to accept my apology.* ○ [+ in] *He was always generous in sharing his knowledge.*

▶ **COLLOCATIONS:**
generous **in** *something*
generous **of** *someone*
generous **support/praise**
a **generous** gesture

▶ **SYNONYMS:** kind, unselfish

▶ **ANTONYMS:** mean, selfish

WORD FAMILY		
generous	ADJECTIVE	○ *Thank you for all your generous gifts.*
generously	ADVERB	○ *Please give generously.*
generosity	UNCOUNT	○ *She is well known for her generosity.*

gen|tle /ˈdʒentəl/ (gentler, gentlest) `PERSONALITY` `SCIENCE & NATURE`

1 **ADJECTIVE** Someone who is **gentle** is kind and calm. ○ *John was a kind and gentle man.* ○ *She spoke to the little girl in a calm, gentle voice.*

▶ **COLLOCATIONS:**
kind/soft/warm and gentle
a gentle **voice/smile**

2 **ADJECTIVE** If you describe the wind as **gentle**, you mean it is pleasant and calm and not strong or violent. ○ *A gentle breeze was blowing.*

WORD FAMILY		
gentle	ADJECTIVE	○ *He smiled in a soft and gentle way.*
gently	ADVERB	○ *She smiled gently at him.*
gentleness	UNCOUNT	○ *the gentleness with which she treated her child*

genu|ine /ˈdʒenjʊɪn/

1 **ADJECTIVE** **Genuine** is used to describe people and things that are exactly what they appear to be, and are not false or an imitation. ○ *They're convinced the picture is genuine.* ○ *genuine leather* ○ *You need to have a genuine reason for missing the class.*

▶ **SYNONYM:** real

▶ **ANTONYM:** fake

2 **ADJECTIVE** **Genuine** refers to emotions and ideas that are real and not pretended. ○ *There was genuine concern in his voice.* ○ *If this offer is genuine, I will gladly accept it.*

▶ **COLLOCATIONS:**
genuine **concern/interest/fear**
genuine **affection/love/friendship**
quite/absolutely genuine
seem/look/sound genuine

▶ **SYNONYM:** sincere

▶ **ANTONYM:** insincere

WORD FAMILY		
genuine	**ADJECTIVE**	○ *Her interest was quite genuine.*
genuinely	**ADVERB**	○ *He was genuinely surprised.*

---

ge|og|ra|phy /dʒiˈɒgrəfi/ `SCIENCE & NATURE`

UNCOUNTABLE NOUN **Geography** is the study of the countries of the world and of the land, seas, climate, towns, and population. ○ *She plans to go to university to study geography.* ○ *a geography lesson on the rainforest*

▶ **COLLOCATIONS:**
study/teach geography
a geography **teacher/student**
a geography **lesson/book/field trip/degree**
the geography **department**
physical/political/human geography

WORD FAMILY		
geography	**UNCOUNT**	○ *He's studying for a degree in political geography.*
geographical	**ADJECTIVE**	○ *a vast geographical area* ○ *geographical features such as rivers*
geographically	**ADVERB**	○ *Geographically, it's the highest point in London.*
geographer	**NOUN**	○ *Geographers recognize that areas change over time.*

ge|ol|ogy /dʒiˈɒlədʒi/ SCIENCE & NATURE

UNCOUNTABLE NOUN Geology is the study of the Earth's structure, surface, and origins. ○ *By studying geology, he could combine his love of science and rock climbing.*

▶ **COLLOCATIONS:**
study/teach geology
a geology **professor/student**
a geology **course/textbook/degree**
the geology **department**

WORD FAMILY		
geology	UNCOUNT	○ *I want to study geography and geology at university.*
geological	ADJECTIVE	○ *a lengthy geological survey* ○ *geological formations*
geologically	ADVERB	○ *Geologically, the island is of great interest.*
geologist	NOUN	○ *Geologists have studied the way that heat flows from the earth.*

g

get away /get əˈweɪ/ TRANSPORT & TRAVEL
(gets away, getting away, got away)

PHRASAL VERB If you **get away**, you go away for a period of time in order to have a holiday. ○ *He is too busy to get away.* ○ [+ for] *It would be good to get away for a holiday.*

▶ **COLLOCATION:** get away **for** *something*

get on /get ˈɒn/ **(gets on, getting on, got on)** SOCIAL LIFE

PHRASAL VERB If you **get on with** someone, you like them and have a friendly relationship with them. ○ *I'm worried the guests won't get on.* ○ [+ with] *What are your neighbours like? Do you get on with them?*

▶ **COLLOCATIONS:**
get on **with** *someone*
get on **well**

▶ **SYNONYM:** get along

get through /get ˈθruː/ COMMUNICATIONS
(gets through, getting through, got through)

PHRASAL VERB If you **get through to** someone, you succeed in contacting them on the telephone. ○ [+ to] *I can't get through to his number.* ○ *I've been trying to call her all day but I couldn't get through.*

▶ **COLLOCATION:** get through **to** *someone*

get to|geth|er (with) /get təˈgeðə/   SOCIAL LIFE
(gets together, getting together, got together)

PHRASAL VERB When people **get together**, they meet in order to spend time together. ○ *We should all get together some time.* ○ [+ with] *One of the best things about holidays is getting together with friends.*

▶ **COLLOCATION:** get together **with** someone

---

gift /gɪft/ **(gifts)**   SOCIAL LIFE

NOUN A **gift** is something that you give someone as a present. ○ [+ of] *Her uncle sent a gift of $50.* ○ *He kept buying me expensive gifts.* ○ [+ from] *This ring was a gift from a friend.*

▶ **COLLOCATIONS:**
a gift **of** something
a gift **from** someone
give/buy/send/take someone a gift
get/receive a gift
wrap a gift
a **small/expensive/free** gift
a **birthday/wedding/Christmas** gift
a gift **shop**
a gift **card/voucher**

▶ **SYNONYM:** present

---

gig /gɪg/ **(gigs)**   MEDIA & CULTURE

NOUN A **gig** is a live performance by a musician or a comedian. [INFORMAL] ○ *Do you want to go to a gig this weekend?* ○ *I'd really like to see more gigs.*

▶ **COLLOCATIONS:**
go to/see a gig
play/do a gig
announce/cancel a gig
a **live/big/good/free** gig
a **one-off** gig
a **club/pub/stadium** gig

▶ **SYNONYM:** show

---

give away /gɪv əˈweɪ/ **(gives away, giving away, gave away, given away)**

PHRASAL VERB If someone **gives away** something that they own, they give it to someone, rather than selling it. ○ *The company is giving the software away for non-commercial use.* ○ *We have six free tickets to give away.*

▶ **ANTONYM:** keep

give back /gɪv 'bæk/ (gives back, giving back, gave back, given back)

PHRASAL VERB If you **give** something **back**, you return it to the person who gave it to you. ○ [+ to] *Can I borrow your textbook? I promise I'll give it back to you.* ○ *I gave the money back politely.*

▸ **COLLOCATION:** give *something* back **to** *someone*

give up /gɪv 'ʌp/ (gives up, giving up, gave up, given up)

PHRASAL VERB If you **give up** something, you stop doing it or having it. ○ *She decided to give up smoking.* ○ *She gave up her university studies to concentrate full-time on acting.* ○ *Coastguards had given up all hope of finding the two divers alive.*

▸ **COLLOCATIONS:**
give up **smoking/drinking**
give up *your* **job/career**
give up **hope**

glad /glæd/

ADJECTIVE If you are **glad** about something, you are happy and pleased about it. ○ [+ to-inf] *I'm so glad to see you.* ○ [+ that] *I'm just glad that she's all right.* ○ [+ of] *She was glad of the opportunity to take two weeks' leave.*

▸ **COLLOCATIONS:**
glad **of** *something*
glad of the **chance/opportunity/excuse**

▸ **SYNONYMS:** happy, pleased

glance /glɑːns, glæns/ (glances, glancing, glanced)

VERB If you **glance at** something or someone, you look at them very quickly and then look away again immediately. ○ [+ at] *He glanced at his watch.* ○ *The man glanced up.* ○ *She glanced nervously in the direction of the door.*

▸ **COLLOCATIONS:**
glance **at/towards/across** *something/someone*
glance **back/around/down/up**, etc.
glance **quickly/nervously**

▸ **SYNONYM:** look

glasses /'glɑːsɪz, 'glæsɪz/ CLOTHES & APPEARANCE

PLURAL NOUN **Glasses** are a set of two lenses in a frame that people wear in front of their eyes to help them see better. ○ *He took off his glasses.* ○ *I usually wear glasses.*

▸ **COLLOCATIONS:**
wear glasses
put on/take off *your* glasses

▸ **SYNONYM:** spectacles

glob|al /ˈɡləʊbəl/

ADJECTIVE You can use **global** to describe something that happens in all parts of the world or affects all parts of the world. ○ *global environmental problems* ○ *E-mail allows us to conduct business on a global scale.* ○ *The global advertising industry spends billions each year persuading us to buy certain brands.*

▶ **COLLOCATIONS:**
a global **company/industry**
a global **network/system**
a global **issue/problem/crisis/threat**
the global **economy**
on a global **scale**
truly global

▶ **SYNONYMS:** worldwide, international

WORD FAMILY		
globe	**NOUN**	○ *underdeveloped countries around the globe*
global	**ADJECTIVE**	○ *the global political system* ○ *Cyber-crime is a global issue.*
globally	**ADVERB**	○ *The UK is competing globally for international students.*

glob|al warm|ing /ˌɡləʊbəl ˈwɔːmɪŋ/　　　SCIENCE & NATURE

UNCOUNTABLE NOUN **Global warming** is the gradual rise in the earth's temperature caused by high levels of carbon dioxide and other gases in the atmosphere. ○ *proposals to combat global warming* ○ *Scientists continue to study the effects of global warming.*

→ see also **climate change**

▶ **COLLOCATIONS:**
contribute to/cause global warming
combat/fight global warming
reduce/increase global warming
the **effects/impact of** global warming
the **threat /danger/problem of** global warming

gloves /ɡlʌvz/　　　CLOTHES & APPEARANCE

PLURAL NOUN **Gloves** are pieces of clothing which cover your hands and wrists and have individual sections for each finger. You wear gloves to keep your hands warm or dry or to protect them. ○ *Always wear gloves in very cold weather.* ○ *a pair of white cotton gloves*

golf /gɒlf/

SPORT & ACTIVITY

UNCOUNTABLE NOUN Golf is a game in which you use long sticks called clubs to hit a small, hard ball into holes that are spread out over a large area of grassy land. ○ *They played golf twice a week.* ○ *He spends most of his weekends on the golf course.*

▶ COLLOCATIONS:
play golf
a golf **course/game**
a golf **club/ball**
a golf **tournament/championship**

goods /gʊdz/

SHOPPING

PLURAL NOUN Goods are things that are made to be sold. ○ *Most mail-order companies will deliver goods within 7 to 10 days.* ○ *Supermarkets are now offering an ever-widening range of food and household goods.*

▶ COLLOCATIONS:
buy/sell/deliver goods
produce/manufacture goods
import/export goods
luxury/consumer goods
household/electrical/electronic goods

go on /gəʊ 'ɒn/ (goes on, going on, went on, gone on)

PHRASAL VERB If a process, activity or event **goes on**, it continues to happen. ○ *Why is it necessary for the war to go on?* ○ [+ for] *This has been going on for months.*

▶ SYNONYM: continue

▶ ANTONYM: end

gos|sip /'gɒsɪp/

MEDIA & CULTURE

UNCOUNTABLE NOUN Gossip is informal conversation about other people's private affairs. **Gossip** is also information about famous people's private lives, in a magazine, newspaper, or on the Internet. ○ *She's been spreading gossip about him being in prison.* ○ *He loved celebrity gossip.*

▶ COLLOCATIONS:
gossip **about** *someone/something*
hear/spread/swap gossip
the **latest** gossip
celebrity/office gossip

gradu|ate (graduates, graduating, graduated)

EDUCATION

The noun is pronounced /'grædʒʊət/. The verb is pronounced /'grædʒʊeɪt/.

1 **NOUN** In Britain, a **graduate** is a person who has successfully completed a degree at a university or college and has received a certificate that shows this. ○ [+ in] *graduates in engineering* ○ [+ of/from] *He is a graduate of the University of Oxford.* ○ *Unemployment among university graduates is rising.*

→ see also **undergraduate, postgraduate**

▶ **COLLOCATIONS:**
a graduate **of/from** *something*
a graduate **in** *something*
a **university/college** graduate
a **recent** graduate
a **law/science/engineering**, etc. graduate

2 **VERB** In Britain, when a student **graduates** from university, they have successfully completed a degree course. ○ [+ from] *After I graduated from university I took the first job I was offered.* ○ [+ in] *He graduated in law in 1967.* ○ [+ with] *Laura has just graduated with a degree in fashion design.*

▶ **COLLOCATIONS:**
graduate **from** *something*
graduate from **college/university**
graduate **in** *something*
graduate in **English/medicine/economics**, etc.
graduate **with** *something*
graduate with a **degree/MA/diploma**

WORD FAMILY		
graduate	NOUN	○ *Applications will be considered from recent graduates.*
graduate	VERB	○ *He graduated recently from Trent University.*
graduation	UNCOUNT	○ *After graduation O'Brien moved to Los Angeles and quickly got a job.*
undergraduate	NOUN	○ *I remember when I was an undergraduate at Oxford.*
postgraduate	NOUN	○ *After getting his bachelor's degree he did some postgraduate courses.*

graf|fi|ti /grəˈfiːti/ PLACES

UNCOUNTABLE NOUN **Graffiti** is words or pictures that are written or drawn in public places, for example on walls or posters. ○ *Buildings are thickly covered with graffiti.* ○ *Raphael was arrested for spraying graffiti on two subway train carriages.*

grate /greɪt/ (grates, grating, grated) FOOD & DRINK

VERB If you **grate** food such as cheese or carrots, you rub it over a metal tool called a grater so that the food is cut into very small pieces. ○ *Grate the cheese into a mixing bowl.* ○ *grated carrot*

green /griːn/ (greener, greenest) SCIENCE & NATURE

ADJECTIVE If you say that someone or something is **green**, you mean they harm the environment as little as possible. ○ *Wind farms supply clean, green energy* ○ *Our children are being educated to be green in everything they do.*

▶ **COLLOCATIONS:**
green **power/energy/technology/electricity**
green **products**
a green **building**
green **policies**

grey /greɪ/ (greyer, greyest) [in AM, use **gray**] CLOTHES & APPEARANCE

ADJECTIVE You use **grey** to describe the colour of people's hair when it changes from its original colour, usually as they get old. ○ *her grey hair* ○ *Eddie was going grey.*

g

grill /grɪl/ (grills, grilling, grilled) FOOD & DRINK

1 NOUN A **grill** is a part of a stove which produces strong heat to cook food that has been placed underneath it. [BRIT; in AM, use **broiler**] ○ *Put the mushrooms under a hot grill and cook on both sides until golden.*

2 VERB When you **grill** food, or when it **grills**, you cook it using very strong heat directly above or below it. [BRIT; in AM, use **broil**] ○ *Grill the meat for 20 minutes each side.* ○ *grilled chicken*

groom /gruːm/ (grooms) SOCIAL LIFE

NOUN A **groom** or **bridegroom** is a man who is getting married. ○ *Now the bride and groom will cut the cake.*

→ see also **bride**

ground /graʊnd/ SCIENCE & NATURE

1 UNCOUNTABLE NOUN The **ground** is the surface of the earth. ○ *I sat down on the ground.* ○ *We slid down the roof and dropped to the ground.* ○ *a hole in the ground*

→ see note at **soil**

2 UNCOUNTABLE NOUN You can refer to an area of land as **ground**, especially of a particular type. ○ *There was snow on high ground.* ○ *The body was found on waste ground near a railway station.*

▶ **COLLOCATIONS:**
on/in the ground
sit on/lie on the ground
high/soft/solid ground

▶ **SYNONYM:** land

grow /grəʊ/ (grows, growing, grew, grown) `SCIENCE & NATURE`

VERB When people, animals, and plants **grow**, they increase in size and change physically over a period of time. ○ *Most young people stop growing by the time they reach their late teens.* ○ *The grass was growing fast.*

grow into/out of `CLOTHES & APPEARANCE`

PHRASAL VERB When a child **grows into** an item of clothing, they become taller or bigger so that it fits them properly. When a child **grows out of** an item of clothing, they become so tall or big that it no longer fits them. ○ *It's a bit big, but she'll soon grow into it.* ○ *You've grown out of your shoes again.*

grown-up (grown-ups) `PEOPLE`

The noun is pronounced /'grəʊn,ʌp/. The adjective is pronounced /,grəʊn'ʌp/.

1 NOUN A **grown-up** is an adult; used by or to children. ○ *We are not allowed there without a grown-up.* ○ *Tell children to tell a grown-up if they're being bullied.*

▶ **SYNONYM:** adult

2 ADJECTIVE Someone who is **grown-up** is physically and mentally mature and no longer depends on their parents or another adult. ○ *I have grown-up children who're doing well.*

▶ **SYNONYM:** adult

WORD FAMILY		
grow	**VERB**	○ *New apple trees grow slowly.*
grow into	**PHRASAL VERB**	○ *Even if you grow into it, you may not wear it.*
grow out of	**PHRASAL VERB**	○ *Children grow out of their clothes so quickly.*
grown-up	**NOUN**	○ *Julie couldn't follow what the grown-ups were talking about.*
grown-up	**ADJECTIVE**	○ *I certainly didn't feel grown-up.*
growth	**UNCOUNT**	○ *Hormones control the growth and development of the body.*

guar|an|tee /,gærən'tiː/ `SHOPPING`
(guarantees, guaranteeing, guaranteed)

1 NOUN A **guarantee** is a written promise by a company to replace or repair a product free of charge if it has any faults within a particular time. ○ *All beds carry a 10-year guarantee.* ○ *It was still under guarantee.*

▶ **COLLOCATIONS:**
be **under** guarantee
come with/carry a guarantee

▶ **SYNONYM:** warranty

2 **VERB** If a company **guarantees** its product or work, they provide a guarantee for it. ○ *Some builders guarantee their work.* ○ [+ *for*] *All suitcases are guaranteed for three years.* ○ [+ *against*] *All goods are guaranteed against defects in manufacturing.*

▸ **COLLOCATIONS:**
be guaranteed **for** *x* years
be guaranteed **against** something

guest /gest/ (guests)

SOCIAL LIFE

NOUN A **guest** is someone who is visiting you or is at an event because you have invited them. ○ [+ *at*] *She was a guest at the wedding.* ○ *The couple had invited 350 guests to the ceremony and dinner.*

▸ **COLLOCATIONS:**
a guest **at** something
a **wedding/party/dinner** guest
invite a guest
greet/welcome a guest
an **invited/uninvited** guest

guide|book /ˈgaɪdbʊk/ (guidebooks)

TRANSPORT & TRAVEL

NOUN A **guidebook** is a book that gives tourists information about a town, area, or country. ○ [+ *to*] *a popular guidebook to Rome* ○ *It is best to buy a good guidebook before setting off on holiday.*

▸ **SYNONYM:** guide

guilty /ˈgɪlti/ (guiltier, guiltiest)

CRIME

1 **ADJECTIVE** If you feel **guilty**, you feel unhappy because you think that you have done something wrong or have failed to do something which you should have done. ○ *Sam sat there looking guilty.* ○ [+ *about*] *She had felt ashamed and guilty about the incident.* ○ [+ *for*] *Now I feel so guilty for what I have done.*

▸ **COLLOCATIONS:**
guilty **about /for** something
feel/look guilty

2 **ADJECTIVE** If someone is **guilty of** a crime, they have committed that crime. ○ [+ *of*] *They were found guilty of murder.* ○ *He pleaded guilty to causing actual bodily harm.*

▸ **COLLOCATIONS:**
guilty **of** something
guilty of a **crime/charge/offence**
guilty of **murder/assault/fraud**
plead guilty
find/prove someone guilty
a guilty **verdict/plea**

▶ **ANTONYMS:** not guilty, innocent

WORD FAMILY		
guilt	**UNCOUNT**	○ *She felt a twinge of guilt over her plans to leave him.*
guilty	**ADJECTIVE**	○ *He felt guilty that he hadn't visited more often.*
guiltily	**ADVERB**	○ *He glanced guiltily over his shoulder.*

gui|tar /gɪˈtɑː/ (guitars)   `MEDIA & CULTURE`

NOUN A **guitar** is a musical instrument with six strings that you pluck or strum.
○ *She could play the guitar better than me.* ○ *a broken guitar string*

▶ **COLLOCATIONS:**
 play the guitar
 an **acoustic/electric** guitar
 a guitar **player**
 a guitar **string**

WORD FAMILY		
guitar	**NOUN**	○ *He was sitting under a tree, strumming a guitar.*
guitarist	**NOUN**	○ *the group's guitarist and songwriter*

gym /dʒɪm/ (gyms)   `HEALTH` `SPORT & ACTIVITY`

NOUN A **gym** is a club, building, or large room, usually containing special
equipment, where people go to do physical exercise and get fit. ○ *Dave had joined
a local gym to keep fit.* ○ *the school gym*

▶ **COLLOCATIONS:**
 join/go to/use a gym
 gym **membership**
 gym **equipment**

gym|nas|tics /dʒɪmˈnæstɪks/   `SPORT & ACTIVITY`

UNCOUNTABLE NOUN **Gymnastics** consists of physical exercises that develop your
strength, co-ordination, and ease of movement. ○ *the Romanian women's
gymnastics team* ○ *She also swam, did gymnastics and played basketball.*

▶ **COLLOCATIONS:**
 do gymnastics
 a gymnastics **team/competition**
 a gymnastics **coach**

gym|nast /ˈdʒɪmnæst/ (gymnasts)   `SPORT & ACTIVITY`

NOUN A **gymnast** is someone who is trained in gymnastics. ○ *His childhood dream
was to be an Olympic gymnast.*

Hh

---

ham /hæm/ `FOOD & DRINK`

UNCOUNTABLE NOUN **Ham** is meat from the top of the back leg of a pig, specially treated so that it can be kept for a long period of time. ○ *ham sandwiches* ○ *a dozen slices of ham*

---

hand in /hænd ˈɪn/ (hands in, handing in, handed in) `EDUCATION`

PHRASAL VERB If you **hand in** something such as homework, you give it to a teacher. ○ *I handed it in a week late.* ○ *Failing to hand homework in on time would result in detention.*

▶ **COLLOCATIONS:**
hand in **homework**
hand in an **essay/dissertation/assignment**

---

hand lug|gage /ˈhænd lʌgɪdʒ/ `TRANSPORT & TRAVEL`

UNCOUNTABLE NOUN When you travel by air, your **hand luggage** is the luggage you have with you in the plane, rather than the luggage that is carried in the hold. ○ *Airlines restrict hand luggage to one piece per person.* ○ *Keep essential items in your hand luggage.*

▶ **COLLOCATIONS:**
in *someone's* hand luggage
a **piece of** hand luggage

---

hang up /hæŋ ˈʌp/ `CLOTHES & APPEARANCE` `COMMUNICATIONS`
(hangs up, hanging up, hung up)

1 **PHRASAL VERB** If a piece of clothing is **hanging up** in a high place, or if you **hang** it **up** there, it is put there so it does not touch the ground. ○ *I found his jacket, which was hanging up in the hallway.* ○ *Diana undressed and hung up her dress.*

2 **PHRASAL VERB** If you **hang up** or you **hang up** the phone, you end a phone call. If you **hang up on** someone you are speaking to on the phone, you end the phone call suddenly and unexpectedly. ○ *She sounded annoyed and hung up without saying goodbye.* ○ [+ on] *He said he'd call again, and hung up on me.*

---

har|bour /ˈhɑːbə/ (harbours) [in AM, use harbor] `PLACES`

NOUN A **harbour** is an area of the sea at the coast which is partly enclosed by land or strong walls, so that boats can be left there safely. ○ *a room with a balcony overlooking the harbour* ○ *The ship was permitted to tie up in Boston harbour.*

harm /hɑːm/ (harms, harming, harmed)

HEALTH

1 **VERB** To **harm** a person or animal means to cause them physical injury, usually on purpose. ○ *The hijackers seemed anxious not to harm anyone.* ○ *I would never harm any child.*

▶ **SYNONYMS:** injure, hurt

2 **UNCOUNTABLE NOUN** **Harm** is physical injury to a person or an animal which is usually caused on purpose. ○ [+ to] *All dogs are capable of doing harm to human beings.* ○ *She's shaken up but she's avoided any physical harm.*

▶ **COLLOCATIONS:**
harm **to** *someone/something*
do/cause harm
suffer harm
serious/physical harm

▶ **SYNONYM:** injury

3 **VERB** To **harm** a thing, or sometimes a person, means to damage them or make them less effective or successful than they were. ○ *Pesticides and other chemicals can harm the environment.*

▶ **COLLOCATIONS:**
harm **the environment/the economy**
harm a **business/industry**
seriously harm

▶ **SYNONYMS:** damage, ruin

harm|ful /ˈhɑːmfʊl/

ADJECTIVE Something that is **harmful** has a bad effect on something else, especially on a person's health. ○ *the harmful effects of smoking* ○ [+ to] *Some drugs can be potentially harmful to an unborn baby.*

▶ **COLLOCATIONS:**
harmful **to** *someone/something*
potentially harmful
a harmful **effect**
harmful **chemicals/substances/emissions**

▶ **SYNONYM:** damaging

▶ **ANTONYM:** harmless

WORD FAMILY		
harm	**VERB**	○ *The dispute has seriously harmed relations between the two countries.*
harm	**UNCOUNT**	○ *These measures will protect the animals from any serious harm.*
harmful	**ADJECTIVE**	○ *non-toxic cleaning products that are free of harmful chemicals*
harmless	**ADJECTIVE**	○ *The virus is common and relatively harmless.*

head|ache /ˈhedeɪk/ (headaches)　　　`HEALTH`

NOUN If you have a **headache**, you have a pain in your head. ○ *I've had a terrible headache for the last two days.* ○ *I began to get very severe headaches.*

▶ COLLOCATIONS:
　have/get a headache
　a **severe/bad/splitting** headache

head|line /ˈhedlaɪn/ (headlines)　　　`MEDIA & CULTURE`

NOUN A **headline** is the title of a news story, especially printed in large letters at the top of a newspaper story on the front page. ○ *The headline read 'Man Linked with Diplomat's Murder'.* ○ *The case made international headlines.*

▶ COLLOCATIONS:
　a **news/newspaper** headline
　a **front-page** headline
　a **national/international** headline
　a headline **reads/says** *something*
　something **makes/hits** the headlines

head teach|er /ˌhed ˈtiːtʃə/ (head teachers)
also **headteacher**　　　`EDUCATION`

NOUN A **head teacher** is a teacher who is in charge of a school. [BRIT] ○ [+ *of/at*] *Evans became headteacher of Priory Park Primary School.* ○ *The school's deputy headteacher said the girl would receive support.*

▶ COLLOCATIONS:
　the headteacher **of/at** *a school*
　a **deputy/assistant** headteacher

▶ SYNONYM: head

health /helθ/　　　`HEALTH`

UNCOUNTABLE NOUN A person's **health** is the condition of their body and the extent to which it is free from illness or is able to resist illness. ○ *Caffeine is bad for your health.* ○ *Leone was in poor health.* ○ *the health benefits of exercise*

▶ COLLOCATIONS:
　affect /damage/endanger *someone's* health
　someone's health **deteriorates/improves**
　good/ill/poor health
　be **in** good/poor health
　physical/mental/general health
　a health **problem/risk**
　the health **benefits** of *something*
　health **care/service/department**
　a health **worker/professional/official**

h

healthy /ˈhelθi/ (healthier, healthiest)

1 **ADJECTIVE** Someone who is **healthy** is well and is not suffering from any illness. ○ *To stay healthy your body needs regular exercise.* ○ *My number one goal is to get healthy .* ○ *a perfectly healthy baby boy*

▶ **COLLOCATIONS:**
be/stay/get healthy
look/feel healthy
a healthy **baby/child/man/woman**
perfectly healthy

▶ **SYNONYMS:** fit, well

▶ **ANTONYMS:** unhealthy, unwell

2 **ADJECTIVE** Something that is **healthy** is good for your health. ○ *I know I don't have a very healthy diet.* ○ *We work with patients to encourage healthier lifestyles.*

▶ **COLLOCATIONS:**
a healthy **diet/lifestyle/meal**
healthy **food/eating/living**

▶ **ANTONYM:** unhealthy

WORD FAMILY		
health	**UNCOUNT**	○ *She had never suffered any major health problems.*
healthy	**ADJECTIVE**	○ *I actually feel healthier than I did when I was younger.*
unhealthy	**ADJECTIVE**	○ *a bad diet and unhealthy lifestyle*
healthily	**ADVERB**	○ *I started to exercise regularly and eat healthily.*

---

health care /ˈhelθ keə/   HEALTH   WORK

UNCOUNTABLE NOUN **Health care** is the jobs and services that involve looking after people's health. ○ *I always wanted to work in health care.* ○ *doctors and other health care workers*

▶ **COLLOCATIONS:**
work in health care
a health care **worker/professional**
health care **services/jobs**
the health care **system**
health care **costs/facilities**

---

heat /hiːt/ (heats, heating, heated)   SCIENCE & NATURE

1 **VERB** When you **heat** something, you raise its temperature, for example by using a flame or a special piece of equipment. ○ *Gently heat the milk until it is warm.* ○ *When liquids and gases are heated, they expand and become less dense.* ○ *a heated swimming pool*

▶ **SYNONYM:** warm

▶ **ANTONYM:** cool

2 **UNCOUNTABLE NOUN** **Heat** is warmth or the quality of being hot. ○ [+ of] *the heat of the sun* ○ [+ from] *The heat from the fire was so intense that it melted the tyres.* ○ *They are thirsty and exhausted by the summer heat.*

▶ COLLOCATIONS:
the heat **from/of** something
generate/produce/absorb heat
intense heat
stifling/searing/sweltering heat
summer/midday/afternoon heat

▶ SYNONYM: warmth

▶ ANTONYM: cold

WORD FAMILY		
hot	ADJECTIVE	○ *Have plenty of cool drinks in hot weather.*
heat	VERB	○ *Wood as a source of energy is excellent for heating houses.*
heat	UNCOUNT	○ *New light bulbs generate less heat with less electricity.*

---

heavy /ˈhevi/ (heavier, heaviest) SCIENCE & NATURE

ADJECTIVE **Heavy** means great in amount, degree, or intensity. ○ *The rain was so heavy that we had difficulty seeing the road.* ○ *The traffic along Fitzjohn's Avenue was heavy.*

▶ COLLOCATIONS:
heavy **rain/snow**
heavy **traffic**

WORD FAMILY		
heavy	ADJECTIVE	○ *On this particular day, heavy snow had fallen.*
heavily	ADVERB	○ *It has been raining heavily all day.*

---

hedge /hedʒ/ (hedges) HOME

NOUN A **hedge** is a row of bushes or small trees, usually along the edge of a garden, field, or road. ○ *It was a large house set back behind a high hedge.*

---

heel /hiːl/ (heels) CLOTHES & APPEARANCE

1 **NOUN** Your **heel** is the back part of your foot, just below your ankle. ○ *The player is recovering from a heel injury.*

2 **NOUN** The **heel** of a shoe is the raised part on the bottom at the back. **Heels** are women's shoes with raised heels. ○ [+ of] *He kicked it shut with the heel of his boot.* ○ *a young woman in a simple red dress and high heels*

h

▶ **COLLOCATIONS:**
the heel **of** something
high/low heels
wear heels

---

hero /ˈhɪərəʊ/ (heroes) MEDIA & CULTURE

1 **NOUN** The **hero** of a book, play, film, or story is the main male character, who usually has good qualities. ○ [+ of] *The hero of Doctor Zhivago dies in 1929.* ○ *the American comic-book hero, Superman*

▶ **COLLOCATIONS:**
the hero **of** something
an **action** hero
a **movie/comic-book** hero

▶ **ANTONYM:** villain

2 **NOUN** A **hero** is someone, especially a man, who has done something brave, new, or good, and who is therefore greatly admired by a lot of people. ○ *He called Mr Mandela a hero who had inspired millions.* ○ *He became a national hero after winning a gold medal at the Olympic Games.*

▶ **COLLOCATIONS:**
become a hero
a **national/local** hero
a **true/real** hero
an **unsung** hero
a **war** hero
a **sporting/football/rugby** hero

WORD FAMILY		
hero	NOUN	○ *Who is your all-time sporting hero?*
heroine	NOUN	○ *Sophia, the novel's heroine, leaves home to start a new life.*
heroic	ADJECTIVE	○ *a heroic rescue attempt*
heroically	ADVERB	○ *Despite injury, Hamilton heroically carried on.*
heroism	UNCOUNT	○ *tales of heroism and sacrifice*

---

high /haɪ/ (higher, highest) SCIENCE & NATURE   HEALTH

ADJECTIVE If a food or other substance is **high in** a particular ingredient, it contains a large amount of that ingredient. ○ [+ in] *Rich sauces and fried food are high in fat.* ○ *Although cheese is quite high in calories, it is a good source of minerals.*

▶ **COLLOCATIONS:**
high **in** something
high in **fat/protein/fibre/sugar**
high in **calories/vitamins**

▶ **ANTONYM:** low

high|er edu|ca|tion /ˌhaɪə edʒʊˈkeɪʃən/

UNCOUNTABLE NOUN **Higher education** is education at universities and colleges. ○ *Around 10% of students in higher education discontinue their studies each year.*

▶ COLLOCATIONS:
  in higher education
  enter higher education
  a **college/institute/institution of** higher education
  a higher education **course/student**

high|lights /ˈhaɪlaɪts/

PLURAL NOUN The **highlights of** an event, activity, or period of time are the most interesting or exciting parts of it. ○ [+ *of*] *Viewers can watch highlights of the performances again on demand.* ○ *Highlights of the trip include visits to Paris and Bruges.* ○ *the football highlights show*

▶ COLLOCATIONS:
  highlights **of** *something*
  TV/football highlights

hik|ing /ˈhaɪkɪŋ/

UNCOUNTABLE NOUN **Hiking** is the activity of going for a long walk in the country. ○ *They went hiking in Switzerland.* ○ *heavy hiking boots*

▶ COLLOCATIONS:
  go hiking
  hiking **boots**
  a hiking **trail**

▶ SYNONYM: walking

WORD FAMILY		
hike	**VERB**	○ *You could hike through the Fish River Canyon.*
hike	**NOUN**	○ *She'd been on a long hike with Greg.*
hiking	**UNCOUNT**	○ *the excellent network of hiking trails*
hiker	**NOUN**	○ *a new 8km trail for cyclists and hikers*

hill /hɪl/ (hills)

NOUN A **hill** is an area of land that is higher than the land that surrounds it. ○ *They were climbing a hill just beyond the village.* ○ *Alston was a nice little town, built on a steep hill.*

▶ COLLOCATIONS:
  on a hill
  up/down a hill
  climb a hill
  a **steep/gentle** hill
  a **low/small/high** hill
  rugged/rolling hills

> **WORD FAMILY**
>
> | hill | **NOUN** | ○ a campsite right on the lakeside, surrounded by wooded hills |
> | hilly | **ADJECTIVE** | ○ The plane had crashed in a hilly area. |

his|to|ry /ˈhɪstəri/

1 UNCOUNTABLE NOUN You can refer to the events of the past as **history**. You can also refer to the past events which concern a particular topic or place as its history. ○ [+ of] the history of Birmingham ○ the greatest figure in modern Turkish history

▶ COLLOCATIONS:
  the history **of** something
  in/throughout history
  modern/recent/ancient history
  British/American/Japanese, etc. history
  art/political/military history
  history **shows/suggests** something

2 UNCOUNTABLE NOUN History is a subject studied in schools, colleges, and universities that deals with events that have happened in the past. ○ My favourite subjects are English and history. ○ She taught history and politics in a large London school.

▶ COLLOCATIONS:
  do/study history
  teach history
  a history **teacher/student/lesson**

his|tor|ic /hɪˈstɒrɪk, AM -ˈtɔːr-/

ADJECTIVE Something that is **historic** is important in history, or likely to be considered important at some time in the future. ○ Saint Petersburg has restored some of its historic buildings, palaces and monuments. ○ She says she's proud to be a part of this historic event.

▶ COLLOCATIONS:
  a historic **building/house**
  a historic **site/landmark**
  a historic **town/city**
  a historic **event/occasion**
  a historic **moment/day**
  a historic **victory/win**
  a historic **decision/agreement**

his|tori|cal /hɪˈstɒrɪkəl, AM -tɔːr-/

ADJECTIVE **Historical** people, situations, or things existed in the past and are considered to be a part of history. ○ Many significant historical figures have been *buried at the Cathedral.* ○ *major historical events, such as the First World War and the Russian Revolution*

▶ **COLLOCATION:** a historical **figure/event/novel**

> **WHICH WORD: historic** or **historical**?
>
> You use **historic** to describe something that is important in history or something that is likely to be considered important in the future. ○ *It will be a historic day for the club.*
>
> You use **historical** to describe people or things that have existed in history or are connected with history. ○ *The historical figure he most admires is Isaac Newton.*

> **WORD FAMILY**
>
> | history | UNCOUNT | ○ books on ancient Greek history |
> |---|---|---|
> | historic | ADJECTIVE | ○ Britain and France signed a historic agreement. |
> | historical | ADJECTIVE | ○ Iraq's many cultural and historical sites |
> | historically | ADVERB | ○ The new film is more historically accurate. |
> | historian | NOUN | ○ Local historians said there had once been a house on the hillside. |

---

hit /hɪt/ (hits) MEDIA & CULTURE

NOUN If a song, film, play, etc. is a **hit**, it is very popular and successful. ○ *The show became a massive hit.* ○ *The Rolling Stones had several hits in the 1960s.* ○ *Ephron's hit comedy 'Sleepless In Seattle'*

▶ **COLLOCATIONS:**
  become a hit
  have a hit
  a **big/huge/massive** hit
  an **instant** hit
  a **box-office** hit
  a hit **show/film/song/movie**
  a hit **single/album**

▶ **ANTONYM:** flop

---

hock|ey /ˈhɒki/ SPORT & ACTIVITY

UNCOUNTABLE NOUN Hockey is an outdoor game played between two teams of 11 players who use long curved sticks to hit a small ball and try to score goals. [BRIT; in AM, usually use **field hockey**] ○ *She played hockey for the national side.* ○ *the British hockey team*

▶ **COLLOCATIONS:**
  play hockey
  a hockey **player/team/game**
  a hockey **stick**

home page /ˈhəʊm peɪdʒ/   SHOPPING   COMMUNICATIONS
(home pages) also homepage

NOUN On the Internet, a person's or organization's **home page** is the main page of information about them, which often contains links to other pages about them. ○ To learn more, visit our home page. ○ On my home page, you will find details of some of my interests.

▸ **COLLOCATIONS:**
  on someone's home page
  visit a home page

home|sick /ˈhəʊmsɪk/   HOME

ADJECTIVE If you are **homesick**, you feel unhappy because you are away from home and are missing your family, friends, and home very much. ○ She's feeling a little homesick. ○ While I'm away I get quite homesick.

home town /ˌhəʊm ˈtaʊn/   HOME   PLACES

NOUN Your **home town** is the town or city where you were born or where you lived when you were a child. ○ [+ of] her home town of Edinburgh ○ She planned to go to stay with a friend in her home town.

▸ **COLLOCATIONS:**
  in someone's home town
  someone's home town **of** somewhere

hon|est /ˈɒnɪst/   PERSONALITY

ADJECTIVE If you describe someone as **honest**, you mean that they always tell the truth, and do not try to deceive people or break the law. ○ My dad was the most honest man I ever met. ○ I know she's honest and reliable.

▸ **SYNONYM:** truthful

▸ **ANTONYM:** dishonest

WORD FAMILY		
honest	**ADJECTIVE**	○ They're two of the most honest people I know.
honesty	**UNCOUNT**	○ Anderson is renowned for his honesty and integrity.
honestly	**ADVERB**	○ First we need to talk openly and honestly with each other.
dishonest	**ADJECTIVE**	○ Gray described Vincent as a 'thoroughly dishonest con-man'.

hood /hʊd/ (hoods)   CLOTHES & APPEARANCE

NOUN A **hood** is a part of a coat or sweater which you can pull up to cover your head. ○ Edward pulled the hood of his sweatshirt up over his head.

hood|ie /'hʊdi/ (hoodies) CLOTHES & APPEARANCE

NOUN A **hoodie** is a type of casual jacket with a hood. [INFORMAL] ○ *She wore jeans and a hoodie.*

hos|tel /'hɒstəl/ (hostels) TRANSPORT & TRAVEL

NOUN A **hostel** is a place where people can stay cheaply when they are travelling. ○ *We stayed in a hostel.* ○ *Australia's backpacker hostels*

▶ COLLOCATIONS:
in a hostel
a **youth/backpacker** hostel

ho|tel /ˌhəʊ'tel/ (hotels) TRANSPORT & TRAVEL

NOUN A **hotel** is a building where people stay, for example on holiday, paying for their rooms and meals. ○ *I had dinner at my hotel.* ○ *The bar here is for hotel guests only.*

▶ COLLOCATIONS:
in/at a hotel
stay in/at a hotel
book a hotel
own/run a hotel
check into/check out of a hotel
a **three-star/four-star**, etc. hotel
a **luxury/cheap/budget** hotel
a **city centre/country** hotel
a hotel **room/suite**
hotel **accommodation**
a hotel **guest/manager/owner**
hotel **staff**
a hotel **pool/restaurant**

house|hold /'haʊshəʊld/ (households) HOME

1 **NOUN** A **household** is all the people in a family or group who live together in a house. ○ *growing up in a male-only household* ○ *The average American household has access to 90 television channels.*

2 **UNCOUNTABLE NOUN** The **household** is your home and everything that is connected with looking after it. ○ *household chores* ○ *I pay all the household bills.*

▶ COLLOCATIONS:
in a household
the **average** household
a **poor/low-income** household
a household **task/chore**
household **goods/items/appliances**
a household **bill**

house|work /ˈhaʊswɜːk/

HOME

UNCOUNTABLE NOUN Housework is the work such as cleaning, washing, and ironing that you do in your home. ○ *My older sister always did the housework.* ○ *Mark and I share the housework.*

> **WHICH WORD: housework** or **homework**?
>
> You use **housework** for the work you do in your house, such as cleaning, washing, and ironing. ○ *I help all I can with childcare and housework.*
>
> You use **homework** for the school work that teachers give you to do at home. ○ *Have you done your English homework?*

hum /hʌm/ (hums, humming, hummed)

1 VERB If something **hums**, it makes a low continuous noise. ○ *The birds sang, the bees hummed.* ○ *There was a low humming sound in the sky.*

2 UNCOUNTABLE NOUN A **hum** is a low continuous noise. ○ [+ of] *the constant hum of traffic* ○ *There was a general hum of conversation around them.*

hu|man /ˈhjuːmən/

PEOPLE

ADJECTIVE Human means relating to or concerning people. ○ *The human body is between 50 and 65 per cent water.* ○ *The crash was the result of human error.*

▶ **COLLOCATIONS:**
the human **body/race/brain**
a human **being**
human **rights/life/nature**
human **error**

hu|man be|ing /ˌhjuːmən ˈbiːɪŋ/ (human beings)

PEOPLE

NOUN A **human being** is a man, woman, or child. ○ *Although they have committed crimes, they are still human beings.* ○ *the belief that human beings are superior to animals*

hu|mor|ous /ˈhjuːmərəs/

MEDIA & CULTURE

ADJECTIVE If someone or something is **humorous**, they are amusing and witty. ○ *The programme deals with politics in a humorous way.* ○ *He was quite humorous, and I liked that about him.*

▶ **SYNONYMS:** amusing, funny, witty

> **WORD FAMILY**
>
> | humour | **UNCOUNT** | ○ *She is a fan of his outrageous humour.* |
> | humorous | **ADJECTIVE** | ○ *a humorous story* |
> | humorously | **ADVERB** | ○ *He regarded the whole thing humorously.* |

hunt /hʌnt/ (hunts, hunting, hunted)

HISTORY

VERB When people or animals **hunt**, they chase and kill wild animals for food or as a sport. ○ *Our ancestors hunted animals and gathered plants for food.* ○ *A leopard hunts alone.*

WORD FAMILY		
hunt	NOUN	○ *a bear hunt* ○ *a fox hunt*
hunt	VERB	○ *As a child I learned to hunt and fish.*
hunting	UNCOUNT	○ *They used to go hunting together.*
hunter	NOUN	○ *a deer hunter* ○ *big-game hunters*

hur|ri|cane /ˈhʌrɪkən, AM ˈhɜːrɪkeɪn/ (hurricanes)

SCIENCE & NATURE

NOUN A **hurricane** is an extremely violent wind or storm. ○ *Many buildings were destroyed by the hurricane.*

▶ **COLLOCATIONS:**
a **major/powerful/strong** hurricane
a hurricane **hits/strikes**
a hurricane **destroys** something
hurricane **season/damage**

h

ice /aɪs/

UNCOUNTABLE NOUN **Ice** is frozen water. ○ *Glaciers are moving rivers of ice.* ○ *The ice is melting.*

▶ COLLOCATIONS:
ice **melts/breaks/forms**
thin/black/crushed ice
an ice **cube/sheet/cap**

WORD FAMILY		
ice	**NOUN**	○ *The road was covered with black ice.*
icy	**ADJECTIVE**	○ *an icy wind* ○ *a bucket of icy water*

ice hock|ey /ˈaɪs hɒki/

UNCOUNTABLE NOUN **Ice hockey** is a game played on ice between two teams of 11 players using long curved sticks. [mainly BRIT; in AM, usually use **hockey**] ○ *They didn't even know we played ice hockey in England*

▶ COLLOCATIONS:
play ice hockey
an ice hockey **match/arena/club**
an ice hockey **player/team**

ig|nore /ɪgˈnɔː/ (ignores, ignoring, ignored)

VERB If you **ignore** someone or something, you pay no attention to them. ○ *I said hello but she completely ignored me.* ○ *She ignored my advice to stay away from her ex-boyfriend.*

▶ COLLOCATIONS:
ignore *someone's* **advice**
ignore a **fact/warning/problem**
completely/virtually/deliberately ignore *someone/something*
choose to/try to ignore *something*
hard to/impossible to ignore

WORD FAMILY

ignore	**VERB**	○ They had ignored the warning signs.
ignorant	**ADJECTIVE**	○ He doesn't ask questions because he doesn't want to seem ignorant.
ignorance	**UNCOUNT**	○ I am embarrassed by my ignorance of European history.

---

im|age /'ɪmɪdʒ/ (images)   ▐ MEDIA & CULTURE ▌

1 NOUN If you have an **image** of something or someone, you have a picture or idea of them in your mind. ○ [+ of] Some people have an image of football fans as thugs. ○ The words 'Cote d'Azur' conjure up images of sunny days in Mediterranean cafes.

▶ **SYNONYM:** picture

2 NOUN The **image** of a person, group, or organization is the way that they appear to other people. ○ I don't think she should change her image at all. ○ The tobacco industry has been trying to improve its image.

▶ **COLLOCATIONS:**
an image **of** someone/something
an image **as** something
conjure up an image
have/create/project an image
improve/change your image
damage someone's image
someone's **public** image
a **new/positive** image
a **powerful** image

---

im|agi|na|tive /ɪ'mædʒɪnətɪv/   ▐ PERSONALITY ▌

ADJECTIVE If you are **imaginative** or you have **imaginative** ideas, you are easily able to think of or create new or exciting things. ○ an imaginative writer ○ Try to think of a more imaginative way of presenting your work.

▶ **SYNONYMS:** inventive, creative

▶ **ANTONYM:** unimaginative

WORD FAMILY

imagine	**VERB**	○ Imagine you're lying on a beach.
imagination	**UNCOUNT**	○ Dressing the same as everyone else shows no imagination.
imaginative	**ADJECTIVE**	○ hundreds of cooking ideas and imaginative recipes
imaginatively	**ADVERB**	○ The hotel is decorated imaginatively and attractively.
unimaginative	**ADJECTIVE**	○ The design of the phone is dull and unimaginative.

im|pact /'ɪmpækt/

SCIENCE & NATURE

NOUN If something has an **impact on** a situation or person, it has a strong effect on them. ○ [+ on] *All methods of making electricity have an impact on the environment.* ○ [+ of] *the impact of technology on the workplace*

▶ **COLLOCATIONS:**
an impact **on** something
the impact **of** something
have/make an impact
the **likely** impact
the **full** impact
the **immediate/long-term** impact
a **big/negative** impact
an **environmental/economic** impact

im|pres|sive /ɪm'presɪv/

ADJECTIVE Something that is **impressive** impresses you, for example because it is great in size or degree, or is done with a lot of skill. ○ *It is an impressive achievement.* ○ *The film's special effects are particularly impressive.*

▶ **COLLOCATIONS:**
an impressive **win/result/achievement**
an impressive **performance/display/start**
an impressive **record/list**
an impressive **number/range**
look/sound impressive

▶ **ANTONYM:** unimpressive

WORD FAMILY		
impress	**VERB**	○ *The boys were trying to impress their girlfriends.*
impression	**NOUN**	○ *I wanted to make a good impression.*
impressive	**ADJECTIVE**	○ *He looked very impressive in his last match.*
impressively	**ADVERB**	○ *The team performed impressively in the football competition.*
impressed	**ADJECTIVE**	○ *I'm very impressed with the new airport.*
unimpressive	**ADJECTIVE**	○ *England gave an unimpressive performance.*

in|come /'ɪnkʌm/ (incomes)

WORK   MONEY

NOUN A person's or organization's **income** is the money that they earn or receive. ○ *Many families on low incomes cannot afford to send their children to college.* ○ [+ of] *an annual income of £15 million*

▶ **COLLOCATIONS:**
on an income
an income **of** something
have/earn/receive an income

increase/reduce/lose your income
someone's income rises/falls
a low/high income
someone's current/annual/total income
income tax

▶ SYNONYMS: pay, salary, wages

---

in|di|vid|ual /ˌɪndɪˈvɪdʒʊəl/ (individuals) `PEOPLE`

1 **ADJECTIVE Individual** means relating to one person or thing, rather than to a
large group. ○ *The charges are £25 for an individual membership and £44 for a family
membership.* ○ *Divide the vegetables among four individual dishes.*

2 **NOUN** An **individual** is a person. ○ *Andy Murray is a very talented individual.*
○ *the rights and responsibilities of the individual.*

▶ SYNONYMS: human being, person

WORD FAMILY		
individual	ADJECTIVE	○ *Wait for the group to decide rather than making individual decisions.*
individual	NOUN	○ *Only a few individuals are to blame for the crisis.*
individually	ADVERB	○ *Individually, many of these pictures are superb.*
individuality	UNCOUNT	○ *People should be free to express their individuality.*

---

in|fec|tion /ɪnˈfekʃən/ (infections) `HEALTH`

NOUN An **infection** is a disease caused by germs or bacteria. ○ *She thought she had
a chest infection.* ○ *Exactly which bacteria cause the infection is still unknown.*

▶ COLLOCATIONS:
have/get/spread an infection
cause/prevent/treat an infection
a serious/common/deadly infection
a viral/bacterial/fungal infection
a chest/ear/throat/eye infection

WORD FAMILY		
infect	VERB	○ *Healthy cells are infected by the virus.*
infection	NOUN	○ *I had an ear infection.*
infectious	ADJECTIVE	○ *The disease is highly infectious.*

---

in|for|ma|tion tech|nol|ogy /ɪnfəˌmeɪʃən tekˈnɒlədʒi/ `WORK`

UNCOUNTABLE NOUN Information technology is the work of using computers to
store and analyse information. The abbreviation **IT** is often used. ○ *My father
works in information technology.* ○ *the IT department*

in|gre|di|ents /ɪnˈgriːdiənts/ FOOD & DRINK

PLURAL NOUN **Ingredients** are all the different foods you use when you are cooking a particular dish. ○ *Mix in the remaining ingredients.* ○ *Their products contain only natural ingredients.*

▶ COLLOCATIONS:
   add/mix/combine ingredients
   contain ingredients
   the main/basic/vital ingredients
   natural/fresh/dry ingredients

---

in|hab|it|ant /ɪnˈhæbɪtənt/ (inhabitants) PEOPLE   PLACES

NOUN The **inhabitants** of a place are the people who live there. ○ [+ *of*] *the inhabitants of Glasgow* ○ *There are only about 40 inhabitants left in the village.*

WORD FAMILY		
inhabit	VERB	○ *the people who inhabit these beautiful islands*
inhabited	ADJECTIVE	○ *An inhabited house is more interesting than an empty one.*
uninhabited	ADJECTIVE	○ *The area is largely uninhabited.*
inhabitant	NOUN	○ *We are the inhabitants of this city.*

---

in|jec|tion /ɪnˈdʒekʃən/ (injections) HEALTH

NOUN If you have an **injection**, a doctor or nurse puts a medicine into your body using a device with a needle called a syringe. ○ *They gave me an injection to help me sleep.* ○ *When did you last have a tetanus injection?*

▶ COLLOCATIONS:
   give *someone* an injection
   have/need/get an injection
   a pain-killing injection
   daily/regular injections
   a steroid/insulin/tetanus injection

WORD FAMILY		
inject	VERB	○ *She was injected with painkillers.*
injection	NOUN	○ *I hate having injections.*

---

in|ju|ry /ˈɪndʒəri/ (injuries) HEALTH

NOUN An **injury** is damage done to someone's body. ○ *He suffered a serious head injury in the crash.* ○ *Physiotherapists can offer advice on how to avoid injuries.*

▶ COLLOCATIONS:
   a serious/minor injury
   internal injuries

a **head/back/knee** injury
suffer/have/cause an injury
prevent/avoid an injury

in|jured /ˈɪndʒəd/

ADJECTIVE An **injured** person has physical damage to part of their body, usually as a result of an accident or fighting. ○ *The team was missing several injured players.* ○ *Many of them died because they were so badly injured.* ○ *an injured left ankle*

▶ COLLOCATIONS:
seriously/badly/critically injured
an injured **soldier/player/worker**
an injured **knee/ankle/shoulder**

WORD FAMILY		
injure	**VERB**	○ *She injured her knee during a dance routine.*
injured	**ADJECTIVE**	○ *He was seriously injured in a car accident.*
injury	**NOUN**	○ *He can't play because he has an injury.*

---

in-law /ˈɪnlɔː/ PEOPLE

COMBINING FORM The word **in-law** is used after the names of some relatives to show that they are related to you by marriage. For example, your **brother-in-law** is the husband of your sister or the brother of your wife. ○ *We visited my sister and brother-in-law in Germany.*

WORD FAMILY		
mother-in-law	**NOUN**	○ *She doesn't get on with her mother-in-law.*
father-in-law	**NOUN**	○ *He wanted to impress his future father-in-law.*
sister-in-law	**NOUN**	○ *My sisters-in-law and I are good friends.*
brother-in-law	**NOUN**	○ *Next week my brother-in-law is coming to stay.*
son-in-law	**NOUN**	○ *Their daughter and son-in-law were injured in the crash.*
daughter-in-law	**NOUN**	○ *She lives with her son and daughter-in-law.*

---

in|no|cent /ˈɪnəsənt/ CRIME

ADJECTIVE If someone is **innocent**, they did not commit a crime which they have been accused of. ○ *The police knew from day one that I was innocent.* ○ *[+ of] He was sure that the man was innocent of any crime.*

▶ COLLOCATIONS:
innocent **of** *something*
innocent of a **crime/charge**
innocent of **murder/assault**
plead innocent
find/prove *someone* innocent
completely/totally innocent

▶ **ANTONYM:** guilty

WORD FAMILY

innocent	ADJECTIVE	○ *A jury found him innocent of murder.*
innocently	ADVERB	○ *The baby smiled innocently.*
innocence	UNCOUNT	○ *He was unable to prove his innocence.*

---

in|no|va|tive /ˈɪnəveɪtɪv/

1 ADJECTIVE Something that is **innovative** is new and original. ○ *an innovative business idea* ○ *products which are more innovative than those of their competitors*

▶ **SYNONYMS:** original, inventive

2 ADJECTIVE An **innovative** person introduces changes and new ideas. ○ *He was one of the most creative and innovative engineers of his generation.*

▶ **SYNONYM:** creative

WORD FAMILY

innovate	VERB	○ *Successful companies are constantly innovating.*
innovation	NOUN	○ *It is the latest innovation in mobile phones.*
innovative	ADJECTIVE	○ *The students tried some innovative ways of raising money.*
innovatively	ADVERB	○ *We were encouraged to think innovatively.*

---

in|sist /ɪnˈsɪst/ (insists, insisting, insisted)   BELIEFS & OPINIONS

VERB If you **insist that** something should be done, you say very firmly that it must be done. ○ [+ *that*] *My parents insisted that I should finish my studies.* ○ [+ *on*] *She insisted on being present at all the interviews.*

▶ **COLLOCATION:** insist **on** *something*

WORD FAMILY

insist	VERB	○ *I didn't want to join in, but Kenneth insisted.*
insistence	UNCOUNT	○ *She had come to the party at her boyfriend's insistence.*
insistent	ADJECTIVE	○ *He was insistent that the matter should be resolved quickly.*
insistently	ADVERB	○ *'What is it?' his wife asked again, gently but insistently.*

---

in|spire /ɪnˈspaɪə/ (inspires, inspiring, inspired)

1 VERB If someone or something **inspires** you **to** do something new or unusual, they make you want to do it. ○ [+ *to-inf*] *What inspired you to change your name?*

▶ **SYNONYM:** motivate

2 VERB If someone or something **inspires** you, they give you new ideas and a strong feeling of enthusiasm. ○ *Jimi Hendrix inspired a generation of guitarists.* ○ *It's a story that should inspire people.*

WORD FAMILY		
inspire	**VERB**	○ *The book was inspired by a real person.*
inspiring	**ADJECTIVE**	○ *She is a brilliant and inspiring teacher.*
inspiration	**UNCOUNT**	○ *I need some inspiration for my next essay.*
inspirational	**ADJECTIVE**	○ *Gandhi was an inspirational figure.*

in|struc|tion /ɪnˈstrʌkʃən/ (instructions)

1 NOUN An **instruction** is something that someone tells you to do. ○ [+ to-inf] *They were given strict instructions to be home before 10 o'clock.* ○ *He lost his job because he refused to obey a direct instruction.*

▶ **COLLOCATIONS:**
   give *someone* an instruction
   receive/get an instruction
   obey/ignore an instruction
   strict/specific instructions

▶ **SYNONYM:** order

2 PLURAL NOUN Instructions are clear and detailed information on how to do something. ○ *Always read the instructions before you start taking the medicine.* ○ [+ on] *some basic instructions on how to use the washing machine*

▶ **COLLOCATIONS:**
   instructions **on** *something*
   read/follow the instructions
   clear/simple/written instructions
   detailed/full instructions
   step-by-step instructions
   on-screen instructions
   an instruction **book/manual/sheet**

▶ **SYNONYM:** directions

WORD FAMILY		
instruct	**VERB**	○ *He was instructed to take his medicine with food.*
instruction	**NOUN**	○ *Follow the on-screen instructions.*
instructor	**NOUN**	○ *his karate instructor* ○ *a driving instructor*

in|stru|ment /ˈɪnstrəmənt/   SCIENCE & NATURE   MEDIA & CULTURE
(instruments)

1 NOUN An **instrument** is a tool or device that is used to do a medical or scientific task. ○ *The spacecraft will have about 60 scientific instruments on board.* ○ [+ for] *instruments for cleaning and polishing teeth*

▶ COLLOCATIONS:
an instrument **for** something
a **scientific/surgical/medical** instrument

2 NOUN A musical **instrument** is an object such as a piano, guitar, or flute. ○ *Do you play any instruments?* ○ *Learning a musical instrument introduces a child to an understanding of music.*

▶ COLLOCATIONS:
play/learn an instrument
a **musical** instrument
a **stringed/wind/brass** instrument

---

in|tel|li|gent /ɪnˈtelɪdʒənt/

PERSONALITY

ADJECTIVE An **intelligent** person has the ability to think, understand, and learn things quickly and well. ○ *Susan's a very bright and intelligent woman.* ○ *We were all impressed by the child's intelligent questions.*

▶ COLLOCATIONS:
very/highly/reasonably intelligent
look/seem intelligent
an intelligent **decision/question**
intelligent **conversation**

▶ SYNONYMS: bright, clever

▶ ANTONYMS: stupid, unintelligent

in|tel|li|gence /ɪnˈtelɪdʒəns/

UNCOUNTABLE NOUN **Intelligence** is the quality of being intelligent. ○ *Her written work shows intelligence and maturity.* ○ *They were given a well-known test for measuring intelligence.*

▶ COLLOCATIONS:
great/low/average intelligence
need/show intelligence
measure/improve/develop someone's intelligence
an intelligence **test**

WORD FAMILY		
intelligent	**ADJECTIVE**	○ *Paul is the most intelligent man I have ever met.*
intelligently	**ADVERB**	○ *She spoke clearly and intelligently.*
intelligence	**UNCOUNT**	○ *Play helps develop a child's intelligence.*

---

in|ten|tion /ɪnˈtenʃən/ (intentions)

NOUN An **intention** is an idea or plan of what you are going to do. ○ [+ to-inf] *It is my intention to study overseas.* ○ *Unfortunately, his good intentions never seemed to last long.*

→ see Useful Phrases **have no/every intention**

▶ **COLLOCATIONS:**
have an intention
express/announce/state an intention
someone's **true/real/original** intention
a **clear** intention
good/bad/evil intentions

WORD FAMILY		
intend	**VERB**	○ *I intend to go to university.*
intention	**NOUN**	○ *Her original intention was to become a nurse.*
intentional	**ADJECTIVE**	○ *The kick was clearly intentional.*
intentionally	**ADVERB**	○ *I've never intentionally hurt anyone.*
unintentional	**ADJECTIVE**	○ *I'm sorry I upset you. It was quite unintentional.*
unintentionally	**ADVERB**	○ *A user who unintentionally deletes a document can use the tool to find it.*

in|ter|est /ˈɪntrəst, -tərest/ **(interests)** `FREE TIME`

1 UNCOUNTABLE NOUN If you have an **interest in** something, you want to learn or hear more about it. ○ [+ in] *His parents tried to discourage his interest in music.* ○ *She'd liked him at first, but soon lost interest.*

▶ **COLLOCATIONS:**
interest **in** *something*
of interest (**to** *someone*)
have/show/take an interest
express/lose/attract interest
hold *someone's* interest
great/little/real interest
a **level of** interest
a **place of** interest

2 NOUN Your **interests** are the things that you enjoy doing. ○ *Her interests include cooking and photography.* ○ *Have you got any other hobbies or interests?*

▶ **SYNONYM:** hobby

in|ter|est|ed /ˈɪntrestɪd/

ADJECTIVE If you are **interested in** something, you think it is important and want to learn more about it or spend time doing it. ○ [+ in] *I thought she might be interested in what I had to say.* ○ [+ to-inf] *I'd be interested to meet her.*

▶ **COLLOCATIONS:**
interested **in** *something*
interested **to see/know/hear** *something*
interested **to read/learn** *something*
very/really/particularly interested
genuinely/seriously interested

become/get interested
seem/look interested
keep *someone* interested

WORD FAMILY		
interest	NOUN	○ Food was of no interest to her at all.
interest	VERB	○ These are the stories that interest me.
interested	ADJECTIVE	○ I started getting interested in astronomy when I was a child.
interesting	ADJECTIVE	○ a very interesting book ○ It was interesting to be in a different environment.
interestingly	ADVERB	○ Interestingly, Benjamin never married.

inter|view /ˈɪntəvjuː/
(interviews, interviewing, interviewed)

`MEDIA & CULTURE` `WORK`

1 NOUN An **interview** is a formal meeting at which someone is asked questions in order to find out if they are suitable for a job or a course of study. ○ *The interview went well.* ○ *[+ for] When I went for my first interview for this job I arrived extremely early.*

▶ COLLOCATIONS:
an interview **for** *something*
an interview for a **job/position/post**
have/get an interview
go for/attend an interview
invite *someone* **for** an interview
conduct an interview
a **job** interview
a **face-to-face/telephone** interview
a **first/second/final/follow-up** interview
an interview **question**
an interview **panel/candidate**
interview **technique/skills**

2 VERB If you **are interviewed** for a particular job or course of study, someone asks you questions about yourself to find out if you are suitable for it. ○ *[+ for] Three candidates were interviewed for the job.* ○ *When Wardell was interviewed, he was very impressive.*

▶ COLLOCATIONS:
interview *someone* **for** *something*
interview *someone* for a **job/position/post**

3 NOUN An **interview** is a conversation in which a journalist puts questions to someone such as a famous person or politician. ○ *He gave an interview to the Chicago Tribune newspaper last month.* ○ *[+ with] There'll be an interview with Mr Brown after the news.*

▶ COLLOCATIONS:
an interview **with** someone
give/do an interview
read/see an interview
publish/broadcast an interview
a **recent/rare/live** interview
a **full/in-depth** interview
an **exclusive** interview
a **television/radio/newspaper/magazine** interview
an interview **request**

4 VERB When a journalist **interviews** someone such as a famous person, they ask them a series of questions. ○ *Her favourite band were being interviewed on television.*

WORD FAMILY		
interview	NOUN	○ *Only the best candidates are invited for an interview.*
interview	VERB	○ *He was interviewed for a management job.*
interviewer	NOUN	○ *Being a good interviewer requires a lot of skill.*
interviewee	NOUN	○ *She waited nervously with the other interviewees.*

---

intro|duce /ˌɪntrəˈdjuːs, AM -ˈduːs/ `HISTORY`
(introduces, introducing, introduced)

VERB To **introduce** something means to cause it to enter a place or exist in a system for the first time. ○ *Electronic entry code systems were introduced in the 1970s.* ○ [+ to] *The word 'Pagoda' was introduced to Europe by the Portuguese.*

▶ COLLOCATIONS:
introduce something **to** something
introduce a **law/rule/system**
introduce a **change/reform**

WORD FAMILY		
introduce	VERB	○ *Many changes were introduced at that time.*
introduction	UNCOUNT	○ *He is best remembered for the introduction of the moving assembly-line.*
introductory	ADJECTIVE	○ *The product is available at an introductory price of £3.99.*

---

in|vade /ɪnˈveɪd/ (invades, invading, invaded) `HISTORY`

VERB To **invade** a country means to enter it by force with an army. ○ *Spanish troops invaded Belgium in 1585.* ○ *The capital city was invaded by hundreds of soldiers.*

▶ COLLOCATIONS:
an **army** invades somewhere
troops/forces/rebels invade somewhere
invade a **country/island/city**

in|va|sion /ɪnˈveɪʒən/ (invasions)

NOUN If there is an **invasion** of a country, a foreign army enters it by force.
   ○ [+ of] the Roman invasion of Britain ○ Argentina was about to launch a full-scale invasion.

▶ **COLLOCATIONS:**
   an invasion **of** somewhere
   launch/lead/order an invasion
   a **military/foreign** invasion
   a **full-scale/massive** invasion

WORD FAMILY		
invade	**VERB**	○ In autumn 1944 the allies invaded the Italian mainland.
invasion	**NOUN**	○ He was commander in chief during the invasion of Panama.
invader	**NOUN**	○ action against a foreign invader ○ invaders from the north

in|vent /ɪnˈvent/ (invents, inventing, invented)   `HISTORY`

VERB If you **invent** something such as a machine or process, you are the first person to think of it or make it. ○ He invented the first electric clock. ○ Writing had not been invented as yet.

▶ **SYNONYMS:** come up with, devise

in|ven|tion /ɪnˈvenʃən/ (inventions)   `SCIENCE & NATURE`

NOUN An **invention** is a machine, device, or system that has been invented by someone. ○ The spinning wheel was a Chinese invention. ○ He is preparing to test his latest invention.

▶ **COLLOCATIONS:**
   a **new/great/ingenious** invention
   a **modern/recent** invention
   someone's **latest** invention

WORD FAMILY		
invent	**VERB**	○ A new type of satellite has been invented by scientists.
invention	**NOUN**	○ His greatest invention came in 1839.
inventor	**NOUN**	○ Alexander Graham Bell, the inventor of the telephone
inventive	**ADJECTIVE**	○ She taught me to be more inventive with my cooking.

in|ves|ti|gate /ɪnˈvɛstɪgeɪt/ `SCIENCE & NATURE` `CRIME`
(investigates, investigating, investigated)

VERB If someone **investigates** something, they try to find out what happened or what is the truth. ○ [+ how] *Police are still investigating how the accident happened.* ○ *The scientists investigated the effects of chemicals found in food.*

▶ **COLLOCATIONS:**
   police/detectives/officials investigate *something*
   scientists/researchers investigate *something*
   investigate a **claim/complaint/allegation**
   investigate a **case/murder/crime**
   investigate the **cause/effects** of *something*
   investigate *something* **thoroughly/fully/properly**
   investigate *something* **further**

WORD FAMILY		
investigate	**VERB**	○ *Gas officials are investigating the cause of an explosion.*
investigation	**NOUN**	○ *He ordered an investigation into the affair.*
investigator	**NOUN**	○ *Police investigators believe he was murdered.*

in|volve /ɪnˈvɒlv/ **(involves, involving, involved)**

VERB If a situation or activity **involves** something, that thing is a necessary part or consequence of it. ○ *Working as a waitress involves a great deal of hard work.* ○ [+ v-ing] *Nicky's job involves spending quite a lot of time with other people.*

in|volved in /ɪnˈvɒlvd ɪn/

1 ADJECTIVE If you are **involved in** a situation or activity, you are taking part in it or have a strong connection with it. ○ [+ v-ing] *She was closely involved in setting up a students' council.* ○ *an organisation for people involved in agriculture*

▶ **COLLOCATIONS:**
   directly/closely/personally involved in *something*
   heavily/actively/deeply involved in *something*

2 ADJECTIVE The things **involved in** something such as a job or system are the necessary parts or consequences of it. ○ *He cannot reveal how much money is involved in the scheme.* ○ [+ v-ing] *The time and hard work involved in completing such an assignment are worthwhile.*

WORD FAMILY		
involve	**VERB**	○ *All sports involve a certain amount of risk.*
involved in	**ADJECTIVE**	○ *She was not directly involved in the decision.*
involvement	**UNCOUNT**	○ *My first involvement in politics was in 1986.*

is|sue /ˈɪsjuː, ˈɪʃuː/ (issues)   `MEDIA & CULTURE`

1 NOUN An **issue** is an important subject that people are arguing about or discussing. ○ [+ *of*] *I will raise the issue of holiday pay when I next see my manager.* ○ *The public are now more aware of environmental issues.*

▶ **COLLOCATIONS:**
the issue **of** *something*
raise/address/discuss an issue
resolve/tackle/settle an issue
consider/examine an issue
be/become an issue
a **big/key/important** issue
the **real** issue
a **sensitive/controversial/serious** issue
a **political/social/environmental** issue
a **safety/health/family** issue

▶ **SYNONYMS:** subject, matter

2 NOUN An **issue** of a magazine or newspaper is a particular edition of it. ○ [+ *of*] *the latest issue of the 'Lancet' magazine*

Jj

jack|et /ˈdʒækɪt/ (jackets)

NOUN A **jacket** is a short coat with long sleeves. ○ *He was wearing a black leather jacket.*

▶ **COLLOCATIONS:**
  wear/put on/take off a jacket
  a **black/dark/short/smart** jacket
  a **tailored/fitted/hooded** jacket
  a **leather/denim** jacket
  a **dinner** jacket

▶ **SYNONYM:** coat

jazz /dʒæz/

UNCOUNTABLE NOUN **Jazz** is a style of music that was invented by African American musicians in the early part of the twentieth century. It has very strong rhythms and the musicians often improvise. ○ *The club has live jazz on Sundays.* ○ *the great American jazz pianist George Shearing*

▶ **COLLOCATIONS:**
  play jazz
  jazz **music**
  a jazz **musician/singer/band**
  a jazz **pianist/guitarist/trumpeter**
  a jazz **club/festival/concert**
  modern/traditional jazz

jeal|ous /ˈdʒeləs/

1 **ADJECTIVE** If someone is **jealous**, they feel angry or bitter because they think that another person is trying to take a partner, friend or possession away from them. ○ *My girlfriend gets jealous if she sees me talking to other girls.*

2 **ADJECTIVE** If you are **jealous of** another person's possessions or qualities, you feel angry or bitter because you do not have them. ○ [+ *of*] *She was jealous of his wealth.* ○ *You're jealous because the record company rejected your idea.*

▶ **COLLOCATIONS:**
  jealous **of** *someone/something*
  very/insanely/really jealous
  a little/a bit jealous
  be/feel jealous

get/become jealous
a jealous **husband/rival/girlfriend**
a jealous **rage**

▶ SYNONYM: envious

WORD FAMILY		
jealous	ADJECTIVE	○ I couldn't help feeling a bit jealous.
jealously	ADVERB	○ The formula is jealously guarded.
jealousy	UNCOUNT	○ Her beauty causes envy and jealousy.

---

jeans /dʒiːnz/

PLURAL NOUN Jeans are casual trousers that are usually made of strong blue denim. ○ She was wearing jeans and a T-shirt.

▶ COLLOCATIONS:
wear jeans
a **pair of** jeans
tight/baggy/skinny/cut-off jeans
blue/black/white jeans
faded/ripped/flared jeans
designer jeans

---

jet lag /ˈdʒet ˌlæg/ [HEALTH] [TRANSPORT & TRAVEL]

UNCOUNTABLE NOUN If you are suffering from **jet lag**, you feel tired and slightly confused after a long journey by aeroplane. ○ I love travelling and don't get jet lag.

▶ COLLOCATIONS:
suffer from/have/get jet lag
reduce/prevent jet lag

WORD FAMILY		
jet lag	UNCOUNT	○ Travelling westwards can help to reduce jet lag.
jet-lagged	ADJECTIVE	○ I'm still jet-lagged from my trip to Australia.

---

jew|el|lery /ˈdʒuːəlri/ [in AM, use **jewelry**] [MEDIA & CULTURE]

UNCOUNTABLE NOUN Jewellery consists of ornaments that people wear such as rings and bracelets. ○ She doesn't wear much jewellery.

▶ COLLOCATIONS:
wear jewellery
make/design jewellery
a **piece of** jewellery
gold/silver jewellery
expensive/cheap jewellery
a jewellery **shop/box/designer**

WORD FAMILY

jewellery	**UNCOUNT**	○ some unusual pieces of silver jewellery
jeweller	**NOUN**	○ I bought the ring from a local jeweller.

---

jig|saw /'dʒɪgsɔː/ (jigsaws)   FREE TIME

NOUN A **jigsaw** or **jigsaw puzzle** is a picture on cardboard or wood that has been cut up into odd shapes. You have to make the picture again by putting the pieces together correctly. ○ I felt like a two-year-old trying to do a jigsaw.

---

job /dʒɒb/ (jobs)   WORK

NOUN A **job** is the work that someone does to earn money. ○ She took a holiday job as a nanny. ○ Thousands have lost their jobs. ○ I felt the pressure of being the first woman in the job.

▶ **COLLOCATIONS:**
a job **as** something
in a job
do/have/hold down a job
get/find/take a job
give/offer someone a job
lose/leave/change your job
a **good/top** job
a **dead-end** job
a **difficult/stressful** job
your **first/old/new** job
your **dream** job
a **part-time/full-time** job
a **summer/holiday/Saturday** job
an **office/factory** job
a job **offer/interview/application**
a job **opportunity/vacancy**
the jobs **market**
job **losses/cuts**
job **security/satisfaction**
your job **prospects**

▶ **SYNONYM:** occupation

WHICH WORD: job, work, or occupation?

You use **job** to talk about the particular activity that someone does to earn money, especially when they are an employee in an organization. ○ After I finish school, I will get a job.

Use **work** to talk more generally about the activity of working, for example when saying whether or not someone has a job or what kind of a job they have. ○ I was out of work at the time. ○ What kind of work do you do?

Occupation is a more formal word for 'job' often used on official forms. ○ Please give your name, address and occupation.

jog|ging /ˈdʒɒgɪŋ/ `SPORT & ACTIVITY`

UNCOUNTABLE NOUN Jogging is the activity of running slowly, often as a form of exercise. ○ *We go jogging in the park every day.*

▶ **SYNONYM:** running

jour|nal|ist /ˈdʒɜːnəlɪst/ **(journalists)** `MEDIA & CULTURE`

NOUN A **journalist** is a person whose job is to collect news and write about it for newspapers, magazines, television, or radio. ○ *He wanted to be a journalist and work for a newspaper.* ○ [+ with] *a journalist with the Financial Times*

▶ **COLLOCATIONS:**
   a journalist **with** something
   be/become a journalist
   a **foreign/local** journalist
   a **political** journalist
   a **television/newspaper/radio** journalist
   a **sports/music/fashion** journalist
   a **freelance** journalist

▶ **SYNONYM:** reporter

jour|nal|ism /ˈdʒɜːnəlɪsm/

UNCOUNTABLE NOUN Journalism is the job of being a journalist. ○ *He began a career in journalism, working on a local newspaper.* ○ *It was an accomplished piece of investigative journalism.*

▶ **COLLOCATIONS:**
   study/teach journalism
   investigative/tabloid/online journalism
   good/serious journalism
   sports/music/fashion journalism
   broadcast/print journalism
   a journalism **course/degree/career**
   a journalism **student/professor**

▶ **SYNONYM:** reporting

jour|ney /ˈdʒɜːni/ **(journeys)** `TRANSPORT & TRAVEL`

NOUN When you make a **journey**, you travel from one place to another. ○ [+ to] *During the journey to the airport he was followed by photographers.* ○ *We were exhausted after the long journey.*

→ see note at **travel**

▶ **COLLOCATIONS:**
   a journey **to** somewhere
   go on/make/do a journey
   start/complete/continue a journey
   a **long/short** journey

a **safe/difficult/dangerous** journey
a **return** journey
a **train/car/bus** journey

judo /ˈdʒuːdəʊ/ SPORT & ACTIVITY

UNCOUNTABLE NOUN **Judo** is a sport in which two people fight and try to throw each other to the ground. ○ *I started doing judo when I was 9 years old.*

▶ COLLOCATIONS:
do judo
a judo **champion/team**
a judo **club/class**

juice /dʒuːs/ FOOD & DRINK

UNCOUNTABLE NOUN **Juice** is the liquid from a fruit. ○ *a glass of fresh orange juice* ○ *Soak the couscous overnight in the juice of about six lemons.*

▶ COLLOCATIONS:
fruit juice
orange/apple/tomato juice
a **glass/bottle** of juice

jump|er /ˈdʒʌmpə/ (jumpers) CLOTHES & APPEARANCE

NOUN A **jumper** is a warm knitted piece of clothing which covers the upper part of your body and your arms. [BRIT; in AM, use **sweater**] ○ *He was wearing a thick woolly jumper.*

▶ COLLOCATIONS:
wear/put on/take off a jumper
make/knit a jumper
a **long/baggy/woolly** jumper

▶ SYNONYMS: sweater, pullover

junk food /ˈdʒʌŋk fuːd/ HEALTH FOOD & DRINK

UNCOUNTABLE NOUN **Junk food** is food that is quick and easy to prepare but is not good for your health. ○ *Children will get fat if they eat too much junk food.* ○ *his junk food diet of cheeseburgers, chocolate and chips*

▶ COLLOCATIONS:
eat/buy/sell junk food
a junk food **diet**

Kk

keen /kiːn/ (keener, keenest)

ADJECTIVE If you are **keen on** doing something, you very much want to do it. If you are **keen that** something should happen, you very much want it to happen. [mainly BRIT] ○ [+ on] *You're not keen on going, are you?* ○ [+ that] *His teachers are keen that he should read as much as possible.* ○ [+ to-inf] *She's still keen to keep in touch.* ○ [+ for] *Her parents are not keen for her to learn to drive.*

▶ COLLOCATIONS:
keen **on/for** something
particularly/really/quite keen
dead/desperately keen
seem/sound/look keen

keep up /kiːp ˈʌp/ (keeps up, keeping up, kept up)

PHRASAL VERB To **keep up with** something that is changing means to be able to cope with the change, usually by changing at the same rate. ○ *Things are changing so fast, it's hard to keep up.* ○ [+ with] *Some girls like to keep up with fashion.*

key|word /ˈkiːˌwɜːd/ (keywords) `SHOPPING` `COMMUNICATIONS`

NOUN A **keyword** is a word that you type into a computer in order to find information on a particular subject on the Internet. ○ *Web surfers can match their skills to jobs by simply entering a keyword.*

▶ COLLOCATIONS:
type/enter a keyword
a keyword **search**
a **specific/exact** keyword

kind /kaɪnd/ (kinder, kindest) `PERSONALITY`

ADJECTIVE Someone who is **kind** behaves in a gentle, caring, and helpful way towards other people. ○ [+ to] *She is warmhearted and kind to everyone.* ○ [+ of] *It was very kind of you to come.*

▶ COLLOCATIONS:
kind **to** someone
kind **of** someone (to do something)
kind and **gentle**
a kind **face**
kind **eyes**

► **SYNONYM:** considerate

> | WORD FAMILY | | |
> |---|---|---|
> | kind | **ADJECTIVE** | ○ *I must thank you for being so kind to me.* |
> | kindly | **ADVERB** | ○ *'You seem tired this morning, Jenny,' she said kindly.* |
> | kindness | **UNCOUNT** | ○ *We have been treated with such kindness by everybody.* |
> | unkind | **ADJECTIVE** | ○ *It's very unkind of you to make up stories about him.* |

kin|der|gar|ten /ˈkɪndəgɑːtən/ (kindergartens)   [EDUCATION]

NOUN A **kindergarten** is an informal kind of school for very young children, where they learn things by playing. ○ *She's in kindergarten now.*

► **COLLOCATIONS:**
   in/at kindergarten
   go to/start kindergarten
   a kindergarten **teacher/class**

► **SYNONYM:** nursery

kitch|en /ˈkɪtʃɪn/ (kitchens)   [HOME]

NOUN The **kitchen** is the room used for cooking and for household jobs such as washing dishes. ○ *She was cooking bacon and eggs in the kitchen.*

► **COLLOCATIONS:**
   in the kitchen
   a **large/modern/open-plan** kitchen
   a **hotel/school** kitchen
   a kitchen **table/sink/cupboard**
   a kitchen **knife/utensil**

k

Ll

la|bel /ˈleɪbəl/ (labels)

1 **NOUN** A **label** is a piece of paper or plastic that is attached to an object in order to give information about it. ○ [+ on] *He peered at the label on the bottle.* ○ *Do the warning labels on cigarette packets stop people smoking?*

▶ **COLLOCATIONS:**
   the label **on** *something*
   a **food/wine** label
   a **warning** label
   a **luggage/address** label

▶ **SYNONYMS:** tag, sticker

2 **NOUN** A **label** is a version of a product made by one particular manufacturer. ○ *She spends a lot of money on designer labels.* ○ *luxury labels such as Gucci*

▶ **COLLOCATIONS:**
   a **designer** label
   a **fashion/clothing** label
   a **luxury** label
   a *company's* **own** label

▶ **SYNONYM:** brand

lake /leɪk/ (lakes)

NOUN A **lake** is a large area of fresh water, surrounded by land. ○ *They can go fishing in the lake.* ○ *The Nile flows from Lake Victoria in East Africa north to the Mediterranean Sea.*

lamb /læm/

UNCOUNTABLE NOUN **Lamb** is the flesh of a young sheep eaten as food. ○ *We are having roast lamb.* ○ *grilled lamb chops*

▶ **COLLOCATIONS:**
   eat lamb
   roast lamb
   a lamb **chop**

land /lænd/

SCIENCE & NATURE   TRANSPORT & TRAVEL

(lands, landing, landed)

1 UNCOUNTABLE NOUN Land is an area of ground, especially one that is used for a particular purpose such as farming or building. ○ *There are also plots of land for sale.* ○ *Many of the new out-of-town stores are being built on land that was previously derelict.* ○ *160 acres of land*

→ see note at **soil**

2 UNCOUNTABLE NOUN Land is the part of the world that consists of ground, rather than sea or air. ○ *It isn't clear whether the plane went down over land or sea.* ○ *He studied the ocean currents that control temperatures on land.*

▶ COLLOCATIONS:
  on land
  a **piece/area/plot** of land
  agricultural/farm land
  industrial/residential land
  public/private land
  undeveloped/derelict/waste land
  own/buy/sell land
  develop/build on land
  reach land

3 VERB When a plane **lands**, it arrives somewhere after a journey. ○ [+ *at*] *The plane was forced to land at an airport in Pennsylvania.* ○ *In Moscow the plane landed to refuel.*

▶ COLLOCATIONS:
  land **at** *somewhere*
  a **plane/helicopter/aircraft/flight** lands

▶ SYNONYM: touch down

▶ ANTONYM: take off

land|scape /ˈlændskeɪp/ (landscapes)

MEDIA & CULTURE

1 UNCOUNTABLE NOUN The **landscape** is everything you can see when you look across an area of land, including hills, rivers, buildings, trees, and plants. ○ *Arizona's desert landscape* ○ *A group of three peaks dominate the landscape.* ○ [+ *of*] *a landscape of hedges and fields*

→ see note at **nature**

▶ COLLOCATIONS:
  a landscape **of** *something*
  something **dominates/dots** the landscape
  an **urban/rural** landscape
  a **desert/mountain** landscape
  a **bleak/barren** landscape
  a **flat/rugged** landscape

2 NOUN A **landscape** is a painting which shows a scene in the countryside. ○ *She painted winter landscapes.* ○ *Constable was a famous English landscape painter.*

▶ COLLOCATIONS:
paint a landscape
a landscape **painting**
a landscape **painter/artist**

---

lane /leɪn/ (lanes)

PLACES   TRANSPORT & TRAVEL

1 NOUN A **lane** is a narrow road, especially in the country. ○ *a quiet country lane* ○ *This narrow lane leads to Porlock Bay.*

▶ COLLOCATIONS:
a **country** lane
a **narrow** lane
a lane **leads** somewhere

2 NOUN A **lane** is a part of a main road which is marked by the edge of the road and a painted line, or by two painted lines. ○ *The lorry was travelling at 20mph in the slow lane.* ○ *In the Netherlands there are cycle lanes on both sides of almost every road.*

▶ COLLOCATIONS:
in a lane
a **bus** lane
a **cycle/bike** lane
the **slow/fast** lane
the **inside/outside/middle** lane
the **southbound/northbound/eastbound/westbound** lane
pull into/move into a lane
change lanes
a lane **closure**

---

lap|top /ˈlæptɒp/ (laptops)

COMMUNICATIONS

NOUN A **laptop** or a **laptop computer** is a small portable computer. ○ *Every student gets a laptop computer when they start school.* ○ *He uses a laptop to do schoolwork.* ○ *At the same time I was making notes on my laptop.*

▶ COLLOCATIONS:
on a laptop
use a laptop
a **wireless** laptop
a laptop **user**

---

last /lɑːst, læst/ (lasts, lasting, lasted)

VERB If an event, situation, or problem **lasts** for a particular length of time, it continues to exist or happen for that length of time. ○ *[+ for] The marriage had lasted for less than two years.* ○ *The ride only lasted five minutes.* ○ *This weather won't last long.*

▶ **COLLOCATIONS:**
last **for** something
last (for) x **minutes/years/hours**
only last 5 minutes, 2 years, etc.
last **forever**
not last **long**

---

law /lɔː/ (laws) `CRIME`

1 **UNCOUNTABLE NOUN** **The law** is a system of rules that a society or government develops in order to deal with crime, business agreements, and social relationships. ○ *If you speed, you are risking lives and breaking the law.* ○ *It is against the law to cycle on pavements.* ○ *Planning permission is required by law for most new development.*

2 **NOUN** A **law** is one of the rules in a system of law which deals with a particular type of agreement, relationship, or crime. ○ [+ on] *new laws on data protection* ○ *The law was passed on a second vote.*

▶ **COLLOCATIONS:**
against the law
by law
the law **on** something
break the law
change the law
introduce/pass a law
relax/tighten a law
something **becomes** law
a law **allows** something
a law **prohibits/bans** something
a **new** law
tax/employment law
law **enforcement**

law|yer /ˈlɔɪə/ (lawyers)

NOUN A **lawyer** is a person who is qualified to advise people about the law and represent them in court. ○ *Many people cannot afford to hire good lawyers to defend themselves.* ○ *lawyers representing the families of Perry's victims* ○ *I consulted a lawyer.*

▶ **COLLOCATIONS:**
get/hire/appoint a lawyer
consult a lawyer
a lawyer **represents** someone
a **good** lawyer
a **leading/top/prominent** lawyer
a **prosecution/defence** lawyer
a **divorce/immigration/employment** lawyer

le|gal /ˈliːgəl/

1 **ADJECTIVE** Legal is used to describe things that relate to the law. ○ *the English legal system* ○ *He vowed to take legal action.* ○ *I sought legal advice on this.*

> ▶ **COLLOCATIONS:**
> the legal **system**
> legal **action**
> a legal **battle/challenge/dispute**
> legal **advice/rights**
> a legal **expert**
> the legal **profession**
> legal **fees/costs**

2 **ADJECTIVE** An action or situation that is **legal** is allowed or required by law. ○ *What I did was perfectly legal.* ○ *The legal age for driving is 17.*

> ▶ **COLLOCATIONS:**
> **perfectly** legal
> the legal **limit**
> a legal **requirement/obligation/responsibility**
> the legal **age** for *something*

> ▶ **ANTONYM:** illegal

il|legal /ɪˈliːgəl/

ADJECTIVE If something is **illegal**, the law says that it is not allowed. ○ [+ to-inf] *It's illegal to sell alcohol to under-18s.* ○ *About 300, mainly young people, die as a result of using illegal drugs each year.*

> ▶ **COLLOCATIONS:**
> illegal **drugs/substances**
> illegal **weapons**
> illegal **activities**
> illegal **trade**
> illegal **immigration/immigrants**
> **do** *something* illegal

> ▶ **SYNONYM:** unlawful

> ▶ **ANTONYM:** legal

WORD FAMILY		
law	NOUN	○ *The law requires you to wear a seat belt.* ○ *a new anti-smoking law*
lawyer	NOUN	○ *He was the best divorce lawyer in the business.*
legal	ADJECTIVE	○ *Campaigners won a three-year legal battle against the government.*
legally	ADVERB	○ *The school is legally responsible for your child's safety.*
illegal	ADJECTIVE	○ *He denied doing anything illegal.*
illegally	ADVERB	○ *The previous government had acted illegally.*

lazy /ˈleɪzi/ (lazier, laziest)

PERSONALITY

ADJECTIVE If someone is **lazy**, they do not want to work or make any effort to do anything. ○ [+ to-inf] *I was too lazy to learn how to read music.* ○ *I was also quite a lazy student.*

▶ **SYNONYM:** idle

▶ **ANTONYM:** hard-working

WORD FAMILY		
lazy	**ADJECTIVE**	○ *He's terribly lazy.*
lazily	**ADVERB**	○ *She yawned, and stretched lazily.*
laziness	**UNCOUNT**	○ *It was sheer laziness that had kept him living with his parents.*

leath|er /ˈleðə/

CLOTHES & APPEARANCE

UNCOUNTABLE NOUN **Leather** is treated animal skin which is used for making shoes, clothes, bags, and furniture. ○ *He wore a leather jacket and dark trousers.* ○ *cream leather sofas*

lec|ture /ˈlektʃə/ (lectures)

EDUCATION

NOUN A **lecture** is a talk someone gives in order to teach people about a particular subject, usually at a university or college. ○ [+ by] *I went to a lecture by the architect Daniel Libeskind.* ○ [+ on] *He asked my father to give a lecture on tourism in Madrid.* ○ *In his lecture, Riemann covered an enormous variety of topics.*

▶ **COLLOCATIONS:**
a lecture **by** someone
a lecture **on** something
in a lecture
give/deliver a lecture
go to/attend a lecture
a lecture **hall/theatre/room**

lec|tur|er /ˈlektʃərə/ (lecturers)

NOUN A **lecturer** is a teacher at a university or college. ○ [+ in] *a lecturer in law at Southampton University* ○ *Her husband became a university lecturer.*

▶ **COLLOCATIONS:**
a lecturer **in** something
a lecturer in **law/psychology/economics**, etc.
a **university/college** lecturer
a **senior** lecturer

lei|sure /ˈleʒə, AM ˈliːʒ-/

WORK **FREE TIME**

UNCOUNTABLE NOUN **Leisure** is the time when you are not working and you can relax and do things that you enjoy. **Leisure** is also the industry or work that involves providing services for people's free time. ○ *There are leisure facilities in the hotel – a pool, gym, sauna, and steam room.* ○ *Reading is her main leisure activity.* ○ *people working in the leisure industry*

▶ COLLOCATIONS:
a leisure **activity/pursuit**
someone's leisure **time**
leisure **facilities**
a leisure **centre/complex**
the leisure **industry**

let down /let ˈdaʊn/ (lets down, letting down, let down)

PHRASAL VERB If you **let** someone **down**, you disappoint them, by not doing something that you have said you will do or that they expected you to do. ○ *Don't worry, Xiao, I won't let you down.* ○ *I realised how much I had let down my parents.*

lev|el /ˈlevəl/ (levels) `EDUCATION`

NOUN A **level** is a point on a scale, for example a scale of difficulty. ○ *The course is suitable for intermediate or advanced level students.* ○ *He reached the 200-hit level in the game.* ○ *[+ of] The exercises are marked according to their level of difficulty.*

▶ COLLOCATIONS:
the level **of** *something*
the level of **difficulty**
reach/achieve a level
beginner/intermediate/advanced level
skill levels

li|brary /ˈlaɪbrəri, AM -breri/ (libraries) `EDUCATION`

NOUN A **library** is a building or part of a building where things such as books, newspapers, and music are kept for people to read, use, or borrow. ○ *We were doing some studying in the school library.* ○ *I have to return some library books.*

▶ COLLOCATIONS:
at/in a library
go to/visit a library
use a library
a **public/local** library
a **school/university** library
a library **book**
a library **card**
library **staff**

WORD FAMILY		
library	NOUN	○ *She issued them with library cards.*
librarian	NOUN	○ *The school librarian made a list of 'must read' books for the kids.*

life|style /ˈlaɪfstaɪl/ (lifestyles) also **life style** also **life-style**

NOUN The **lifestyle** of a particular person or group of people is the living conditions, behaviour, and habits that are typical of them or are chosen by them. ○ *He was enjoying the student lifestyle.* ○ *My parents have been encouraging me to do more exercise and have a more healthy lifestyle.*

▶ COLLOCATIONS:
lead/enjoy/have a lifestyle
change your lifestyle
a **healthy/unhealthy/active** lifestyle
a **comfortable** lifestyle
a **busy/hectic** lifestyle
a lifestyle **change**

light /laɪt/ (lights, lighter, lightest)

1 **UNCOUNTABLE NOUN** A **light** is something such as an electric lamp which produces light. ○ *She switched on the bedside light.* ○ *The janitor comes round to turn the lights out.*

▶ COLLOCATIONS:
turn on/switch on/put on a light
turn off/out a light
switch off/out a light
a **wall/bedside/kitchen** light
street lights

2 **ADJECTIVE** When you use **light** to describe a colour, you are referring to a shade of that colour which is very pale. ○ *She was wearing a light green dress.* ○ *light brown, curly hair*

▶ COLLOCATION: light **green/blue/brown**

▶ SYNONYM: pale

▶ ANTONYM: dark

lim|it|ed /ˈlɪmɪtɪd/

ADJECTIVE Something that is **limited** is not very great in amount, range, or degree. ○ *The offer is valid for a limited period only.* ○ *There was a very limited choice of vegetarian dishes on the menu.*

▶ COLLOCATIONS:
a limited **number/amount**
a limited **period/time**
a limited **selection/range/choice**
a limited **supply**
limited **success**
very/extremely limited

<table>
<tr><td colspan="3">WORD FAMILY</td></tr>
<tr><td>limit</td><td>NOUN</td><td>○ If a user exceeds their monthly download limit, they are charged extra.</td></tr>
<tr><td>limit</td><td>VERB</td><td>○ Poor education can limit the range of opportunities available.</td></tr>
<tr><td>limited</td><td>ADJECTIVE</td><td>○ He achieved only limited success.</td></tr>
<tr><td>unlimited</td><td>ADJECTIVE</td><td>○ The service allows users to download an unlimited amount of music.</td></tr>
<tr><td>limitation</td><td>NOUN</td><td>○ She knows her limitations and operates within them.</td></tr>
</table>

lin|guis|tics /lɪŋˈgwɪstɪks/

UNCOUNTABLE NOUN Linguistics is the study of the way in which language works. ○ courses in English language and linguistics ○ He's studying linguistics at New York University.

<table>
<tr><td colspan="3">WORD FAMILY</td></tr>
<tr><td>linguistic</td><td>ADJECTIVE</td><td>○ Many international companies are keen to take on graduates with high linguistic skills.</td></tr>
<tr><td>linguistics</td><td>UNCOUNT</td><td>○ She has written many books and articles about linguistics.</td></tr>
<tr><td>linguistically</td><td>ADVERB</td><td>○ The area south of Los Angeles is one of the most linguistically diverse regions in the country.</td></tr>
<tr><td>linguist</td><td>NOUN</td><td>○ He was a very good linguist, able to speak eight or nine languages.</td></tr>
</table>

link /lɪŋk/ (links) `TRANSPORT & TRAVEL` `COMMUNICATIONS`

1 **NOUN** A **link between** two things or places is a physical connection between them. ○ [+ between] Other proposals include improving the rail link between North and South Wales. ○ The village is a long way from the city and the transport links aren't great.

> ▸ COLLOCATIONS:
> a link **between** two things
> a link **with** something
> a **direct** link
> a **high-speed** link
> a **rail/transport/road** link

2 **NOUN** In computing, a **link** is a connection between different documents, or between different parts of the same document, using hypertext. ○ Check out tracks from the new album by clicking on the links below. ○ [+ to] He posted a link to the forum on his website.

▶ COLLOCATIONS:
a link **to** something
click on a link
post/add a link

lit|era|ture /ˈlɪtrətʃə, AM -tərətʃʊr/ `MEDIA & CULTURE`

UNCOUNTABLE NOUN Novels, plays, and poetry are referred to as **literature**, especially when they are considered to be good or important. ○ *He studied French literature at university in Paris.* ○ *It's one of the best novels in English literature.* ○ *classic works of literature*

▶ COLLOCATIONS:
in literature
English/French/American, etc. literature
modern/contemporary literature
study/teach literature
a **work of** literature

WORD FAMILY		
literature	**UNCOUNT**	○ *Harry Potter is one of the most popular characters in modern literature for young people.*
literary	**ADJECTIVE**	○ *Literary critics analyse a writer's use of language.*

lit|ter /ˈlɪtə/ `PLACES`

UNCOUNTABLE NOUN **Litter** is rubbish that is left lying around outside. ○ *If you see litter in the corridor, pick it up.* ○ *There are fines of up to £400 for dropping litter.*

▶ COLLOCATION: **drop/leave** litter

▶ SYNONYM: rubbish

live /laɪv/ `MEDIA & CULTURE`

ADJECTIVE A **live** performance is given in front of an audience, rather than being recorded and then broadcast or shown in a film. ○ *There's a club with live music every night.* ○ *The band was forced to cancel a string of live dates.*

▶ COLLOCATIONS:
live **music/entertainment**
a live **show/performance/concert/gig**
live **coverage**
a live **broadcast/recording**
a live **audience**
a live **game/match**

live|ly /ˈlaɪvli/ (livelier, liveliest) `PERSONALITY`

ADJECTIVE You can describe someone as **lively** when they behave in an enthusiastic and cheerful way. ○ *She had a sweet, lively personality.* ○ *Josephine was bright, lively and cheerful.*

WORD FAMILY		
lively	**ADJECTIVE**	○ *Jamie is an affectionate, lively child.*
liveliness	**UNCOUNT**	○ *He loved the liveliness of the young generation.*

liv|ing /ˈlɪvɪŋ/ `WORK`

NOUN The work that you do for a **living** is the work that you do in order to earn the money that you need. ○ *I'm not sure what he does for a living.* ○ [+ from] *He made a comfortable living from his job as a driver.*

▶ **COLLOCATIONS:**
   do something **for** a living
   earn/make a living **from** something
   a **good/decent/comfortable** living

liv|ing room /ˈlɪvɪŋ ruːm/ (living rooms) also **living-room** `HOME`

NOUN The **living room** in a house is the room where people sit and relax. ○ *We were sitting in the living room watching TV.*

▶ **COLLOCATION: in** the living room
▶ **SYNONYMS:** sitting room, lounge

lo|cal /ˈləʊkəl/ `PLACES`

ADJECTIVE Local means existing in or belonging to the area where you live, or to the area that you are talking about. ○ *I saw an ad in the local newspaper.* ○ *He went to the local high school.*

▶ **COLLOCATIONS:**
   local **people/residents**
   the local **community**
   the local **area**
   local **news**
   the local **newspaper/paper**
   the local **school/hospital/library**
   local **shops/businesses**
   a local **artist/farmer**

WORD FAMILY		
local	**ADJECTIVE**	○ *Plans for the new runway have been opposed by local residents.*
locally	**ADVERB**	○ *locally produced food* ○ *The monument is known locally as the Giant's Stone.*

lo|ca|tion /ləʊˈkeɪʃən/ (locations)   PLACES

1 NOUN A **location** is the place where something happens or is situated. ○ *The Amba is a friendly hotel, in a handy central location.* ○ [+ for] *Scotland is an ideal location for a holiday.*

▶ **SYNONYMS:** setting, site

2 NOUN The **location** of someone or something is their exact position. ○ [+ of] *A GPS system is used to pinpoint the location of vehicles in trouble.* ○ *The exact location is being kept secret .*

▶ **SYNONYM:** position

3 NOUN A **location** is a place away from a studio where a film or part of a film is made. ○ *an art movie with dozens of exotic locations* ○ *We're shooting on location.*

▶ **COLLOCATIONS:**
in a location
on location
a location **for** something
the location **of** something
a **secret** location
a **central** location
an **ideal/good/convenient** location
the **exact/precise** location

WORD FAMILY		
locate	**VERB**	○ *He looked around, trying to locate the source of the noise.*
location	**NOUN**	○ *He was immediately taken by police to an undisclosed location.*

look af|ter /lʊk ˈɑːftə, ˈæftə/ (looks after, looking after, looked after)

1 PHRASAL VERB If you **look after** someone or something, you do what is necessary to keep them healthy, safe, or in good condition. ○ *I had to stay at home to look after my three younger brothers.* ○ *Sian's mother arrived to look after the kids.*

▶ **SYNONYM:** take care of

2 PHRASAL VERB If you **look after** something, you are responsible for it and deal with it or make sure it is all right, especially because it is your job to do so. ○ *My job is to look after reception and make sure everything is running properly.* ○ *We'll help you look after your finances.*

▶ **SYNONYM:** deal with

look for|ward to /lʊk ˈfɔːwəd tə/   COMMUNICATIONS
(looks forward to, looking forward to, looked forward to)

PHRASAL VERB If you **are looking forward to** something that is going to happen, you want it to happen because you think you will enjoy it. ○ [+ v-ing] *I'm really* *looking forward to seeing her again.* ○ *She had been looking forward to the school concert.*

> **USAGE**
>
> You often use **look forward to** at the end of letters and emails to talk about what you hope will happen. You usually use the present tense form of the verb. ○ *I look forward to hearing from you soon.* ○ *I look forward to seeing you next month.*

---

low /ləʊ/ **(lower, lowest)** SCIENCE & NATURE HEALTH

1 ADJECTIVE Something that is **low** measures only a short distance from the bottom to the top, or from the ground to the top. ○ *She put it down on the low table.* ○ *There was a low wall that separated the two gardens.*

▶ **ANTONYM:** high

2 ADJECTIVE If something is **low**, it is close to the ground, to sea level, or to the bottom of something. ○ *He bumped his head on the low beams.* ○ *It was late afternoon and the sun was low in the sky.*

▶ **ANTONYM:** high

3 ADJECTIVE If a food or other substance is **low in** a particular ingredient, it contains only a small amount of that ingredient. ○ [+ *in*] *They look for foods that are low in calories.* ○ *Eat a diet high in raw foods and low in fat and sugar.*

▶ **COLLOCATIONS:**
low **in** *something*
low in **fat/sugar/salt**
low in c**arbohydrates/fibre**
low in **calories**

▶ **ANTONYM:** high

---

loy|al /ˈlɔɪəl/ PERSONALITY

ADJECTIVE Someone who is **loyal** remains firm in their friendship or support for a person or thing. ○ *Loyal fans travelled to the Czech Republic to watch their team play.* ○ [+ *to*] *He is very loyal to his family and friends.*

▶ **COLLOCATIONS:**
loyal **to** *someone/something*
fiercely loyal
a loyal **fan/friend/customer/servant**
a loyal **supporter/follower**
a loyal **following**
remain loyal

▶ **SYNONYM:** faithful

▶ **ANTONYM:** disloyal

lug|gage /ˈlʌɡɪdʒ/ TRANSPORT & TRAVEL

UNCOUNTABLE NOUN Luggage is the suitcases and bags that you take with you when travel. ○ *Each passenger was allowed two pieces of luggage.* ○ *Passengers with hand luggage can go straight to the departure gate.*

▶ COLLOCATIONS:
a **piece of** luggage
carry luggage
hand/carry-on luggage
heavy luggage
a luggage **rack/compartment**

luxu|ry /ˈlʌkʃəri/ (luxuries)

1 NOUN A **luxury** is something expensive which is not necessary but which gives you pleasure. ○ *He felt that cars were expensive luxuries.* ○ *Holidays are not a luxury, they are a necessity.*

▶ COLLOCATIONS:
a **rare** luxury
an **expensive/affordable** luxury

▶ SYNONYMS: extravagance, treat

2 ADJECTIVE A **luxury** item is something expensive which is not necessary but which gives you pleasure. ○ *They have been staying at a luxury hotel, with swimming pool, tennis courts and golf range.* ○ *The aim is to convert the building into 35 luxury apartments.*

▶ COLLOCATIONS:
a luxury **car/hotel**
a luxury **home/apartment/suite/villa**
a luxury **yacht/liner**
a luxury **cruise/holiday**

lyr|ics /ˈlɪrɪks/

MEDIA & CULTURE

PLURAL NOUN The **lyrics** of a song are its words. ○ [+ for] *Keith wrote the lyrics for the album.* ○ [+ by] *the Beatles' song 'Hey Jude' with lyrics by Paul McCartney*

> ▶ **COLLOCATIONS:**
> the lyrics **for/of** *something*
> lyrics **by** *someone*
> **write** the lyrics
> **sing** the lyrics

Mm

ma|chine /məˈʃiːn/ (machines)

NOUN A **machine** is a piece of equipment which uses electricity or an engine in order to do a particular kind of work. ○ *How do you use the coffee machine?* ○ *The seeds are sown by machine.*

▶ COLLOCATIONS:
by machine
use/operate a machine
design/make/build/invent a machine
install a machine
a **washing/sewing** machine
a **cash/coffee** machine
an **automatic** machine

▶ SYNONYM: appliance

WORD FAMILY		
machine	NOUN	○ There are plans to install ticket machines at the station.
machinery	UNCOUNT	○ Heavy machinery was used to clear the road after the landslide.

maga|zine /ˌmægəˈziːn, AM ˈmægəziːn/ (magazines)

MEDIA & CULTURE

NOUN A **magazine** is a publication with a paper cover which is issued regularly, usually every week or every month, and which contains articles, stories, photographs, and advertisements. ○ *I read an article about exam stress in a magazine.* ○ *Many parents want tougher controls on the content of teen magazines and pop videos.*

▶ COLLOCATIONS:
in a magazine
a magazine **for** *someone*
read a magazine
a magazine **article/interview/report/ad**
a magazine **cover**
a magazine **editor**
a **glossy** magazine

a **weekly/monthly** magazine
a **teen/children's/women's/men's** magazine
a **fashion/music/computer/celebrity** magazine

---

ma|jor /ˈmeɪdʒə/

ADJECTIVE You use **major** when you want to describe something that is more important, serious, or significant than other things in a group or situation. ○ *Lack of clean drinking water was a major problem.* ○ *Exercise has a major part to play in preventing and combating disease.*

▶ COLLOCATIONS:
a major **problem/issue/concern**
a major **change**
a major **part/factor/role**
a major **company/city**
a major **event/tournament**

▶ SYNONYMS: key, crucial, critical

▶ ANTONYMS: unimportant, minor

ma|jor|ity /məˈdʒɒrɪti, AM -ˈdʒɔːr-/

UNCOUNTABLE NOUN The **majority** of people or things in a group is more than half of them. ○ [+ of] *The majority of my friends live nearby.* ○ *The vast majority of teenagers have mobile phones.*

▶ COLLOCATIONS:
the majority **of** *something*
the **vast/overwhelming/great** majority

▶ ANTONYM: minority

---

make sure

1 PHRASE If you **make sure that** something is done, you take action so that it is done. ○ *Make sure that you follow the instructions carefully.*

2 PHRASE If you **make sure that** something is the way that you want or expect it to be, you check that it is that way. ○ *He looked in the bathroom to make sure that he was alone.*

▶ SYNONYM: check

---

make-up /ˈmeɪkʌp/ also **makeup**   CLOTHES & APPEARANCE

UNCOUNTABLE NOUN **Make-up** consists of things such as lipstick, eye shadow, and powder which some women put on their faces to make themselves look more attractive or which actors use to change or improve their appearance. ○ *Normally she wore little make-up.* ○ *She hurriedly applied make-up without a mirror.*

▶ COLLOCATIONS:
wear make-up

put on/apply make-up
remove make-up
full/heavy make-up
eye make-up
a make-up **bag**

---

make up /meɪk ˈʌp/ (makes up, making up, made up)

1 **PHRASAL VERB** The people or things that **make up** something are the members or parts that form that thing. ○ *Women officers make up 13 per cent of the police force.* ○ *Insects are made up of tens of thousands of proteins.*

▶ COLLOCATIONS:
be made up **of** something
be **largely/entirely/mainly** made up **of** something
make up **the majority**

▶ SYNONYMS: form, constitute

2 **PHRASAL VERB** If you **make up** something such as a story or excuse, you invent it, sometimes in order to deceive people. ○ *He made up an excuse so he didn't have to go to the party.* ○ *You're not making it up, are you? I have actually passed the exam?*

▶ COLLOCATION: make up a **story/excuse**

▶ SYNONYM: invent

---

male /meɪl/ PEOPLE

ADJECTIVE Someone who is **male** is a man or a boy. ○ *Around 47 per cent of teachers are male.* ○ *male friends* ○ *male students*

→ see also **female**

---

man|ag|er /ˈmænɪdʒə/ (managers) WORK

NOUN A **manager** is a person who is responsible for running part of or the whole of a business organization. ○ *My father is a bank manager.* ○ [+ of] *The managers of a company know their business better than anybody.*

▶ COLLOCATIONS:
the manager **of** something
the **general** manager
a **senior/top** manager
an **assistant/deputy** manager
a **regional** manager
a **project/campaign** manager
a **marketing/sales** manager
a **bank** manager
an **office/branch** manager

m

WORD FAMILY		
manage	VERB	○ *The family business is now managed by the three brothers.*
manager	NOUN	○ *He was product marketing manager at Microsoft.*
management	UNCOUNT	○ *The zoo needed better management rather than more money.*
managerial	ADJECTIVE	○ *an increase in the number of women in managerial roles*

mar|ket /ˈmɑːkɪt/ (markets)   PLACES   WORK

1 NOUN A **market** is a place where goods are bought and sold, usually outdoors.
○ *He sold boots on a market stall.* ○ *I went to the market to get a few things for our lunch.*

→ see also **stall**

▶ COLLOCATIONS:
  go to a market
  a **street/local** market
  a market **stall**
  a market **trader**

2 NOUN The **market** for a particular type of thing is the number of people who want to buy it, or the area of the world in which it is sold. ○ [+ for] *The market for games software has grown.* ○ *America is the biggest market for pain-relieving drugs.*

▶ COLLOCATIONS:
  the market **for** *something*
  a **large/big/huge/major** market
  the **European/American**, etc. market
  the **foreign/international/domestic** market

WORD FAMILY		
market	NOUN	○ *Japan is a major market for lumber and building products.*
market	VERB	○ *Companies have innovative ways of marketing their products in stores.*
marketing	UNCOUNT	○ *They were planning a separate marketing campaign.*

marks /mɑːks/   EDUCATION

PLURAL NOUN If someone gets good or high **marks** for doing something, they have done it well. If they get poor or low **marks**, they have done it badly.
○ *She had been getting some of the best marks in the class for her essays.* ○ *Students sometimes got upset with teachers who gave them low exam marks.*

▶ COLLOCATIONS:
  give/get good/bad marks
  good/high/top marks
  bad/low/poor marks

mar|tial arts /ˌmɑːʃəl ˈɑːts/ SPORT & ACTIVITY

PLURAL NOUN Martial arts are the methods of fighting, often without weapons, that come from the Far East, for example kung fu, karate, or judo. ○ *Outside of school, I do martial arts.* ○ *a martial arts instructor*

match /mætʃ/ CLOTHES & APPEARANCE SPORT & ACTIVITY
(matches, matching, matched)

1 VERB If clothes **match**, they have the same colour or design, or have a pleasing appearance when they are worn together. ○ *I wore a pink T-shirt and shoes which matched my skirt.* ○ *The mother's dress is peach taffeta, with shoes dyed to match.*

2 NOUN A **match** is an organized game of football, tennis, cricket, or some other sport. [mainly BRIT] ○ *He was watching a football match.* ○ *France won the match 28-19.* ○ [+ against] *a rugby match against another school*

▶ **COLLOCATIONS:**
  a match **against** someone
  a match **between** two teams
  win/lose a match
  watch a match
  play a match
  a **football/tennis/cricket/rugby** match
  a **boxing** match
  a **home/away** match
  a match **referee**

▶ **SYNONYM:** game

math|emat|ics /ˌmæθəˈmætɪks/ or **maths** SCIENCE & NATURE

UNCOUNTABLE NOUN Mathematics or **maths** is the study of numbers, quantities, or shapes. ○ *I've done maths at school.* ○ *He studied for a mathematics degree at the local university.*

▶ **COLLOCATIONS:**
  do mathematics
  teach/study mathematics
  a mathematics **teacher/student**
  a mathematics **exam/test**
  a mathematics **course/lesson**
  a mathematics **degree**

WORD FAMILY		
mathematics	UNCOUNT	○ *He was a schoolteacher, teaching mathematics and physics.*
maths	UNCOUNT	○ *At school I hated maths.*
mathematical	ADJECTIVE	○ *Teachers show children easy methods of solving mathematical problems.*
mathematically	ADVERB	○ *The analysis was mathematically correct.*
mathematician	NOUN	○ *He was a good mathematician.*

m

mean /miːn/ (meaner, meanest)   PERSONALITY

ADJECTIVE If you describe someone as **mean**, you are being critical of them because they are unwilling to spend much money or to use very much of a particular thing. [mainly BRIT] ○ *He was too mean to pay for a taxi.* ○ [+ with] *Her parents were mean with money.*

▶ COLLOCATIONS:
mean **with** *something*
mean with **money**

▶ SYNONYM: stingy

meat /miːt/   FOOD & DRINK

UNCOUNTABLE NOUN Meat is flesh taken from a dead animal that people cook and eat. ○ *Vegans eat no meat or animal products of any kind.* ○ *Wash your hands after handling raw meat.*

▶ COLLOCATIONS:
eat meat
raw meat
fresh/processed meat
grilled/roast meat
a meat **pie**

me|chan|ic /mɪˈkænɪk/ (mechanics)   WORK

NOUN A **mechanic** is someone whose job is to repair and maintain machines and engines, especially car engines. ○ *A mechanic was working on his car.* ○ *Her mother was a nurse and her father a car mechanic.*

▶ COLLOCATION: a **car/motor** mechanic

WORD FAMILY		
mechanic	NOUN	○ *I decided to become a mechanic.*
mechanical	ADJECTIVE	○ *Initial investigations pointed to mechanical failure as the cause of the crash.*
mechanically	ADVERB	○ *The gates were mechanically operated.*

me|dia /ˈmiːdiə/   MEDIA & CULTURE

UNCOUNTABLE NOUN You can refer to television, radio, newspapers, and magazines as **the media**. ○ *There has been a lot about the case in the media.* ○ *Widespread media coverage on food safety has increased public concern about the food we eat.*

▶ COLLOCATIONS:
in the media
media **coverage**
media **attention/interest**
a media **report/interview**

a media **company/empire**
the **news** media
digital/online/print/broadcast media

---

medi|cine /ˈmedsən, AM ˈmedɪsɪn/ `HEALTH`

1 **UNCOUNTABLE NOUN** Medicine is the treatment of illness and injuries by doctors and nurses. ○ *He pursued a career in medicine.* ○ *I was interested in alternative medicine.*

▶ **COLLOCATIONS:**
study medicine
practise medicine
modern/traditional medicine
alternative/orthodox medicine
Chinese/Western medicine

2 **NOUN** Medicine is a substance that you drink or swallow in order to cure an illness. ○ *Does taking medicine make a cold go away any quicker?* ○ *Tell the doctor if you are taking any medicine or tablets.*

▶ **COLLOCATIONS:**
take medicine
prescribe medicine
an **over-the-counter/prescription** medicine
cough medicine

WORD FAMILY		
medicine	**UNCOUNT**	○ *Doctors who want to practise medicine need to be registered with the General Medical Council.*
medical	**ADJECTIVE**	○ *High blood-pressure needs expert medical treatment.*
medically	**ADVERB**	○ *He was medically unfit to fly.*

---

menu /ˈmenjuː/ (menus) `COMMUNICATIONS`

NOUN On a computer screen, a **menu** is a list of choices. Each choice represents something that you can do using the computer. ○ *Click on the 'Start' menu and choose 'Run'.* ○ *He scrolled through the menu options.*

▶ **COLLOCATIONS:**
a **drop-down/pull-down** menu
a **pop-up** menu
click on a menu
navigate a menu
a menu **option**

m

messy /'mesi/ (messier, messiest)   `HOME`

1 **ADJECTIVE** A **messy** person or activity makes things dirty or untidy. ○ *Very young kids are messy eaters.* ○ *As the work tends to be a bit messy you'll need to wear old clothes.*

2 **ADJECTIVE** Something that is **messy** is dirty or untidy. ○ *Mum made me clean up my messy room.* ○ *His writing is very messy.*

▶ COLLOCATIONS:
get messy
a messy **room/kitchen/bedroom/office**
a messy **house/desk**
messy **hair**

WORD FAMILY		
mess	**UNCOUNT**	○ *They cleaned up the mess with a broom.*
messy	**ADJECTIVE**	○ *Children love getting messy.*
messily	**ADVERB**	○ *She wrote it hastily and messily on a scrap of paper.*

me|ter /'miːtə/ (meters)   `TRANSPORT & TRAVEL`

NOUN A **meter** is a device that measures and records something such as how far a taxi has travelled and how much you must pay the driver. ○ *When the taxi stopped, the meter said 58 euros.*

middle-aged /ˌmɪdəl'eɪdʒd/   `PEOPLE`

ADJECTIVE If you describe someone as **middle-aged**, you mean that they are neither young nor old. People between the ages of 40 and 60 are usually considered to be middle-aged. ○ *His parents are middle-aged.* ○ *a middle-aged woman*

mild /maɪld/ (milder, mildest)   `SCIENCE & NATURE`

ADJECTIVE **Mild** weather is pleasant because it is neither extremely hot nor extremely cold. ○ *The weather is mild throughout the year.* ○ *The area is famous for its very mild winter climate.*

▶ COLLOCATIONS:
mild **weather**
a mild **climate**
a mild **winter**
a mild **day**
unusually/unseasonably mild

▶ ANTONYMS: severe, harsh

> **WHICH WORD: cool, mild, cold, or warm?**
>
> You use **cool** to describe weather which is slightly cold in a pleasant way.
> ○ It's time to get outside and enjoy the cooler weather.
>
> You use **mild** to describe weather which is pleasant because it is neither
> extremely hot nor extremely cold. ○ It was a mild spring day.
>
> You use **cold** to describe weather in which the temperature of the air is low.
> ○ Being by the sea is great if the weather isn't too cold.
>
> You use **warm** to describe weather which is slightly hot in a pleasant way.
> ○ The plant thrives in a warm climate.

---

milk /mɪlk/

FOOD & DRINK

UNCOUNTABLE NOUN Milk is the white liquid produced by cows, goats, and some
other animals, which people drink and use to make butter, cheese, and yoghurt.
○ He went to buy a pint of milk. ○ I don't drink much milk.

▶ COLLOCATIONS:
drink milk
produce milk
skimmed/semi-skimmed milk
pasteurized milk
cow's/goat's milk
a **pint/litre** of milk
a **glass/carton/bottle** of milk
a milk **carton/bottle**

---

mi|nor /ˈmaɪnə/

ADJECTIVE You use **minor** when you want to describe something that is less
important, serious, or significant than other things in a group or situation.
○ Many of the changes were relatively minor. ○ She is known in Italy for a number of
minor roles in films.

▶ COLLOCATIONS:
a minor **problem/issue**
a minor **change**
a minor **difference/detail**
a minor **role**
minor **damage**
a minor **illness/injury**
relatively/fairly minor

▶ SYNONYMS: small, insignificant

▶ ANTONYM: major

mi|nor|ity /mɪˈnɒrɪti, AM -ˈnɔːr-/

UNCOUNTABLE NOUN The **minority** of people or things in a group is less than half of them. ○ [+ of] *Only a small minority of the participants were teenagers.* ○ *A substantial minority of school leavers are unable to find work.*

▸ **COLLOCATIONS:**
  a minority **of** something
  a **small/tiny** minority
  a **large/significant/substantial** minority

▸ **ANTONYM:** majority

mis|er|able /ˈmɪzərəbəl/

ADJECTIVE If you are **miserable**, you are very unhappy. ○ *I was in a job that was making me absolutely miserable.* ○ *I had a bad cold and felt miserable.*

▸ **COLLOCATIONS:**
  absolutely/utterly miserable
  feel/look miserable
  make someone miserable

▸ **SYNONYM:** unhappy

▸ **ANTONYM:** happy

WORD FAMILY		
miserable	**ADJECTIVE**	○ *I saw you sitting in here looking miserable.*
miserably	**ADVERB**	○ *He looked miserably down at his plate.*
misery	**UNCOUNT**	○ *Back pain causes misery to millions of people each year.*

mix /mɪks/ (mixes, mixing, mixed)   `FOOD & DRINK`

VERB If you **mix** one substance **with** another, you stir or shake them together, or combine them in some other way, so that they become a single substance. ○ [+ with] *Mix the cinnamon with the rest of the sugar.* ○ *Mix the ingredients together slowly.*

▸ **COLLOCATIONS:**
  mix something **with** something
  mix two things **together**
  mix the **ingredients**
  thoroughly mix something

mo|bile phone /ˌməʊbaɪl ˈfəʊn, AM -bəl/   `COMMUNICATIONS`
(mobile phones)

NOUN A **mobile phone** or a **mobile** is a telephone that you can carry with you and use to make or receive calls wherever you are. [BRIT; in AM, use **cellular phone**, **cellphone**] ○ *I called my Dad on his mobile.* ○ *We're not allowed to use mobile phones during class.*

→ see also **smart phone**

▶ **COLLOCATIONS:**
on a mobile phone
use a mobile phone
charge (up) a mobile phone
a mobile phone **call/number**

mod|ern /ˈmɒdən/ HOME

1 ADJECTIVE Modern means relating to the present time. ○ *the problems of modern society* ○ *the changing role of women in the modern world*

▶ **COLLOCATIONS:**
modern **life/society/culture/civilization/times**
the modern **world/era**

▶ **SYNONYMS:** contemporary, present, current

2 ADJECTIVE Something that is **modern** is new and involves the latest ideas or equipment. ○ *Their house is very modern.* ○ *a modern kitchen* ○ *Modern technology has made instant communication possible across the world.*

▶ **COLLOCATIONS:**
modern **technology/conveniences/equipment**
modern **house/furniture/style**

▶ **SYNONYMS:** new, up-to-date

mod|est /ˈmɒdɪst/ PERSONALITY

ADJECTIVE If you say that someone is **modest**, you approve of them because they do not talk much about their abilities or achievements. ○ [+ *about*] *He is modest about his success.* ○ *She is an incredibly talented artist but very modest.*

▶ **COLLOCATIONS:**
modest **about** *something*
be/remain modest
a modest **man**

▶ **ANTONYM:** boastful

WORD FAMILY		
modest	ADJECTIVE	○ *I found him a modest and unassuming man.*
modestly	ADVERB	○ *'It was nothing,' she said modestly.*
modesty	UNCOUNT	○ *He shows surprising modesty about his achievements.*
immodest	ADJECTIVE	○ *It would be immodest to repeat the praise I received.*

mon|soon /mɒnˈsuːn/ (monsoons) SCIENCE & NATURE

NOUN The **monsoon** is the season in Southern Asia when there is a lot of very heavy rain. ○ *the end of the monsoon* ○ *monsoon flooding*

month|ly /'mʌnθli/

ADJECTIVE A **monthly** event or publication happens or appears every month. ○ Register for our monthly newsletter. ○ She makes monthly payments of £20 for her mobile phone contract.

▶ COLLOCATIONS:
a monthly **payment/instalment/fee/rent**
a monthly **newsletter/magazine/bulletin**

mood /muːd/ (moods)

NOUN Your **mood** is the way you are feeling at a particular time. ○ He is clearly in a good mood today. ○ When he came back, he was in a foul mood. ○ [+ for] I was in the mood for dancing. ○ [+ to-inf] We were not in the mood to celebrate.

▶ COLLOCATIONS:
in a mood
a **good/bad/foul** mood
a **depressed/positive/tense** mood
someone's mood **changes/swings**

moody /'muːdi/ (moodier, moodiest)   PERSONALITY

ADJECTIVE A **moody** person often becomes angry or sad without any warning. ○ David's mother was irritable and moody.

WORD FAMILY		
mood	NOUN	○ Her mood changed completely when she saw him.
moody	ADJECTIVE	○ Tom can be quite moody and unpredictable.
moodiness	UNCOUNT	○ I've had enough of his moodiness.

mosque /mɒsk/ (mosques)   PLACES

NOUN A **mosque** is a building where Muslims go to worship. ○ Prayers were said for them at the mosque. ○ worshippers at a local mosque ○ the site of an ancient mosque

▶ COLLOCATIONS:
at/in a mosque
go to/visit a mosque
the **local/main/central** mosque

mo|tor|ist /'məʊtərɪst/ (motorists)   TRANSPORT & TRAVEL

NOUN A **motorist** is a person who drives a car. [mainly BRIT] ○ Police warned motorists to look out for bikers. ○ The road was closed to motorists and pedestrians.

▶ SYNONYM: driver

moun|tain /ˈmaʊntɪn, AM -tən/ (mountains) SCIENCE & NATURE

NOUN A **mountain** is a very high area of land with steep sides. ○ *They climbed Ben Nevis, Britain's highest mountain.* ○ *a skiing village in the mountains* ○ *a little mountain stream*

▶ **COLLOCATIONS:**
in the mountains
go up/climb a mountain
go down/descend a mountain
a **high/snowy/snow-capped** mountain
a mountain **village/road/path/stream**
a mountain **peak/top**

> WORD FAMILY
>
> | **mountain** | NOUN | ○ *In the distance you can see snowy mountains.* |
> | **mountainous** | ADJECTIVE | ○ *The remote village is in a mountainous region, 240 miles south of Quito.* |

mud /mʌd/ SCIENCE & NATURE

UNCOUNTABLE NOUN **Mud** is a sticky mixture of earth and water. ○ *His football boots were covered with mud.* ○ *Their car got stuck in the mud.*

▶ **COLLOCATION:** **in** the mud

> WORD FAMILY
>
> | **mud** | UNCOUNT | ○ *The field had turned to mud.* |
> | **muddy** | ADJECTIVE | ○ *Don't walk in here with your muddy boots!* |

m

mur|der /ˈmɜːdə/ (murders, murdering, murdered) CRIME

1 UNCOUNTABLE NOUN **Murder** is the crime of deliberately killing a person.
○ *The three men were charged with attempted murder.* ○ *He was jailed for life for murder.*
○ *a murder victim*

▶ **COLLOCATIONS:**
commit murder
be accused of/be charged with murder
guilty of murder
attempted murder
a murder **charge/trial/victim**

▶ **SYNONYM:** homicide

2 VERB To **murder** someone means to commit the crime of killing them deliberately. ○ *She was accused of murdering her husband.* ○ *a murdered religious leader*

▶ **SYNONYM:** kill

WORD FAMILY		
murder	NOUN	○ He is on trial, accused of murder.
murder	VERB	○ Police think the dead man was murdered.
murderer	NOUN	○ The murderer was sentenced to life imprisonment.

mu|si|cal /ˈmjuːzɪkəl/ (musicals)

MEDIA & CULTURE

1 **ADJECTIVE** You use **musical** to indicate that something is connected with playing or studying music. ○ We have a lot of musical talent in our school. ○ I'd like to learn a musical instrument.

▶ COLLOCATIONS:
  musical **talent/ability**
  a musical **instrument**

2 **NOUN** A **musical** is a play or film that uses singing and dancing in the story. ○ They went to see a musical in the West End.

WORD FAMILY		
music	UNCOUNT	○ I like all kinds of music, especially rap and R&B.
musical	ADJECTIVE	○ He plays a range of musical styles.
musical	NOUN	○ Have you seen the musical 'Les Miserables'?
musically	ADVERB	○ The band are both popular and musically talented.
musician	NOUN	○ She is a good musician who plays several instruments.

m

Nn

---

nar|row /ˈnærəʊ/ (narrower, narrowest)

PLACES

ADJECTIVE Something that is **narrow** measures a very small distance from one side to the other. ○ *We wandered through the narrow streets of the old town.* ○ *My bed was too narrow.* ○ *She had long, narrow feet.*

▶ COLLOCATIONS:
  a narrow **street/path/road/corridor/river**
  a narrow **strip/band**
  a narrow **gap/space/opening**
  a narrow **bed**
  narrow **shoulders/feet**
  long and narrow

▶ ANTONYMS: wide, broad

---

na|ture /ˈneɪtʃə/

SCIENCE & NATURE

UNCOUNTABLE NOUN **Nature** is all the animals, plants, and other things in the world that are not made by people or caused by people. ○ *She writes a column about nature and science.* ○ *The nature trail leads through woodland to a viewpoint overlooking a spectacular waterfall.* ○ *the ecological balance of nature*

▶ COLLOCATIONS:
  the **wonders/beauty/balance** of nature
  a nature **trail/reserve**
  nature **conservation**

natu|ral /ˈnætʃərəl/

ADJECTIVE **Natural** things exist or occur in nature and are not made or caused by people. ○ *We need to be careful how we use our natural resources.* ○ *I prefer to wear natural fibres such as cotton.* ○ *The typhoon was the worst natural disaster in many years.*

▶ COLLOCATIONS:
  natural **resources**
  natural **fibres/fabrics**
  natural **beauty**
  the natural **world**
  a natural **disaster**

▶ ANTONYMS: artificial, man-made

n

WHICH WORD: nature, countryside, wildlife, or landscape?

Nature refers to everything that is not made by people, and includes landscape, animals, plants, and weather. ○ *When I'm walking I feel very close to nature.*

You use **countryside** to refer to land which is away from towns and cities. ○ *We love going for walks in the countryside.*

You use **wildlife** to refer to animals and plants that live wild in a place. ○ *Pollution is harming the local wildlife.*

You use **landscape** to refer to the natural physical features of land, such as hills and forests. ○ *Here the landscape becomes more rocky.*

WORD FAMILY

nature	UNCOUNT	○ *He writes songs about the beauty of nature.*
natural	ADJECTIVE	○ *our understanding of the natural world*
naturally	ADVERB	○ *Nitrates can occur naturally in water and soil.*
unnatural	ADJECTIVE	○ *The acting in the play seemed very unnatural.*
unnaturally	ADVERB	○ *His skin looked unnaturally pale.*

---

neck|lace /'neklɪs/ (necklaces)   CLOTHES & APPEARANCE

NOUN A **necklace** is a piece of jewellery such as a chain or a string of beads which someone wears round their neck. ○ *She wore a silver necklace and bracelet.* ○ *a diamond necklace*

▶ COLLOCATIONS:
   a **gold/silver/diamond/pearl** necklace
   wear a necklace

---

nega|tive /'neɡətɪv/

ADJECTIVE A situation, experience, or reaction that is **negative** is bad, unpleasant, or harmful. ○ *We welcome your comments, positive and negative.* ○ *Internet bullying has an extremely negative effect on people.* ○ *Reaction to the film was overwhelmingly negative.*

▶ COLLOCATIONS:
   a negative **effect/impact/result/consequence**
   a negative **feeling/reaction/attitude**
   a negative **image**
   negative **news/publicity/comments**
   extremely/overwhelmingly/strongly negative

▶ ANTONYM: positive

> **WORD FAMILY**
>
> | | | |
> |---|---|---|
> | **negative** | ADJECTIVE | ○ The company has a very negative image among young people. |
> | **negatively** | ADVERB | ○ This will negatively affect the result. |

---

neigh|bour /ˈneɪbə/ (neighbours) [in AM, use neighbor]   PEOPLE

NOUN Your **neighbour** is someone who lives near you. ○ We could hear our upstairs neighbours having a party. ○ a good neighbour

▶ **COLLOCATIONS:**
a **good** neighbour
someone's **next-door/upstairs/downstairs** neighbour

> **WORD FAMILY**
>
> | | | |
> |---|---|---|
> | **neighbour** | NOUN | ○ I was talking to my neighbour in the street. |
> | **neighbouring** | ADJECTIVE | ○ The fire spread to neighbouring houses. |
> | **neighbourhood** | NOUN | ○ They live in a very nice neighbourhood. |
> | **neighbourly** | ADJECTIVE | ○ People here are very neighbourly and help each other. |

---

neph|ew /ˈnefjuː, ˈnev-/ (nephews)   PEOPLE

NOUN Someone's **nephew** is the son of their sister or brother. ○ I took my nephew to the zoo.

---

news|paper /ˈnjuːspeɪpə, AM ˈnuːz-/ (newspapers)   MEDIA & CULTURE

NOUN A **newspaper** is a publication consisting of large sheets of folded paper, on which news is printed. ○ He sat down to read his newspaper. ○ They saw the story in the newspaper. ○ a newspaper article about a new band

▶ **COLLOCATIONS:**
in the newspaper
read/buy a newspaper
read/see/write something **in** a newspaper
a **local/national/daily** newspaper
a newspaper **article/feature/headline**

---

niece /niːs/ (nieces)   PEOPLE

NOUN Someone's **niece** is the daughter of their sister or brother. ○ I went to my niece's birthday party.

---

noo|dles /ˈnuːdəlz/   FOOD & DRINK

PLURAL NOUN **Noodles** are long, thin, curly strips of pasta. They are used especially in Chinese and Italian cooking. ○ a bowl of noodles ○ chicken served with noodles

no|tice /ˈnəʊtɪs/ (notices, noticing, noticed)

VERB If you **notice** something or someone, you become aware of them. ○ *The teacher began to notice a difference in her attitude.* ○ [+ that] *I noticed that nobody was laughing.* ○ [+ who] *She didn't notice who he was with.* ○ *She noticed a bird sitting on the garage roof.* ○ *I had my hair cut, but nobody noticed.*

▶ COLLOCATIONS:
  notice a **change/difference**
  begin/fail to notice

▶ SYNONYMS: observe, see

WORD FAMILY		
notice	**VERB**	○ *Did you notice anything different about him?*
noticeable	**ADJECTIVE**	○ *There has been a noticeable change in his behaviour.*
noticeably	**ADVERB**	○ *He was noticeably taller than when I last saw him.*

nov|el /ˈnɒvəl/ (novels)   `MEDIA & CULTURE`

NOUN A **novel** is a long written story about imaginary people and events.
  ○ *She writes historical novels set in the time of Henry VIII.* ○ [+ by] *a novel by J.K Rowling*
  ○ [+ about] *a novel about life in rural Ireland*

▶ COLLOCATIONS:
  a novel **by** someone
  a novel **about** something
  a novel **set** somewhere
  write/read/publish a novel
  a **historical/crime/romantic** novel
  a **fantasy/science fiction** novel
  a **best-selling/new/first** novel

▶ SYNONYM: book

nov|el|ist /ˈnɒvəlɪst/ (novelists)

NOUN A **novelist** is a person who writes novels. ○ *a best-selling romantic novelist*

▶ COLLOCATIONS:
  a **romantic/crime/comic/fantasy/historical** novelist
  a **best-selling** novelist

▶ SYNONYMS: writer, author

nurse|ry school /ˈnɜːsəri skuːl/ (nursery schools)   `EDUCATION`

NOUN A **nursery school** or a **nursery** is a school for very young children.
  ○ *From the ages of 2 to 4 they go to nursery school.*

▶ COLLOCATIONS:
  go to nursery school
  a **local/private** nursery school
  a nursery school **teacher**

▶ SYNONYM: kindergarten

Oo

ob|serve /əbˈzɜːv/ (observes, observing, observed) SCIENCE & NATURE

VERB If you **observe** a person or thing, you watch them carefully. ○ *Professor Simms observes the behaviour of babies.* ○ *Researchers observed the birds returning to their nests.*

▶ **COLLOCATIONS:**
  observe **behaviour/animals/children**
  a **researcher/scientist** observes *something/someone*
  observe **closely/carefully**

▶ **SYNONYMS:** study, watch

ob|ser|va|tion /ˌɒbzəˈveɪʃən/ (observations)

1 UNCOUNTABLE NOUN Observation is the action or process of carefully watching someone or something. ○ [+ *of*] *careful observation of the movement of the planets* ○ *You can learn a lot through observation.*

▶ **COLLOCATIONS:**
  observation **of** *someone/something*
  under observation
  through/by observation
  careful/close observation
  direct observation

2 NOUN An **observation** is something that you have learned by seeing or watching something and thinking about it. ○ [+ *about*] *This book contains observations about the causes of addiction.*

▶ **COLLOCATIONS:**
  an observation **about** *something*
  make an observation

WORD FAMILY		
observe	**VERB**	○ *Are there any classes I could observe?*
observation	**UNCOUNT**	○ *Trainee teachers are under observation most of the time.*
observation	**NOUN**	○ *During our research we made some interesting observations.*
observer	**NOUN**	○ *Observers said he was to blame for the crash.*
observant	**ADJECTIVE**	○ *Observant readers pointed out a spelling mistake in the article.*

o

oc|cu|pa|tion /ˌɒkjʊˈpeɪʃən/ (occupations) WORK

NOUN Your **occupation** is your job or profession. ○ *Her main occupation was writing.* ○ *Please state your name, age, and occupation.*

→ see note at **job**

▶ COLLOCATIONS:
someone's **main** occupation
a **full-time** occupation

ocean /ˈəʊʃən/ (oceans) SCIENCE & NATURE

1 **NOUN** The **ocean** is the sea. ○ *They looked out at the ocean.* ○ *creatures that live in the ocean* ○ *a ship sailing on the ocean*

2 **NOUN** An **ocean** is one of the five very large areas of sea on the Earth's surface. ○ *She sailed alone across the Atlantic Ocean.* ○ *the Indian Ocean*

▶ COLLOCATIONS:
on the ocean
in the ocean
the **Atlantic/Pacific/Indian/Arctic/Antarctic** Ocean

of|fer /ˈɒfə, AM ˈɔːfər/ MEDIA & CULTURE · SHOPPING
(offers, offering, offered)

1 **VERB** If you **offer** something to someone, you ask them if they would like to have it or use it. ○ *She offered me a lift to the station.* ○ [+ to] *The company is offering summer jobs to students.* ○ *The clinic offers free health checks.*

▶ COLLOCATIONS:
offer *something* **to** *someone*
offer **help/advice/support**
offer *someone* **work/a job**
offer a **chance/opportunity**

2 **VERB** If you **offer to** do something, you say that you are willing to do it. ○ [+ to-inf] *Peter offered to teach them water-skiing.*

3 **NOUN** An **offer** in a shop is a special low price for a product, or something extra that you get if you buy the product. ○ [+ on] *They have great offers on smartphones and tablets.* ○ *Today's special offer is two main courses for the price of one.* ○ *Many new books are on offer at 50 per cent off.*

▶ COLLOCATIONS:
an offer **on** *something*
be **on** offer
a **special** offer
a **good/great** offer

o

on|line /ˈɒnlaɪn, ɒnˈlaɪn/ also on-line `COMMUNICATIONS` `SHOPPING`

1 ADJECTIVE Online means available on or connected to the Internet. ○ *You can chat to other people who are online.* ○ *I went online to check my messages.* ○ *an online dating service* ○ *online gaming*

▶ **COLLOCATIONS:**
 be/go online
 an online **store/retailer/bank**
 an online **business/company**
 an online **service/system**
 online **shopping/learning/advertising**

2 ADVERB If you do something **online**, you do it on the Internet. ○ *You can find some really good deals online.* ○ *I bought my plane tickets online.* ○ *They play online against friends.*

▶ **COLLOCATIONS:**
 shop online
 get/buy/find *something* online
 look/search online
 play online
 available online

opin|ion /əˈpɪnjən/ (opinions) `BELIEFS & OPINIONS`

NOUN Your **opinion** about something is what you think or believe about it. ○ [+ *of*] *What is your opinion of this plan?* ○ *I wasn't asking for your opinion.* ○ *We want the opportunity to express our opinions.* ○ *In his opinion, the Internet should not be censored.*

▶ **COLLOCATIONS:**
 an opinion **about/of** *something*
 in *someone's* opinion
 have/hold an opinion
 express/give/share/offer an opinion
 ask for/seek an opinion
 a **strong** opinion
 a **good/favourable/bad/poor** opinion

▶ **SYNONYM:** view

op|por|tu|nity /ˌɒpəˈtjuːnɪti, AM -ˈtuːn-/ (opportunities)

NOUN An **opportunity** is a situation in which it is possible for you to do something that you want to do. ○ [+ *to-inf*] *I had an opportunity to go to New York and study.* ○ *The course was a great opportunity to meet new people.* ○ [+ *for*] *I want to see more opportunities for young people.*

▶ **COLLOCATIONS:**
 an opportunity **for** *something/someone*
 have/get an opportunity
 miss an opportunity

take/take advantage of/seize an opportunity
a **great/good/golden** opportunity
a **rare/unique** opportunity
a **job/educational/business** opportunity

▶ SYNONYM: chance

---

op|pose /əˈpəʊz/ (opposes, opposing, opposed) [BELIEFS & OPINIONS]

VERB If you **oppose** a plan or idea or **oppose** someone, you disagree with what someone wants to do and try to prevent them from doing it. ○ *He bitterly opposed the idea of women's rights.* ○ *She was elected, although many people opposed her.*

▶ COLLOCATIONS:
oppose a **plan/bill/idea**
strongly/vehemently/vigorously oppose *something/someone*

▶ ANTONYM: support

WORD FAMILY		
oppose	**VERB**	○ *Local people oppose the planned road.*
opposition	**UNCOUNT**	○ *The increase in fees met with a lot of opposition from students.*
opposing	**ADJECTIVE**	○ *an opportunity for the opposing sides to talk*
opposed to	**ADJECTIVE**	○ *I am completely opposed to the death penalty.*
opponent	**NOUN**	○ *She debated calmly with her opponents.*

---

op|ti|cian /ɒpˈtɪʃən/ (opticians) [WORK] [HEALTH]

1 NOUN An **optician** is someone whose job involves testing people's eyesight and making or selling glasses and contact lenses. ○ *She decided to train as an optician.*

2 NOUN An **optician** or an **optician's** is a shop where you can have your eyes tested and buy glasses and contact lenses. ○ *I went for a sight test at the optician's.*

▶ COLLOCATION: **at** the optician

---

op|ti|mis|tic /ˌɒptɪˈmɪstɪk/ [BELIEFS & OPINIONS]

ADJECTIVE Someone who is **optimistic** is hopeful about the future or the success of something in particular. ○ [+ that] *I am optimistic that I'll pass the exam.* ○ [+ about] *People are feeling more optimistic about the future.* ○ *She has a very optimistic view of human nature.*

▶ COLLOCATIONS:
optimistic **about** *something*
be/feel/seem optimistic
an optimistic **mood**
an optimistic **view/outlook/forecast**
cautiously/wildly/overly optimistic

▶ SYNONYM: hopeful

▶ ANTONYM: pessimistic

op|tion|al /ˈɒpʃənəl/

ADJECTIVE If something is **optional**, you can choose whether or not you do it or have it. ○ *Attendance at the summer school is optional, but recommended.* ○ *You pay more for optional extras such as headphones and a carry case.* ○ *optional excursion to Roman site available*

▶ **COLLOCATIONS:**
   an optional **extra**
   an optional **excursion/trip/tour**
   an optional **course**

▶ **ANTONYM:** compulsory

WORD FAMILY		
optional	ADJECTIVE	○ *The school uniform includes a tie, but this is optional.*
option	NOUN	○ *For an extra charge you have the option of a private bathroom.*

---

or|ches|tra /ˈɔːkɪstrə/ (orchestras) `MEDIA & CULTURE`

NOUN An **orchestra** is a large group of musicians who play a variety of different instruments together. ○ *The orchestra played the opening theme.* ○ *He has conducted the City of Birmingham Symphony Orchestra.*

▶ **COLLOCATIONS:**
   an orchestra **plays**
   play in/conduct an orchestra
   a **symphony/chamber** orchestra

WORD FAMILY		
orchestra	NOUN	○ *the strings section of an orchestra*
orchestral	ADJECTIVE	○ *orchestral instruments such as the flute*

---

or|gan|ic /ɔːˈɡænɪk/ `SCIENCE & NATURE`

ADJECTIVE Organic farming or gardening uses only natural animal and plant products and does not use artificial fertilizers or pesticides. ○ *Organic farming is expanding everywhere.* ○ *They grow their own organic vegetables.*

▶ COLLOCATIONS:
organic **farming/gardening**
organic **food/fruit/vegetables/milk**

WORD FAMILY		
organic	ADJECTIVE	○ She prefers to buy organic food.
organically	ADVERB	○ All our vegetables are grown organically.

---

or|ga|nized /ˈɔːɡənaɪzd/ [in BRIT, also use **organised**] `PERSONALITY`

ADJECTIVE Someone who is **organized** plans their work and activities efficiently.
○ We need an efficient, organized manager. ○ He's clever, but not very organized.

▶ ANTONYM: disorganized

USAGE
You can also say that someone is **well-organized**. This has the same meaning as **organized**: ○ You have to be well-organized to do this job.

---

origi|nal /əˈrɪdʒɪnəl/ `HISTORY` `MEDIA & CULTURE`

1 ADJECTIVE You use **original** when referring to something that existed at the beginning of a process, or the characteristics that something had when it first existed. ○ The original plan was to camp, but the weather was too bad. ○ The inhabitants voted to restore the city's original name.

▶ COLLOCATIONS:
the original **plan/idea/design/version**
something's original **name/title**

▶ SYNONYM: initial

2 ADJECTIVE An **original** piece of writing or music was written recently and has not been published or performed before. ○ The movie had an original soundtrack by Jay-Z. ○ a remake of an original film from the 1950s

▶ COLLOCATION: an original **work/song/soundtrack**

▶ SYNONYM: new

3 ADJECTIVE If you describe someone or their work as **original**, you mean that they are very imaginative and have new ideas. ○ It is one of the most original movies I've ever seen. ○ His ideas are so original. ○ a highly original writer

▶ SYNONYMS: innovative, unique

WORD FAMILY		
origin	NOUN	○ theories about the origin of life
original	ADJECTIVE	○ changes to the original design
originally	ADVERB	○ The hotel was originally a monastery.
originate	VERB	○ Nobody knows where this custom originated.

out|doors /ˌaʊtˈdɔːz/

ADVERB If something happens **outdoors**, it happens outside rather than in a building. ○ *It was warm enough to eat outdoors.* ○ *I prefer playing sport outdoors to going to the gym.*

▶ **SYNONYM:** out of doors

▶ **ANTONYM:** indoors

out|fit /ˈaʊtfɪt/ (outfits)

NOUN An **outfit** is a set of clothes. ○ *I bought a new outfit for the interview.* ○ *I like your outfit.*

▶ **COLLOCATIONS:**
wear/buy/choose an outfit
a **new** outfit

out|going /ˌaʊtˈɡəʊɪŋ/

ADJECTIVE Someone who is **outgoing** is very friendly and likes talking to people. ○ *She's very outgoing and loves meeting new people.* ○ *an outgoing personality*

▶ **SYNONYM:** extrovert

▶ **ANTONYMS:** shy, introvert

out-of-town /ˌaʊt əv ˈtaʊn/

ADJECTIVE **Out-of-town** shops are situated away from the centre of a town or city. ○ *She usually shops at a big out-of-town supermarket.*

▶ **COLLOCATIONS:**
an out-of-town **shop/supermarket/shopping centre**
out-of-town **shopping**

out|ra|geous /aʊtˈreɪdʒəs/

ADJECTIVE If you describe something as **outrageous**, you are emphasizing that it is unacceptable or very shocking. ○ *He apologised for his outrageous behaviour.* ○ *Charges when using your mobile abroad can be outrageous.*

▶ **COLLOCATIONS:**
outrageous **behaviour**
outrageous **charges/prices/fees**
outrageous **claims/demands**
absolutely/completely outrageous

WORD FAMILY		
outrage	**VERB**	○ *We were outraged by his comments.*
outrage	**UNCOUNT**	○ *The decision provoked outrage from women.*
outrageous	**ADJECTIVE**	○ *His claims are absolutely outrageous and untrue.*
outrageously	**ADVERB**	○ *Designer clothes can be outrageously expensive.*

out|skirts /'aʊtskɜːts/ `PLACES`

PLURAL NOUN The **outskirts of** a city or town are the parts of it that are farthest away from its centre. ○ [+ of] *We reached the outskirts of a town.* ○ *a house on the outskirts of London*

▸ **COLLOCATIONS:**
  the outskirts **of** *something*
  on the outskirts
  the outskirts of the **city/town/capital/village**

out|stand|ing /ˌaʊt'stændɪŋ/

ADJECTIVE If you describe someone or something as **outstanding**, you think that they are remarkable and very impressive. ○ *He is an outstanding athlete.* ○ *Her performance was absolutely outstanding.* ○ *an area of outstanding natural beauty*

▸ **COLLOCATIONS:**
  an outstanding **player/athlete**
  an oustanding **performance/achievement/contribution**
  outstanding **beauty**
  absolutely outstanding

▸ **SYNONYM:** exceptional

oven /'ʌvən/ (ovens) `FOOD & DRINK`

NOUN An **oven** is a cooker or part of a cooker that you can cook food inside.
  ○ *Put the potatoes in the oven and roast them for one hour.* ○ *Heat the oven to 200° C.*

▸ **COLLOCATIONS:**
  in the oven
  put/cook/bake/roast *something* in the oven
  heat/set/turn on/put on an oven
  a **gas/electric/microwave** oven

over|take /ˌəʊvə'teɪk/ `TRANSPORT & TRAVEL`
(overtakes, overtaking, overtook, overtaken)

VERB If you **overtake** a moving vehicle or person, you pass them because you are moving faster in the same direction. [mainly BRIT] ○ *A motorbike overtook me going about 80 miles an hour.* ○ *The red car was signalling, ready to overtake.*

over|time /'əʊvətaɪm/ `WORK`

UNCOUNTABLE NOUN **Overtime** is time that you spend doing your job in addition to your normal working hours. ○ *He would work overtime to finish a job.* ○ *I sometimes do overtime to earn extra cash.*

▸ **COLLOCATION:** **work/do** overtime

owe /əʊ/ (owes, owing, owed)

`MONEY`

VERB If you **owe** money to someone, they have lent it to you and you have not yet paid it back. ○ [+ to] *The company owes money to the bank.* ○ *His brother owed him nearly £50.* ○ *I owe two months' rent.*

▶ **COLLOCATIONS:**
owe *something* **to** *someone*
owe **money/rent/taxes**

o

Pp

---

pack /pæk/ (packs, packing, packed) TRANSPORT & TRAVEL

VERB When you **pack** a bag, you put clothes and other things into it, because you are leaving a place or going on holiday. ○ *I packed my bags and left home.* ○ *Don't forget to pack your swimming costume.* ○ *I packed the night before.*

▶ COLLOCATIONS:
  pack your **bags/things/belongings**
  pack a **bag/suitcase**

---

pack|ag|ing /ˈpækɪdʒɪŋ/ SHOPPING

UNCOUNTABLE NOUN Packaging is the container or covering that something is sold in. ○ *It sells well because the packaging is so attractive.* ○ *plastic food packaging*

▶ COLLOCATIONS:
  plastic/cardboard/paper packaging
  biodegradable packaging
  wasteful/unnecessary packaging
  food/product packaging

---

paint /peɪnt/ (paints, painting, painted) MEDIA & CULTURE

VERB If you **paint** something or **paint** a picture of it, you produce a picture of it using paint. ○ *I painted a picture of a horse.* ○ *His portrait was painted by Holbein.* ○ *She loves to paint.*

▶ COLLOCATIONS:
  paint a **picture/portrait**
  paint a **scene/landscape**

WORD FAMILY		
paint	**VERB**	○ *Who painted 'The Mona Lisa'?*
paint	**UNCOUNT**	○ *a tin of white paint*
painting	**NOUN**	○ *A painting of sunflowers hung on the wall.*
painter	**NOUN**	○ *My favourite painter is Picasso.*

---

pale /peɪl/ (paler, palest) CLOTHES & APPEARANCE

1 ADJECTIVE If something is **pale**, it is very light in colour or almost white. ○ *He wore a pale green shirt.* ○ *People with pale skin should protect themselves in the sun.*

▶ **COLLOCATIONS:**
a pale **colour/shade**
pale **blue/pink/green/yellow/grey**
pale **skin/complexion**

▶ **ANTONYM:** dark

2 **ADJECTIVE** If someone looks **pale**, their face is a lighter colour than usual, because they are ill, frightened, or shocked. ○ *She looked pale and tired.* ○ *He went deathly pale.*

▶ **COLLOCATIONS:**
look/turn/go pale
deathly pale

---

par|ticu|lar /pə'tɪkjʊlə/

ADJECTIVE You use **particular** to emphasize that you are talking about one thing or one kind of thing rather than other similar ones. ○ *Are there particular things you're interested in?* ○ *Check the index to find information on your particular problem.* ○ *The group which has attracted particular attention is young males.*

▶ **COLLOCATIONS:**
a particular **thing/reason/area/case**
a particular **problem/concern**
particular **attention/interest**

WORD FAMILY		
particular	**ADJECTIVE**	○ *In this particular case I agree.*
particularly	**ADVERB**	○ *I would particularly like to go to Rio.*

---

par|ty /'pɑːti/ (parties)　　　　　`SOCIAL LIFE`

NOUN A **party** is a social event at which people enjoy themselves doing things such as eating, drinking, or dancing. ○ *The couple met at a party.* ○ *We threw a huge birthday party.* ○ *I'm going to a party on Saturday.* ○ *She gets invited to lots of parties.*

▶ **COLLOCATIONS:**
at a party
have/throw a party
go to a party
invite *someone* **to** a party
a **birthday/Christmas/engagement** party
a **garden/dinner/drinks** party
a party **dress/invitation/game**

---

pass /pɑːs, pæs/ (passes, passing, passed)

1 **VERB** When a period of time **passes**, it happens and finishes. ○ *As time passed it became clear that the system was not working.* ○ *My first day at work passed very slowly.* ○ *Several hours passed before anyone noticed they were missing.*

► **COLLOCATIONS:**
time passes
minutes/hours/days pass
weeks/months/years pass
time passes **slowly/quickly**

► SYNONYM: go by

2 VERB If you **pass** time in a particular way, you spend it in that way. ○ *The children passed the time playing in the streets.* ○ *To pass the time they sang songs.*

---

pass|port /'pɑːspɔːt, 'pæs-/ (passports)   `TRANSPORT & TRAVEL`

NOUN Your **passport** is an official document which you need to show when you enter or leave a country. ○ *You need to show a valid passport in order to travel.* ○ *Her children hold British passports.*

► **COLLOCATIONS:**
have/hold/carry a passport
show/produce your passport
a **British/American/German/EU**, etc. passport
a **valid** passport
a **false/fake** passport

pass|port con|trol /,pɑːspɔːt kən'trəʊl, ,pæs-/

UNCOUNTABLE NOUN **Passport control** is a place, for example at an airport or port, where you need to show your passport when entering or leaving a country. ○ *First you have to go through security and passport control.* ○ *He was stopped at passport control.*

► **COLLOCATIONS:**
at passport control
go through passport control

---

pass|word /'pɑːswɜːd, 'pæs-/ (passwords)   `COMMUNICATIONS`

NOUN A **password** is a secret word or phrase that you must know in order to be allowed to use a computer system. ○ *Enter your username and password.* ○ *Click here if you have forgotten your password.*

► **COLLOCATIONS:**
type in/enter a password
ask for/require a password
change/remember/forget your password
set/create/choose a password
a **secret/secure/strong** password

---

path /pɑːθ, pæθ/ (paths)   `SCIENCE & NATURE`

NOUN A **path** is a long strip of ground which people walk along to get from one place to another. ○ *We followed the path along the clifftops.* ○ *He went up the garden path and knocked on the door.*

▶ **COLLOCATIONS:**
up/down/along a path
a **clifftop/garden** path

---

pa|tient /ˈpeɪʃənt/ (patients) `HEALTH` `PERSONALITY`

1 NOUN A **patient** is a person who is receiving treatment from a doctor or who is registered with a doctor. ○ *The doctor has a lot of patients to see.* ○ *Nurses play a vital role in caring for patients.* ○ *cancer patients*

▶ **COLLOCATIONS:**
see/care for/treat a patient
a **cancer/heart/transplant** patient
a **hospital** patient

2 ADJECTIVE If you are **patient**, you stay calm and do not get annoyed, for example when something takes a long time. ○ *Please be patient – your cheque will arrive.* ○ [+ with] *He was very kind and patient with children.*

▶ **COLLOCATIONS:**
patient **with** someone
extremely/endlessly/incredibly patient

▶ **ANTONYM:** impatient

WORD FAMILY		
patient	ADJECTIVE	○ She was an extremely patient teacher.
patiently	ADVERB	○ She waited patiently for me to finish.
patience	NOUN	○ Thank you for your patience - your call will be answered as soon as possible.
impatient	ADJECTIVE	○ After waiting for an hour, the crowd was getting impatient.
impatiently	ADVERB	○ 'Where is he?' she asked impatiently.
impatience	NOUN	○ I remember his impatience with long speeches.

---

pay /peɪ/ (pays, paying, paid) `MONEY`

1 VERB When you **pay** an amount of money **to** someone, you give it to them in exchange for something. When you **pay** something such as a bill or a debt, you pay the amount that you owe. ○ [+ for] *We paid £35 for the tickets.* ○ [+ for] *All you pay for is your meals.* ○ *My uncle offered to pay the bill.* ○ *You can pay by credit card.*

▶ **COLLOCATIONS:**
pay **for** something
pay something **to** someone
pay a **price/fee/bill**
pay **more/less/extra**
pay **money**
pay **tax/a fine**
pay **in cash/by credit card**

2 VERB When you **are paid**, you get your wages or salary from your employer. ○ *The lawyer was paid a huge salary.* ○ *I get paid monthly.* ○ *[+ for] They pay $10 an hour for waitressing.*

▶ **COLLOCATIONS:**
pay someone **for** something
get/be paid
pay someone **weekly/monthly/by the hour**
pay **well/badly**

WORD FAMILY		
pay	VERB	○ He paid $50 to the owner. ○ It's OK, I'll pay.
payment	NOUN	○ He didn't expect any payment for his help.

peace|ful /ˈpiːsfʊl/

ADJECTIVE Someone who is **peaceful** is calm and free from worry. ○ *I feel relaxed and peaceful.* ○ *She fell into a deep, peaceful sleep.*

▶ **COLLOCATIONS:**
feel/look peaceful
a peaceful **sleep**

▶ **SYNONYMS:** calm, relaxed

▶ **ANTONYMS:** worried, anxious

WORD FAMILY		
peace	UNCOUNT	○ I need peace and quiet so I can work.
peaceful	ADJECTIVE	○ In the morning everything was quiet and peaceful.
peacefully	ADVERB	○ The baby was sleeping peacefully.
peacefulness	NOUN	○ They love the peacefulness of the countryside.

peak /piːk/ (peaks)   SCIENCE & NATURE

NOUN A **peak** is a mountain or the top of a mountain. ○ *the snow-capped peak of Mont Blanc* ○ *You could see tall mountain peaks in the distance.*

▶ **COLLOCATIONS:**
a **mountain** peak
a **snowy/snow-capped** peak

pe|des|trian /pɪˈdestriən/ (pedestrians)   TRANSPORT & TRAVEL

NOUN A **pedestrian** is a person who is walking, especially in a town or city, rather than travelling in a vehicle. ○ *Cars are supposed to give way to pedestrians on the pedestrian crossing.* ○ *A 16-year-old pedestrian was killed by a hit-and-run driver.*

peel /piːl/ (peels, peeling, peeled)

`FOOD & DRINK`

VERB When you **peel** fruit or vegetables, you remove their skins. ○ *She sat down in the kitchen and began peeling potatoes.*

▶ **COLLOCATIONS:**
   peel a **potato/onion/carrot**
   peel a **banana/apple/orange**

---

pen|sion /ˈpenʃən/ (pensions)

`WORK`

NOUN Someone who has a **pension** receives a regular sum of money from the state or from a former employer because they have retired or because they are widowed or disabled. ○ *Some people on pensions are struggling to buy food.* ○ *She receives a pension of £73.46 per week.*

▶ **COLLOCATIONS:**
   be **on** a pension
   get/receive/have a pension
   a **state/company** pension
   a pension **scheme**

WORD FAMILY		
pension	**NOUN**	○ *I'm already a member of my company's pension scheme.*
pensioner	**NOUN**	○ *Single pensioners will receive a £3-a-week increase.*

---

per cent /pɜː ˈsent/ (per cent) also **percent**

NOUN You use **per cent** to talk about amounts. For example, if an amount is 10 per cent (10%) of a larger amount, it is equal to 10 hundredths of the larger amount. ○ [+ *of*] *Ten per cent of the school's students are American.* ○ *The area has an unemployment level of 40 per cent.*

WORD FAMILY		
per cent	**NOUN**	○ *56 percent said snack products, such as crisps and chocolate, contributed most to children's obesity.*
percentage	**NOUN**	○ *A high percentage of people now do at least some of their shopping online.*

---

per|for|mance /pəˈfɔːməns/ (performances)

`MEDIA & CULTURE`

NOUN A **performance** involves entertaining an audience by doing something such as singing, dancing, or acting. ○ [+ *by*] *There will be performances by local bands.* ○ [+ *of*] *The singer gave a solo performance of a song called 'Goodbye'.*

▶ **COLLOCATIONS:**
   a performance **of** *something*
   a performance **by** *someone*

give a performance
go to/attend a performance
a **live** performance
a **solo** performance
a **stage/dance/concert** performance

WORD FAMILY		
perform	VERB	○ *The band performed a new song, 'Silence Is Easy'.*
performance	NOUN	○ *She attended a performance of 'Swan Lake' at the Bolshoi Theatre.*
performer	NOUN	○ *He has won 12 awards as a solo performer and member of 'Take That'.*

---

per|ma|nent /'pɜːmənənt/ [WORK]

ADJECTIVE A **permanent** employee is one who is employed for an unlimited length of time. ○ *The company now employs 1,300 permanent staff.* ○ *They offered me a permanent job.*

▶ **COLLOCATIONS:**
permanent **staff**
a permanent **employee/worker**
a permanent **job/contract**
permanent **employment**

▶ **ANTONYM:** temporary

WORD FAMILY		
permanent	ADJECTIVE	○ *A lot of young people are struggling to find permanent employment.*
permanently	ADVERB	○ *230 people are permanently employed at the factory.*
permanence	UNCOUNT	○ *The jobs offer flexibility rather than permanence.*

---

per|son|al|ity /ˌpɜːsəˈnælɪti/ (personalities) [PERSONALITY]

1 UNCOUNTABLE NOUN Your **personality** is your whole character and nature. ○ *He has such a warm and outgoing personality.* ○ *Your expectations are determined by your personality type.*

▶ **COLLOCATIONS:**
have a x personality
a **warm/outgoing/bubbly** personality
a **strong** personality
your personality **type**
a personality **trait**

2 NOUN You can refer to a famous person, especially in entertainment, broadcasting, or sport, as a **personality**. ○ *Many celebrities and sports personalities will be coming along to support the event.* ○ *The show features well-known personalities from the world of entertainment.*

▶ COLLOCATIONS:
a **well-known** personality
a **television/radio** personality
a **sports** personality

▶ SYNONYM: celebrity

---

pes|si|mis|tic /ˌpesɪˈmɪstɪk/

ADJECTIVE Someone who is **pessimistic** thinks that bad things are going to happen. ○ [+ about] *Not everyone is so pessimistic about the future.* ○ *He has an excessively pessimistic view of life.*

▶ COLLOCATIONS:
pessimistic **about** something
a pessimistic **view/outlook**
deeply pessimistic

▶ ANTONYM: optimistic

WORD FAMILY		
pessimistic	ADJECTIVE	○ They are deeply pessimistic about the prospect for success.
pessimistically	ADVERB	○ 'But it won't happen,' she concluded pessimistically.
pessimism	UNCOUNT	○ There has been a mood of growing pessimism about the economy.
pessimist	NOUN	○ Stop being such a pessimist!

---

pet /pet/ (pets)

FREE TIME

P

NOUN A **pet** is an animal that you keep in your home to give you company and pleasure. ○ *Mum won't let us have any pets.* ○ *The bird had obviously been kept as a pet.*

▶ COLLOCATIONS:
have/keep/own a pet
keep something **as** a pet
a **family** pet
a pet **owner**
a pet **shop**
pet **food**
a pet **dog/cat/rabbit**

---

pet|rol /ˈpetrəl/

TRANSPORT & TRAVEL

UNCOUNTABLE NOUN **Petrol** is a liquid which is used as a fuel for motor vehicles. [BRIT; in AM, use **gas**, **gasoline**] ○ *We stopped to fill up with petrol.* ○ *The car's petrol tank was empty.*

▶ **COLLOCATIONS:**
fill (*something*) **up with** petrol
unleaded petrol
a petrol **station/pump**
a petrol **tank**

phi|loso|phy /fɪˈlɒsəfi/   `BELIEFS & OPINIONS`

UNCOUNTABLE NOUN Philosophy is the study or creation of theories about basic
things such as the nature of existence, knowledge, and thought, or about how
people should live. ○ *He studied philosophy and psychology at Cambridge.*
○ *traditional Chinese philosophy*

WORD FAMILY		
philosophy	UNCOUNT	○ *At this time, people were deeply influenced by Greek philosophy.*
philosopher	NOUN	○ *the Greek philosopher, Plato*
philosophical	ADJECTIVE	○ *philosophical discussion*
philosophically	ADVERB	○ *He's philosophically opposed to war.*

phone call /ˈfəʊn kɔːl/ (phone calls)   `COMMUNICATIONS`

NOUN If you make a **phone call**, you dial someone's phone number and speak to
them by phone. ○ *I have to make a phone call.* ○ [+ *from/to*] *I got a phone call last
night from Peter.*

▶ **COLLOCATIONS:**
a phone call **to/from** *someone*
make a phone call
get/have/receive a phone call

photo|graph /ˈfəʊtəɡrɑːf, -ɡræf/ (photographs)

NOUN A **photograph**, or a **photo**, is a picture that is made using a camera.
○ [+ *of*] *He wants to take some photographs of the house.* ○ *In the photograph they
looked happy together.*

▶ **COLLOCATIONS:**
a photograph **of** *someone/something*
in a photograph
take a photograph
a photograph **shows** *something*
a **black-and-white/colour** photograph
a **family/wedding** photograph
a photograph **album/frame**

WORD FAMILY

photograph	NOUN	○ *Lindsay looked absolutely stunning in her wedding photographs.*
photo	NOUN	○ *She showed me a photo of her boyfriend.*
photography	UNCOUNT	○ *With digital photography it's easier to view your pictures.*
photographer	NOUN	○ *He became a highly successful fashion photographer.*
photographic	ADJECTIVE	○ *Photographic images can be stored on computer.*

---

physi|cal /ˈfɪzɪkəl/

SPORT & ACTIVITY

ADJECTIVE Physical qualities, actions, or things are connected with a person's body, rather than with their mind. ○ *Children are being encouraged to do more physical exercise.* ○ *What sports or physical activities do you enjoy?*

▶ COLLOCATIONS:
physical **activities/exercise**
physical **health/fitness**
physical **strength**
physical **appearance**
a physical **disability**

WORD FAMILY

physical	ADJECTIVE	○ *My mother was obsessed with weight and physical appearance.*
physically	ADVERB	○ *You may be physically and mentally exhausted after a long flight.*

---

phys|ics /ˈfɪzɪks/

SCIENCE & NATURE

UNCOUNTABLE NOUN Physics is the scientific study of forces such as heat, light, sound, pressure, gravity, and electricity. ○ *He is now at St Andrews University studying physics.* ○ *It is a basic law of physics that energy cannot be created nor destroyed.*

▶ COLLOCATIONS:
study/teach physics
a physics **professor/teacher/student**
a physics **class/lesson/course**
the physics **department**
a physics **lab/experiment/exam**

WORD FAMILY

physics	UNCOUNT	○ *I did have a very good physics teacher.*
physicist	NOUN	○ *He was a nuclear physicist.*

P

pi|ano /pi'ænəʊ/ (pianos)

MEDIA & CULTURE

NOUN A **piano** is a large musical instrument with a row of black and white keys that you press with your fingers. ○ *I taught myself how to play the piano.* ○ *He started piano lessons at the age of 7.*

▶ COLLOCATIONS:
  play the piano
  a piano **lesson/teacher/player**
  piano **music**
  a piano **key/stool**

WORD FAMILY		
piano	NOUN	○ *The room was filled with the soft sound of piano music.*
pianist	NOUN	○ *Billy is a superb jazz pianist.*

pick up /pɪk 'ʌp/
(picks up, picking up, picked up)

COMMUNICATIONS | TRANSPORT & TRAVEL

1 PHRASAL VERB When you **pick** the phone **up**, you lift the receiver so you can make or receive a call. ○ *He picked up the phone and called Marcus.* ○ *I picked up the receiver and hit the re-dial button.*

2 PHRASAL VERB When you **pick up** someone or something that is waiting to be collected, you go to the place where they are and take them away, often in a car. ○ *We drove to the airport to pick up my brother.* ○ *She went over to her parents' house to pick up some clean clothes.*

pic|tur|esque /ˌpɪktʃə'resk/

PLACES

ADJECTIVE A **picturesque** place is attractive and interesting, and has no ugly modern buildings. ○ *Barnetby was a very picturesque little village.* ○ *The harbour is one of the most picturesque in the country.*

▶ COLLOCATIONS:
  a picturesque **village/town/city**
  a picturesque **island/harbour/lake/beach**
  a picturesque **setting/spot**
  picturesque **countryside**

plain /pleɪn/ (plainer, plainest)

CLOTHES & APPEARANCE

ADJECTIVE A **plain** object, surface, or fabric is entirely in one colour and has no pattern, design, or writing on it. ○ *He wore a plain blue shirt.* ○ *The fabric comes in a wide range of plain colours and printed designs.*

plas|ter /ˈplɑːstə, ˈplæs-/ (plasters)　　　HEALTH

1 **NOUN** A **plaster** is a strip of sticky material used for covering small cuts or sores on your body. [BRIT; in AM, usually use **Band-Aid**] ○ *Mum put a plaster on my knee.* ○ *The waiter was wearing a blue sticking plaster on his finger.*

▶ **COLLOCATIONS:**
　put/stick a plaster **on** *something*
　a **sticking** plaster

2 **UNCOUNTABLE NOUN** If you have a leg or arm **in plaster**, you have a cover made of plaster of Paris around your leg or arm, in order to protect a broken bone and allow it to mend. [mainly BRIT; in AM, use **in a cast**] ○ *Her wrist was in plaster.*

plat|form /ˈplætfɔːm/ (platforms)　　　TRANSPORT & TRAVEL

NOUN A **platform** in a railway station is the area beside the rails where you wait for or get off a train. ○ *There were several people waiting on the platform already.* ○ *The train left from platform four.*

▶ **COLLOCATIONS:**
　on a platform
　a **station/train/subway** platform

play /pleɪ/ (plays)　　　MEDIA & CULTURE

NOUN A **play** is a piece of writing which is performed in a theatre, on the radio, or on television. ○ *He is going to be in the school play.* ○ [+ about] *The company put on a play about two couples who fall in love.*

▶ **COLLOCATIONS:**
　a play **about** *something*
　be **in** a play
　go to (see) a play
　watch a play
　put on/perform a play
　write/produce/direct a play
　a **school** play

play|ground /ˈpleɪɡraʊnd/ (playgrounds)　　　FREE TIME　EDUCATION

NOUN A **playground** is a piece of land, at school or in a public area, where children can play. ○ *The boys were playing football in their school playground.* ○ *There are plans for new playground equipment in parks.*

▶ **COLLOCATIONS:**
　in the playground
　a **school** playground
　build a playground
　playground **equipment**
　a playground **game**

pleas|ant /ˈplezənt/ (pleasanter, pleasantest)

ADJECTIVE Something that is **pleasant** is nice, enjoyable, or attractive. ○ *Jane and I had a pleasant day looking round the shops.* ○ *We've had sun which makes a pleasant change from all the rain.*

▶ **COLLOCATIONS:**
a pleasant **surprise/experience/change**
a pleasant **place/town**
a pleasant **day/evening**
a pleasant **atmosphere/environment**

▶ **SYNONYM:** nice

▶ **ANTONYM:** unpleasant

WORD FAMILY		
pleasant	**ADJECTIVE**	○ *It was a pleasant surprise to discover that I had passed the exam.*
pleasantly	**ADVERB**	○ *The room was pleasantly warm.*

pleased /pliːzd/

ADJECTIVE If you are **pleased**, you are happy about something or satisfied with something. ○ [+ at] *Felicity seemed pleased at the suggestion.* ○ [+ that] *She was secretly pleased that Alex was going to be at the party.* ○ [+ to-inf] *They're pleased to be going home.*

▶ **COLLOCATIONS:**
pleased **at** *something*
seem/look/feel pleased
a pleased **smile/expression**
obviously/secretly pleased

▶ **SYNONYMS:** happy, satisfied, content

▶ **ANTONYMS:** displeased, unhappy

pleas|ure /ˈpleʒə/

UNCOUNTABLE NOUN If something gives you **pleasure**, you get a feeling of happiness, satisfaction, or enjoyment from it. ○ *Watching sport gave him great pleasure.* ○ [+ in] *Everybody takes pleasure in eating.*

▶ **COLLOCATIONS:**
pleasure **in** *something*
pleasure **from** *something*
give/bring *someone* pleasure
get/take pleasure
great/much/enormous/real pleasure

▶ **SYNONYMS:** happiness, enjoyment

WORD FAMILY		
please	VERB	○ You can't please everyone.
pleasing	ADJECTIVE	○ It was a very pleasing result.
pleased	ADJECTIVE	○ He glanced at her with a pleased smile.
pleasure	UNCOUNT	○ He gets a lot of pleasure from his hobbies.

plot /plɒt/ (plots)   MEDIA & CULTURE

NOUN The **plot** of a film, novel, or play is the connected series of events which make up the story. ○ The plot revolves around a missing diamond. ○ As the plot unfolds, we discover what happened to the child.

▶ COLLOCATIONS:
the plot **revolves around** someone/something
the plot **unfolds**
follow the plot
a **complex/convoluted** plot
an **implausible** plot
a **good/strong** plot
the **main** plot

▶ SYNONYM: storyline

plumb|er /ˈplʌmə/ (plumbers)   WORK

NOUN A **plumber** is a person whose job is to connect and repair things such as water and drainage pipes, baths, and toilets. ○ He had to call the plumber out to fix the boiler.

WORD FAMILY		
plumbing	UNCOUNT	○ I worked with my dad in his plumbing business.
plumber	NOUN	○ He started training to become a plumber.

P

pock|et /ˈpɒkɪt/ (pockets)   CLOTHES & APPEARANCE

NOUN A **pocket** is a kind of small bag which forms part of a piece of clothing, and which is used for carrying small things such as money or a handkerchief. ○ The man stood with his hands in his pockets. ○ Tommy fumbled in the back pocket of his trousers for his wallet.

▶ COLLOCATIONS:
in/inside a pocket
a **back/front/side** pocket
a **jacket/coat/trouser/shirt** pocket

poem /ˈpəʊɪm/ (poems)   MEDIA & CULTURE

NOUN A **poem** is a piece of writing in which the words are chosen for their beauty and sound and are carefully arranged, often in short lines. ○ [+ about] He has written a poem about love. ○ [+ by] I read a poem by John Betjeman.

▶ **COLLOCATIONS:**
a poem **about/on** something
a poem **by** someone
in a poem
write a poem
read/recite a poem
a **long/short** poem

po|et|ry /ˈpəʊɪtri/

UNCOUNTABLE NOUN Poems, considered as a form of literature, are referred to as **poetry**. ○ *Lawrence Durrell wrote a great deal of poetry.* ○ *She's the author of a children's poetry book.*

▶ **COLLOCATIONS:**
English/American/Japanese, etc. poetry
read/write poetry
a poetry **book/collection**
a poetry **competition**

WORD FAMILY		
poem	NOUN	○ *David read a short poem at the wedding.*
poetry	UNCOUNT	○ *They were discussing French poetry.*
poet	NOUN	○ *Pushkin is one of Russia's most famous poets.*
poetic	ADJECTIVE	○ *artistic and poetic talents*

po|lice of|fic|er /pəˈliːs ˌɒfɪsə, AM ɔːf-/   `WORK` `CRIME`
(police officers)

NOUN A **police officer** is a member of the police force. ○ *An off-duty police officer gave chase, but the attackers got away.* ○ *Undercover police officers attended the club posing as customers.*

▶ **COLLOCATIONS:**
a **senior** police officer
an **off-duty** police officer
an **undercover/plain-clothes** police officer

USAGE

You can use **police officer** to talk about a male or a female member of **the police**. You can also use **policeman** to refer to a male officer or **policewoman** to refer to a female officer.

po|lite /pəˈlaɪt/ (politer, politest)   `PERSONALITY`

ADJECTIVE Someone who is **polite** has good manners and is not rude to other people. ○ [+ to] *We were polite to each other.* ○ [+ to-inf] *It's not polite to point or talk about strangers in public.*

▶ **COLLOCATIONS:**
polite **to** *someone*
polite **conversation/applause**
a polite **request/question**
a polite **smile**

▶ **SYNONYMS:** well-mannered, courteous

▶ **ANTONYMS:** rude, impolite

WORD FAMILY		
polite	ADJECTIVE	○ *His speech was greeted by polite applause.*
politely	ADVERB	○ *'Your home is beautiful,' I said politely.*
politeness	UNCOUNT	○ *She listened to him, but only out of politeness.*
impolite	ADJECTIVE	○ *It would have been impolite to ask as we didn't know each other very well.*

poli|tics /'pɒlɪtɪks/ BELIEFS & OPINIONS

UNCOUNTABLE NOUN Politics is the actions or activities concerned with achieving and using power in a country or society. ○ *I come from a family which enjoys discussing politics.* ○ *There has been an increase in the number of women entering politics.*

▶ **COLLOCATIONS:**
in politics
talk about/discuss politics
enter/leave politics
British/Russian/Japanese, etc. politics
international/national/local politics

po|liti|cal /pə'lɪtɪkəl/

ADJECTIVE Political means relating to the way power is achieved and used in a country or society. ○ *the major political parties* ○ *The government is facing another political crisis.*

▶ **COLLOCATIONS:**
a political **party**
the political **system/process**
a political **leader**
political **power**
a political **issue/crisis**
political **change/reform**

poli|ti|cian /ˌpɒlɪ'tɪʃən/ (politicians)

NOUN A **politician** is a person whose job is in politics, especially a member of the government. ○ *Local politicians demanded action.* ○ *His comments angered some Conservative politicians.*

p

▶ COLLOCATIONS:
a **leading/senior/prominent** politician
a **local** politician
a **Conservative/Liberal/Republican** politician
an **opposition** politician

WORD FAMILY		
politics	UNCOUNT	○ He quickly involved himself in local politics.
political	ADJECTIVE	○ the American political system
politically	ADVERB	○ They do not believe the killings were politically motivated.
politician	NOUN	○ Mr Darling was a prominent local politician in Edinburgh.

pol|lu|tion /pəˈluːʃən/

SCIENCE & NATURE

UNCOUNTABLE NOUN **Pollution** is the process of making water, air, or land dirty, especially with poisonous chemicals. ○ [+ of] Pollution of the river is being caused by oil and diesel from boats. ○ [+ from] Air pollution from cars and power stations may have caused an increase in lung disease.

▶ COLLOCATIONS:
pollution **from** something
pollution **of** something
air/water pollution
environmental/atmospheric pollution
industrial pollution
cause/increase pollution
reduce/cut/tackle pollution
pollution **affects/threatens** something
a pollution **problem**
pollution **control**

pol|lute /pəˈluːt/ (pollutes, polluting, polluted)

VERB To **pollute** water, air, or land means to make it dirty and dangerous to live in or to use, especially with poisonous chemicals or sewage. ○ [+ with] Heavy industry pollutes our rivers with chemicals. ○ A number of beaches have been polluted by sewage pumped into the sea.

▶ COLLOCATIONS:
pollute something **with** something
pollute the **environment/atmosphere/air**
pollute **soil/land/water**
pollute a **river/lake/stream/sea**
pollute a **beach/shore**

WORD FAMILY		
pollute	**VERB**	○ Wind and other renewable energy sources don't pollute the air.
polluted	**ADJECTIVE**	○ The river was too heavily polluted for any fish to survive.
pollution	**UNCOUNT**	○ There is no easy way to solve the city's traffic and pollution problem.
polluter	**NOUN**	○ The country is the world's biggest polluter.

pop (mu|sic) /ˈpɒp mjuːzɪk/   MEDIA & CULTURE

UNCOUNTABLE NOUN Pop is modern music that usually has a strong rhythm and uses electronic equipment. ○ a programme of classical, rock, pop and jazz concerts ○ She had posters of pop stars all over her bedroom walls. ○ Which great British pop band had a hit with 'In the Army Now'?

▶ **COLLOCATIONS:**
a pop **star/singer**
a pop **group/band**
a pop **song**
a pop **concert**
the pop **charts**

popu|lar /ˈpɒpjʊlə/

ADJECTIVE Someone who is **popular** is liked by a lot of people. ○ He is one of the most popular players in the team. ○ [+ with] At school I was always popular with the boys.

▶ **COLLOCATIONS:**
popular **with** someone
extremely/hugely/immensely popular
a popular **figure/player/leader**

▶ **ANTONYM:** unpopular

WORD FAMILY		
popular	**ADJECTIVE**	○ The President remains hugely popular.
popularly	**ADVERB**	○ India's film industry is popularly known as Bollywood.
popularity	**UNCOUNT**	○ It is his popularity with ordinary people that sets him apart.
unpopular	**ADJECTIVE**	○ He was deeply unpopular with his colleagues.

p

popu|la|tion /ˌpɒpjʊˈleɪʃən/ (populations)   `PEOPLE`

NOUN The **population** of a country or area is all the people who live in it.
○ [+ of] *Bangladesh now has a population of about 110 million.* ○ *The world's population has reached 7 billion.* ○ *The number and proportion of elderly people in the population is increasing.*

▶ COLLOCATIONS:
the population **of** somewhere
in the population
the population **grows/increases/declines**
the population **reaches** x
population **growth/size**

pork /pɔːk/   `FOOD & DRINK`

UNCOUNTABLE NOUN **Pork** is meat from a pig, usually fresh and not smoked or salted. ○ *Muslims don't generally eat pork.* ○ *a packet of pork sausages*

▶ COLLOCATIONS:
eat pork
roast pork
a pork **chop/sausage**

por|trait /ˈpɔːtreɪt/ (portraits)   `MEDIA & CULTURE`

NOUN A **portrait** is a painting, drawing, or photograph of a particular person.
○ [+ of] *Lucian Freud was asked to paint a portrait of the Queen.* ○ *Always use a tripod when you are taking portraits.*

▶ COLLOCATIONS:
a portrait **of** someone
in a portrait
paint/do a portrait
take a portrait
a portrait **painter/artist/photographer**
a **family/self** portrait

po|si|tion /pəˈzɪʃən/ (positions)   `WORK`

NOUN A **position** in a company or organization is a job. [FORMAL] ○ *He left a career in teaching to take up a position with the Arts Council.* ○ [+ of] *He rose to the position of Public Relations Manager.*

▶ COLLOCATIONS:
the position **of** something
a position **as** something
take (up) a position
hold a position
a **full-time/part-time** position
a **permanent/temporary** position

▶ SYNONYMS: post, job

posi|tive /'pɒzɪtɪv/

ADJECTIVE A **positive** situation or e perience is pleasant, good, or helpful to you in some way. ○ *A good diet and exercise can have a positive effect on your health.* ○ *Studying abroad should be an exciting and positive experience.*

▶ **COLLOCATIONS:**
a positive **impact/effect/result/outcome**
a positive **aspect/change/experience**
positive **news/comments**
extremely/overwhelmingly positive
generally positive

▶ **ANTONYM:** negative

WORD FAMILY		
positive	**ADJECTIVE**	○ *Feedback from last year's courses was overwhelmingly positive.*
positively	**ADVERB**	○ *Literacy programmes have positively affected the lives of many people.*

post|er /'pəʊstə/ (posters)   `SHOPPING`

NOUN A **poster** is a large notice or picture that you stick on a wall or board, often in order to advertise something. ○ [+ of] *The walls of the room were covered with posters of Justin Bieber.* ○ [+ for] *We're going to make posters for the dance.* ○ *I'm putting posters up in all the local shops.*

▶ **COLLOCATIONS:**
a poster **of** *someone/something*
a poster **for** *something*
on a poster
a poster **advertises/shows** *something*
make/design a poster
put up/display a poster

post|gradu|ate /ˌpəʊstˈɡrædʒʊət/   `EDUCATION`
(postgraduates) also **post-graduate**

1 **NOUN** A **postgraduate** or a **postgraduate student** is a student with a first degree from a university who is studying or doing research at a more advanced level. [BRIT; in AM, use **graduate student**] ○ *Courses are for undergraduates and postgraduates.*

→ see also **graduate, undergraduate**

2 **ADJECTIVE Postgraduate** study or research is done by a student who has a first degree and is studying or doing research at a more advanced level. [BRIT; in AM, use **graduate**] ○ *She's doing a postgraduate course in English Literature.* ○ *Dr Hoffman did his postgraduate work at Leicester University.*

▸ COLLOCATIONS:
a postgraduate **course**
a postgraduate **qualification/degree/diploma**
postgraduate **study/education/research/work**

---

pour /pɔː/

(pours, pouring, poured)

FOOD & DRINK SCIENCE & NATURE

1 VERB If you **pour** a liquid or other substance, you make it flow steadily out of a container by holding the container at an angle. ○ *Francis poured the orange juice into a fresh glass.* ○ *Carefully pour the mixture over the vegetables.*

2 VERB When it rains very heavily, you can say that **it is pouring** or **it is pouring with rain**. ○ *It has been pouring with rain all week.* ○ *It had poured relentlessly for a full twenty four hours.* ○ *We drove through pouring rain.*

---

pre|dict /prɪˈdɪkt/ (predicts, predicting, predicted)

VERB If you **predict** an event, you say that it will happen. ○ *Teachers predict the grade their pupils will achieve in end-of-year exams.* ○ [+ that] *Experts predict that by 2050 global energy use could increase fourfold.*

▸ COLLOCATIONS:
predict the **result/outcome**
predict the **future**
accurately/correctly/reliably predict *something*
something is predicted **to increase/rise/fall**

WORD FAMILY		
predict	VERB	○ *The country's population is predicted to increase.*
prediction	NOUN	○ *Students read part of the story, and make predictions about what will later happen.*
predictable	ADJECTIVE	○ *I hate films that have a predictable ending.*
unpredictable	ADJECTIVE	○ *Take an umbrella to protect you from the unpredictable British weather.*

---

pre|fer /prɪˈfɜː/ (prefers, preferring, preferred)

VERB If you **prefer** someone or something, you like that person or thing better than another, and so you are more likely to choose them if there is a choice. ○ [+ to] *I prefer tea to coffee.* ○ [+ to-inf] *Most people prefer to live close to where they work.* ○ [+ v-ing] *I prefer going to the beach with friends in the summer.*

▸ COLLOCATIONS:
prefer *something* **to** *something*
much/strongly prefer *something*
personally prefer *something*

USAGE

Note that **prefer** can often sound rather formal in ordinary conversation. Expressions such as **like ... better** and **would rather** are more common. For example, instead of saying '*I prefer football to tennis*', you can say '*I like football better than tennis*', and instead of '*I'd prefer to walk*', you can say '*I'd rather walk*'.

WORD FAMILY

prefer	VERB	○ *I much prefer shopping online.*
preference	NOUN	○ *Please specify if you have any food preferences.*
preferable	ADJECTIVE	○ *Prevention of a problem is preferable to trying to cure it.*
preferably	ADVERB	○ *Select an image, preferably one that's not too big.*

---

preg|nant /ˈpregnənt/   PEOPLE

ADJECTIVE If a woman or female animal is **pregnant**, she has a baby or babies developing in her body. ○ *When I first got pregnant , my mother was thrilled.* ○ [+ with] *Tina was pregnant with their first daughter.*

▶ COLLOCATIONS:
   be pregnant **with** *a baby*
   be pregnant with your **child/baby/son/daughter**
   be pregnant with **twins**
   get/become pregnant
   a pregnant **woman/mother**
   heavily pregnant

WORD FAMILY

pregnant	ADJECTIVE	○ *By then Stella was heavily pregnant.*
pregnancy	NOUN	○ *Smoking during pregnancy is harmful to the unborn baby.*

---

pre|scrip|tion /prɪˈskrɪpʃən/ (prescriptions)   HEALTH

NOUN A **prescription** is the piece of paper on which your doctor writes an order for medicine and which you give to a chemist or pharmacist to get the medicine. ○ [+ for] *The doctor gave me a prescription for antibiotics.* ○ *Marion was taking two prescription drugs.*

▶ COLLOCATIONS:
   a prescription **for** *something*
   write a prescription
   give *someone* a prescription
   get a prescription
   a prescription **medicine/drug**

pres|ent /ˈprezənt/ (presents)   `SOCIAL LIFE`

NOUN A **present** is something that you give to someone, for example on their birthday or when you visit them. ○ [+ *for*] *I bought a birthday present for my mother.* ○ [+ *from*] *The vase was a present from a friend.* ○ *This book would make a great Christmas present.*

▶ **COLLOCATIONS:**
a present **from/for** *someone*
a **birthday/Christmas/wedding** present
buy/give *someone* a present
get a present
wrap/open a present

▶ **SYNONYM:** gift

presi|dent /ˈprezɪdənt/ (presidents)

NOUN The **president** of a country that has no king or queen is the person who is the head of state of that country. ○ *President Obama* ○ *the former French president, Nicolas Sarkozy* ○ [+ *of*] *Within two years she had been elected president of the country.*

▶ **COLLOCATIONS:**
the president **of** *somewhere*
the **American/Iraqi/French**, etc. president
become president
elect a president
be **elected** president

press /pres/   `MEDIA & CULTURE`

UNCOUNTABLE NOUN Newspapers or journalists are referred to as **the press**. ○ *I'd read about it in the local press.* ○ *Christie looked relaxed and calm as he faced the press.* ○ *He was giving several press interviews to promote his new film.*

▶ **COLLOCATIONS:**
in the press
the press **reports** *something*
the **local/national** press
the **British/German**, etc. press
the **tabloid** press
tell the press *something*
face the press
a press **report/interview**
a press **photographer**
press **freedom**

pride /praɪd/

1 UNCOUNTABLE NOUN Pride is a feeling of satisfaction which you have because you or people close to you have done something good or possess something good. ○ [+ *in*] *He took genuine pride in the achievements of his children.* ○ *They can look back on their endeavours with pride.*

▶ **COLLOCATIONS:**
pride **in** something
with pride
take pride **in** something
feel pride
immense/enormous pride
personal/national pride
professional pride

2 UNCOUNTABLE NOUN Pride is a sense of the respect that other people have for you, and that you have for yourself. ○ *It was a severe blow to Kendall's pride.* ○ *No one was physically hurt, but hurt pride is harder to heal.*

▶ **SYNONYM:** self-esteem

proud /praʊd/ (prouder, proudest)

ADJECTIVE If you feel **proud**, you feel pleased about something good that you possess or have done, or about something good that a person close to you has done. ○ [+ of] *I felt proud of his efforts.* ○ [+ that] *They are proud that she is doing well at school.* ○ [+ to-inf] *I am proud to be a Canadian.*

▶ **COLLOCATIONS:**
proud **of** something
feel proud
extremely/immensely proud
justifiably proud
proud **parents/grandparents**
a proud **father/mother**
be the proud **owner of** something

▶ **ANTONYM:** ashamed

WORD FAMILY		
proud	**ADJECTIVE**	○ *Nicos was the proud owner of the Park Hotel.*
proudly	**ADVERB**	○ *'That's the first part finished,' he said proudly.*
pride	**UNCOUNT**	○ *His achievements are a source of personal pride.*

priest /priːst/ (priests)

NOUN A **priest** is a member of the Christian clergy in the Catholic, Anglican, or Orthodox church. ○ *He had trained to be a Catholic priest.* ○ *The Roman Catholic church does not have women priests.*

▶ **COLLOCATIONS:**
become a priest
a **Catholic** priest
a **parish** priest
a **woman** priest

▶ **SYNONYM:** vicar

pri|ma|ry school /ˈpraɪməri skuːl, AM -meri/ EDUCATION
(primary schools)

NOUN A **primary school** is a school for children between the ages of 5 and 11. [mainly BRIT; in AM, usually use **elementary school**] ○ I remember my first day at primary school. ○ She became a primary school teacher. ○ Greenside Primary School

▶ **COLLOCATIONS:**
 at/in primary school
 a primary school **teacher**
 primary school **children/pupils**

---

pris|on /ˈprɪzən/ (prisons) CRIME

NOUN A **prison** is a building where criminals are kept as punishment. ○ He spent six years in prison. ○ Clark was sent to prison for killing his two sons.

▶ **COLLOCATIONS:**
 in prison
 go to prison
 be **sent to** prison
 be **released from** prison
 escape from prison
 a prison **sentence**
 a prison **cell/officer**
 the prison **system/population**

▶ **SYNONYM:** jail

WORD FAMILY		
prison	**NOUN**	○ He's serving a long prison sentence.
prisoner	**NOUN**	○ Hundreds of prisoners are serving sentences of 25 years or more.

---

pro|cessed /ˈprəʊsest, AM ˈprɑːsest/ FOOD & DRINK HEALTH

ADJECTIVE **Processed** foods, have been prepared in factories. ○ Avoid fatty and processed foods. ○ Nitrites are found in processed meats, such as sausages, bacon and ham.

WORD FAMILY		
process	**NOUN**	○ They began the process of choosing a new leader.
process	**VERB**	○ The plant processes milk products.
processed	**ADJECTIVE**	○ Refined and processed foods make it harder for our body to do its work.
processing	**UNCOUNT**	○ Food processing also removes many essential nutrients.

pro|duce /prəˈdjuːs, AM -ˈduːs/ (produces, producing, produced)

VERB If you **produce** something, you make or create it. ○ *In that year Japan produced 5 million cars.* ○ *All pies served in the restaurant are made with locally produced meat.*

▶ **COLLOCATIONS:**
produce a **product**
produce **goods/work**
produce **food/wine/cars**
produce a **report/document**
locally produced

▶ **SYNONYMS:** make, create

WORD FAMILY		
produce	**VERB**	○ *They produce a fine range of wines by traditional methods.*
production	**UNCOUNT**	○ *The firm aims to increase production.*
product	**NOUN**	○ *I'm often tempted by special offers and new products.*
producer	**NOUN**	○ *Spain is the world's leading producer of olives and olive oil.*
productive	**ADJECTIVE**	○ *Training makes workers more productive.*
productively	**ADVERB**	○ *Farmers want to farm the land as productively as possible.*
productivity	**UNCOUNT**	○ *Employees had to work harder and productivity automatically increased.*
unproductive	**ADJECTIVE**	○ *Employers can still fire unproductive workers.*

pro|fes|sion|al /prəˈfeʃənəl/ (professionals)   WORK

1 **ADJECTIVE** **Professional** means relating to a person's work, especially work that requires special training. ○ *List three specific goals you want to achieve in your professional life.* ○ *What academic or professional qualifications have you achieved?*

▶ **COLLOCATIONS:**
someone's professional **life/career**
professional **advice/help**
professional **training/development**
professional **qualifications/skills**
professional **experience**

2 **NOUN** **Professionals** are people who have jobs that require advanced education or training. ○ *highly qualified professional people like doctors and engineers* ○ *doctors, nurses, and other healthcare professionals*

▶ **COLLOCATION: medical/healthcare** professionals

WORD FAMILY		
profession	**NOUN**	○ *She left the teaching profession to become a politician.*
professional	**ADJECTIVE**	○ *I believe that professional training is less important than experience.*
professionally	**ADVERB**	○ *She's a professionally-qualified architect.*

---

pro|fes|sor /prəˈfesə/ (professors)   `EDUCATION`

NOUN A **professor** in a British university is the most senior teacher in a department. ○ *Professor Cameron* ○ [+ *of*] *He's a professor of medicine at University College London.*

▶ COLLOCATIONS:
  a professor **of** *something*
  a professor of **science/medicine/law** etc.
  a **university** professor
  a **science/history/psychology**, etc. professor

---

pro|gramme /ˈprəʊɡræm/
(programmes) [in AM, use **program**]   `MEDIA & CULTURE`

NOUN A television or radio **programme** is something that is broadcast on television or radio. ○ [+ *about*] *I've seen programmes about vets on TV.* ○ *He has been in several children's programmes.*

▶ COLLOCATIONS:
  a programme **about/on** *something*
  in a programme
  watch/see a programme
  make/broadcast/show a programme
  a **television/TV/radio** programme
  a **news/children's** programme

---

pro|gress /ˈprəʊɡres, AM ˈprɑː-/

UNCOUNTABLE NOUN Progress is the process of gradually improving or getting nearer to achieving or completing something. ○ *The teacher said I was making good progress.* ○ *We're continuing to make progress in the fight against cancer.*

▶ COLLOCATIONS:
  make progress
  monitor/measure progress
  good/real/steady/great progress
  slow progress

WORD FAMILY		
progress	UNCOUNT	○ He was very impatient with the slow progress.
progress	VERB	○ The test measures how well a student is progressing.
progression	UNCOUNT	○ Employees are concerned about job security and career progression.
progressive	ADJECTIVE	○ One symptom of the disease is progressive loss of memory.
progressively	ADVERB	○ The pain got progressively worse.

---

proj|ect /ˈprɒdʒekt/ (projects) EDUCATION

1 NOUN A **project** is a task that requires a lot of time and effort. ○ *The organization encourages young people to get involved in community projects.* ○ *The project was funded by the Australian Film Commission.*

▶ COLLOCATIONS:
 undertake/start a project
 complete/abandon a project
 fund/finance/support a project
 manage/run/plan a project
 a **new/major/ambitious** project
 a **joint** project
 a **research/science/development** project
 a **construction/building** project
 a **community/arts** project

2 NOUN A **project** is a detailed study of a subject by a pupil or student. ○ [+ on] *I'm doing a project on comedy.* ○ [+ about] *We had to do a school project about favourite hobbies.*

▶ COLLOCATIONS:
 a project **on/about** *something*
 do a project
 a **school** project

---

prom|ise /ˈprɒmɪs/ (promises, promising, promised)

1 VERB If you **promise that** you will do something, you say to someone that you will definitely do it. ○ [+ to-inf] *He promised to call me.* ○ [+ that] *I promised that I wouldn't tell anyone else.*

2 VERB If you **promise** someone something, you tell them that you will definitely give it to them or make sure that they have it. ○ *My dad has promised me a new laptop if I pass my exams.* ○ *The company promises a reply to queries within 24 hours.*

prom|is|ing /ˈprɒmɪsɪŋ/ PERSONALITY

ADJECTIVE Someone or something that is **promising** seems likely to be very good or successful. ○ *He had been a promising student at Cambridge.* ○ *After a promising start, the film soon deteriorates.*

▶ **COLLOCATIONS:**
a promising **start**
a promising **career/future**
a promising **player/youngster/student**
promising **results**
a promising **sign**
very/highly promising

---

pro|mote /prə'məʊt/ (promotes, promoting, promoted)   [WORK]

VERB If someone **is promoted**, they are given a more important job or rank in the organization that they work for. ○ [+ from/to] *She was promoted to editor and then editorial director.* ○ *My Dad's been promoted.*

▶ **COLLOCATION:** be promoted **to/from** *something*

pro|mo|tion /prə'məʊʃən/

UNCOUNTABLE NOUN If you are given **promotion** or a **promotion** in your job, you are given a more important job or rank in the organization that you work for. ○ *She had just been given a promotion.* ○ [+ to] *Since his promotion to assistant manager Trevor had an office of his own.*

▶ **COLLOCATIONS:**
promotion **to** *something*
get a promotion
offer/give *someone* a promotion
seek/want a promotion

---

proof /pruːf/   [CRIME]

UNCOUNTABLE NOUN **Proof** is a fact, argument, or piece of evidence which shows that something is definitely true or definitely exists. ○ [+ that] *There was no conclusive proof that Frei was guilty.* ○ [+ of] *Young people will need to provide proof of age.*

▶ **COLLOCATIONS:**
proof **of** *something*
have proof
provide/offer proof
need proof
further/conclusive proof
scientific proof

WORD FAMILY		
proof	UNCOUNT	○ *This is further proof that we need to reduce traffic on the roads.*
prove	VERB	○ *We have no clear evidence to prove that the two men were involved in the attack.*

pro|pose /prə'pəʊz/ (proposes, proposing, proposed)

VERB If you **propose** something such as a plan or an idea, you suggest it for people to think about and decide upon. ○ *None of the proposed solutions to congestion seems to work.* ○ [+ that] *Elspeth proposed that they should go to Portugal.*

▶ COLLOCATIONS:
propose **changes**
propose a **law/rule**
propose a **plan/solution/deal/idea**
first/initially/originally proposed *something*

▶ SYNONYMS: suggest, put forward

WORD FAMILY		
propose	**VERB**	○ *They had proposed building a new museum in Zurich.*
proposal	**NOUN**	○ *The teachers were told of the proposal to close the school in July.*

pro|spec|tus /prə'spektəs, AM prɑː-/ (prospectuses) EDUCATION

NOUN A **prospectus** is a detailed document produced by a college, school, or university, which gives details about it. ○ *This information is available in the prospectus.* ○ *The prospectus contains details of the school's policy on bullying.*

▶ COLLOCATIONS:
in a prospectus
read a prospectus
a prospectus **contains** *something*
a **school/university/college** prospectus

pro|tect /prə'tekt/ (protects, protecting, protected)

VERB To **protect** someone or something means to prevent them from being harmed or damaged. ○ [+ from] *Always protect your skin from the sun.* ○ [+ against] *What can women do to protect themselves against heart disease?*

▶ COLLOCATIONS:
protect *someone/something* **from/against** *something*
protect *someone/something* from the **sun/wind**
protect against a **disease/cancer**
protect against **attack/damage**
adequately protect *someone/something*

WORD FAMILY		
protect	**VERB**	○ *The current laws do not adequately protect individuals.*
protection	**UNCOUNT**	○ *Sunscreens do not provide total protection against skin cancer.*
protective	**ADJECTIVE**	○ *Always wear protective clothing whilst using chemicals.*
protectively	**ADVERB**	○ *He wrapped his arms protectively around his body.*

psy|chol|ogy /saɪˈkɒlədʒi/

UNCOUNTABLE NOUN Psychology is the scientific study of the human mind and the reasons for people's behaviour. ○ *She studied psychology at university.* ○ *I took a psychology course.*

▶ COLLOCATIONS:
study psychology
a psychology **professor/lecturer/student**
the psychology **department**
a psychology **course/degree**
child/human/social/educational psychology

WORD FAMILY		
psychology	**UNCOUNT**	○ *There are plenty of books on child psychology.*
psychological	**ADJECTIVE**	○ *Robyn's loss of memory is a psychological problem, not a physical one.*
psychologically	**ADVERB**	○ *Some soldiers have been psychologically damaged by their experiences during the war.*
psychologist	**NOUN**	○ *Psychologists now believe that our sense of well-being is partially genetic.*

pub|lic /ˈpʌblɪk/

1 UNCOUNTABLE NOUN You can refer to people in general, or to all the people in a particular country or community, as **the public**. ○ *Lauderdale House is now open to the public.* ○ *The campaign is aimed at educating the public about the dangers of smoking.*

→ see Useful Phrases **in public**

▶ COLLOCATIONS:
the **general** public
the **American/British/French**, etc. public
a **member of** the public
open to the public
tell/inform/educate the public
protect/reassure the public

2 ADJECTIVE Public buildings and services are provided for everyone to use. ○ *Public buildings were lit up at night.* ○ *Birmingham has about 150 public parks.*

▶ COLLOCATIONS:
a public **building/library/toilet/park**
public **services**
public **land**

▶ ANTONYM: private

WORD FAMILY		
public	**UNCOUNT**	○ *The site is not accessible to members of the public.*
public	**ADJECTIVE**	○ *I went into town, to the public library.*
publicly	**ADVERB**	○ *He has never spoken publicly about the situation.*

pub|lic|ity /pʌˈblɪsɪti/ [SHOPPING]

UNCOUNTABLE NOUN Publicity is information or actions that are intended to attract the public's attention to someone or something. ○ [+ for] *It's a big game for the players and great publicity for the club.* ○ *a massive publicity campaign* ○ *It was all a publicity stunt.*

▶ **COLLOCATIONS:**
publicity **for** something
a publicity **campaign/stunt**
publicity **material**
a publicity **photo/shot**

WORD FAMILY		
publicity	UNCOUNT	○ *We're doing some publicity shots for the play.*
publicize	VERB	○ *Organizers are putting a major effort into publicizing the event.*
publicist	NOUN	○ *The film's publicists tried to raise its profile.*

pub|lic trans|port /ˌpʌblɪk ˈtrænspɔːt/ [TRANSPORT & TRAVEL]

UNCOUNTABLE NOUN Public transport is the system of buses and trains that people use to get from one place to another. ○ *I travel to college by public transport.* ○ *Japan and France have fast, efficient public transport systems.*

▶ **COLLOCATIONS:**
on/by public transport
travel on/use public transport
the public transport **system/network**
a **form of** public transport

P

pub|lish /ˈpʌblɪʃ/ (publishes, publishing, published)

VERB When a company **publishes** a book or magazine, it prints copies of it, which are sent to shops to be sold. ○ *They publish reference books.* ○ *His latest book of poetry will be published by Faber in May.*

▶ **COLLOCATIONS:**
publish a **book/novel/biography**
publish a **magazine/journal**

WORD FAMILY		
publish	VERB	○ *The novel was first published in 1957.*
publishing	NOUN	○ *My girlfriend works in publishing.*
publisher	NOUN	○ *America's biggest book publisher*
publication	NOUN	○ *He has become more well-known since the publication of his first book in 1991.*

pun|ish /'pʌnɪʃ/ (punishes, punishing, punished) `CRIME`

VERB To **punish** someone means to make them suffer in some way because they
have done something wrong. ○ [+ for] *She deserved to be punished for those crimes.*
○ *Such behaviour is unacceptable and will be punished.* ○ *I hope they are caught and
punished severely.*

▶ **COLLOCATIONS:**
punish *someone* **for** *something*
punish *someone* **severely/harshly**

pun|ish|ment /'pʌnɪʃmənt/ (punishments)

1 **UNCOUNTABLE NOUN** **Punishment** is the act of punishing someone or of being
punished. ○ [+ of] *She supports a total ban on the physical punishment of children.*

2 **NOUN** A **punishment** is a particular way of punishing someone. ○ *The usual
punishment is a fine.* ○ [+ for] *The government is proposing tougher punishments
for officials convicted of corruption.*

▶ **COLLOCATIONS:**
a punishment **for** *something*
punishment **of** *someone*
face/receive punishment
escape/deserve punishment
a **severe/harsh** punishment
an **appropriate** punishment
physical punishment

---

pu|pil /'pjuːpɪl/ (pupils) `EDUCATION`

NOUN The **pupils** of a school are the children who go to it. ○ *The school has only
125 pupils.* ○ [+ of/at] *He's a former pupil of Latymer Upper School in London.*

▶ **COLLOCATIONS:**
a pupil **of/at** *a school*
a **school** pupil
primary school/secondary school pupils
a **former** pupil
a **star/model/bright** pupil
a **disruptive** pupil

▶ **SYNONYM:** student

---

put on /pʊt 'ɒn/ `CLOTHES & APPEARANCE` `HEALTH`
(puts on, putting on, put on)

1 **PHRASAL VERB** When you **put on** clothing or make-up, you place it on your
body in order to wear it. ○ *She put on her coat and went out.* ○ *I haven't even put any
lipstick on.*

→ see note at **wear**

▶ **ANTONYM:** take off

2 PHRASAL VERB If someone **puts on** weight, they become heavier. ○ *I can eat what I want but I never put on weight.* ○ *Luther's put on three stone.*

▶ **COLLOCATIONS:**
put on **weight**
put on *x* **pounds/stone/kilograms**

▶ **SYNONYM:** gain

▶ **ANTONYM:** lose

---

put up with /pʊt ˈʌp wɪθ/ (puts up with, putting up with, put up with)

PHRASAL VERB If you **put up with** something, you tolerate or accept it, even though you find it unpleasant or unsatisfactory. ○ *Families living near the airport have to put up with the noise of aircraft taking off and landing.* ○ *Don't put up with any nonsense from Howard.*

---

py|ja|mas /pɪˈdʒɑːməz/   CLOTHES & APPEARANCE

PLURAL NOUN A pair of **pyjamas** consists of loose trousers and a loose T-shirt or jacket that people wear in bed. ○ *My brother was still in his pyjamas.* ○ *He was wearing only pyjama bottoms.*

▶ **COLLOCATIONS:**
be **in** your pyjamas
wear pyjamas
a **pair of** pyjamas
a pyjama **top**
pyjama **bottoms**
silk/cotton pyjamas

Qq

quali|fi|ca|tions /ˌkwɒlɪfɪˈkeɪʃənz/

PLURAL NOUN Your **qualifications** are the examinations that you have passed. ○ *He has the right qualifications for the job.* ○ *My parents are trying to persuade me to stay at school and get more qualifications.* ○ [+ in] *qualifications in business and accountancy*

▶ **COLLOCATIONS:**
qualifications **in** *something*
have/get/gain qualifications
need qualifications
academic/vocational/professional qualifications
formal /educational qualifications

WORD FAMILY		
qualify	**VERB**	○ *Tom had qualified as a doctor.*
qualified	**ADJECTIVE**	○ *She's a qualified nurse.*
qualification	**NOUN**	○ *What qualifications do you need to be a teacher?*

queue /kjuː/

(queues, queuing, queued)

1 NOUN A **queue** is a line of people or vehicles that are waiting for something. [mainly BRIT; in AM, usually use **line**] ○ *She waited in the bus queue.* ○ [+ for] *There was still a queue for tickets.* ○ [+ of] *Ahead of us was a long queue of cars waiting to leave the carpark .*

▶ **COLLOCATIONS:**
a queue **of** *something*
a queue of **people/cars/traffic**
a queue **for** *something*
a queue for **tickets/food/the toilet**
join/wait in/form a queue
jump the queue
a **long/short/orderly** queue
a **bus** queue

2 VERB When people **queue**, they stand in a line waiting for something. [mainly BRIT] ○ [+ to-inf] *Fans queued for hours to see the band.* ○ [+ for] *People were already queuing for taxis in front of the station.*

Rr

---

rack|et /'rækɪt/ (rackets) also **racquet** SPORT & ACTIVITY

NOUN A **racket** is an oval-shaped bat with strings across it. Rackets are used in tennis, squash, and badminton. ○ *Tennis rackets and balls are provided.* ○ *a badminton racket* ○ *a squash racket*

---

radi|cal /'rædɪkəl/ BELIEFS & OPINIONS

1 ADJECTIVE Radical changes and differences are very important and great in degree. ○ *Recent improvements have made a radical difference .* ○ *New mothers have to cope with radical changes in their lives.*

▶ **COLLOCATIONS:**
a radical **change/reform**
a radical **difference**

▶ **SYNONYM:** fundamental

2 ADJECTIVE Radical people believe that there should be great changes in society and try to bring about these changes. ○ *Radical student groups clashed with police.* ○ *radical religious leaders*

▶ **COLLOCATIONS:**
a radical **group/party/faction**
a radical **leader/politician**

▶ **ANTONYM:** conservative

WORD FAMILY		
radical	**ADJECTIVE**	○ *This is a radical overhaul of how we manage the organization.*
radically	**ADVERB**	○ *They are two large groups of people with radically different beliefs and cultures.*

---

rain /reɪn/ (rains, raining, rained) SCIENCE & NATURE

1 UNCOUNTABLE NOUN Rain is water that falls from the clouds in small drops. ○ *She stood on the pavement in the pouring rain.* ○ *A spot of rain fell on her hand.*

▶ **COLLOCATIONS:**
in the rain
heavy/pouring/torrential rain
light/steady rain

rain **pours down/falls**
rain **starts/stops**
rain is **forecast**
a **drop of/spot of** rain

2 VERB When rain falls, you can say that **it is raining**. ○ It rained the whole weekend.
○ It was raining hard, and she didn't have an umbrella.

▶ **COLLOCATION:** rain **heavily/hard**

WORD FAMILY		
rain	**UNCOUNT**	○ The rain was falling harder.
rain	**VERB**	○ It began to rain heavily.
rainy	**ADJECTIVE**	○ It was a cold and rainy day.

---

rain|for|est /'reɪnfɒrɪst, AM -fɔːr-/ **(rainforests)**
[in AM, also use **rain forest**]   SCIENCE & NATURE

NOUN A **rainforest** is a thick forest of tall trees which is found in tropical areas
where there is a lot of rain. ○ There is worldwide concern about the destruction of the
rainforests. ○ Many rare plants are found in the tropical rainforests.

▶ **COLLOCATIONS:**
in a rainforest
save/preserve the rainforests
destroy the rainforest
a **tropical** rainforest

---

re|act /ri'ækt/ **(reacts, reacting, reacted)**

VERB When you **react to** something that has happened to you, you behave in a
particular way because of it. ○ [+ to] They reacted violently to the news. ○ [+ with]
Fans reacted with anger. ○ You have to be able to react quickly when things don't go to
plan.

▶ **COLLOCATIONS:**
react **to** something
react **with** something
react with **anger/outrage/shock**
react **angrily/furiously**
react **positively/negatively**
react **quickly/immediately/differently**

▶ **SYNONYM:** respond

re|ac|tion /ri'ækʃən/

NOUN Your **reaction** to something that has happened or something that you have
experienced is what you feel, say, or do because of it. ○ [+ to] Most job applicants
are tense; it's a natural reaction to an interview. ○ He was surprised his answer caused
such a strong reaction.

▶ **COLLOCATIONS:**
reaction **to** something
cause/provoke a reaction
someone's **first/initial/immediate** reaction
a **strong** reaction
a **positive/negative/mixed** reaction
a **violent/angry** reaction
a **natural** reaction

▶ **SYNONYM:** response

---

re|al|is|tic /ˌriːəˈlɪstɪk/ `MEDIA & CULTURE`

ADJECTIVE You say that a painting, story, or film is **realistic** when the people and things in it are like people and things in real life. ○ *The graphics are unsophisticated but the realistic sound effects make up for this.* ○ *This is a very realistic film with some sensational acting.*

▶ **SYNONYM:** lifelike

▶ **ANTONYM:** unrealistic

WORD FAMILY		
real	**ADJECTIVE**	○ *Real diamonds are more expensive.*
realistic	**ADJECTIVE**	○ *This is the most realistic soccer game on the market.*
realistically	**ADVERB**	○ *The film starts off realistically and then develops into a ridiculous fantasy.*
unrealistic	**ADJECTIVE**	○ *We are bombarded with unrealistic images of women in magazines.*

---

re|al|ity TV /riˈælɪti tiː ˌviː/ `MEDIA & CULTURE`

UNCOUNTABLE NOUN **Reality TV** is a type of television programme which aims to show how ordinary people behave in everyday life, or in situations, often created by the programme makers, which are intended to represent everyday life. ○ *Dave and I both love reality TV.* ○ *a reality TV show* ○ *a reality TV star*

---

re|ceipt /rɪˈsiːt/ (receipts) `SHOPPING`

NOUN A **receipt** is a piece of paper that you get from someone as proof that they have received money from you. ○ [+ for] *Keep all receipts for equipment when you buy it.* ○ *Make sure you get a receipt.*

▶ **COLLOCATIONS:**
a receipt **for** something
get/keep a receipt
give someone a receipt

r

re|cep|tion /rɪˈsepʃən/ (receptions) `WORK` `SOCIAL LIFE`

1 **UNCOUNTABLE NOUN** The **reception** in a hotel is the desk or office that books rooms for people and answers their questions. [mainly BRIT; in AM, use **front desk**] ○ *I waited in the hotel reception to meet the others.* ○ *She called reception to complain about the noise.*

2 **UNCOUNTABLE NOUN** The **reception** in an office or hospital is the place where people's appointments and questions are dealt with. [mainly BRIT] ○ *Wait at reception for me.* ○ *The reception area was clean and bright.*

▶ **COLLOCATIONS:**
at/in reception
the reception **desk/area**

3 **NOUN** A **reception** is a formal party which is given to welcome someone or to celebrate a special event. ○ *At the reception they served smoked salmon.* ○ *He had been invited to the wedding reception.*

▶ **COLLOCATIONS:**
at a reception
a **wedding** reception
a **champagne** reception
attend/hold/host a reception

re|cep|tion|ist /rɪˈsepʃənɪst/ (receptionists) `WORK`

1 **NOUN** In a hotel, the **receptionist** is the person whose job is to book rooms for people and answer their questions. [mainly BRIT; in AM, use **desk clerk**] ○ *Lisa had been offered a job as hotel receptionist.*

2 **NOUN** In an office or hospital, the **receptionist** is the person whose job is to answer the telephone, arrange appointments, and deal with people when they first arrive. ○ *The receptionist told me that Heike had left the office.*

reci|pe /ˈresɪpi/ (recipes) `FOOD & DRINK`

NOUN A **recipe** is a list of ingredients and a set of instructions that tell you how to cook something. ○ [+ for] *Do you have a recipe for chocolate cake?* ○ *I spent most of yesterday afternoon trying a new recipe.*

▶ **COLLOCATIONS:**
a recipe **for** something
have a recipe
try (out)/follow a recipe
a **new/delicious** recipe
someone's **favourite** recipe
a recipe **book**

rec|ord /ˈrekɔːd, AM -kərd/ (records) `HISTORY`

NOUN If you keep a **record of** something, you keep a written account or photographs of it so that it can be referred to later. ○ [+ of] *Keep a record of all the payments.* ○ *the historical record of the period*

▶ **COLLOCATIONS:**
a record **of** something
keep/compile a record
a record **shows/indicates** something
medical/historical/financial records
a **public/official** record
a **written/electronic** record
a **detailed/accurate** record

---

re|cy|cle /ˌriːˈsaɪkəl/ (recycles, recycling, recycled) [SCIENCE & NATURE]

VERB If you **recycle** things that have already been used, such as bottles or sheets of paper, you process them so that they can be used again. ○ *All glass bottles can be recycled.* ○ *The aim is to recycle 98 per cent of domestic waste.*

WORD FAMILY		
recycle	**VERB**	○ *Re-use and recycle everyday things.*
recycled	**ADJECTIVE**	○ *It is printed on recycled paper.*
recyclable	**ADJECTIVE**	○ *The packaging is made of recyclable steel.*
recycling	**UNCOUNT**	○ *Recycling helps save the Earth's natural resources.*

---

re|dun|dant /rɪˈdʌndənt/ [WORK]

ADJECTIVE If you are made **redundant**, your employer tells you to leave because your job is no longer necessary or because your employer cannot afford to keep paying you. [BRIT; in AM, use **be dismissed**] ○ *My Dad was made redundant last year.* ○ *redundant workers*

---

ref|er|ence /ˈrefərəns/ [MEDIA & CULTURE]

ADJECTIVE Reference books are ones that you look at when you need specific information or facts about a subject. ○ *I checked a few facts in some reference books and made brief notes.* ○ *This is a list of websites where you will find useful reference material.*

▶ **COLLOCATIONS:**
a reference **book/guide/work**
reference **material**

---

re|fresh|ments /rɪˈfreʃmənts/ [TRANSPORT & TRAVEL]

PLURAL NOUN Refreshments are drinks and small amounts of food that are provided, for example, during a meeting or a journey. ○ *Drinks and other light refreshments will be available.* ○ *Airlines have a duty to provide refreshments for delayed passengers.*

▶ **COLLOCATIONS:**
serve/provide refreshments
light refreshments

WORD FAMILY		
refresh	**VERB**	○ Holidays are intended to relax and refresh you.
refreshing	**ADJECTIVE**	○ a refreshing drink
refreshments	**PLURAL NOUN**	○ Along the route, they stopped for refreshments.

---

re|fund (refunds, refunding, refunded) `SHOPPING`

The noun is pronounced /ˈriːfʌnd/. The verb is pronounced /rɪˈfʌnd/.

1 **NOUN** A **refund** is a sum of money which is returned to you, for example because you have paid too much or because you have returned goods to a shop. ○ Can I get a refund if my flight is cancelled? ○ [+ on] Fans were told they will receive a full refund on the $85 tickets.

▶ **COLLOCATIONS:**
a refund **on** something
get/receive a refund
ask for/demand a refund
give/offer someone a refund
a **full** refund

2 **VERB** If someone **refunds** your money, they return it to you, for example because you have paid too much or because you have returned goods to a shop. ○ We guarantee to refund your money if you're not delighted with your purchase. ○ Take the goods back to your retailer who will refund you the purchase price.

---

re|fuse /rɪˈfjuːz/ (refuses, refusing, refused)

1 **VERB** If you **refuse to** do something, you deliberately do not do it, or you say firmly that you will not do it. ○ [+ to-inf] He refused to discuss any of his plans. ○ I suggested she see a counsellor but she has flatly refused.

▶ **COLLOCATIONS:**
steadfastly/flatly/stubbornly refuse
simply refuse
repeatedly/consistently refuse

2 **VERB** If someone **refuses** you something, they do not give it to you or do not allow you to have it. ○ The United States has refused him a visa. ○ The town council had refused permission for the march.

▶ **COLLOCATIONS:**
refuse (someone) **permission**
refuse someone **entry/access/admission**
refuse someone a **visa/licence**

WORD FAMILY

| refuse | **VERB** | ○ He simply refused to accept defeat. |
| refusal | **UNCOUNT** | ○ His refusal to take anything seriously could be frustrating at times. |

re|gion /ˈriːdʒən/ (regions)

PLACES

NOUN A **region** is an area of a country or the world ○ [+ of] Badakshan province is a remote mountainous region of Afghanistan. ○ villages in the southwestern coastal region

▸ COLLOCATIONS:
in a region
a region **of** somewhere
a **remote/mountainous/coastal** region
the **border** region
a **mountain/desert** region
a **farming/wine-growing** region

WORD FAMILY

region	**NOUN**	○ We selected favourite dishes from the whole region.
regional	**ADJECTIVE**	○ Faro is the regional capital of the Algarve.
regionally	**ADVERB**	○ In Italy, lifestyles and customs vary regionally.

re|gret /rɪˈɡret/ (regrets, regretting, regretted)

1 **VERB** If you **regret** something that you have done, you wish that you had not done it. ○ I decided to go to university and have never regretted that decision. ○ [+ that] Ellis seemed to be regretting that he had asked the question. ○ [+ v-ing] My mother bitterly regretted leaving.

▸ COLLOCATIONS:
regret a **decision/incident**
come to regret something
bitterly/deeply regret something
immediately regret something

2 **VERB** You can say that you **regret** something as a polite way of saying that you are sorry about it. You use expressions such as **I regret to say** or **I regret to inform you** to show that you are sorry about something. ○ We regret any inconvenience this may cause. ○ [+ to-inf] We regret to announce flight EZY 68 to London has been cancelled.

regu|lar /ˈreɡjʊlə/

1 **ADJECTIVE** **Regular** events have equal amounts of time between them, so that they happen, for example, at the same time each day or each week. ○ Take regular exercise. ○ We're going to be meeting there on a regular basis.

2 **ADJECTIVE Regular** events happen often. ○ *Flooding is a regular occurrence in the area.* ○ *This condition usually clears up with regular shampooing.*

▶ COLLOCATIONS:
on a regular **basis**
at regular **intervals**
regular **exercise/contact/use**
regular **meetings/updates/visits/checks**
a regular **occurrence**

WORD FAMILY

regular	ADJECTIVE	○ *Pilots have to have regular health checks.*
regularly	ADVERB	○ *The lecture room at the centre is regularly used for talks.*
regularity	UNCOUNT	○ *The team has been losing with increasing regularity.*
irregular	ADJECTIVE	○ *He was suffering from an irregular heartbeat.*

---

re|hearse /rɪˈhɜːs/
(rehearses, rehearsing, rehearsed)

MEDIA & CULTURE

VERB When people **rehearse** a play, dance, or piece of music, they practise it in order to prepare for a performance. ○ [+ for] *We were rehearsing for the school play.* ○ *Ben and I had to rehearse these two scenes.*

▶ COLLOCATIONS:
rehearse **for** *something*
rehearse a **play/scene/song**

re|hears|al /rɪˈhɜːsəl/ (rehearsals)

NOUN A **rehearsal** of a play, dance, or piece of music is a practice of it in preparation for a performance. ○ [+ for] *The band was scheduled to begin rehearsals for a concert tour.* ○ *The acting is going pretty well in rehearsals .*

▶ COLLOCATIONS:
a rehearsal **for** *something*
in a rehearsal
begin rehearsals
the **first/final** rehearsal

---

re|la|tion|ship /rɪˈleɪʃənʃɪp/ (relationships)

PEOPLE

1 **NOUN** The **relationship** between two people or groups is the way in which they feel and behave towards each other. ○ [+ between] *The quality of the relationship between teachers and students is very important.* ○ [+ with] *I wanted to build a relationship with my team.*

2 **NOUN** A **relationship** is a close friendship between two people, especially one involving romantic or sexual feelings. ○ [+ with] *She was in a relationship with an older man.* ○ *Her last serious relationship ended a year ago.*

> ▶ **COLLOCATIONS:**
> a relationship **with** someone
> a relationship **between** two people
> be **in** a relationship
> **have/start/end** a relationship
> **build/establish/form** a relationship
> a relationship **ends/breaks up**
> a **loving/romantic** relationship
> a **close/good/strong** relationship
> a **serious/long-term** relationship
> a **personal/professional/family** relationship
> relationship **problems**

WORD FAMILY		
relation	NOUN	○ The country has good relations with the USA.
relationship	NOUN	○ Primary school teachers build up a very personal relationship with children.

---

rela|tive /ˈrelətɪv/ (relatives)   PEOPLE

NOUN Your **relatives** are the members of your family. ○ [+ of] He's a distant relative of mine ○ She had an elderly relative to care for as well as teenage children.

> ▶ **COLLOCATIONS:**
> a relative **of** someone
> a **close/distant** relative
> an **elderly** relative
> a **blood** relative
> **visit** relatives

> ▶ **SYNONYM:** relation

---

re|lax /rɪˈlæks/ (relaxes, relaxing, relaxed)   TRANSPORT & TRAVEL

VERB If you **relax**, you rest and do enjoyable things so that you feel more calm and less worried or tense. ○ When I'm on holiday I just want to relax. ○ [+ with] You can relax with a drink on the poolside terrace.

> ▶ **COLLOCATIONS:**
> relax **with** someone/something
> relax **completely**
> relax **and enjoy** something

> ▶ **SYNONYM:** unwind

re|laxed /rɪˈlækst/

ADJECTIVE If you are **relaxed**, you are calm and not worried or tense. ○ She looked more relaxed than I had ever seen her. ○ I felt very relaxed after my holiday in New Zealand.

> ▶ **ANTONYMS:** unrelaxed, tense

re|lax|ing /rɪˈlæksɪŋ/

ADJECTIVE Something that is **relaxing** is pleasant and helps you to relax. ○ *France is a brilliant place for a relaxing holiday.* ○ *The hotel has a comfortable and relaxing atmosphere.*

▶ **COLLOCATIONS:**
   a relaxing **atmosphere**
   a relaxing **holiday/break**
   a relaxing **day/evening/weekend**
   a relaxing **massage/bath**
   relaxing **music**

WORD FAMILY		
relax	**VERB**	○ *Just relax and enjoy the view!*
relaxing	**ADJECTIVE**	○ *She had been enjoying a relaxing day by the pool.*
relaxed	**ADJECTIVE**	○ *He felt more relaxed now the exams were over.*
relaxation	**UNCOUNT**	○ *Some kind of relaxation technique will help him unwind.*
unrelaxed	**ADJECTIVE**	○ *Informal conversation is difficult between unrelaxed polite people.*

rel|evant /ˈreləvənt/

ADJECTIVE Something that is **relevant to** a situation or person is important or significant in that situation or to that person. ○ [+ to] *Some of these ideas and suggestions may be relevant to you.* ○ *We have passed all relevant information on to the police.*

▶ **COLLOCATIONS:**
   relevant **to** *someone/something*
   relevant **information/experience**
   a relevant **question/fact**

▶ **ANTONYM:** irrelevant

WORD FAMILY		
relevant	**ADJECTIVE**	○ *Unless you have relevant work experience, you are unlikely to get the job.*
relevance	**UNCOUNT**	○ *All this information was fascinating, but I couldn't see its relevance.*
irrelevant	**ADJECTIVE**	○ *Your age is irrelevant – what matters is whether you can do the job.*
irrelevance	**UNCOUNT**	○ *I believe this highlights the irrelevance of the royal family to life today.*

re|li|able /rɪˈlaɪəbəl/ WORK PERSONALITY

ADJECTIVE People or things that are **reliable** can be trusted to work well or to behave in the way that you want them to. ○ *She was efficient and reliable.* ○ *Japanese cars are so reliable.*

➔ see also **rely on**

▶ **SYNONYM:** dependable

▶ **ANTONYM:** unreliable

re|lieved /rɪˈliːvd/

ADJECTIVE If you are **relieved**, you feel happy because something unpleasant has not happened or is no longer happening. ○ [+ to-inf] *She looked relieved to see him.* ○ [+ *that*] *I am very relieved that the exams are over.* ○ [+ *at*] *He was relieved at the result.*

▶ **COLLOCATIONS:**
relieved **at** *something*
feel/look relieved
relieved to **see/hear/find** *someone/something*
very/greatly relieved

WORD FAMILY

relieve	**VERB**	○ *Drugs can relieve the pain.*
relieved	**ADJECTIVE**	○ *Joe is now perfectly healthy and back home with his relieved parents.*
relief	**UNCOUNT**	○ *I felt a great sense of relief when we'd finished.*

re|li|gion /rɪˈlɪdʒən/ (religions) BELIEFS & OPINIONS

1 **UNCOUNTABLE NOUN** **Religion** is belief in a god or gods and the activities that are connected with this belief. ○ *Some people think that religion and science are not compatible.* ○ *Discrimination based on race or religion is outlawed.*

2 **NOUN** A **religion** is a particular system of belief in a god or gods and the activities that are connected with this system. ○ *the Christian religion* ○ *the major world religions* ○ *In many religions, eating pork is prohibited.*

▶ **COLLOCATIONS:**
in a religion
the **Islamic/Jewish/Christian** religion
world religions

WORD FAMILY

religion	**NOUN**	○ *He had no interest in religion.*
religious	**ADJECTIVE**	○ *religious beliefs* ○ *a deeply religious family*

r

rely on /rɪˈlaɪ ɒn/ (relies on, relying on, relied on)   `PERSONALITY`

1 VERB If you **rely on** someone or something, you need them and depend on them in order to live or work properly. ○ *The country relies heavily on imported oil.* ○ [+ *for*] *19% young people said they were relying solely on their parents for financial support.*

▶ **COLLOCATIONS:**
 rely on *someone* **for** *something*
 rely **heavily** on *someone/something*
 rely **solely/entirely** on *someone/something*
 rely **mainly/largely/increasingly** on *someone/something*

2 VERB If you can **rely on** someone to work well or to behave as you want them to, you can trust them to do this. ○ *You can rely on me.* ○ [+ *to-inf*] *I know I can rely on you to sort it out.*

WORD FAMILY		
rely on	VERB	○ *She relied increasingly on her son, Sanjay.*
reliable	ADJECTIVE	○ *Modern cars are more reliable.*
reliably	ADVERB	○ *The equipment has been working reliably for years.*
reliability	UNCOUNT	○ *New trains will improve reliability and journey times.*

re|mark|able /rɪˈmɑːkəbəl/

ADJECTIVE Someone or something that is **remarkable** is unusual or special in a way that makes people notice them and be surprised or impressed. ○ *He was a remarkable man.* ○ *It was a remarkable achievement.*

▶ **COLLOCATIONS:**
 a remarkable **achievement/feat/performance**
 a remarkable **story/recovery/ability**
 a remarkable **result/success**
 a remarkable **woman/man**
 quite/truly remarkable

▶ **SYNONYM:** amazing

▶ **ANTONYM:** unremarkable

WORD FAMILY		
remarkable	ADJECTIVE	○ *The change in her was quite remarkable.*
remarkably	ADVERB	○ *Remarkably, no one was injured in the crash.*
unremarkable	ADJECTIVE	○ *The room was cold, but otherwise unremarkable.*

re|mote con|trol /rɪˌməʊt kənˈtrəʊl/   `MEDIA & CULTURE`
(remote controls)

NOUN A **remote control** is a device which allows you to control a television or other equipment from a distance, by pressing the buttons on it. ○ *He reached for the remote control and switched off the television.* ○ *She used the remote control to close the gates.*

re|peat /rɪ'piːt/ (repeats)　　　`MEDIA & CULTURE`

NOUN A **repeat** is a television or radio programme that has been broadcast before.
[BRIT; in AM, use **re-run**] ○ *There's nothing except repeats on TV.* ○ [+ *of*] *Lenz spends his days off watching repeats of 'I Love Lucy'.*

▶ **COLLOCATIONS:**
　a repeat **of** something
　watch/run a repeat
　endless repeats

WORD FAMILY		
repeat	**NOUN**	○ *One channel ran endless repeats of the sitcom.*
repeat	**VERB**	○ *The programme is repeated on Sundays at 6.15.*
repetitive	**ADJECTIVE**	○ *Many people do a boring, repetitive job simply because they need the money.*
repetitively	**ADVERB**	○ *Children with the condition play repetitively with the same toy.*

re|port /rɪ'pɔːt/ (reports, reporting, reported)　　　`MEDIA & CULTURE`

1 **VERB** If you **report on** an event or subject, you tell people about it, because it is your job or duty to do so. ○ [+ *on*] *Many journalists enter the country to report on political affairs.* ○ *Jane Howard reports from the Turkish capital, Ankara.*

2 **NOUN** A **report** is a news article or broadcast which gives information about something that has just happened. ○ [+ *on*] *With a report on these developments, here's Jim Fish in Belgrade.* ○ *Press reports said that 65mm of water fell in twenty four hours.*

▶ **COLLOCATIONS:**
　a report **on** something
　in a report
　a **news/newspaper/press/media** report
　a report **says** something

re|port|er /rɪ'pɔːtə/ (reporters)

NOUN A **reporter** is someone who writes news articles or who broadcasts news reports. ○ *a TV reporter* ○ *a trainee sports reporter* ○ *He told reporters that he had no plans to retire from the game.*

▶ **COLLOCATIONS:**
　a **political/business/sports/health** reporter
　a **news** reporter
　an **undercover/investigative** reporter
　a **newspaper/TV/radio** reporter

▶ **SYNONYM:** journalist

r

re|quire /rɪˈkwaɪə/ (requires, requiring, required)

VERB To **require** something means to need it. [FORMAL] ○ *If you require further information, you should consult the headteacher.* ○ *Learning music does require you to be disciplined.*

WORD FAMILY		
require	VERB	○ *The doctor will advise you whether surgery is required.*
requirement	NOUN	○ *Car insurance is a legal requirement in Britain.*

res|cue /ˈreskjuː/ (rescues, rescuing, rescued)

VERB If you **rescue** someone, you get them out of a dangerous or unpleasant situation. ○ [+ from] *Helicopters rescued 20 people from the roof of the burning building.* ○ *The film is about a man who is trying to rescue his friend from a life of crime.*

WORD FAMILY		
rescue	VERB	○ *She had to be rescued by firefighters after becoming trapped.*
rescue	NOUN	○ *The dramatic rescue happened after the horse became stuck in mud.*
rescuer	NOUN	○ *It took rescuers 90 minutes to reach the trapped men.*

re|search /rɪˈsɜːtʃ/

SCIENCE & NATURE

(researches, researching, researched)

1 UNCOUNTABLE NOUN Research is work that involves studying something and trying to discover facts about it. ○ [+ into] *Scientists are carrying out research into the causes of the disease.* ○ *Recent research has shown that young women are more likely than young men to take up smoking.*

▶ **COLLOCATIONS:**
research **into** something
do/carry out/conduct research
publish research
research **shows/suggests/reveals** something
new/recent/the latest research
scientific/medical/academic research
extensive research
a research **project/findings**
a research **team/group/scientist**
a research **lab**

2 VERB If you **research** something, you try to discover facts about it. ○ *I am researching my family history.* ○ *She spent two years in South Florida researching her book.*

▶ **COLLOCATIONS:**
research a **book/story/article**
research the **history of** something
research an **issue/subject/topic**

WORD FAMILY		
research	UNCOUNT	○ Dr Zava has also done extensive research into the effects of food.
research	VERB	○ If you want to research the topic, there are dozens of articles online.
researcher	NOUN	○ Medical researchers have found new evidence that the drug may be harmful.

re|serve /rɪˈzɜːv/ (reserves, reserving, reserved)   SOCIAL LIFE

VERB If you **reserve** something such as a table, ticket, or place on a course or trip, you arrange for it to be kept specially for you, rather than sold or given to someone else. ○ I'll reserve a table for five. ○ To reserve a place on the course, please contact Denise Jones.

▶ **COLLOCATIONS:**
reserve a **place/seat/table/room**
reserve a **ticket**

WORD FAMILY		
reserve	VERB	○ They had reserved a room at the Tudor Rose Hotel for their wedding night.
reservation	NOUN	○ An increasing number of people are making hotel reservations online.

resi|dent /ˈrezɪdənt/ (residents)   PEOPLE   PLACES

NOUN The **residents** of a house or area are the people who live there. ○ Local residents objected to the plans. ○ [+ of] The offer is open to residents of the UK.

▶ **COLLOCATIONS:**
a resident **of** somewhere
local residents
a **permanent/former** resident

▶ **SYNONYM:** inhabitant

WORD FAMILY		
resident	NOUN	○ Residents in the building were told to leave.
residence	NOUN	○ He had taken up residence in Switzerland.
residential	ADJECTIVE	○ Drive slowly in residential areas.

r

re|sign /rɪˈzaɪn/ (resigns, resigning, resigned) `WORK`

VERB If you **resign** from a job or position, you formally announce that you are leaving it. ○ [+ *as*] *He resigned as head of the oil company, Yukos.* ○ [+ *from*] *My father resigned from the job last year.*

▶ **COLLOCATION:** resign **as/from/over** *something*

▶ **SYNONYM:** quit

WORD FAMILY		
resign	**VERB**	○ *A hospital administrator has resigned over claims that he lied to get the job.*
resignation	**UNCOUNT**	○ *His resignation was announced last week.*

re|sources /rɪˈzɔːsɪz, AM ˈriːsɔːrsɪz/ `SCIENCE & NATURE`

1 PLURAL NOUN The **resources** of an organization or person are the materials, money, and other things that they have and can use in order to function properly. ○ *Only a limited amount of time and resources are available.* ○ *Some families don't have the resources to feed themselves properly.*

2 PLURAL NOUN A country's **resources** are the things that it has and can use to increase its wealth, such as coal, oil, or land. ○ *This part of the country has more natural resources, including coal and iron ore.* ○ *We need to encourage more use of renewable energy resources, such as the wind.*

▶ **COLLOCATIONS:**
natural resources
water/energy/oil/mineral resources
financial resources
limited/scarce resources
valuable/precious resources
renewable resources
use/provide/lack resources

re|spon|sible /rɪˈspɒnsɪbəl/ `PERSONALITY` `WORK`

1 ADJECTIVE If you are **responsible for** something, it is your job or duty to deal with it. ○ [+ *for*] *Parents are responsible for their children's safety.* ○ *The vice-principal is responsible for the day-to-day management of the school.*

2 ADJECTIVE Responsible people behave properly and sensibly, without needing to be supervised. ○ *He's a very responsible sort of person.* ○ *The media should be more responsible in what they report.* ○ *Mature students generally take a more responsible attitude towards their studies.*

▶ **COLLOCATIONS:**
responsible **for** *something*
a responsible **adult/citizen/person**
a responsible **attitude/approach**
in a responsible **way/manner**

res|tau|rant /ˈrestərɒnt, AM -rənt/ FOOD & DRINK SOCIAL LIFE
(restaurants)

NOUN A **restaurant** is a place where you can eat a meal and pay for it. In restaurants your food is usually served to you at your table by a waiter or waitress. ○ *We're going to a Japanese restaurant in town.* ○ *They had dinner in the hotel's restaurant.*

▶ COLLOCATIONS:
in a restaurant
go to a restaurant
eat in a restaurant
run/own a restaurant
a **Chinese/Italian/Indian**, etc. restaurant
a **fast-food** restaurant
a restaurant **serves** *something*

▶ SYNONYM: cafe

re|sults /rɪˈzʌlts/ EDUCATION

NOUN Your **results** are the marks or grades that you get for examinations you have taken. [mainly BRIT; in AM, usually use **scores**] ○ *Kate's exam results were excellent.* ○ *schools with poor examination results*

▶ SYNONYMS: marks, grades

re|tire /rɪˈtaɪə/ (retires, retiring, retired) WORK

VERB When older people **retire**, they leave their job and usually stop working completely. ○ [+ *from*] *In 2012 he retired from the museum.* ○ [+ *at*] *Firemen usually retire at the age of 50.*

▶ COLLOCATIONS:
retire **from** *a job*
retire **at** *an age*
retire **as** *something*

r

re|view /rɪˈvjuː/ (reviews)

MEDIA & CULTURE

NOUN A **review** is a report in the media in which someone gives their opinion of something such as a new book or film. ○ *The play got mixed reviews.* ○ [+ of] *reviews of the latest books*

▶ COLLOCATIONS:
  a review **of** something
  a review **in** something
  get/receive/win a ... review
  write/read a review
  a **good/bad** review
  mixed reviews
  a **book/film/restaurant/TV** review

WORD FAMILY		
review	NOUN	○ *his weekly restaurant review in The Sunday Times*
reviewer	NOUN	○ *He was a regular book reviewer for 'The Observer'.*

re|vise /rɪˈvaɪz/ (revises, revising, revised)

EDUCATION

VERB When you **revise for** an examination, you read things again and make notes in order to be prepared for the examination. [BRIT; in AM, use **review**] ○ [+ for] *I have to revise for maths.* ○ *I'd better skip the party and stay at home to revise.*

▶ COLLOCATIONS:
  revise **for** something
  revise for an **exam/test**
  revise for **maths/English**, etc.

WORD FAMILY		
revise	VERB	○ *I was supposed to be revising for exams.*
revision	UNCOUNT	○ *I need to do some chemistry revision today.*

ring /rɪŋ/
(rings, ringing, rang, rung)

COMMUNICATIONS   CLOTHES & APPEARANCE

1 VERB When you **ring** someone, or **ring** them **up**, you telephone them. [mainly BRIT; in AM, usually use **call**] ○ [+ to-inf] *I rang a friend to tell her what had happened.* ○ [+ about] *He was ringing up about the party next week.* ○ [+ for] *Could someone ring for a taxi?*

▶ COLLOCATIONS:
  ring (up) **about** something
  ring (up) **for** something
  ring for a **taxi/ambulance**

▶ SYNONYMS: phone, call

2 NOUN A **ring** is a small circle of metal that you wear on your finger. ○ *She wore several diamond rings.* ○ *a gold wedding ring*

▸ **COLLOCATIONS:**
wear a ring
a **gold/silver/diamond** ring
a **wedding/engagement** ring

---

rise /raɪz/ (rises, rising, rose, risen)   `SCIENCE & NATURE`

VERB If the temperature of something **rises**, it increases. ○ [+ to] In summer the temperature can rise to over 40°C. ○ [+ by] Over the last 25 years, the average global temperature has risen by 0.6°C.

▸ **COLLOCATIONS:**
rise **to** x
rise **by** x
rise **above** x
rise **rapidly/steadily/slightly**

▸ **SYNONYM:** increase

▸ **ANTONYM:** fall

---

riv|er /ˈrɪvə/ (rivers)   `SCIENCE & NATURE`

NOUN A **river** is a large amount of fresh water flowing continuously in a long line across the land. ○ We had a picnic on the river bank. ○ They were rowing down the River Thames.

---

roast /rəʊst/ (roasts, roasting, roasted)   `FOOD & DRINK`

1 **VERB** When you **roast** meat or other food, you cook it by dry heat in an oven or over a fire. ○ I roasted the chicken for about ten minutes longer than normal.

2 **ADJECTIVE** **Roast** meat or vegetables have been cooked by roasting. ○ I ordered the roast beef.

▸ **COLLOCATIONS:**
roast **beef/chicken/lamb/pork**
roast **potatoes**

---

rob /rɒb/ (robs, robbing, robbed)   `CRIME`

VERB If a person, bank, or shop **is robbed**, they have money or property stolen from them. ○ [+ of] Mrs Yacoub was robbed of her £3,000 watch. ○ The gang tried to rob a bank.

▸ **COLLOCATIONS:**
be robbed **of** something
rob a **bank/shop/store**

rob|bery /ˈrɒbəri/ (robberies)

NOUN **Robbery** is the crime of stealing money or property from a bank, shop, or vehicle, often by using force or threats. ○ The gang members committed dozens of armed robberies. ○ He was jailed for six years for a bank robbery.

▶ COLLOCATIONS:
commit a robbery
an **armed/attempted** robbery
a **bank** robbery

WORD FAMILY		
rob	VERB	○ *Police said Stefanovski had robbed a man just hours earlier.*
robber	NOUN	○ *Armed robbers stole £3 million from a security van.*
robbery	NOUN	○ *Wood pleaded guilty to two attempted robberies.*

---

rock (mu|sic) /ˈrɒk mjuːzɪk/ `MEDIA & CULTURE`

UNCOUNTABLE NOUN **Rock** is loud music with a strong beat that is usually played and sung by a small group of people using instruments such as electric guitars and drums. ○ *I like rock music.* ○ *They're playing at the Glastonbury rock festival.*

▶ COLLOCATIONS:
a rock **band/group**
a rock **star/singer/musician**
a rock **concert/festival**
a rock **song/album**

---

round|about /ˈraʊndəbaʊt/ (roundabouts) `TRANSPORT & TRAVEL`

NOUN A **roundabout** is a circular structure in the road at a place where several roads meet. You drive round it until you come to the road that you want. [BRIT; in AM, use **traffic circle**] ○ *At the roundabout, he took the second exit.* ○ *Go straight on at the roundabout.*

▶ COLLOCATION: **at** a roundabout

---

route /ruːt, AM raʊt/ (routes) `TRANSPORT & TRAVEL`

1 **NOUN** A **route** is a way from one place to another. ○ *He always took the same route home.* ○ *All escape routes were blocked by armed police.* ○ *Cheering crowds lined the route.*

2 **NOUN** A bus, air, or shipping **route** is the way between two places along which buses, planes, or ships travel regularly. ○ *This is one of Britain's busiest rail routes.* ○ *The hospital is on the 73 bus route.*

▶ COLLOCATIONS:
take/follow a route
a **bus/rail/air** route
a **direct/alternative** route
the **main** route
a **scenic** route

rou|tine /ruːˈtiːn/ (routines)

NOUN A **routine** is the usual series of things that you do at a particular time and in a particular order. ○ *The players had to change their daily routine and lifestyle.* ○ *She was following a daily exercise routine.*

▶ **COLLOCATIONS:**
  in a routine
  a **daily** routine
  someone's **normal/regular/usual** routine
  a morning **routine**
  a **fitness/exercise** routine
  follow a routine

WORD FAMILY		
routine	**NOUN**	○ *There was never time in her morning routine for a cup of coffee.*
routinely	**ADVERB**	○ *It's a drug which is routinely used in hospitals.*

rub|bish /ˈrʌbɪʃ/   SCIENCE & NATURE

UNCOUNTABLE NOUN **Rubbish** consists of unwanted things or waste material such as used paper, empty tins and bottles, and waste food. [mainly BRIT; in AM, usually use **garbage**, **trash**] ○ *25% of all household rubbish must be recycled.* ○ *It's your turn to put the rubbish out.*

▶ **COLLOCATIONS:**
  household rubbish
  put/take the rubbish **out**
  collect /dump rubbish

▶ **SYNONYM:** waste

rude /ruːd/ (ruder, rudest)   PERSONALITY

ADJECTIVE When people are **rude**, they behave in an impolite way towards other people. ○ [+ to] *I'm sorry that I was rude to you on the phone.* ○ [+ about] *He was very rude about my essay.*

▶ **COLLOCATIONS:**
  rude **to** someone
  rude **about** someone/something
  a rude **remark/comment/question**

▶ **SYNONYM:** disrespectful

▶ **ANTONYM:** polite

WORD FAMILY		
rude	**ADJECTIVE**	○ *I ignored the man's rude comment.*
rudely	**ADVERB**	○ *If customers are treated rudely, they won't go back to the restaurant.*
rudeness	**UNCOUNT**	○ *She was angry at Steve's rudeness.*

r

rug|by /ˈrʌgbi/

SPORT & ACTIVITY

UNCOUNTABLE NOUN **Rugby** or **rugby football** is a game played by two teams who try to score by kicking or carrying an oval ball to their opponents' end of the field. ○ *I played rugby when I went to university.* ○ *the Welsh rugby team* ○ *English rugby fans*

▶ **COLLOCATIONS:**
  play/watch/love rugby
  a rugby **team/club**
  a rugby **player/coach/fan**
  a rugby **match/game**
  a rugby **pitch/ball/shirt**

ruined /ˈruːɪnd/

PLACES

ADJECTIVE A **ruined** building or place has been very badly damaged or has gradually fallen down because no-one has taken care of it. ○ *There's an old town with a ruined castle.* ○ *Beyond the gate you can see the ruined walls of a few houses.*

▶ **COLLOCATIONS:**
  a ruined **building/castle/house**
  a ruined **church/abbey/temple**
  a ruined **city**
  ruined **walls**

WORD FAMILY		
ruin	**NOUN**	○ *You can visit the ruins of the Roman city of Baelo Claudia.*
ruin	**VERB**	○ *Cars and heavy lorries are ruining our environment.*
ruined	**ADJECTIVE**	○ *We stopped to explore a ruined house.*

run /rʌn/ (runs, running, ran)

SPORT & ACTIVITY

1 VERB When you **run**, you move more quickly than when you walk, for example because you are in a hurry to get somewhere, or for exercise. ○ *He ran back home.* ○ *She's running in the London marathon.* ○ *I started an exercise programme, running 6 miles a week.*

2 NOUN A **run** is the act of running for pleasure or exercise. ○ *I go for a run twice a week.* ○ *After a six-mile run, Jackie returns home for a substantial breakfast.*

▶ **COLLOCATIONS:**
  go for a run
  a **five-mile/ten-kilometre**, etc. run

run|ner /ˈrʌnə/ (runners)

NOUN A **runner** is a person who runs, especially for sport or pleasure. ○ *I am a very keen runner and am out training most days.* ○ *She's one of Britain's top marathon runners.*

▶ **COLLOCATIONS:**
  a **marathon/long-distance** runner
  a **good/fast** runner

run|ning /ˈrʌnɪŋ/

UNCOUNTABLE NOUN **Running** is the activity of moving fast on foot, especially as a sport. ○ *He goes running every morning.* ○ *You should wear a good pair of running shoes.*

▶ **COLLOCATIONS:**
  go running
  long-distance/marathon/cross-country running
  running **shoes**

WORD FAMILY		
run	VERB	○ *Michael ran to catch up with his friends.*
run	NOUN	○ *I might go for a run.*
running	UNCOUNT	○ *Marathon running has become more popular.*
runner	NOUN	○ *I'm one of the fastest runners in my school.*

run-down /ˈrʌndaʊn/ also **rundown**   HEALTH   PLACES

1 **ADJECTIVE** If someone is **run-down**, they are tired or slightly ill. [INFORMAL]
  ○ *You do look a bit run-down.* ○ *The infection had left him feeling tired and run-down.*

▶ **SYNONYM:** under the weather

2 **ADJECTIVE** A **run-down** building or area is in very poor condition. ○ *It is one of the most run-down areas in Scotland.* ○ *The house was damp and run-down when they moved in.*

▶ **COLLOCATIONS:**
  a run-down **area**
  a run-down **house/building/property**
  a run-down **estate/neighbourhood**

▶ **SYNONYMS:** neglected, dilapidated

run through /rʌn ˈθruː/ (runs through, running through, ran through)

1 **PHRASAL VERB** If you **run through** a list of items, you read or mention all the items quickly. ○ *I ran through the options with him.* ○ *She ran through a mental list of what she had to do today.*

▶ **COLLOCATIONS:**
  run through a **list/checklist**
  run through the **options**

▶ **SYNONYM:** go through

2 **PHRASAL VERB** If you **run through** a performance or a series of actions, you practise it. ○ *He ran through the song a couple of times before going on stage.* ○ *She started to run through her presentation again.*

▶ **SYNONYMS:** go through, practise, rehearse

---

run up against /rʌn ˈʌp əˌgenst, əˌgeɪnst/ (runs up against, running up against, ran up against)

PHRASAL VERB If you **run up against** problems, you suddenly begin to experience them. ○ *The project ran up against all sorts of cultural and financial problems.* ○ *He ran up against a solid wall of opposition.*

▶ **SYNONYM:** encounter

---

ru|ral /ˈrʊərəl/   PLACES

ADJECTIVE **Rural** places are far away from large towns or cities. ○ *Public transport is often scarce in rural areas.* ○ *Many rural schools have been forced to close.*

→ see also **urban**

▶ **COLLOCATIONS:**
a rural **area/community**
a rural **town/village**
a rural **school/road**
rural **life**

---

rush /rʌʃ/ (rushes, rushing, rushed)

VERB If you **rush** somewhere, you go there quickly. ○ *The children rushed out of the classroom.* ○ [+ to-inf] *People rushed to help the injured driver.*

---

rush hour /ˈrʌʃ ˌaʊə/ also **rush-hour**   TRANSPORT & TRAVEL

UNCOUNTABLE NOUN The **rush hour** is one of the periods of the day when most people are travelling to or from work. ○ *The journey can take even longer in the rush hour.* ○ *We left earlier to avoid rush-hour traffic.*

▶ **COLLOCATIONS:**
at/during rush hour
in the rush hour
the **morning/evening** rush hour
rush-hour **traffic**

Ss

sail|ing /ˈseɪlɪŋ/

UNCOUNTABLE NOUN **Sailing** is the activity or sport of sailing boats. ○ *Dad's arranged for us to go sailing.* ○ *There was swimming and sailing down on the lake.*

▶ **COLLOCATIONS:**
go/enjoy sailing
a sailing **club/school**
a sailing **trip/holiday**

WORD FAMILY		
sail	**VERB**	○ *Ben wanted to sail around the world.*
sailing	**UNCOUNT**	○ *He joined the sailing club.*
sailor	**NOUN**	○ *Six sailors died when huge storms hit their boat.*

sal|ad /ˈsæləd/ (salads)

NOUN A **salad** is a mixture of raw or cold foods such as lettuce, cucumber, and tomatoes. It is often served with other food as part of a meal. ○ *I made a salad to go with the kebabs.* ○ *The peppery flavoured leaves are good in salads.*

▶ **COLLOCATIONS:**
in a salad
a salad **of** *something*
make/prepare a salad
a **green/mixed** salad
a **pasta/potato** salad
a **chicken/tuna/cheese** salad
a **side** salad
a salad **bowl/dressing**

USAGE

Salad is not the name of a vegetable, it is a mixture of raw or cold foods.
Lettuce is a vegetable with green leaves that is often used in salads.
○ *The dish came with a salad of lettuce, cucumber, and celery.*

S

sala|ry /ˈsæləri/ (salaries)   WORK MONEY

NOUN A **salary** is the money that someone is paid each month by their employer. ○ *Adam was earning a very good salary as a lawyer.* ○ *She couldn't afford to buy a house on her salary.* ○ [+ of] *My friends are on salaries of £25,000 or more.*

▶ COLLOCATIONS:
  on a salary
  a salary **of** x
  earn/receive/get a salary
  pay a salary
  a salary **increases/rises**
  a **high/good/huge** salary
  a **low/average** salary
  an **annual** salary

▶ SYNONYMS: wages, income

> **WHICH WORD: salary** or **wages**?
>
> A salary is usually a fixed amount that someone is paid per year, divided into monthly payments. ○ *an annual salary of £48,000*
>
> Wages are weekly or monthly payments, usually based on how many hours someone has worked. ○ *an hourly wage of £5.71*

sale /seɪl/ (sales)   WORK SHOPPING

1 PLURAL NOUN The part of a company that deals with **sales** deals with selling the company's products. ○ *Until 2010 he worked in sales and marketing.* ○ *She was their sales manager.*

▶ COLLOCATIONS:
  work in sales
  a sales **manager/director**
  a **sales rep/representative**
  the sales **team**
  sales **and marketing**

2 NOUN A **sale** is an occasion when a shop sells things at less than their normal price. ○ *I got these jeans half-price in a sale.* ○ *Many stores have started their January sales a month early.*

▶ COLLOCATIONS:
  in a sale
  a **summer/winter** sale
  a **clearance/closing-down** sale

salt /sɔːlt/   HEALTH FOOD & DRINK

UNCOUNTABLE NOUN **Salt** is a strong-tasting substance, in the form of white powder or crystals, which is used to improve the flavour of food or to preserve it. ○ *Add a pinch of salt.* ○ *Soya sauce has a very high salt content, so don't use too much.*

▶ COLLOCATIONS:
add/use salt
season *something* **with** salt
a **pinch of** salt
salt **and pepper**
salt **content/intake**

WORD FAMILY		
salt	UNCOUNT	○ *I try to use less salt in cooking.*
salty	ADJECTIVE	○ *Cut down on crisps, nuts and other salty snacks.*

---

sand /sænd/ (sands, sanding, sanded)
SCIENCE & NATURE

UNCOUNTABLE NOUN **Sand** is a substance that looks like powder, and consists of extremely small pieces of stone. Some deserts and many beaches are made up of sand. ○ *They walked across the sand to the water's edge.* ○ *There is a long stretch of beach with fine white sand.*

▶ COLLOCATIONS:
fine/coarse sand
white/golden sand
a **grain of** sand

---

san|dals /'sændəlz/
CLOTHES & APPEARANCE

PLURAL NOUN **Sandals** are light shoes that you wear in warm weather, which have straps instead of a solid part over the top of your foot. ○ *She wore a pair of white sandals.*

▶ COLLOCATIONS:
a **pair of** sandals
wear sandals
high-heeled/flat sandals
leather/plastic/rubber sandals

---

sat|is|fied /'sætɪsfaɪd/

ADJECTIVE If you are **satisfied with** something, you are happy because you have got what you wanted or needed. ○ [+ with] *Professor Wilkinson said he was satisfied with the exam results.* ○ *The interviewer seemed reasonably satisfied with my answers.*

▶ COLLOCATIONS:
satisfied **with** *something*
a satisfied **smile**
a satisfied **customer**
completely/fully/entirely satisfied
reasonably satisfied

S

WORD FAMILY		
satisfy	VERB	○ This decision may not satisfy everyone.
satisfied	ADJECTIVE	○ The company has hundreds of satisfied customers.
unsatisfied	ADJECTIVE	○ Several hotel guests were unsatisfied with the service they received.
satisfying	ADJECTIVE	○ This is the most satisfying job I have ever done.
unsatisfying	ADJECTIVE	○ He is concerned that the huge arena might provide an unsatisfying experience for fans.
satisfaction	UNCOUNT	○ She felt a sense of satisfaction.
satisfactory	ADJECTIVE	○ There's been no satisfactory answer to the question.
unsatisfactory	ADJECTIVE	○ It is totally unsatisfactory that students are having to wait so long for their results.

sauce /sɔːs/ (sauces)   FOOD & DRINK

NOUN A **sauce** is a thick liquid which is served with other food. ○ I had vanilla ice cream with chocolate sauce. ○ [+ of] The pasta is cooked in a sauce of garlic, tomatoes, and cheese.

▶ COLLOCATIONS:
a sauce **of** something
make/pour/spoon a sauce
a **hot/spicy** sauce
a **rich/creamy/sweet** sauce
chocolate/cheese/tomato sauce

sauce|pan /'sɔːspən, AM -pæn/ (saucepans)   FOOD & DRINK

NOUN A **saucepan** is a deep metal cooking pot, usually with a long handle and a lid. ○ Cook the potatoes in a large saucepan.

▶ COLLOCATIONS:
in a saucepan
a **large/small/medium** saucepan

▶ SYNONYM: pan

sau|sage /'sɒsɪdʒ, AM 'sɔːs-/ (sausages)   FOOD & DRINK

NOUN A **sausage** consists of minced meat, usually pork, mixed with other ingredients and is contained in a tube made of skin or a similar material. ○ sausages and chips ○ a packet of pork sausages

save /seɪv/ (saves, saving, saved)   MONEY

1 VERB If you **save**, you gradually collect money by spending less than you get, usually in order to buy something that you want. ○ [+ for] I'm saving for a car. ○ Many people on low wages find it difficult to save.

▶ COLLOCATIONS:
save **for** something
save **money**

2 VERB If you **save** something such as time or money, you prevent the loss or waste of it. ○ *To save time I got the bus to school.* ○ [+ on] *You can save on travel costs by booking your tickets in advance.*

▶ COLLOCATIONS:
save **on** something
save **time/money**

▶ ANTONYM: waste

WORD FAMILY		
save	**VERB**	○ *Save money by buying your clothes in the sales.*
savings	**PLURAL NOUN**	○ *She used all her savings to pay for the course.*
saver	**NOUN**	○ *Internet banks give savers a better deal.*

sa|voury /ˈseɪvəri/ [in AM, use **savory**]

FOOD & DRINK

ADJECTIVE **Savoury** food has a salty or spicy flavour rather than a sweet one. ○ *The spice can be used in sweet and savoury dishes.* ○ *People in Britain eat a lot of crisps and savoury snacks.*

→ see also **sweet**

▶ COLLOCATIONS:
a savoury **dish/snack**
savoury **food**

scales /skeɪlz/

HEALTH

PLURAL NOUN **Scales** are a piece of equipment used for weighing things, for example for weighing yourself or for weighing amounts of food. ○ *a pair of kitchen scales* ○ *I step on the scales practically every morning.*

▶ COLLOCATIONS:
get on/step on/stand on the scales
kitchen/bathroom scales
a **pair of/set of** scales

S

scar /skɑː/ (scars)

HEALTH

NOUN A **scar** is a mark on the skin which is left after a wound has healed. ○ [+ on] *He had a scar on his forehead.* ○ *The facial injuries he received left permanent scars.*

▶ COLLOCATIONS:
a scar **on** something
have a scar
something **leaves** a scar

hide a scar
a **permanent/visible** scar
a **long/small/deep** scar

---

scared /skeəd/

1 **ADJECTIVE** If you are **scared of** someone or something, you are frightened of them. ○ [+ of] I'm really scared of spiders. ○ [+ to-inf] I was too scared to move.

▶ **SYNONYM:** frightened

2 **ADJECTIVE** If you are **scared that** something unpleasant might happen, you are nervous and worried because you think that it might happen. ○ [+ that] I was scared that I might be sick. ○ [+ of] He was scared of letting us down.

▶ **COLLOCATIONS:**
scared **of** someone/something
get/feel scared

▶ **SYNONYM:** worried

WORD FAMILY		
scare	VERB	○ You're scaring me.
scared	ADJECTIVE	○ Sometimes I get really scared.
scary	ADJECTIVE	○ I love scary movies.

---

scarf /skɑːf/ (scarfs, scarves) `CLOTHES & APPEARANCE`

NOUN A **scarf** is a piece of cloth that you wear round your neck or head, usually to keep yourself warm. ○ She was wearing a red scarf. ○ an orange silk scarf

---

sci|ence /saɪəns/ (sciences) `SCIENCE & NATURE`

1 **UNCOUNTABLE NOUN** **Science** is the study of the nature and behaviour of natural things and the knowledge that we obtain about them. ○ The best discoveries in science are very simple. ○ Teachers are careful to lock up chemicals used for science experiments.

2 **NOUN** A **science** is a particular branch of science such as physics, chemistry, or biology. ○ You need to do sciences at school if you want to be a doctor. ○ [+ of] the science of microbiology

▶ **COLLOCATIONS:**
in science
the science **of** something
study/teach science
a science **teacher/student/writer**
a science **class/lesson/course**
the science **department**
a science **lab/experiment**
computer/health/environmental science

sci|en|tif|ic /ˌsaɪən'tɪfɪk/

ADJECTIVE **Scientific** is used to describe things that relate to science or to a particular science. ○ *Scientific research has shown that people who eat lots of fruits and vegetables live longer, healthier lives.* ○ *The use of animals in scientific experiments is very controversial.*

▶ **COLLOCATIONS:**
scientific **research/study**
a scientific **experiment/investigation**
scientific **evidence/knowledge**
a scientific **discovery/instrument**

WORD FAMILY		
science	**UNCOUNT**	○ *a university science lab* ○ *the department of biological sciences*
scientific	**ADJECTIVE**	○ *Many important scientific discoveries have been stumbled across by accident.*
scientifically	**ADVERB**	○ *This claim has never been scientifically proved.*
scientist	**NOUN**	○ *Some scientists believe that the temperature will continue to rise.*

sci|ence fic|tion /ˌsaɪəns 'fɪkʃən/

MEDIA & CULTURE

UNCOUNTABLE NOUN **Science fiction** consists of stories in books and films about events that take place in the future or in other parts of the universe. ○ *Robots are popular characters in science fiction.* ○ *Surely you don't just read science fiction?*

▶ **COLLOCATIONS:**
in science fiction
a science fiction **book/film/story**
a science fiction **writer/author**
read/write science fiction

screen /skriːn/ (screens)

MEDIA & CULTURE

NOUN A **screen** is a flat vertical surface on which pictures or words are shown. Television sets and computers have screens, and films are shown on a screen in cinemas. ○ *A message flashed up on the screen.* ○ *Suddenly the screen went blank.*

▶ **COLLOCATIONS:**
on a screen
a **computer/TV/cinema** screen
a **huge/big/small** screen
a **blank** screen
a **flat** screen

S

script /skrɪpt/ (scripts)

MEDIA & CULTURE

NOUN The **script** of a play, film, or television programme is the written version of it. ○ *Jenny's writing a film script.* ○ *The script writers have got rid of one of the show's best characters.*

▶ **COLLOCATIONS:**
write/read a script
a **TV/film** script
a script **writer**

sculp|ture /ˈskʌlptʃə/ (sculptures)

MEDIA & CULTURE

1 NOUN A **sculpture** is a work of art that is produced by carving or shaping stone, wood, clay, or other materials. ○ [+ of] *stone sculptures of animals* ○ *The museum houses a collection of 20th-century art and sculpture.*

2 UNCOUNTABLE NOUN **Sculpture** is the art of creating sculptures. ○ *Both studied sculpture.*

▶ **COLLOCATIONS:**
a sculpture **of** something
make/create a sculpture
a **bronze/ice/stone** sculpture

WORD FAMILY		
sculpture	NOUN	○ *He's well-known for making glass sculptures.*
sculptor	NOUN	○ *She was a talented painter and sculptor.*

sea /siː/ (seas)

SCIENCE & NATURE

1 UNCOUNTABLE NOUN **The sea** is the salty water that covers about three-quarters of the Earth's surface. ○ *a day by the sea* ○ *We can swim in the sea.* ○ *The sea was too rough for fishing.*

▶ **SYNONYM:** ocean

2 NOUN A **sea** is a large area of salty water that is part of an ocean or is surrounded by land. ○ *the North Sea* ○ *the huge inland sea of Turkana*

▶ **COLLOCATIONS:**
by/in the sea
at sea
overlook the sea
the sea is **rough/choppy/calm**
a sea **breeze/creature/voyage**

sea|side /ˈsiːsaɪd/

TRANSPORT & TRAVEL   PLACES

UNCOUNTABLE NOUN You can refer to an area that is close to the sea, especially one where people go for their holidays, as **the seaside**. ○ *I went to spend a few days at the seaside.* ○ *Brighton is an elegant seaside resort.*

▶ **COLLOCATIONS:**
at the seaside
go to the seaside
a seaside **resort/town/village**
a seaside **holiday/hotel**

▶ **SYNONYMS:** coast, beach

---

sea|son /'siːzən/ (seasons) SCIENCE & NATURE

NOUN The **seasons** are the main periods into which a year can be divided and which each have their own typical weather conditions. ○ *Autumn's my favourite season.* ○ *In the rainy season, water pours off the mountains.*

▶ **COLLOCATIONS:**
in a season
the **rainy/wet/dry** season

WORD FAMILY		
season	**NOUN**	○ *I went in April , in the dry season.*
seasonal	**ADJECTIVE**	○ *seasonal changes in weather*

---

seat belt /'siːt ˌbelt/ TRANSPORT & TRAVEL
(seat belts) also **seatbelt**

NOUN A **seat belt** is a strap attached to a seat in a car or an aircraft. You fasten it across your body and it stops you being thrown out of your seat in an accident. ○ *The fact I was wearing a seat belt saved my life.* ○ *Anna got in and fastened her seat belt.*

▶ **COLLOCATIONS:**
wear a seat belt
fasten/undo a seatbelt

▶ **SYNONYM:** safety belt

---

sec|ond|ary school /'sekəndri skuːl, AM -deri/ EDUCATION
(secondary schools)

NOUN A **secondary school** is a school for pupils between the ages of 11 or 12 and 17 or 18. ○ *My sister's now at secondary school.* ○ *He absolutely loved his job as a secondary school teacher.*

▶ **COLLOCATIONS:**
at/in secondary school
start/leave secondary school
a secondary school **teacher/pupil/student**

▶ **SYNONYM:** high school

S

second-hand /ˌsekənd'hænd/

ADJECTIVE Second-hand things are not new and have been owned by someone else. ○ *I like to buy second-hand clothes.* ○ *Buying a second-hand car can be a risky business.*

→ see also **brand-new**

▶ COLLOCATIONS:
a second-hand **car**
second-hand **clothes/books/furniture**

sec|tion /'sekʃən/ (sections, sectioning, sectioned)

NOUN A section of something is one of the parts into which it is divided or from which it is formed. ○ [+ of] *You can comment on the issues in the 'Have Your Say' section of this website.* ○ *I always read the sports section of the newspaper first.*

▶ COLLOCATIONS:
a section **of** something
in a section

> **WHICH WORD: section, stage, or part?**
>
> You use **section** to talk about one of the parts that something such as a newspaper, a piece of writing, a book, a piece of music etc. is divided into. ○ *This section of the book provides practice exercises.*
>
> You use **stage** to talk about something which is part of a long process. ○ *The next stage of the project is already underway.*
>
> **Part** is a more general word that you can use in most situations. ○ *The second part of the project will involve more people.* ○ *the final part of the book* ○ *one of the poorest parts of the city*

se|cure /sɪ'kjʊə/

ADJECTIVE A secure website, internet connection, etc. is one which has good protection and is safe to use, for example when making payments. ○ *Check the website you are visiting is secure before submitting sensitive information.* ○ *Use sites with secure connections to take card details.*

se|cu|rity /sɪ'kjʊərɪti/

UNCOUNTABLE NOUN Security refers to all the measures that are taken to protect a place. ○ *Airport security has been tightened.* ○ *All airline passengers are required to go through security.*

▶ COLLOCATIONS:
airport security
go through security
improve/increase/tighten security
tight security

a security **check**
security **measures**

WORD FAMILY		
secure	**ADJECTIVE**	○ We all want to feel safe and secure.
securely	**ADVERB**	○ He checked that all the windows and doors were securely locked.
security	**UNCOUNT**	○ You'll have to go through a security check where your bag will be searched.

self|ish /'selfɪʃ/

PERSONALITY

ADJECTIVE If you say that someone is **selfish**, you mean that he or she cares only about himself or herself, and not about other people. ○ I did it for purely selfish reasons. ○ My Dad said I was lazy and selfish.

▶ **ANTONYMS:** unselfish, considerate

WORD FAMILY		
selfish	**ADJECTIVE**	○ Andrew was a very selfish man.
selfishly	**ADVERB**	○ She had selfishly gone out for the evening instead of staying at home to help.
unselfish	**ADJECTIVE**	○ Paul was one of the most generous and unselfish people I have ever met.

semi|nar /'semɪnɑː/ (seminars)

EDUCATION

NOUN A **seminar** is a class at a college or university in which the teacher and a small group of students discuss a topic. ○ During the day, students attend lectures and seminars. ○ [+ on] a seminar on civil rights

▶ **COLLOCATIONS:**
   at/in a seminar
   a seminar **on** something
   go to/attend a seminar

sen|sible /'sensɪbəl/

PERSONALITY

ADJECTIVE **Sensible** people make good decisions and do not do things which are silly . ○ She was a sensible girl and did not panic. ○ [+ about] Top athletes have to be sensible about their diet.

→ see note at **sensitive**

▶ **COLLOCATIONS:**
   sensible **about** something
   a sensible **person**
   a sensible **approach/decision/idea**

WORD FAMILY		
sensible	ADJECTIVE	○ *You two seem to be sensible people.*
sensibly	ADVERB	○ *They very sensibly decided that it was time to go home.*

sen|si|tive /ˈsensɪtɪv/

PERSONALITY

ADJECTIVE If you are **sensitive to** other people's needs, problems, or feelings, you show understanding and awareness of them. ○ [+ to] *The classroom teacher must be sensitive to a child's needs.* ○ *He was always so sensitive and caring.*

▶ **COLLOCATION:** sensitive **to** *something*

▶ **ANTONYM:** insensitive

WHICH WORD: sensitive or sensible?

You use **sensitive** to describe someone who is very aware of other people's needs, feelings, or problems. ○ *He is very sensitive to the moods of other people.*

You use **sensible** to describe someone who makes good decisions and does not do silly things. ○ *Most young people are sensible enough never to use drugs.*

WORD FAMILY		
sensitive	ADJECTIVE	○ *He seemed to be sensitive and considerate.*
sensitively	ADVERB	○ *The situation could have been handled more sensitively.*
sensitivity	UNCOUNT	○ *I should have had the sensitivity to consider their feelings.*
insensitive	ADJECTIVE	○ *It was a stupid, insensitive remark.*

se|ries /ˈsɪəriːz/ (series)

MEDIA & CULTURE

NOUN A radio or television **series** is a set of programmes of a particular kind which have the same title. ○ *He stars in the BBC drama series 'Casualty'.* ○ *the hit cartoon series, 'South Park'* ○ [+ about] *'Friends' was a series about the lives of six friends.*

▶ **COLLOCATIONS:**
a series **about** *something*
in a series
a **TV/television/radio** series
watch a series
present a series
a **drama/documentary/cartoon** series
a **comedy/detective** series
a **new/hit** series

se|ri|ous /ˈsɪəriəs/

PERSONALITY

ADJECTIVE Serious people are thoughtful and quiet, and do not laugh very often. ○ *He's quite a serious person.* ○ *She looked at me with big, serious eyes.*

> **WORD FAMILY**
>
> | **serious** | **ADJECTIVE** | ○ *Ahmed was a thoughtful, serious man.* |
> | **seriously** | **ADVERB** | ○ *They spoke to me very seriously but politely.* |

serve /sɜːv/ (serves, serving, served)

FOOD & DRINK

VERB When you **serve** food and drink, you give people food and drink. ○ *There's also a cafe serving drinks and ice cream.* ○ [+ with] *The soup is delicious served with French bread.*

▶ COLLOCATIONS:
serve *something* **with** *something*
a **restaurant/cafe/bar** serves *something*
serve *something* **warm/cold**

ser|vice /ˈsɜːvɪs/ (services)

TRANSPORT & TRAVEL

1 **NOUN** A **service** is an organization or system that provides something for the public. ○ *My father works in the health service.* ○ *the postal service* ○ *service industries, such as banks and airlines*

▶ COLLOCATIONS:
the **health/security/prison** service
the **emergency** services
Internet/broadband/phone service
customer services
public/social/medical services
basic/essential services
provide/offer/use a service
a service **provider/company/industry**

2 **NOUN** A bus or train **service** is a route or regular journey that is part of a transport system. ○ *There's a regular bus service into town.*

▶ COLLOCATIONS:
bus/train service
regular/free service
Sunday service

set /set/

MEDIA & CULTURE

ADJECTIVE If a play, film, or story is **set** in a particular place or period of time, the events in it take place in that place or period. ○ [+ in] *The play is set in a small Midwestern town.* ○ *an action adventure film set in 1898* ○ *a novel set during the Russian revolution*

set out /set 'aʊt/ (sets out, setting out, set out) `TRANSPORT & TRAVEL`

PHRASAL VERB When you **set out**, you start a journey. ○ [+ for] *We set out for school at 8 o'clock.* ○ [+ on] *If you set out on a long walk, you need to wear suitable boots.*

▶ **COLLOCATIONS:**
set out **for** *something*
set out **on** *something*

▶ **SYNONYM:** set off

set|tle /'setəl/ (settles, settling, settled) `HISTORY`

VERB When people **settle** in a place, they start living there permanently. ○ [+ in] *My parents settled in France after moving from Algeria.* ○ *About 80 colonists settled on the island of St. Croix.*

WORD FAMILY		
settle	VERB	○ *It was not until a century later that the first Europeans settled in the area.*
settlement	NOUN	○ *Carlisle was an important Roman settlement.*
settler	NOUN	○ *the early settlers in North America*

set up /set 'ʌp/ (sets up, setting up, set up)

PHRASAL VERB If you **set** something **up**, you create or arrange it. ○ *A few of the students set up a study group.* ○ *How do you set up a new business?*

▶ **COLLOCATIONS:**
set up a **company/school/office**
set up a **group**
set up a **system/scheme/meeting**

shade /ʃeɪd/ `SCIENCE & NATURE`

UNCOUNTABLE NOUN **Shade** is a cool area of darkness where the sun does not reach. ○ *I don't like the heat – I prefer to sit in the shade.* ○ [+ of] *He parked his car under the shade of a tree.*

▶ **COLLOCATIONS:**
in the shade
the shade **of** *something*
shade **from** *something*

shal|low /'ʃæləʊ/ (shallower, shallowest) `SCIENCE & NATURE`

ADJECTIVE A **shallow** container, hole, or area of water measures only a short distance from the top to the bottom. ○ *The water is too shallow to dive into.* ○ *Put the milk in a shallow dish.*

▶ **COLLOCATIONS:**
shallow **water**

a shallow **pool/lake/river**
the shallow **end**
a shallow **dish/bowl**

▶ **ANTONYM:** deep

---

shift /ʃɪft/ (shifts)

WORK

NOUN A **shift** is a set period of work in a place like a factory or hospital. ○ *My father is a policeman and works shifts.* ○ *workers coming home from the afternoon shift*

▶ **COLLOCATIONS:**
work shifts
the **night/morning/afternoon** shift
the **late/early** shift
a **long** shift
shift **work**

---

shoes /ʃuːz/

CLOTHES & APPEARANCE

PLURAL NOUN **Shoes** are objects which you wear on your feet. ○ *My mother has over thirty pairs of shoes.* ○ *Flat comfortable shoes are best.*

▶ **COLLOCATIONS:**
a **pair of** shoes
put on/take off your shoes
new shoes
high-heeled/flat shoes
sensible/comfortable shoes
leather/suede/canvas shoes
tennis/dancing/ballet/walking shoes

---

shop|ping /ʃɒpɪŋ/

SHOPPING

UNCOUNTABLE NOUN When you do **the shopping**, you go to shops and buy things. ○ *I'll do the shopping this afternoon.* ○ *My dad hates going clothes shopping.* ○ *Internet shopping is getting more and more popular.*

▶ **COLLOCATIONS:**
go shopping
do the shopping
online/home/Internet shopping
food/clothes shopping
Christmas/holiday shopping
a shopping **bag/list**

shop|ping cen|tre /ʃɒpɪŋ ˌsentə/ (shopping centres) [in AM, use shopping center]

NOUN A **shopping centre** is a specially built area containing a lot of different shops. ○ *There's a big shopping centre right next to where we live.*

WORD FAMILY

shop	NOUN	○ My mother works in an antiques shop.
shop	VERB	○ He always shops at the local supermarket.
shopping	UNCOUNT	○ New York is a great place to go shopping.
shopping centre	NOUN	○ A new shopping centre has just been opened.
shopper	NOUN	○ The shops were full of Christmas shoppers.

---

shore /ʃɔː/ (shores)　　　SCIENCE & NATURE

NOUN The **shore** of a sea, lake, or wide river is the land along the edge of it.
○ We walked down to the shore to look at the boats. ○ You will spend the night on shore and return to your boat in the morning.

▶ **COLLOCATIONS:**
　on shore
　the shore(s) **of** somewhere
　reach/leave the shore
　the **sea/lake** shore
　a **rocky/sandy/wild** shore

▶ **SYNONYM:** coast

---

shorts /ʃɔːts/　　　CLOTHES & APPEARANCE

PLURAL NOUN **Shorts** are trousers with very short legs, that people wear in hot weather or for taking part in sports. ○ I decided to put on a pair of shorts.
○ two women in bright cotton shorts

▶ **COLLOCATIONS:**
　in shorts
　a **pair of** shorts
　wear shorts
　baggy/tight shorts
　knee-length/long shorts
　cycling/football shorts

---

show /ʃəʊ/ (shows)　　　MEDIA & CULTURE

1 NOUN A television or radio **show** is a programme on television or radio. ○ What's your favourite TV show? ○ I'd be too embarrassed to go on a game show. ○ a popular talk show on the radio

▶ **SYNONYM:** programme

2 NOUN A **show** in a theatre is an entertainment or concert, especially one that includes different items such as music, dancing, and comedy. ○ How about going shopping and seeing a show in London? ○ The band are playing a handful of shows at smaller venues.

▶ **COLLOCATIONS:**
　on a show

watch/see a show
a **good/popular/funny** show
a **new/live/big** show
a **TV/radio** show
a **talk/reality/talent** show
a **comedy/news** show
a **game/quiz** show
a **fashion/stage** show
the **breakfast/morning/late** show

---

show|er /ʃaʊə/ (showers)   SCIENCE & NATURE

NOUN A **shower** is a short period of rain, especially light rain. ○ *There will be scattered showers this afternoon.* ○ *Heavy showers are forecast for next week.*

▶ **COLLOCATIONS:**
  forecast showers
  heavy/thundery showers
  scattered/light showers
  a **snow/rain** shower

---

shut|ters /ˈʃʌtəz/   HOME

PLURAL NOUN **Shutters** are wooden or metal covers fitted on the outside of a window. ○ *If you close the shutters, it gets very dark in the house.*

▶ **COLLOCATIONS:**
  open/close the shutters
  wooden/metal shutters

---

shy /ʃaɪ/ (shyer, shyest)   PERSONALITY

ADJECTIVE A **shy** person is nervous and uncomfortable in the company of other people. ○ *I was too shy to ask for help.* ○ [+ of] *He is painfully shy of women.*

▶ **COLLOCATIONS:**
  shy **of** someone/something
  painfully/very/quite shy
  a bit/a little shy
  a shy **smile**

▶ **SYNONYMS:** nervous, quiet

▶ **ANTONYM:** confident

WORD FAMILY		
shy	**ADJECTIVE**	○ *My little sister's a bit shy.*
shyly	**ADVERB**	○ *The children smiled shyly.*
shyness	**UNCOUNT**	○ *Eventually he overcame his shyness.*

S

sight|see|ing /ˈsaɪtsiːɪŋ/

`TRANSPORT & TRAVEL`

UNCOUNTABLE NOUN If you go **sightseeing**, you travel around visiting the interesting places that tourists usually visit. ○ *On our first day in Paris, we went sightseeing.* ○ *a sightseeing tour of the United States* ○ *an open-top sightseeing bus*

▶ **COLLOCATIONS:**
go sightseeing
do *some* sightseeing
a sightseeing **tour/trip**
a sightseeing **bus/boat/flight**

WORD FAMILY		
sightseeing	UNCOUNT	○ *We did a little sightseeing before lunch.*
sightseer	NOUN	○ *The cathedral was full of sightseers.*

sig|nifi|cant /sɪɡˈnɪfɪkənt/

1 **ADJECTIVE** A **significant** amount or effect is large enough to be important or noticeable. ○ *There's no significant difference in price between the two computers.* ○ *A significant number of 11-year-olds can't read.*

▶ **SYNONYM:** considerable

▶ **ANTONYM:** insignificant

2 **ADJECTIVE** A **significant** fact, event, or thing is one that is important or shows something. ○ [+ *that*] *I think it was significant that he never knew his own father.* ○ *The police must have missed something significant.*

▶ **COLLOCATIONS:**
a significant **change/difference/increase**
a significant **number/amount**
a significant **impact/effect**
a significant **role/contribution**
very/statistically significant

▶ **SYNONYM:** important

▶ **ANTONYM:** insignificant

WORD FAMILY		
significant	ADJECTIVE	○ *The drug has had a significant effect on the disease.*
significantly	ADVERB	○ *Cars can be made significantly more fuel-efficient.*
significance	UNCOUNT	○ *No-one realized the significance of what she said.*
insignificant	ADJECTIVE	○ *It was so insignificant that he didn't even mention it.*

sign in /saɪn ˈɪn/
(signs in, signing in, signed in)

`SHOPPING` `COMMUNICATIONS`

PHRASAL VERB When someone **signs in**, or when they **sign into** a computer system, they gain access to the system, usually by typing their name and a password. ○ *Before you can buy anything from Amazon, you have to sign in.* ○ *What password do you use to sign into your account?*

▶ **SYNONYM:** log in

---

silk /sɪlk/

CLOTHES & APPEARANCE

UNCOUNTABLE NOUN Silk is a very smooth, fine cloth made from a substance produced by a kind of moth. ○ *I bought a shirt made of pure silk.* ○ *He was wearing a dark suit and a red silk tie.*

▶ **COLLOCATIONS:**
   pure silk
   a silk **dress/shirt/tie/scarf**

---

simi|lar /'sɪmɪlə/

CLOTHES & APPEARANCE

ADJECTIVE If one thing is **similar to** another, or if two things are **similar**, they have features that are the same. ○ [+ to] *My sister looks very similar to me.* ○ [+ in] *Venus is very similar in size to the Earth.* ○ *a group of similar pictures*

▶ **COLLOCATIONS:**
   similar **to** *someone/something*
   similar **in** *something*
   similar in **size/style/appearance**
   be/look/sound similar
   very/remarkably similar
   quite/pretty/fairly similar

▶ **SYNONYM:** alike

▶ **ANTONYM:** different

WORD FAMILY		
similar	**ADJECTIVE**	○ *In some ways, hockey is quite similar to football.*
similarly	**ADVERB**	○ *Our parents treat all their children similarly.*
similarity	**UNCOUNT**	○ *There is a striking similarity between the two boys.*

---

sin|gle /'sɪŋɡəl/ (singles)

MEDIA & CULTURE

NOUN A **single** is a CD which has a few short songs on it or it is a song that can be downloaded from the Internet. ○ *The winner of the contest gets a chance to release their own single.* ○ *The collection includes all the band's hit singles.*

▶ **COLLOCATIONS:**
   release/produce/record a single
   a **hit** single
   someone's **new/first/latest** single

S

sink /sɪŋk/ (sinks) `HOME`

1 **NOUN** The **sink** is the container with taps in a kitchen, where you wash dishes.
○ *There was a pile of dirty dishes in the sink.*

2 **NOUN** A **sink** is a container with taps in a bathroom, in which you wash your
hands and face. ○ *He filled the bathroom sink with hot water and shaved.*

▶ **COLLOCATIONS:**
in the sink
fill/block/clean the sink
a **kitchen/bathroom** sink

▶ **SYNONYMS:** basin, washbasin

site /saɪt/ (sites) `HISTORY`

1 **NOUN** A **site** is a piece of ground that is used for a particular purpose or where a
particular thing happens. ○ *My brother works on a building site.* ○ *The site has
pitches for caravans and tents.*

2 **NOUN** The **site of** an important event is the place where it happened. ○ [+ *of*]
It is the site of the worst ecological disaster on Earth.

3 **NOUN** A **site** is a piece of ground where something such as a statue or building
stands or used to stand. ○ [+ *of*] *the site of Moses' tomb* ○ *The temple is Nepal's
holiest site.*

▶ **COLLOCATIONS:**
the site **of** *something*
a **building/burial/camp** site
an **industrial/archaeological** site
a **holy/historic** site
a **crash** site

size /saɪz/ (sizes) `SHOPPING`

NOUN A **size** is one of a series of graded measurements, especially for things such
as clothes or shoes. ○ *My sister and I wear each others' clothes because we're the same
size.* ○ *I tried them on and they were the right size.* ○ *I take a size nine shoe.*

▶ **COLLOCATIONS:**
the **same/right** size
a **different/standard/bigger/smaller** size
size **10/12/38**, etc.
take/wear a size *x*
someone's **shoe/dress** size

skate|board /ˈskeɪtbɔːd/ (skateboards) `SPORT & ACTIVITY`

NOUN A **skateboard** is a narrow board with wheels at each end, which people
stand on and ride for pleasure. ○ *He loves to do tricks on his skateboard.*

▶ **COLLOCATIONS:**
ride a skateboard
a skateboard **park/ramp**

ski /skiː/ (skis, skiing, skied)

`SPORT & ACTIVITY`

1 **NOUN** **Skis** are long, flat, narrow pieces of wood, metal, or plastic that are fastened to boots so that you can move easily on snow. ○ *I borrowed a pair of skis from a friend.*

2 **VERB** When people **ski**, they move over snow on skis. ○ *I want to learn to ski.* ○ [+ *down*] *There's nothing like the feeling of skiing down a mountain.*

▸ **COLLOCATIONS:**
  ski **down** something
  a ski **resort/slope/school**
  a ski **instructor**

ski|ing /ˈskiːɪŋ/

UNCOUNTABLE NOUN **Skiing** is the sport of moving over snow on skis. ○ *We go skiing every winter.* ○ *She's on a skiing holiday in the Alps.*

▸ **COLLOCATIONS:**
  go skiing
  a skiing **holiday/trip**
  a skiing **accident**
  cross-country/downhill skiing

WORD FAMILY		
ski	NOUN	○ One of my skis broke in half when I fell.
ski	VERB	○ He skied off in the opposite direction.
skiing	UNCOUNT	○ My hobbies are skiing and scuba diving.
skier	NOUN	○ He is an enthusiastic skier.

skill /skɪl/ (skills)

`WORK` `EDUCATION`

NOUN A **skill** is a type of work or activity which requires special training and knowledge. ○ *It is important to keep learning new skills.* ○ *She doesn't have the right skills to do the job.* ○ *Being in the Guides has helped develop my leadership skills.*

→ see also **communication skills**

▸ **COLLOCATIONS:**
  have/learn/develop a skill
  a **necessary/important/useful** skill
  the **right** skills
  a **new/special** skill
  basic/social/technical skills
  language/reading skills
  leadership/computer/study skills

▸ **SYNONYM:** ability

S

skirt /skɜːt/ (skirts) `CLOTHES & APPEARANCE`

NOUN A **skirt** is a piece of clothing worn by women and girls. It fastens at the waist and hangs down around the legs. ○ *We are not allowed to wear short skirts for school.*

▶ COLLOCATIONS:
  wear a skirt
  a **short/long/knee-length** skirt
  a **full/tight/straight** skirt
  a **mini** skirt
  a **demin/leather/cotton** skirt

sleep /sliːp/ (sleeps, sleeping, slept) `HEALTH`

1 UNCOUNTABLE NOUN Sleep is the natural state of rest in which your eyes are closed, your body is inactive, and your mind does not think. ○ *I went to bed but couldn't get to sleep.* ○ *It's important to get enough sleep.* ○ *Be quiet and go to sleep.* ○ *Sometimes my brother talks in his sleep.*

▶ COLLOCATIONS:
  in your sleep
  go to/get to sleep
  need sleep
  disturb/disrupt someone's sleep
  lack of sleep
  deep/disturbed sleep
  little/enough sleep

2 VERB When you **sleep**, you rest with your eyes closed and your mind and body inactive. ○ *There weren't enough beds, so I slept on the floor.* ○ *I couldn't sleep last night.*

▶ COLLOCATIONS:
  can't/couldn't sleep
  sleep **well/soundly/peacefully**
  sleep **badly**

sleeves /sliːvz/ `CLOTHES & APPEARANCE`

PLURAL NOUN The **sleeves** of a coat, shirt, or other item of clothing are the parts that cover your arms. ○ *The dress has long sleeves and buttons up the back.* ○ *His sleeves were rolled up to his elbows.*

▶ COLLOCATIONS:
  long/short sleeves
  shirt/jacket/coat sleeves
  roll up your sleeves

slice /slaɪs/ (slices, slicing, sliced)

1 **NOUN** A **slice of** bread, meat, fruit, or other food is a thin piece that has been cut from a larger piece. ○ [+ of] *How many slices of bread do you want?* ○ [+ of] *water flavoured with a slice of lemon*

  ▶ **COLLOCATIONS:**
  a slice **of** something
  a slice of **bread/toast**
  a slice of **cake/pizza/cheese**
  a slice of **lemon/melon/tomato**
  a **large/big/thick** slice
  a **thin/small** slice

2 **VERB** If you **slice** bread, meat, fruit, or other food, you cut it into thin pieces. ○ *Helen sliced the cake.* ○ [+ into] *Slice the steak into long thin slices.* ○ [+ up] *Slice up the onion, tomatoes and olives.*

  ▶ **COLLOCATIONS:**
  slice *something* **into** *something*
  slice *something* **up**
  slice **bread/fruit/meat**
  slice a **tomato/onion/apple**
  slice *something* **thinly/finely/thickly**

slim /slɪm/ (slimmer, slimmest)

ADJECTIVE A **slim** person has an attractively thin and well-shaped body. ○ *Most young girls want to be tall and slim.* ○ *How do you stay so slim?*

  ▶ **COLLOCATIONS:**
  look/stay/get slim
  a slim **figure/build**

  ▶ **SYNONYM:** thin

  ▶ **ANTONYM:** fat

slip|pers /ˈslɪpəz/

PLURAL NOUN **Slippers** are loose, soft shoes that you wear at home. ○ *I always wear slippers in the house.* ○ *a pair of pink fluffy slippers*

  ▶ **COLLOCATIONS:**
  wear slippers
  put on/take off your slippers
  a **pair of** slippers

slip|pery /ˈslɪpəri/

ADJECTIVE Something that is **slippery** is smooth, wet, or oily and is therefore difficult to walk on or to hold. ○ *Be careful not to fall – the floor's slippery.* ○ *The car went out of control on the slippery road.*

  ▶ **COLLOCATION:** a slippery **road/floor/surface**

slo|gan /ˈsləʊgən/ (slogans) [SHOPPING]

NOUN A **slogan** is a short phrase that is easy to remember and is used in advertisements. ○ *It sounds like an advertising slogan.* ○ *The pencils carried the slogan 'Too Cool for Drugs'.*

▶ COLLOCATIONS:
use/carry/write a slogan
a **marketing/advertising** slogan
a **good/catchy/simple** slogan

slope /sləʊp/ (slopes) [SCIENCE & NATURE]

NOUN A **slope** is the side of a mountain, hill, or valley. ○ *You have to walk up a steep slope to get to the hotel.* ○ *Saint-Christo is on a mountain slope.*

▶ COLLOCATIONS:
up/down a slope
on a slope
a **steep/gentle** slope
a **grassy/rocky/wooded** slope
a **ski/mountain** slope

slow down /sləʊ ˈdaʊn/ (slows down, slowing down, slowed down) [TRANSPORT & TRAVEL]

PHRASAL VERB If something **slows down** or if something **slows** it **down**, it starts to move or happen more slowly. ○ *The car slowed down.* ○ *This lever is used to slow the boat down.*

▶ ANTONYM: speed up

smart /smɑːt/ (smarter, smartest) [CLOTHES & APPEARANCE] [PERSONALITY]

1 ADJECTIVE **Smart** people and things are pleasantly neat and clean in appearance. ○ *It's important to look smart when you go for an interview.* ○ *a smart navy blue suit* ○ *smart new offices*

▶ COLLOCATIONS:
look smart
a smart **suit**
smart **clothes**
a smart **restaurant/hotel**

▶ ANTONYMS: untidy, messy

2 **ADJECTIVE** You can describe someone who is clever as **smart**. ○ *He is one of the smartest people I know.* ○ *Buying expensive furniture is not always a smart move.*

▶ **COLLOCATIONS:**
a smart **man/woman**
a smart **guy/kid**
a smart **move/idea/choice**

▶ **SYNONYMS:** clever, intelligent, bright

▶ **ANTONYM:** stupid

WORD FAMILY		
smart	**ADJECTIVE**	○ *We ate at a very smart restaurant.* ○ *Gary's a smart guy.*
smartly	**ADVERB**	○ *He always dresses very smartly.*
smartness	**UNCOUNT**	○ *the smartness of a soldier's uniform*

---

smart phone /'smɑːt fəʊn/ (smart phones) [COMMUNICATIONS]

NOUN A **smart phone** is a type of mobile phone that can perform many of the operations that a computer does, such as accessing the Internet. ○ *Most young people now have some kind of smart phone.*

→ see also **mobile phone**

---

smell /smel/ (smells, smelling, smelled, smelt)

1 **VERB** If something **smells** a particular way, it has a quality you become aware of through your nose. If you say that something **smells**, you mean that it smells unpleasant. ○ *Do my feet smell?* ○ *The sauce smells nice and has a lovely golden colour.* ○ [+ like] *a poisonous gas that smells like rotten eggs* ○ [+ of] *Her clothes smelt of smoke.*

2 **VERB** If you **smell** something, you become aware of it when you breathe in through your nose. ○ *We could smell the gas as soon as we opened the front door.* ○ *You can smell the sea air.*

▶ **COLLOCATIONS:**
smell **like/of** something
smell **good/bad/sweet/nice**
smell **smoke/burning/gas**

WORD FAMILY		
smell	**NOUN**	○ *What's that funny smell?*
smell	**VERB**	○ *I can smell burning.* ○ *Something smells really bad!*
smelly	**ADJECTIVE**	○ *He had extremely smelly feet.*

smok|ing /ˈsməʊkɪŋ/

HEALTH

UNCOUNTABLE NOUN **Smoking** is the act or habit of smoking cigarettes, cigars, or a pipe. ○ *Smoking is banned in many places of work.* ○ *Heavy smoking is very bad for you.* ○ *a no-smoking area*

▶ COLLOCATIONS:
allow/ban smoking
passive/heavy smoking
cigarette smoking
a smoking **ban**
a smoking **room/area/section**

> | WORD FAMILY | | |
> | --- | --- | --- |
> | smoke | **VERB** | ○ *Do you smoke?* |
> | smoking | **UNCOUNT** | ○ *Smoking is not allowed on most trains.* |
> | smoker | **NOUN** | ○ *He is not a heavy smoker.* |

snack /snæk/ (snacks)

FOOD & DRINK

NOUN A **snack** is a simple meal that is quick to cook and to eat. ○ *Let's have a quick snack before we go out.* ○ *Try to eat healthy snacks instead of cakes and sweets.*

▶ COLLOCATIONS:
eat/have a snack
make/buy a snack
a **healthy/tasty/sugary** snack
a **quick** snack
a snack **bar**

sniff /snɪf/ (sniffs, sniffing, sniffed)

1 VERB When you **sniff**, you breathe in air noisily through your nose, for example when you are trying not to cry, or in order to show disapproval. ○ *I can't stop sniffing – I've got a cold.* ○ *She wiped her face and sniffed loudly.*

2 VERB If you **sniff** something or **sniff at** it, you smell it by sniffing. ○ *He sniffed the perfume.* ○ *[+ at] She sniffed at the parcel suspiciously.*

▶ SYNONYM: smell

snow /snəʊ/ (snows, snowing, snowed)

SCIENCE & NATURE

1 NOUN **Snow** consists of a lot of soft white bits of frozen water that fall from the sky in cold weather. ○ *I don't like driving in the snow.* ○ *The ground was covered in snow.* ○ *falling snow*

▶ COLLOCATIONS:
in the snow
snow **falls/melts/drifts**
snow **covers** something
clear snow

heavy/deep/thick snow
new/fresh snow
a snow **storm/shower/drift**

2 VERB When **it snows**, snow falls from the sky. ○ *It had been snowing all night.*

WORD FAMILY		
snow	UNCOUNT	○ *The snow is starting to melt.*
snow	VERB	○ *Look – it's snowing!*
snowy	ADJECTIVE	○ *a snowy day* ○ *snowy mountains*

---

snow|board|ing /ˈsnəʊbɔːdɪŋ/ SPORT & ACTIVITY

UNCOUNTABLE NOUN Snowboarding is the sport or activity of travelling down snowy slopes using a snowboard. ○ *You can ski or go snowboarding.*

WORD FAMILY		
snowboard	NOUN	○ *I will rent a snowboard for the day.*
snowboard	VERB	○ *Can you snowboard?*
snowboarding	UNCOUNT	○ *Snowboarding is great fun.*
snowboarder	NOUN	○ *Experienced snowboarders can go really fast.*

---

soap op|era /ˈsəʊp ˌɒpərə/ (soap operas) MEDIA & CULTURE

NOUN A **soap opera** is a television drama about the daily lives of a group of people. ○ *I don't really like watching soap operas.* ○ *Her life is like a soap opera.*

---

so|ci|ety /səˈsaɪɪti/

UNCOUNTABLE NOUN Society is people in general, thought of as a large organized group. ○ *Priests were the most important people in society.* ○ *He thinks Islam must adapt to modern society.*

▸ **COLLOCATIONS:**
in society
modern/Western society
American/British, etc. society

---

so|cia|ble /ˈsəʊʃəbəl/ PERSONALITY

ADJECTIVE Sociable people are friendly and enjoy talking to other people. ○ *Martin is very sociable and friendly.* ○ *I'm not feeling very sociable this morning.*

▸ **ANTONYM:** unsociable

---

so|cial /ˈsəʊʃəl/ SOCIAL LIFE

1 ADJECTIVE Social means relating to society or to the way society is organized. ○ *It is a poor area with a lot of social problems.* ○ *Social conditions influence crime.* ○ *changing social attitudes*

▶ COLLOCATIONS:
a social **issue/problem**
social **change**
a social **class/group**
a social **worker/service**

2 ADJECTIVE **Social** means relating to leisure activities that involve meeting other people. ○ *We ought to organize more social events.* ○ *What social activities do you enjoy?*

WORD FAMILY		
society	UNCOUNT	○ *They are among the poorest people in society.*
social	ADJECTIVE	○ *I've got a well-paid job and a good social life.*
socially	ADVERB	○ *Socially he is great fun.*
antisocial	ADJECTIVE	○ *The police are cracking down on antisocial behaviour.*
sociable	ADJECTIVE	○ *She's a warm, sociable person.*
unsociable	ADJECTIVE	○ *He is aggressive and unsociable.*

socks /sɒks/

CLOTHES & APPEARANCE

PLURAL NOUN **Socks** are pieces of clothing which cover your foot and ankle and are worn inside shoes. ○ *I took off my shoes and socks.* ○ *a pair of knee-length socks*

▶ COLLOCATIONS:
wear socks
take off/put on *your* socks
pull *your* socks **up**
ankle/knee-length socks
thick/long/dirty socks
a **pair of** socks

soft|ware /'sɒftweə, AM 'sɔːf-/

SCIENCE & NATURE

UNCOUNTABLE NOUN Computer programs are referred to as **software**. ○ *The software is very easy to use.* ○ *It is important to update your anti-virus software regularly.*

▶ COLLOCATIONS:
use/install/run software
develop/design/write software
free/special/sophisticated software
computer software
anti-virus software
a software **company/developer**
a software **package/program/tool**

'soft|ware en|gi|neer (software engineers) `WORK`

NOUN A **software engineer** is someone who designs computer software or who makes sure that it continues to work as it should. ○ *My father is a software engineer at Microsoft.*

soil /sɔɪl/ `SCIENCE & NATURE`

UNCOUNTABLE NOUN Soil is the substance on the surface of the earth in which plants grow. ○ *You have to keep the soil moist.* ○ *Planting trees helps prevent soil erosion.* ○ *the fertile soil of Britain*

▶ **COLLOCATIONS:**
  rich/fertile soil
  sandy/moist/heavy soil
  garden soil
  soil **erosion**
  a soil **sample**

▶ **SYNONYM:** earth

> **WHICH WORD: soil, earth, ground, or land?**
>
> You use **soil** and **earth** to refer to the brown substance in which plants grow. ○ *The soil is heavy and difficult to dig.* ○ *Plants need earth, water and sun to grow.*
>
> You use **the earth** or **the ground** to refer to the surface of the Earth. ○ *As the bomb exploded, the earth shook.* ○ *The ground was covered with snow.*
>
> You use **land** to refer to an area of ground, especially one that is used for a particular purpose or that is owned by a particular person. ○ *agricultural land* ○ *a piece of private land*

so|lar pan|el /ˌsəʊlə ˈpænəl/ (solar panels) `SCIENCE & NATURE`

NOUN A **solar panel** is a device that absorbs light from the sun and converts it into electricity. Solar panels are often found on the roofs of buildings. ○ *My parents have had solar panels installed on their roof.*

so|lici|tor /səˈlɪsɪtə/ (solicitors) `CRIME` `WORK`

NOUN In Britain, a **solicitor** is a lawyer who gives legal advice, prepares legal documents and cases, and represents clients in the lower courts of law. ○ *His solicitor advised him to plead guilty.* ○ *Robin is training to become a solicitor.*

▶ **COLLOCATIONS:**
  be/become a solicitor
  consult/see/use a solicitor
  a solicitor **represents/advises** someone
  a **trainee/qualified** solicitor

▶ **SYNONYM:** lawyer

solo /ˈsəʊləʊ/ (solos)
MEDIA & CULTURE

NOUN A **solo** is a piece of music or a dance performed by one person. ○ *I was asked to sing a solo in the school concert.* ○ *My favourite part of the song is the guitar solo.*

▶ **COLLOCATIONS:**
   play/sing a solo
   a **guitar/piano/trumpet**, etc. solo

solve /sɒlv/ (solves, solving, solved)

VERB If you **solve** a problem or a question, you find a solution or an answer to it. ○ *Arguing won't solve anything.* ○ *This problem is easily solved.* ○ *Maybe you can solve this mystery for us.*

▶ **COLLOCATIONS:**
   solve a **problem/mystery**
   solve a **crime/case/murder**
   solve a **puzzle/riddle**
   solve something **easily/quickly/completely**
   finally/eventually solve something

so|lu|tion /səˈluːʃən/ (solutions)

NOUN A **solution to** a problem or difficult situation is a way of dealing with it so that the difficulty is removed. ○ *[+ to] There is a very simple solution to this problem.* ○ *We'll keep thinking until we find a solution* ○ *To an outsider, the solution is obvious.*

▶ **COLLOCATIONS:**
   a solution **to** something
   a **simple/obvious/good** solution
   a **possible/likely** solution
   a **peaceful/practical** solution
   a **short-term/long-term** solution
   find/have/suggest a solution
   offer/provide a solution

sore throat /ˌsɔː ˈθrəʊt/
HEALTH

NOUN If you have a **sore throat**, the back of your mouth feels painful when you swallow. ○ *The next day I had a sore throat.* ○ *Tom's in bed with a sore throat.*

▶ **COLLOCATIONS:**
   with a sore throat
   have a sore throat

sound|track /ˈsaʊndtræk/ (soundtracks)
MEDIA & CULTURE

NOUN The **soundtrack** of a film is its sound, speech, and especially the music. ○ *Cher sang on the soundtrack of the original film.*

▶ **COLLOCATIONS:**
   the soundtrack **of** something

a **film** soundtrack
the **original** soundtrack

---

space /speɪs/

SCIENCE & NATURE

UNCOUNTABLE NOUN **Space** is the area beyond the Earth's atmosphere, where the stars and planets are. ○ *The astronauts will spend ten days in space.* ○ *Satellites are being launched into space all the time* ○ *a visitor from outer space*

▶ **COLLOCATIONS:**
  in/into space
  outer space
  a space **station/agency/flight**
  space **travel**
  the space **shuttle**

---

spe|cial ef|fect /ˌspeʃəl ɪˈfekt/ **(special effects)**

MEDIA & CULTURE

NOUN In films, **special effects** are unusual pictures or sounds that are created by using special techniques. ○ *The special effects in Avatar are amazing.*

---

spe|cies /ˈspiːʃiz/ **(species)**

SCIENCE & NATURE

NOUN A **species** is a class of plants or animals whose members have the same main characteristics and are able to breed with each other. ○ *Pandas are an endangered species.* ○ [+ of] *There are several thousand species of trees here.*

▶ **COLLOCATIONS:**
  a species **of** *something*
  a species of **fish/bird/plant/animal**
  a **rare/endangered** species
  a **new** species

---

spend /spend/ **(spends, spending, spent)**

MONEY

1 VERB When you **spend** money, you pay money for things that you want. ○ *By the end of the holiday I had spent all my money.* ○ [+ on] *Juventus have spent £23m on new players.* ○ [+ v-ing] *They spend hundreds of pounds going to concerts.*

▶ **COLLOCATIONS:**
  spend *something* **on** *something*
  spend **money**
  spend **hundreds/thousands/billions**
  spend **a lot**
  not spend **much**
  can/can't afford to spend

2 VERB If you **spend** time or energy doing something, you use your time or effort doing it. ○ [+ v-ing] *I always spend a lot of time thinking about what to write.* ○ *This energy could be much better spent doing something positive.*

3 VERB If you **spend** a period of time in a place, you stay there for a period of time. ○ [+ in] *We spent the night in a hotel.* ○ [+ at] *They spent a few days at their grandparents house.*

▶ COLLOCATIONS:
spend something **in/at/on** something
spend a **night/day/week/month** somewhere
spend **hours/days/weeks** somewhere

---

splash /splæʃ/ (splashes, splashing, splashed)

1 VERB If you **splash** a liquid somewhere or if it **splashes**, it hits someone or something and scatters in a lot of small drops. ○ [+ on] *Splash some water on your face.* ○ [+ in] *The water splashed in my face.* ○ [+ with] *A lorry went past, splashing them with dirty water.*

▶ COLLOCATIONS:
splash something **on/in/with** something
splash **water/paint**

2 NOUN A **splash** is the sound made when something hits water or falls into it. ○ *It hit the water with a huge splash.*

▶ COLLOCATIONS:
with a splash
hear/make a splash
a **big/huge/small** splash

---

spot /spɒt/ (spots, spotting, spotted)

VERB If you **spot** something, you notice it. ○ *Nobody spotted the mistake.* ○ *Who can spot the difference between these two pictures?* ○ [+ v-ing] *We spotted smoke coming up the stairs.*

▶ COLLOCATIONS:
spot a **sign/problem/opportunity**
spot the **difference**
spot something **first**
spot something **easily/immediately/quickly**
spot something **finally/eventually**

▶ SYNONYMS: notice, see

---

sprint /sprɪnt/ (sprints, sprinting, sprinted)   SPORT & ACTIVITY

1 NOUN A **sprint** is a short race in which competitors run, drive, ride, or swim very fast. ○ *the women's 100-metres sprint* ○ *an Olympic sprint final*

▶ COLLOCATIONS:
win/run a sprint
a sprint **champion/team/race/event**

2 VERB If you **sprint**, you run as fast as you can over a short distance. ○ [+ to] *I sprinted to the car.* ○ [+ away] *He sprinted away on the last lap of the race.*

▶ **COLLOCATIONS:**
sprint **to/from** something
sprint **through/across/down** something
sprint **past** someone/something
sprint **away/back/out**
sprint **hard**

▶ **SYNONYM:** run

WORD FAMILY

sprint	NOUN	○ Tor Arne Hetland won the men's sprint event.
sprint	VERB	○ A man came sprinting down the road.
sprinter	NOUN	○ At school I was quite a good sprinter.

square /skweə/ (squares) `PLACES`

NOUN In a town or city, a **square** is a flat open place, often in the shape of a square. ○ We ate at a restaurant in the main square. ○ They crossed the square and went up to the church. ○ St Mark's square

▶ **COLLOCATIONS:**
in a square
the **main/central** square
a **public** square
a **town/market/village** square
cross the square

squash /skwɒʃ/ `SPORT & ACTIVITY`

UNCOUNTABLE NOUN Squash is a game in which two players hit a small rubber ball against the walls of a court using rackets. ○ Does anyone want a game of squash? ○ I've booked a squash court for 3pm.

▶ **COLLOCATIONS:**
play squash
a **game of** squash
a squash **court/ball/racket**
a squash **player/champion**
a squash **club**

sta|dium /ˈsteɪdiəm/ `PLACES` `SPORT & ACTIVITY`
(stadiums, stadia /ˈsteɪdiə/)

NOUN A **stadium** is a large sports ground with rows of seats all round it. ○ There were 57,000 people in the stadium. ○ The land will be used for building a football stadium.

▶ **COLLOCATIONS:**
in a stadium
a **sports/football/baseball** stadium

S

an **Olympic** stadium
a **packed/empty** stadium

▶ **SYNONYM:** ground

---

staff /stɑːf, stæf/ `WORK` `EDUCATION`

UNCOUNTABLE NOUN The **staff** of an organization are the people who work for it.
○ *There's free internet access for staff and students anywhere on campus.* ○ *150 full-time staff are employed at the site.* ○ [+ of] *He was on the staff of St Bartholomew's Hospital for 37 years.*

▶ **COLLOCATIONS:**
the staff **of** *something*
on the staff
employ/recruit/hire staff
train staff
keep/retain/cut staff
full-time/part-time staff
permanent/temporary staff
medical/academic/teaching staff
hospital/office/school staff
a **member of** staff/a staff **member**

> **USAGE**
>
> Remember **staff** is an uncountable noun so you do not talk about 'a staff' or 'staffs'. ○ *In total there are 320 staff working for the company.*
>
> You can talk about **a member of staff** or **members of staff**. ○ *Speak to a member of staff if you have any questions.* ○ *At night there are two members of staff on duty.*

---

stage /steɪdʒ/ (stages) `MEDIA & CULTURE`

1 NOUN In a theatre, the **stage** is an area where actors or other entertainers perform. ○ *I went on stage and did my show.* ○ *The crew needed 24 hours to move and rebuild the stage after a concert.*

2 UNCOUNTABLE NOUN You can refer to acting and the production of plays in a theatre as **the stage**. ○ *I got the part of Beth in a stage version of 'Little Women'.* ○ *He was the first comedian I ever saw on the stage.*

▶ **COLLOCATIONS:**
on stage
go on stage
a stage **play/production/performance**
a stage **version of** *something*
a stage **actor/manager/director**
make *your* stage **debut**

stall /stɔːl/ (stalls)

SHOPPING

NOUN A **stall** is a large table on which you put goods that you want to sell, or information that you want to give people. ○ *There was a food stall selling fresh oysters and smoked salmon.* ○ *I sometimes help my Dad on his market stall.*

▶ COLLOCATIONS:
  on a stall
  a **market/street** stall
  a **food** stall
  a **fruit/cake/flower** stall
  a stall **sells** something
  a stall **holder**

stand|ard /'stændəd/ (standards)

NOUN A **standard** is a level of quality or achievement, especially a level that is thought to be acceptable. ○ [+ of] *The standard of education in this country is very good.* ○ *The school sets a high standard for its plays.*

▶ COLLOCATIONS:
  the standard **of** something
  a **high/low/good/acceptable** standard
  set a standard
  meet/maintain a standard
  raise/improve the standard

stand|ard of liv|ing /ˌstændəd əv 'lɪvɪŋ/ (standards of living)

NOUN Your **standard of living** is the level of comfort and wealth which you have. ○ *Over the past 50 years, the standard of living has risen dramatically for most people.* ○ *a minimum level of standard of living for any family*

→ see also **cost of living**

▶ COLLOCATIONS:
  a standard of living **for/of** someone
  the standard of living **in** a place
  a **high/good/decent** standard of living
  a **comfortable/reasonable** standard of living
  a **low/minimum** standard of living

stare /steə/ (stares, staring, stared)

VERB If you **stare at** someone or something, you look at them for a long time. ○ [+ at] *Alice was staring intently at the screen.* ○ *She knew people were staring, but she didn't care.*

▶ COLLOCATIONS:
  stare **at** someone/something
  stare **in disbelief/amazement/horror**
  stare **blankly/intently**

sta|tion /ˈsteɪʃən/ (stations) MEDIA & CULTURE

NOUN If you talk about a particular radio or television **station**, you are referring to the company that broadcasts programmes or the programmes that it broadcasts. ○ *He works for the Polish television station, TVP.* ○ *The song has been played on radio stations around the world.*

▶ **COLLOCATIONS:**
  on a station
  a **radio/television/TV** station
  a **local/commercial/independent** station

▶ **SYNONYM:** channel

sta|tis|tics /stəˈtɪstɪks/ SCIENCE & NATURE

1 PLURAL NOUN Statistics are facts which are obtained from analysing information expressed in numbers, for example information about the number of times that something happens. ○ [+ on] *Official statistics on crime are notoriously unreliable.* ○ *Statistics show that the number of teens who visit adult chat rooms has increased.*

▶ **COLLOCATIONS:**
  statistics **on** *something*
  official/government statistics
  compile statistics
  release/publish statistics
  statistics **show/suggest/reveal** *something*
  recent/the latest statistics
  reliable statistics
  crime/unemployment/health statistics

▶ **SYNONYM:** figures

2 UNCOUNTABLE NOUN Statistics is a branch of mathematics concerned with the study of information that is expressed in numbers. ○ *He's doing a maths and statistics degree.*

WORD FAMILY		
statistics	**PLURAL NOUN**	○ *The latest unemployment statistics show nine million Americans out of work.*
statistical	**ADJECTIVE**	○ *According to statistical evidence most of us marry for the first time in our twenties.*
statistically	**ADVERB**	○ *Statistically, young men are more likely to be injured or killed than young women.*
statistician	**NOUN**	○ *According to official statisticians, ...*

steak /steɪk/ (steaks) FOOD & DRINK

NOUN A **steak** is a large flat piece of beef without much fat on it. You cook it by grilling or frying it. ○ *grilled steaks* ○ *We ate steak and chips with salad.*

steal /stiːl/ (steals, stealing, stole, stolen)

VERB If you **steal** something **from** someone, you take it away from them without their permission and without intending to return it. ○ *A thief stole her parents' car.* ○ [+ from] *She was stealing money from the till.*

▶ **COLLOCATION:** steal *(something)* **from** *someone/something*

steep /stiːp/ (steeper, steepest) SCIENCE & NATURE

ADJECTIVE A **steep** slope rises at a very sharp angle and is difficult to go up. ○ *A steep path led up to the farmhouse.* ○ *San Francisco is built on 40 hills and some are very steep.*

▶ **COLLOCATIONS:**
   a steep **slope/hill/cliff/mountain**
   a steep **hillside/path**

step- /step/ PEOPLE

COMBINING FORM **Step-** is used with nouns to show a family relationship that exists because of a second marriage. ○ *One of my clearest memories is of a holiday with my mother, stepfather and stepsister.*

WORD FAMILY		
stepsister	**NOUN**	○ *My stepsister, Lucy, was very jealous of me.*
stepbrother	**NOUN**	○ *Henri had a stepbrother from his father's second marriage.*
stepmother	**NOUN**	○ *That's Nicole, my stepmother.*
stepfather	**NOUN**	○ *I live with my mother and stepfather.*
stepson	**NOUN**	○ *When I first met my future stepson I was 25 and he was six.*
stepdaughter	**NOUN**	○ *He married Melanie and acquired a 4-year-old stepdaughter.*

stir /stɜː/ (stirs, stirring, stirred) FOOD & DRINK

VERB If you **stir** a liquid or other substance, you move it around or mix it in a container using something such as a spoon. ○ [+ into] *Stella stirred some sugar into her coffee.* ○ *Stir all the ingredients together.*

▶ **COLLOCATIONS:**
   stir *something* **into** *something*
   stir *something* **in/together**
   stir *something* **constantly/occasionally**
   stir *something* **gently**

stitch /stɪtʃ/ (stitches) HEALTH

NOUN A **stitch** is a piece of thread that has been used to sew the skin of a wound together. ○ [+ in] *He had six stitches in a head wound.* ○ *At the hospital I needed stitches inside my mouth.*

▶ **COLLOCATIONS:**
a stitch **in** something
have/need stitches
take out/remove stitches

---

stone /stəʊn/ (stones) `SCIENCE & NATURE`

1 **UNCOUNTABLE NOUN** **Stone** is a hard solid substance found in the ground and often used for building houses. ○ *They lived in a big stone house.* ○ *People often don't realize that marble is a natural stone.*

▶ **COLLOCATIONS:**
a stone **house/building/bridge**
a stone **wall/floor/fireplace**
stone **steps**
be **made/built/carved** out of stone

2 **NOUN** A **stone** is a small piece of rock that is found on the ground. ○ *He removed a stone from his shoe.* ○ *The crowd began throwing stones.*

---

sto|rey /'stɔːri/ (storeys) [in AM, use **story**] `HOME`

NOUN A **storey** of a building is one of its different levels, which is situated above or below other levels. ○ *Houses must not be more than two storeys high.* ○ *Seafield House is a five-storey building.*

→ see note at **floor**

▶ **COLLOCATIONS:**
be *x* storeys **high**
a **two/three**-storey **building**

---

storm /stɔːm/ (storms) `SCIENCE & NATURE`

NOUN A **storm** is very bad weather, with heavy rain, strong winds, and often thunder and lightning. ○ *Violent storms hit the state of Ohio.* ○ *The tree blew down in a storm.*

▶ **COLLOCATIONS:**
in a storm
a **severe/violent/fierce/bad** storm
a **tropical** storm
a **winter/summer** storm
a storm **hits/strikes** *somewhere*
storm **damage**
storm **clouds**

WORD FAMILY		
storm	NOUN	○ *The building was closed because of storm damage.*
stormy	ADJECTIVE	○ *There were gale winds and stormy weather that night.*

S

straight /streɪt/ (straighter, straightest)　　`CLOTHES & APPEARANCE`

1 ADJECTIVE If something is **straight**, it continues in the same direction and does not bend or curve. ○ *Draw a straight line between the two points.* ○ *His teeth were perfectly straight.* ○ *a long, straight road*

▶ **COLLOCATIONS:**
  a straight **line/edge**
  a straight **road/path**
  perfectly straight

▶ **ANTONYMS:** curved, bent

2 ADJECTIVE **Straight** hair has no curls or waves in it. ○ *She had short, straight blonde hair.*

▶ **ANTONYMS:** curly, wavy

stream /striːm/ (streams)　　`SCIENCE & NATURE`

NOUN A **stream** is a small narrow river. ○ *There was a small stream running through the garden.* ○ *You can go swimming in the cool mountain streams.*

▶ **COLLOCATIONS:**
  in a stream
  a stream **runs/flows** *somewhere*
  a **mountain/underground** stream
  a **shallow** stream

stress /stres/　　`HEALTH`

UNCOUNTABLE NOUN If you feel under **stress**, you feel worried and tense because of difficulties in your life. ○ *Students under exam stress say they have trouble sleeping.* ○ *Regular exercise reduces stress and boosts your energy.*

▶ **COLLOCATIONS:**
  be **under** stress
  suffer stress
  cause stress
  reduce/relieve stress
  cope with/handle stress
  severe/great stress
  emotional/psychological stress
  work-related/job/exam stress
  someone's stress **levels**

WORD FAMILY		
stress	**UNCOUNT**	○ *It is important to reduce your stress levels.*
stressed	**ADJECTIVE**	○ *I was stressed and needed a break.*
stressful	**ADJECTIVE**	○ *Exam time is a stressful time for any young person.*

S

striped /straɪpt/

CLOTHES & APPEARANCE

ADJECTIVE Something that is **striped** has a pattern of lines of different colours. ○ *He was wearing a striped shirt and jeans.* ○ *a green and white striped tie* ○ *striped wallpaper*

> **WORD FAMILY**
>
> | stripe | NOUN | ○ *The fabric was black with white stripes.* |
> | striped | ADJECTIVE | ○ *He is wearing green, striped pyjamas* |
> | stripy | ADJECTIVE | ○ *Polly was in a stripy top and jeans.* |

stroke /strəʊk/ (strokes, stroking, stroked)

VERB If you **stroke** someone or something, you move your hand slowly and gently over them. ○ *Em had been stroking the cat.* ○ *Kathryn gently stroked his cheek.*

stroll /strəʊl/ (strolls, strolling, strolled)

VERB If you **stroll** somewhere, you walk there in a slow, relaxed way. ○ *He strolled casually into the kitchen.* ○ *We were strolling back to the hotel after a day on the beach.*

▶ **SYNONYMS:** walk, wander

strug|gle /ˈstrʌgəl/ (struggles, struggling, struggled)

VERB If you **struggle to** do something, you try hard to do it, even though other people or things may be making it difficult for you to succeed. ○ [+ to-inf] *I'm still struggling to cope with all the work.* ○ [+ against/with] *They had to struggle against all kinds of problems.*

▶ **COLLOCATIONS:**
struggle **against/with** *something*
struggle **financially**

stu|dio /ˈstjuːdiəʊ, ˈstuː-/ (studios)

MEDIA & CULTURE

1 NOUN A **studio** is a room where a painter, photographer, or designer works. ○ *She was in her studio again, painting onto a large canvas.*

2 NOUN A **studio** is a room where radio or television programmes are recorded, music is recorded, or films are made. ○ *She's much happier performing live than in a recording studio.* ○ *They had filmed the show without a studio audience.*

▶ **COLLOCATIONS:**
in a studio
a **recording** studio
a **film/TV/television** studio
a **photographic/art/design** studio
a studio **audience/recording**

stun|ning /ˈstʌnɪŋ/

ADJECTIVE A **stunning** person or thing is extremely beautiful or impressive. ○ *Kelly looked stunning in a backless black dress.* ○ *The hotel offers stunning views of the surrounding countryside.*

▶ **COLLOCATIONS:**
a stunning **view/display/image**
stunning **scenery**
a stunning **woman/girlfriend**
look stunning
absolutely stunning

▶ **SYNONYMS:** striking, gorgeous, amazing, breathtaking

style /staɪl/ (styles) `MEDIA & CULTURE`

NOUN In the arts, a particular **style** is characteristic of a particular period or group of people. ○ [+ *of*] *Tom and I like totally different styles of music.* ○ *We're learning a variety of dance styles.*

▶ **COLLOCATIONS:**
a style **of** *something*
a style of **music/writing/painting/architecture**
in a style
a **dance/art/performance** style

WORD FAMILY		
style	**NOUN**	○ *He began to paint in a more photographic style.*
stylish	**ADJECTIVE**	○ *The band love wearing stylish clothes.*
stylishly	**ADVERB**	○ *She's always stylishly dressed.*

sub|ti|tles /ˈsʌbtaɪtəlz/ `MEDIA & CULTURE`

PLURAL NOUN **Subtitles** are a printed translation of the words of a foreign film that are shown at the bottom of the picture. ○ *The dialogue is in Spanish, with English subtitles.*

sub|urb /ˈsʌbɜːb/ (suburbs) `PLACES`

1 **NOUN** A **suburb of** a city or large town is an area which is part of the city or town but is outside its centre. ○ [+ *of*] *Anna was born in Ardwick, a suburb of Manchester.* ○ *She has an apartment in one of Sydney's most affluent suburbs.*

2 **PLURAL NOUN** If you live **in the suburbs**, you live in an area of houses outside the centre of a large town or city. ○ *His family lived in the suburbs.* ○ *Bombay's suburbs*

▶ **COLLOCATIONS:**
in a suburb/the suburbs
a suburb **of** *a city*

an **affluent/wealthy/leafy** suburb
a **working-class/poor** suburb
the **northern/western/eastern/southern** suburbs

WORD FAMILY		
suburb	**NOUN**	○ *Only 44 per cent of people in the poorest suburbs have a job.*
suburban	**ADJECTIVE**	○ *Pollution is also a problem in rural and suburban areas.*

---

sug|ar /ˈʃʊgə/ `HEALTH` `FOOD & DRINK`

UNCOUNTABLE NOUN Sugar is a sweet substance that is used to make food and drinks sweet. ○ *a bag of sugar* ○ *Ice cream is high in fat and sugar.* ○ *Parents worry about the sugar content of fizzy drinks.*

▶ **COLLOCATIONS:**
brown/white sugar
add/contain sugar
sugar **content**
be **high in/low in** sugar

---

suit /suːt/ (suits, suiting, suited) `CLOTHES & APPEARANCE`

1 NOUN A man's **suit** consists of a jacket and trousers made from the same fabric. ○ *He was wearing a dark pin-striped business suit.* ○ *He was so handsome in his suit and tie.*

▶ **COLLOCATIONS:**
wear a suit
a **business** suit
a **dark/black/grey**, etc. suit

2 VERB If a piece of clothing or a particular style or colour **suits** you, it makes you look attractive. ○ *Green suits you.* ○ *The red dress suits her better than it did me.*

---

suit|able /ˈsuːtəbəl/

ADJECTIVE Someone or something that is **suitable for** a particular purpose, occasion, or person is right or acceptable for them. ○ [+ *for*] *The dish is suitable for vegetarians.* ○ *This course is particularly suitable for students seeking employment in the water industry.* ○ *We found a suitable place to camp.* ○ [+ *to-inf*] *They need somewhere suitable to live.*

▶ **COLLOCATIONS:**
suitable **for** *someone/something*
a suitable **place/site/location**
a suitable **candidate**

▶ **SYNONYM:** appropriate

▶ **ANTONYM:** unsuitable

suit|case /ˈsuːtkeɪs/ (suitcases)   TRANSPORT & TRAVEL

NOUN A **suitcase** is a case in which you carry your clothes when you are travelling. ○ It did not take Andrew long to pack a suitcase. ○ She put her things in the suitcase.

▶ COLLOCATIONS:
   in a suitcase
   pack/unpack a suitcase
   carry a suitcase
   a **small/large** suitcase

sun /sʌn/   SCIENCE & NATURE

1 **UNCOUNTABLE NOUN The sun** is the ball of fire in the sky that the Earth goes round, and that gives us heat and light. ○ The sun was shining. ○ The sun came out, briefly. ○ the sun's rays

2 **UNCOUNTABLE NOUN** You refer to the light and heat that reach us from the sun as **the sun**. ○ Dena took them into the courtyard to sit in the sun. ○ They were out enjoying the sun.

▶ COLLOCATIONS:
   in the sun
   the sun **shines**
   the sun **comes out/goes in**
   the sun **goes down/sets**
   the sun **comes up/rises**
   the sun is **high/low**
   the **hot/warm/blazing** sun
   the **midday/afternoon/morning/evening** sun
   the **summer/winter** sun
   enjoy the sun
   something **catches/gets** the sun

sun|bathe /ˈsʌnbeɪθ/
(sunbathes, sunbathing, sunbathed)

`TRANSPORT & TRAVEL` `HEALTH`

VERB When people **sunbathe**, they sit or lie in a place where the sun shines on them, so that their skin becomes browner. ○ *Franklin swam and sunbathed at the pool every morning.*

WORD FAMILY		
sunbathe	VERB	○ *She was sunbathing on a balcony.*
sunbathing	UNCOUNT	○ *Excessive sunbathing is the very worst thing you can do to your skin.*
sunbather	NOUN	○ *The unspoilt beaches are popular with sunbathers and swimmers.*

sun|burnt /ˈsʌnbɜːnt/ also **sunburned**

`HEALTH`

ADJECTIVE Someone who is **sunburnt** has sore bright pink skin because they have spent too much time in hot sunshine. ○ *I don't want to get sunburnt.* ○ *A badly sunburned face or back is extremely painful.*

▶ **COLLOCATIONS:**
 be/get sunburnt
 badly sunburnt

▶ **SYNONYM:** burnt

WORD FAMILY		
sunburn	UNCOUNT	○ *The dangers of sunburn are well known these days.*
sunburnt	ADJECTIVE	○ *I'm badly sunburnt all over my face and shoulders.*

super|vise /ˈsuːpəvaɪz/ **(supervises, supervising, supervised)**

`WORK`

VERB If you **supervise** a workplace, activity or worker, you ensure that the work is done properly. ○ *He supervises a team of five people.* ○ *The work was supervised by our architect.*

super|vi|sor /ˈsuːpəˌvaɪzə/ **(supervisors)**

VERB A **supervisor** is a person who supervises activities or people, especially workers or students. ○ *He was a supervisor at a factory.* ○ *Each student is given a supervisor.*

WORD FAMILY		
supervise	VERB	○ *She is now supervising the special security office.*
supervision	UNCOUNT	○ *Young children need close supervision.*
supervisor	NOUN	○ *The campsite supervisor came to see what was wrong.*

sup|port /sə'pɔːt/   BELIEFS & OPINIONS   SHOPPING   COMMUNICATIONS
(supports, supporting, supported)

1 VERB If you **support** someone or their ideas or aims, you agree with them, and perhaps help them because you want them to succeed. ○ *Most teachers and parents actively supported the plan.* ○ *I didn't support the war.*

▶ **COLLOCATIONS:**
strongly/fully/actively support *someone/something*
publicly support *someone/something*
support **the government**
support a **plan/proposal/bill**
support **military action/war**

▶ **SYNONYM:** back

▶ **ANTONYM:** oppose

2 UNCOUNTABLE NOUN Support is help that a company offers to people who have bought its products. ○ *The company says customer support has been improved.* ○ *We will continue to provide product support for all versions of the software.*

▶ **COLLOCATIONS:**
customer support
IT/software/product support
technical support
provide/offer support

WORD FAMILY		
support	**VERB**	○ He strongly supports the government controls on the media.
support	**UNCOUNT**	○ I know he'll give you his full support.
supporter	**NOUN**	○ She was a supporter of the ban on smoking in public places.
supportive	**ADJECTIVE**	○ They were always supportive of each other.

surf|ing /'sɜːfɪŋ/   SPORT & ACTIVITY   **s**

UNCOUNTABLE NOUN Surfing is the sport of riding on the top of a wave while standing or lying on a special board. ○ *I took an afternoon off to go surfing.* ○ *a surfing competition* ○ *a surfing beach*

WORD FAMILY		
surf	**VERB**	○ A group of local boys were surfing.
surfing	**UNCOUNT**	○ I love surfing, diving, and things like that.
surfer	**NOUN**	○ The beach is popular with surfers.
surfboard	**NOUN**	○ I could barely stand up on the surfboard.

sur|gery /ˈsɜːdʒəri/

`HEALTH`

UNCOUNTABLE NOUN **Surgery** is medical treatment in which someone's body is cut open so that a doctor can repair, remove, or replace a diseased or damaged part. ○ [+ on] *She underwent surgery on both knees.* ○ *His father is recovering from heart surgery.*

▶ **COLLOCATIONS:**
surgery **on** *something*
have/undergo/need surgery
perform surgery
recover from surgery
major/minor surgery
emergency surgery
knee/heart/brain surgery

▶ **SYNONYM:** operation

WORD FAMILY		
surgery	UNCOUNT	○ He had emergency surgery for a brain tumour.
surgeon	NOUN	○ Dr Koshal, one of the leading heart surgeons in Canada

sur|prised /səˈpraɪzd/

ADJECTIVE If you are **surprised** at something, you have a feeling of surprise, because it is unexpected or unusual. ○ [+ at/by] *I was pleasantly surprised at how well I did.* ○ [+ to-inf] *Maya seemed surprised to see me.* ○ [+ that] *I'm not surprised that James was upset.*

▶ **COLLOCATIONS:**
surprised **at/by** *something*
surprised **to see/find/hear** *something/someone*
surprised **to learn/discover** *something*
pleasantly/genuinely surprised
really/quite surprised
look/seem/sound surprised

sur|pris|ing /səˈpraɪzɪŋ/

ADJECTIVE Something that is **surprising** is unexpected or unusual and makes you feel surprised. ○ [+ that] *It is not surprising that children learn to read at different rates.* ○ *A surprising number of people are allergic to milk.*

▶ **COLLOCATIONS:**
a surprising **number/amount**
a surprising **result**
a surprising **finding/discovery/development**
hardly surprising
seem surprising

▶ **ANTONYM:** unsurprising

WORD FAMILY		
surprise	**NOUN**	○ Well, this is a pleasant surprise.
surprise	**VERB**	○ The news did not surprise Adrina.
surprised	**ADJECTIVE**	○ Billy seemed genuinely surprised by her question.
surprising	**ADJECTIVE**	○ The overall response is hardly surprising.
surprisingly	**ADVERB**	○ Lucy got surprisingly good exam results.
unsurprising	**ADJECTIVE**	○ With so much hard work, it is unsurprising that she has done so well.

sur|vive /sə'vaɪv/ (survives, surviving, survived) `HISTORY`

1 **VERB** If a person or living thing **survives** in a dangerous situation such as an accident or an illness, they do not die. ○ She survived a car crash which killed her mother. ○ The people who survived were in a state of deep shock.

▶ COLLOCATIONS:
survive a **crash/accident**
survive a **war/attack/fire**
survive **cancer**
survive an **operation**
miraculously survive

2 **VERB** If you **survive** in difficult circumstances, you manage to live or continue in spite of them and do not let them affect you very much. ○ He survived high school despite being bullied. ○ I'm not sure how I'm going to survive the next few weeks.

WORD FAMILY		
survive	**VERB**	○ Josie miraculously survived the attack.
survival	**UNCOUNT**	○ Doctors believe the baby's chances of survival are good.
survivor	**NOUN**	○ Four days after the earthquake, hopes of finding survivors are fading.

sus|tain|able /sə'steɪnəbəl/ `SCIENCE & NATURE`

ADJECTIVE You use **sustainable** to describe the use of natural resources when this use is kept at a steady level that is not likely to damage the environment. ○ The technologies to deliver clean, sustainable energy already exist. ○ Try to buy wood that you know has come from a sustainable source.

▶ COLLOCATIONS:
environmentally/ecologically sustainable
a sustainable **source/forest**
sustainable **agriculture/farming/forestry**
sustainable **energy/development**

WORD FAMILY		
sustain	VERB	○ It's difficult to sustain this level of concentration for long.
sustainable	ADJECTIVE	○ We need an environmentally sustainable transport system.
sustainably	ADVERB	○ The paper is produced from sustainably managed forests.
sustainability	UNCOUNT	○ There is growing concern about environmental sustainability.
unsustainable	ADJECTIVE	○ Current rates of consumption harm the environment and are unsustainable.

sweat|shirt /ˈswetʃɜːt/ (sweatshirts)   `CLOTHES & APPEARANCE`
also **sweat shirt**

NOUN A **sweatshirt** is a loose warm piece of casual clothing, usually made of thick stretchy cotton, which covers the upper part of your body and your arms. ○ *On most days she wears a sweatshirt and jeans.* ○ *a grey hooded sweatshirt*

sweet /swiːt/ (sweeter, sweetest, sweets)   `FOOD & DRINK`

1 ADJECTIVE **Sweet** food and drink contains a lot of sugar. ○ *The cake was too sweet for me.* ○ *The beans have a nutty, slightly sweet taste.*

→ see also **savoury**

▶ COLLOCATION: a sweet **taste/flavour**

2 NOUN **Sweets** are small sweet things such as toffees, chocolates, and mints. [BRIT; in AM, use **candy**] ○ *I try not to eat too many sweets.* ○ *a bag of sweets*

▶ COLLOCATIONS:
  eat sweets
  a **bag/packet** of sweets
  a sweet **shop**

WORD FAMILY		
sweet	ADJECTIVE	○ He was drinking a mug of sweet tea.
sweeten	VERB	○ The tea had been sweetened with a little honey.
sweetened	ADJECTIVE	○ Avoid sweetened drinks.

swim|ming /ˈswɪmɪŋ/   `SPORT & ACTIVITY`

UNCOUNTABLE NOUN **Swimming** is the activity of moving through water using your arms and legs, especially as a sport or for pleasure. ○ *I always go swimming on a Thursday night.* ○ *She has been having swimming lessons.*

▶ COLLOCATIONS:
  go/enjoy/love swimming
  a swimming **pool**

swimming **trunks**
a swimming **costume**
a swimming **lesson/coach/team**

WORD FAMILY		
swim	**VERB**	○ All the children swam in the river.
swim	**NOUN**	○ He decided to have a swim in the hotel pool.
swimming	**UNCOUNT**	○ We went swimming and snorkeling.
swimmer	**NOUN**	○ Gemma was not a very strong swimmer.

sym|pa|thet|ic /ˌsɪmpəˈθetɪk/   `PERSONALITY`

ADJECTIVE If you are **sympathetic** to someone who is in a bad situation, you are kind to them and show that you understand their feelings. ○ If you have problems, talk to your family or a sympathetic friend. ○ [+ to] She was very sympathetic to the problems of adult students.

▶ **COLLOCATION:** sympathetic **to/towards** someone/something

▶ **ANTONYM:** unsympathetic

WORD FAMILY		
sympathetic	**ADJECTIVE**	○ She was very sympathetic and helpful when I was ill.
sympathetically	**ADVERB**	○ She nodded sympathetically.
sympathy	**UNCOUNT**	○ I had very little sympathy for him.
unsympathetic	**ADJECTIVE**	○ Many sufferers of the disease have found their doctors unsympathetic.

symp|tom /ˈsɪmptəm/ (symptoms)   `HEALTH`

NOUN A **symptom** of an illness is something wrong with your body or mind that is a sign of the illness. ○ [+ of] Sudden weight loss can be a symptom of serious disease. ○ Most sufferers develop mild symptoms such as fever and headache.

▶ **COLLOCATIONS:**
a symptom **of** something
have/suffer/experience symptoms
develop/show symptoms
cause/treat symptoms
a symptom **appears/develops**
a **common** symptom
severe/mild symptoms

S

Tt

---

tab|let /ˈtæblət/ (tablets)

COMMUNICATIONS

NOUN A **tablet** is a small flat computer that you operate by touching the screen. ○ *There is a free guide to the best tablets on the market.* ○ *The tablet is very easy to use.*

---

ta|ble ten|nis /ˈteɪbəl tenɪs/
also **table-tennis**

SPORT & ACTIVITY

UNCOUNTABLE NOUN **Table tennis** is a game played inside by two or four people. The players stand at each end of a table which has a low net across the middle and hit a small light ball over the net, using small bats. ○ *My hobbies are playing table tennis and reading.*

▶ **COLLOCATIONS:**
   play table tennis
   a table tennis **table/bat/ball**
   a table tennis **player**

---

tab|loid /ˈtæblɔɪd/ (tabloids)

MEDIA & CULTURE

NOUN A **tabloid** is a newspaper that has small pages, short articles, and lots of photographs. Tabloids are often considered to be less serious than other newspapers. ○ *Reports in the tabloid press claimed that the footballer was having an affair.* ○ *Photographs of them kissing have appeared in the tabloids.*

▶ **COLLOCATIONS:**
   in a tabloid
   read a tabloid
   a tabloid **newspaper/paper**
   a tabloid **headline/report/story**
   tabloid **news/journalism**
   the tabloid **press**
   a tabloid **journalist/reporter**

---

take af|ter /teɪk ˈɑːftə, ˈæftə/ (takes after, taking after, took after)

PEOPLE

PHRASAL VERB If you **take after** a member of your family, you look or behave like them. ○ *Becky definitely takes after her dad.* ○ *He takes after his mother in looks.*

take back /teɪk 'bæk/ `SHOPPING`
(takes back, taking back, took back, taken back)

PHRASAL VERB If you **take** something **back**, you return it to the place where you bought it or where you borrowed it from, because it is unsuitable or broken, or because you have finished with it. ○ *I went to the library and took your books back.* ○ *I took a pair of shoes back that fell apart after a week.*

take off /teɪk 'ɒf/ `TRANSPORT & TRAVEL` `CLOTHES & APPEARANCE`
(takes off, taking off, took off, taken off)

1 **PHRASAL VERB** When an aeroplane **takes off**, it leaves the ground and starts flying. ○ *The plane was ready to take off.* ○ *We eventually took off at 11 o'clock and arrived in Venice at 1.30.*

▶ **ANTONYM:** land

2 **PHRASAL VERB** If you **take** a piece of clothing **off**, you remove it. ○ *He wouldn't take his hat off.* ○ *I always take off my shoes as soon as I get in the house.*

▶ **SYNONYM:** remove

▶ **ANTONYM:** put on

take over /teɪk 'əʊvə/ `WORK`
(takes over, taking over, took over, taken over)

PHRASAL VERB If you **take over** a job or role or if you **take over**, you become responsible for the job after someone else has stopped doing it. ○ *I drove as far as Glasgow, then Tom took over.* ○ [+ from] *Someone was due to take over from me twenty minutes ago.* ○ [+ as] *She took over as chief executive of the Book Trust.*

▶ **COLLOCATIONS:**
take over **from** someone
take over **as** something

take up /teɪk 'ʌp/ **(takes up, taking up, took up, taken up)**

1 **PHRASAL VERB** If you **take up** an activity or a subject, you become interested in it and spend time doing it, either as a hobby or as a career. ○ *You ought to take up running.* ○ *He left a job in the City to take up farming.*

2 **PHRASAL VERB** If something **takes up** a particular amount of time, space, or effort, it uses that amount. ○ *The job was taking up a lot of my time.* ○ *His bicycle took up most of the space in the shed.* ○ [+ with] *Half the page was taken up with a picture of the boat.*

▶ **COLLOCATIONS:**
be taken up **with** something
take up **time/space/room**

t

tal|ent /'tælənt/ (talents) PERSONALITY

NOUN **Talent** is the natural ability to do something well. ○ [+ for] *It soon became obvious he had a real talent for the game.* ○ *Singing is easy to Caitlin because she has natural talent.*

▶ COLLOCATIONS:
 a talent **for** something
 have/show a talent
 great talent
 a **natural/special** talent
 musical/creative/artistic talent

▶ SYNONYMS: ability, aptitude, gift

WORD FAMILY		
talent	**NOUN**	○ *She showed exceptional musical talent from early childhood.*
talented	**ADJECTIVE**	○ *He is one of the most talented rugby players in this country.*

tap /tæp/ (taps) HOME

NOUN A **tap** is a device that controls the flow of a liquid or gas from a pipe or container, for example on a sink. [mainly BRIT; in AM, use **faucet**] ○ *She turned on the taps.* ○ *Don't leave taps running.*

▶ COLLOCATIONS:
 turn on/off a tap
 the **cold/hot** tap
 a tap **runs/drips**
 tap **water**

task /tɑːsk, tæsk/ (tasks) WORK

NOUN A **task** is an activity or piece of work which you have to do, usually as part of a larger project. ○ [+ of] *The boys were given the task of planning a menu.* ○ *Organizing the show was perhaps the most difficult task that I've ever faced.*

▶ COLLOCATIONS:
 the task **of** something
 do/perform/tackle a task
 face/have a task
 give someone a task
 complete a task
 a **difficult/tough/impossible** task
 an **easy/simple** task
 household tasks

▶ SYNONYM: job

t

taste /teɪst/ (tastes, tasting, tasted)

FOOD & DRINK

1 **VERB** If food or drink **tastes of** something, it has that particular flavour, which you notice when you eat or drink it. ○ [+ of/like] *It tastes like chocolate.* ○ *The pizza tastes delicious.*

▸ COLLOCATIONS:
   taste **of/like** *something*
   taste **good/great/delicious**
   taste **bad/awful**
   taste **sweet/bitter/salty/sour**

2 **VERB** If you **taste** some food or drink, you eat or drink a small amount of it in order to try its flavour, for example to see if you like it or not. ○ *Don't add salt until you've tasted the food.*

tasty /'teɪsti/ (tastier, tastiest)

ADJECTIVE If you say that food, especially savoury food, is **tasty**, you mean that it has a fairly strong and pleasant flavour which makes it good to eat. ○ *Try this tasty dish for supper with a crispy salad.* ○ *I thought the food was very tasty.*

WHICH WORD: tasty or **tasteful?**

You use **tasty** to describe food which has a pleasant flavour that makes it good to eat. ○ *Popcorn is a tasty snack and is easy to make.*

You use **tasteful** to describe something that you think is attractive and elegant. ○ *The silk shirts come in a range of tasteful colours.*

WORD FAMILY

taste	**VERB**	○ *The grapes tasted quite sweet.*
taste	**NOUN**	○ *He liked the salty taste of the crisps.*
tasty	**ADJECTIVE**	○ *We enjoyed a tasty tapas meal at a lovely bar.*
tasteful	**ADJECTIVE**	○ *The restaurant was softly lit, with tasteful furnishings.*
tastefully	**ADVERB**	○ *Their house was tastefully decorated.*

---

tech|ni|cal /'teknɪkəl/

SCIENCE & NATURE

ADJECTIVE **Technical** means involving the sorts of machines, processes, and materials that are used in industry, transport, and communications. ○ *The aircraft had been delayed due to technical problems.* ○ *They offer free technical support on all hardware and software products.*

▸ COLLOCATIONS:
   a technical **problem/issue/difficulty**
   technical **skills/knowledge/expertise**
   technical **support/assistance**
   a technical **expert**
   technical **staff**

WORD FAMILY

technical	ADJECTIVE	○ *Special technical knowledge is required for this job.*
technically	ADVERB	○ *It is one of the most technically advanced cars ever produced.*

tech|nique /tekˈniːk/ (techniques)

NOUN A **technique** is a particular method of doing an activity, usually a method that involves practical skills. ○ *I use relaxation techniques when I'm feeling stressed.* ○ *Medical science has developed many new techniques aimed at saving lives.*

▶ COLLOCATIONS:
   use/employ/apply a technique
   develop/learn/teach a technique
   a **new/traditional** technique
   a **simple/basic** technique
   a **sophisticated/advanced** technique
   a **management/interview/sales** technique

▶ SYNONYM: method

tech|nol|ogy /tekˈnɒlədʒi/ (technologies)   SCIENCE & NATURE

NOUN **Technology** refers to methods, systems, and devices which are the result of scientific knowledge being used for practical purposes. ○ *We are developing new technologies to combat cybercrime.* ○ *The scheme brought broadband internet technology to rural areas.*

→ see also **information technology**

▶ COLLOCATIONS:
   new/modern/the latest technology
   advanced/sophisticated technology
   use/develop technology
   technology **allows** *something*
   internet/computer technology
   digital/mobile/wireless technology
   medical/military technology

WORD FAMILY

technology	NOUN	○ *Tests have been carried out using the latest technology.*
technological	ADJECTIVE	○ *The past 100 years have seen major technological advances.*
technologically	ADVERB	○ *It is the most modern and technologically advanced cruise ship in the world.*

teen|ager /ˈtiːneɪdʒə/ (teenagers)

NOUN A **teenager** is someone who is between thirteen and nineteen years old. ○ *Children and teenagers spend a lot of time online.* ○ *The magazine is aimed at young teenagers.*

▶ **COLLOCATIONS:**
a **young** teenager
American/British, etc. teenagers
local teenagers
a **typical/rebellious** teenager
children and teenagers

WORD FAMILY

teenage	ADJECTIVE	○ *She has two teenage daughters.*
teenager	NOUN	○ *He was a typical teenager who liked movies, girls, and parties.*

---

teens /tiːnz/

PLURAL NOUN If you are in your **teens**, you are between thirteen and nineteen years old. ○ *Her father died when she was still in her teens.* ○ *When I was in my late teens, we moved to New York.*

▶ **COLLOCATIONS:**
be **in** your teens
reach your teens
early/late teens

tele|phone /ˈtelɪfəʊn/
(telephones, telephoning, telephoned)

VERB If you **telephone** someone, you dial their telephone number and speak to them by telephone. ○ *I telephoned Owen to say I was sorry.* ○ *They usually telephone first to see if she is at home.*

▶ **SYNONYMS:** call, ring, phone

tem|pera|ture /ˈtemprətʃə/

UNCOUNTABLE NOUN The **temperature** of something is a measure of how hot or cold it is. ○ *The temperature soared to above 100 degrees in the shade.* ○ [+ of] *The temperature of the water was about 40 degrees.* ○ *These plants are kept at a constant temperature of 25 degrees C.*

▶ **COLLOCATIONS:**
the temperature **of** something
a temperature **of** x **degrees**
at a temperature
the temperature **rises/soars**
the temperature **drops/falls**

a **high/low/constant** temperature
a **change in/rise in/drop in** temperature
reach a temperature
the **average** temperature
the **water/air/sea** temperature

---

tem|ple /'tempəl/ (temples) `PLACES`

NOUN A **temple** is a building used for the worship of a god or gods, especially in the Buddhist and Hindu religions, and in ancient Greek and Roman times. ○ *a small Hindu temple* ○ [+ *of*] *the Temple of Diana at Ephesus* ○ *Cover up when visiting temples – no shorts or bikini tops.*

▶ COLLOCATIONS:
the temple **of** *someone/something*
visit/build a temple
an **ancient** temple
a **Sikh/Buddhist/Hindu** temple
a **Greek/Chinese/Egyptian** temple

---

tem|po|rary /'tempərəri, AM -reri/ `WORK`

ADJECTIVE A **temporary** employee is one who is employed for only a limited time. ○ *Hotels take on a lot of temporary staff for the summer period.* ○ *When I left college I took a temporary job as a receptionist.*

▶ COLLOCATIONS:
temporary **staff**
a temporary **worker/employee**
a temporary **job/contract**
temporary **employment**

▶ ANTONYM: permanent

WORD FAMILY		
temporary	ADJECTIVE	○ *Many students want temporary employment during the vacations.*
temporarily	ADVERB	○ *The bridge will be temporarily closed for repairs.*

---

tense /tens/ (tenser, tensest)

ADJECTIVE If you are **tense**, you are worried and nervous, and cannot relax. ○ *I felt very tense as I waited.* ○ *She appeared tense and nervous.*

▶ COLLOCATIONS:
feel/look tense
a tense **mood**

▶ SYNONYMS: nervous, stressed

▶ ANTONYM: relaxed

term /tɜːm/ (terms) EDUCATION

NOUN A **term** is one of the periods of time that a school, college, or university divides the year into. ○ *There are usually three school terms in a year.* ○ *the summer term* ○ *the last day of term*

▶ COLLOCATIONS:
a **school** term
the **autumn/spring/summer** term
the **start/end** of term

▶ SYNONYM: semester

ter|ri|fied /ˈterɪfaɪd/

ADJECTIVE If you are **terrified**, you feel extremely frightened. ○ [+ *of*] *He was terrified of heights.* ○ [+ *that*] *She was absolutely terrified that her parents would find out.* ○ *The people on the rollercoaster looked terrified.*

▶ COLLOCATIONS:
terrified **of** *something/someone*
look/feel terrified
absolutely terrified

▶ SYNONYM: petrified

ter|ri|fy|ing /ˈterɪfaɪɪŋ/

ADJECTIVE If something is **terrifying**, it makes you extremely frightened. ○ *She finds speaking in public terrifying.* ○ *It is a terrifying thought that one in three people gets cancer.*

▶ COLLOCATIONS:
find *something* terrifying
absolutely terrifying
a terrifying **thought/idea**
a terrifying **speed/rate**

▶ SYNONYM: frightening

text /tekst/ (texts, texting, texted) `COMMUNICATIONS`

1 **NOUN** A **text** is a written message that you send using a mobile phone. ○ *He sent me about 20 texts.* ○ [+ *from*] *I got a text from my dad asking where I was.*

▶ **COLLOCATIONS:**
   a text **from** *someone*
   send/get/receive a text

▶ **SYNONYM:** text message

2 **VERB** If you **text** someone, you send them a text on a mobile phone. ○ *Text me when you get there.* ○ *We will text you your booking reference.*

text|book /ˈtekstbʊk/ (textbooks) `MEDIA & CULTURE` `EDUCATION`

NOUN A **textbook** is a book about a particular subject that is intended for students. ○ *She wrote a university textbook on international law.* ○ *a chemistry textbook*

▶ **COLLOCATIONS:**
   a textbook **on** *something*
   a **chemistry/science/history/geography/maths** textbook
   a **school/college/university** textbook
   write/read/use a textbook

thea|tre /ˈθiːətə/ (theatres) [in AM, use **theater**] `MEDIA & CULTURE`

NOUN A **theatre** is a building with a stage on which plays and other entertainments are performed. ○ *We went to the theatre on Saturday.* ○ *Her play is on at the Grand Theatre.*

▶ **COLLOCATIONS:**
   at the theatre
   go to/visit the theatre

WORD FAMILY		
theatre	**NOUN**	○ *Do you often go to the theatre?*
theatrical	**ADJECTIVE**	○ *The actor had a successful theatrical career.*
theatrically	**ADVERB**	○ *He shrugged theatrically to show he didn't care.*

theo|ry /ˈθɪəri/ (theories) `SCIENCE & NATURE`

NOUN A **theory** is a formal idea or set of ideas that is intended to explain something. ○ *We need more data to test this theory.* ○ [+ *of*] *Einstein formulated the Theory of Relativity.*

→ see Useful Phrases **in theory**

▶ **COLLOCATIONS:**
   a theory **of** *something*
   develop/formulate/propose a theory
   test a theory

a **scientific** theory
evidence/support for a theory

theo|reti|cal /θiːəˈretɪkəl/

ADJECTIVE **Theoretical** means based on or using the ideas and abstract principles of a particular subject, rather than the practical aspects of it. ○ *theoretical physics* ○ *a theoretical model of the universe*

WORD FAMILY		
theory	NOUN	○ *Scientists developed a new theory of climate change.*
theoretical	ADJECTIVE	○ *There is a theoretical risk but it is extremely small.*
theoretically	ADVERB	○ *It is theoretically possible to travel into the future.*

ther|mom|eter /θəˈmɒmɪtə/ (thermometers) `HEALTH`

NOUN A **thermometer** is an instrument for measuring the temperature of a place or a person's body. ○ *The nurse put a thermometer into his mouth.* ○ *The thermometer showed 80 degrees in the shade.*

thick /θɪk/ (thicker, thickest) `CLOTHES & APPEARANCE`

1 ADJECTIVE Something that is **thick** has a large distance between its two opposite sides. ○ *I had a thick slice of bread and jam.* ○ *The ice is so thick you can walk on it.* ○ *a thick black line*

▶ COLLOCATIONS:
a thick **slice/layer**
a thick **wall/book/line**
thick **ice/glass**

▶ ANTONYM: thin

2 ADJECTIVE You can use **thick** to talk or ask about how wide or deep something is. ○ *The folder was two inches thick.* ○ *How thick is this glass?*

3 ADJECTIVE If you have **thick** hair, you have a lot of hair on your head. ○ *He has thick, wavy hair.* ○ *shampoos to make your hair look thick and shiny*

▶ ANTONYM: thin

WORD FAMILY		
thick	ADJECTIVE	○ *It was impossible to hear through the thick walls.*
thickly	ADVERB	○ *Slice the meat thickly.*
thickness	NOUN	○ *The shell had a thickness of 0.14 mm.*

thief /θiːf/ (thieves /θiːvz/) `CRIME`

NOUN A **thief** is a person who steals something. ○ *The thieves snatched his camera.* ○ *Police have arrested a car thief.*

▶ **COLLOCATIONS:**
catch/chase/arrest a thief
a thief **steals/takes/snatches** *something*
a **car/jewel/art** thief

theft /θeft/

UNCOUNTABLE NOUN **Theft** is the crime of stealing. ○ *The gangsters were involved in art theft.* ○ [+ *of*] *the theft of a laptop from a car*

▶ **COLLOCATIONS:**
the theft **of** *something*
art/car theft
identity theft

> **WHICH WORD: thief, robber,** or **burglar?**
>
> You can use **thief** to talk about anyone who steals something. ○ *A thief must have taken it.*
>
> You use **robber** to talk about someone who uses violence to steal from a place such as a bank or shop. ○ *a gang of bank robbers*
>
> You use **burglar** to talk about someone who breaks into a house or building to steal things. ○ *Burglars stole their TV while they were out.*

thin /θɪn/ (thinner, thinnest) `CLOTHES & APPEARANCE`

1 **ADJECTIVE** If something is **thin**, there is a small distance between its two opposite surfaces. ○ *You could hear everything through the thin wall.* ○ *The material was too thin.* ○ *a thin cable* ○ *a thin layer of ice*

▶ **COLLOCATIONS:**
thin **walls/ice/material**
a thin **layer/slice/strip**

▶ **ANTONYM:** thick

2 **ADJECTIVE** A person or animal that is **thin** has no extra fat on their body. ○ *They exercise because they want to be thin.* ○ *a tall, thin man* ○ *thin, bony fingers*

▶ **COLLOCATIONS:**
a thin **man/woman**
thin **legs/fingers/hands**
too/very thin

▶ **SYNONYM:** slim
▶ **ANTONYM:** fat

thought|ful /ˈθɔːtfʊl/ `PERSONALITY`

ADJECTIVE If you describe someone as **thoughtful**, you approve of them because they remember what other people want, need, or feel, and try not to upset them. ○ *a thoughtful and caring man* ○ [+ *of*] *Thank you. That's very thoughtful of you.*

▶ **COLLOCATIONS:**
thoughtful **of** someone
a thoughtful **man/woman/person**
a thoughtful **gesture/gift**

▶ **SYNONYM:** considerate

▶ **ANTONYM:** thoughtless

WORD FAMILY		
think	VERB	○ I've been thinking about what we should do tomorrow.
thought	NOUN	○ She told me her thoughts about the plan.
thoughtful	ADJECTIVE	○ It was a very kind and thoughtful gesture.
thoughtfully	ADVERB	○ He thoughtfully offered me his chair.
thoughtfulness	UNCOUNT	○ I really appreciate your thoughtfulness.
thoughtless	ADJECTIVE	○ It was thoughtless of me not to invite her.
thoughtlessness	UNCOUNT	○ I apologize for my thoughtlessness.

---

threat|en /ˈθretən/ (threatens, threatening, threatened)

VERB If someone **threatens to** do something unpleasant or **threatens** someone, they say that they will do something unpleasant if they do not get what they want. ○ [+ to-inf] *She threatened to resign over the issue.* ○ [+ with] *The robbers threatened him with a knife.* ○ *Are you threatening me?*

▶ **COLLOCATIONS:**
threaten *someone* **with** *something*
threaten *someone* with a **knife/gun**
threaten to **resign/leave/strike/sue**
threaten to **attack/kill**

WORD FAMILY		
threat	NOUN	○ Criminals made threats against his family.
threaten	VERB	○ They threatened to kill the hostages.
threatening	ADJECTIVE	○ I received a threatening letter.

---

thrilled /θrɪld/

ADJECTIVE If someone is **thrilled**, they are extremely pleased about something. ○ [+ to-inf] *I was so thrilled to get a good report.* ○ [+ with] *The team is thrilled with this award.* ○ [+ that] *I'm really thrilled that we won.* ○ [+ at] *He's thrilled to bits at the news.*

▶ **COLLOCATIONS:**
thrilled **with/at** *something*
really/so/absolutely thrilled
thrilled **to bits/pieces**

▶ **SYNONYM:** delighted

thrill|er /ˈθrɪlə/ (thrillers)

NOUN A **thriller** is a book, film, or play that tells an exciting story about something such as criminal activities or spying. ○ *a thriller about a man who has to save his kidnapped daughter*

WORD FAMILY		
thrill	**NOUN**	○ *It's such a thrill to reach the finals of the competition.*
thrilled	**ADJECTIVE**	○ *I'm so thrilled that you got the job.*
thrilling	**ADJECTIVE**	○ *It was an absolutely thrilling game.*
thriller	**NOUN**	○ *She reads a lot of spy thrillers.*

thunder|storm /ˈθʌndəstɔːm/ (thunderstorms)

NOUN A **thunderstorm** is a storm in which there is thunder, lightning, and heavy rain. ○ *There was a big thunderstorm last night.*

tie /taɪ/ (ties)

NOUN A **tie** is a long narrow piece of cloth that is worn round the neck under a shirt collar and tied in a knot at the front. Ties are usually worn by men. ○ *Men are often expected to wear a suit and tie to work.* ○ *Do you know how to tie a bow tie?*

▶ COLLOCATIONS:
wear a tie
tie/loosen/undo a tie
a **suit/jacket/shirt** and tie
a **bow** tie
a **school** tie

time|table /ˈtaɪmteɪbəl/ (timetables)

1 NOUN In a school or college, a **timetable** is a list that shows the times in the week at which particular subjects are taught. [BRIT; in AM, usually use **class schedule**] ○ *Check on the timetable for your lesson time and classroom number.* ○ *My timetable is very full because I am studying ten subjects.*

▶ COLLOCATIONS:
on a timetable
a **full** timetable
a **school/college/exam** timetable

2 NOUN A **timetable** is a list of the times when trains, boats, buses, or aeroplanes arrive at or depart from a place. [mainly BRIT; in AM, usually use **schedule**] ○ *We checked the bus timetable before we left.*

▶ COLLOCATION: a **bus/train/ferry/rail/flight** timetable

tip /tɪp/ (tips, tipping, tipped)

1 VERB If you **tip** someone such as a waiter, you give them some money for their services. ○ *Is it customary to tip taxi drivers?* ○ *She tipped the waiter 10 dollars.*

2 NOUN If you give a **tip** to someone such as a waiter, you give them some money for their services. ○ *I usually give the hairdresser a tip.* ○ *The customer left a generous tip.*

▶ **COLLOCATIONS:**
give *someone* a tip
leave a tip
a **big/generous** tip

tod|dler /ˈtɒdlə/ (toddlers)   PEOPLE

NOUN A **toddler** is a young child who has recently learned to walk. ○ *a toddler of about two and a half* ○ *a pool for babies and toddlers*

tool /tuːl/ (tools)

NOUN A **tool** is any instrument or simple piece of equipment, for example a hammer or a knife, that you hold in your hands and use to do a particular kind of work. ○ [+ for] *The best tool for this job is a pair of scissors.* ○ *a shed for storing garden tools*

▶ **COLLOCATIONS:**
a **good/useful** tool
a **garden/kitchen/household** tool
use a tool

tour /tʊə/ (tours)   MEDIA & CULTURE   TRANSPORT & TRAVEL

1 NOUN A **tour** is an organized trip that people such as musicians, politicians, or theatre companies go on to several different places, stopping to meet people or perform. ○ [+ of] *The band are currently on a two-month tour of Europe.* ○ *She went on a lecture tour to promote her book.*

▶ **COLLOCATIONS:**
a tour **of** *somewhere*
on (a) tour
a **national/international/world** tour
do a tour
go on tour
an **American/European**, etc. tour
a **concert/lecture** tour
a **rugby/cricket/hockey** tour

2 NOUN A **tour** is a trip or journey to an interesting place or around several interesting places. ○ [+ of] *a guided tour of a ruined Scottish castle* ○ *We went on a tour of Thailand, Malaysia and Hong Kong.* ○ *He took us on a tour of the old town.*

▶ **COLLOCATIONS:**
a tour **of** *something*

a **guided/organized** tour
go on a tour
do a tour
take *someone* **on** a tour
give *someone* a tour

---

tour guide /ˈtʊə gaɪd/ (tour guides)　[TRANSPORT & TRAVEL]

NOUN A **tour guide** is a person who shows tourists around interesting places such as museums or cities. ○ *The tour guide pointed out the sights.* ○ *He works as a tour guide in New York City.*

---

tour|ist /ˈtʊərɪst/ (tourists)

NOUN A **tourist** is a person who is visiting a place for pleasure, especially when they are on holiday. ○ *The Olympic Stadium will attract foreign tourists.* ○ *The Forbidden City is one of China's top tourist attractions.* ○ *The town is very busy in the tourist season.*

▶ COLLOCATIONS:
foreign/international/Western tourists
a **Japanese/German/American**, etc. tourist
attract/bring in tourists
a tourist **attraction/sight**
a tourist **town/resort/destination/centre**
the tourist **season**

WORD FAMILY		
tourist	**NOUN**	○ *A guide was showing a group of tourists around the square.*
tourism	**UNCOUNT**	○ *Tourism is very important to France's economy.*
touristy	**ADJECTIVE**	○ *The village is quiet and not too touristy.*

---

tour|na|ment /ˈtʊənəmənt/ (tournaments)　[SPORT & ACTIVITY]

NOUN A **tournament** is a sports competition in which players who win a match continue to play further matches until just one person or team is left. ○ *I took part in a table tennis tournament.* ○ *He won a major golf tournament.*

▶ COLLOCATIONS:
take part in/play in a tournament
win a tournament
a **golf/tennis/basketball/hockey/football** tournament
a **major** tournament

---

tow|el /ˈtaʊəl/ (towels)

NOUN A **towel** is a piece of thick soft cloth that you use to dry yourself. ○ *She dried her hair with a towel.* ○ *a bath towel* ○ *a wet towel*

▶ COLLOCATIONS:
a **bath/beach/hand** towel
a **wet/dry/clean** towel

---

town /taʊn/ (towns) `PLACES`

NOUN A **town** is a place with many streets and buildings where people live and work. ○ [+ of] *They were married in her home town of Libertyville, Illinois.* ○ *Brecon is a pleasant little market town.* ○ *She likes going shopping in the town centre.*

▶ COLLOCATIONS:
a **small/little/big** town
someone's **home** town
a **market/tourist/spa** town
a **mining/fishing/industrial** town
a **seaside/border/mountain** town
a **university/college** town
the town **centre/hall/square**

---

track /træk/ (tracks) `MEDIA & CULTURE`

NOUN A **track** is one song or piece of music, for example, on an album or that can be downloaded. ○ *This is my favourite track on the album.* ○ *The DJ played some great dance tracks.*

▶ COLLOCATIONS:
the **title** track
the **opening/first/last** track
a **dance** track
an **album** track

---

tra|di|tion /trəˈdɪʃən/ (traditions) `SOCIAL LIFE`

NOUN A **tradition** is a custom or belief that has existed for a long time. ○ [+ of] *the rich traditions of Afro-Cuban music* ○ [+ of] *We have a family tradition of giving home-made gifts.* ○ *The story became part of local tradition.*

▶ COLLOCATIONS:
a tradition **of** *something*
a **family/folk/local** tradition
have/continue/maintain a tradition
become a tradition

▶ SYNONYM: custom

tra|di|tion|al /trəˈdɪʃənəl/

ADJECTIVE **Traditional** customs, beliefs, or methods are ones that have existed for a long time without changing. ○ *traditional teaching methods* ○ *traditional Indian music*

▶ COLLOCATIONS:
traditional **methods/values/ways**
traditional **music/dance/song/dress**

t

tradition	**NOUN**	○ *They have continued the tradition of wearing white to funerals.*
traditional	**ADJECTIVE**	○ *They performed a traditional Scottish dance.*
traditionally	**ADVERB**	○ *The dish was traditionally eaten at weddings.*

traf|fic /ˈtræfɪk/

`TRANSPORT & TRAVEL`

UNCOUNTABLE NOUN **Traffic** refers to all the vehicles that are moving along the roads in an area. ○ *There was heavy traffic on the roads.* ○ *We're late because we got stuck in traffic.* ○ *the problems of city life, such as traffic congestion*

▶ COLLOCATIONS:
heavy/light/bad traffic
rush-hour traffic
road traffic
city traffic
stuck in/caught in traffic
avoid/escape the traffic
traffic **congestion/problems**

traf|fic jam /ˈtræfɪk ˌdʒæm/ (traffic jams)

NOUN A **traffic jam** is a long line of vehicles that cannot move forward because there is too much traffic, or because the road is blocked. ○ *A truck broke down, causing a huge traffic jam.*

▶ SYNONYM: congestion

traf|fic lights /ˈtræfɪk ˌlaɪts/

`TRANSPORT & TRAVEL`

PLURAL NOUN **Traffic lights** are coloured lights at road junctions that control the flow of traffic. ○ *Turn left at the traffic lights.* ○ *Wait for the traffic lights to turn green.*

▶ COLLOCATIONS:
at the traffic lights
traffic lights **turn/go** red/green
traffic lights **change**

trail|er /ˈtreɪlə/ (trailers)

`MEDIA & CULTURE`

NOUN A **trailer** for a film or television programme is a set of short extracts which are shown to advertise it. ○ [+ for] *The trailer for her new film looks really good.* ○ *He does voice-overs for ads and movie trailers.*

▶ COLLOCATIONS:
a trailer **for** something
a **movie/film** trailer

t

train|ers /ˈtreɪnəz/

PLURAL NOUN **Trainers** are shoes with rubber soles that people wear for sports or with casual clothes. [BRIT; in AM, use **sneakers**] ○ *He usually wears jeans and trainers.* ○ *I bought a new pair of trainers.*

▶ COLLOCATIONS:
  wear trainers
  a pair of trainers
  new/old trainers

train|ing /ˈtreɪnɪŋ/

UNCOUNTABLE NOUN **Training** is the process of learning the skills that you need for a particular job or activity. ○ [+ *as*] *She had no formal training as a dancer.* ○ [+ *for*] *You get special computer training for this job.* ○ *a one-day training course*

▶ COLLOCATIONS:
  training **for** *something*
  training **as** *something*
  receive/get/have training
  provide/give/offer training
  formal/special training
  computer/management/medical/military training
  teacher/pilot/officer training
  staff training
  a training **course/day/session**
  education and training

> **USAGE**
>
> Remember, **training** is an uncountable noun, so you do not talk about 'trainings' or 'a training'. ○ *We were given some training on how to use the new equipment.*

> **WORD FAMILY**
>
> | train | **VERB** | ○ *She trained as an architect.* |
> |---|---|---|
> | **training** | **UNCOUNT** | ○ *The shop is closed Tuesday mornings for staff training.* |
> | **trainer** | **NOUN** | ○ *a trainer specialising in career development* |

trav|el /ˈtrævəl/ **(travels, travelling, travelled)** [in AM, use **traveling**, **traveled**]

1 **VERB** If you **travel**, you go from one place to another, often to a place that is far away. ○ [+ *to*] *We travelled to Scotland for a wedding.* ○ [+ *by*] *She travelled down by train.* ○ *I've been traveling all day.* ○ *Pilgrims travel thousands of miles to get here.* ○ [+ *at*] *The train was travelling at 160 kilometres an hour.*

▶ **COLLOCATIONS:**
travel **to/from** somewhere
travel **by** something
travel **at** a speed
travel **abroad/overseas**
travel x **miles/kilometres**

2 UNCOUNTABLE NOUN Travel is the activity of travelling. ○ *Information on travel in New Zealand is available online.* ○ *He hated air travel.* ○ *a writer of travel books*

▶ **COLLOCATIONS:**
air/rail/bus travel
a travel **book/guide/website**
a travel **company/agent**
travel **plans/arrangements**

WHICH WORD: travel, trip, or journey?

You use **travel** to talk about the general activity of travelling. You cannot say 'a travel'. ○ *First-class rail travel to Paris is included.*

You use **trip** to talk about a particular time when you visit somewhere and come back. ○ *I bought them recently on a trip to Manhattan.*

You use **journey** to talk about the time you spend travelling from one place to another. ○ *His journey to work takes almost two hours.*

WORD FAMILY

travel	**VERB**	○ *She travels a lot as part of her job.*
travel	**UNCOUNT**	○ *International travel is much cheaper than it used to be.*
traveller	**NOUN**	○ *On the boat he talked to some of the other travellers.*

---

tribe /traɪb/ (tribes)   HISTORY

NOUN Tribe is sometimes used to refer to a group of people of the same race, language, and customs, especially in a developing country or in the past. Some people disapprove of this use. ○ *an ancient warrior tribe* ○ *members of the Xhosa tribe*

▶ **COLLOCATIONS:**
an **ancient/primitive/stone-age** tribe
Indian/Native American tribes

WORD FAMILY

tribe	**NOUN**	○ *a nomadic tribe from North Africa*
tribal	**ADJECTIVE**	○ *the tribal customs of the Navajo people*

---

tricky /ˈtrɪki/ (trickier, trickiest)

ADJECTIVE A **tricky** task or problem is difficult to deal with. ○ *Some of the questions on the test are quite tricky.* ○ *It's a very tricky problem.*

trip /trɪp/ (trips)

NOUN A **trip** is a journey that you make to a particular place. ○ [+ *to*] *We're going on a school trip to the museum.* ○ *Mark is in China on a business trip.* ○ *You can take a bus trip around the city to see the sights.*

→ see note at **travel**

▶ **COLLOCATIONS:**
a trip **to** *somewhere*
on a trip
make/take/go on a trip
plan a trip
a **business/school/field** trip
a **day/weekend** trip
a **short** trip
a **boat/bus/train/plane/road** trip
a **shopping/camping/sightseeing** trip

▶ **SYNONYMS:** journey, visit

trol|ley /ˈtrɒli/ (trolleys) `TRANSPORT & TRAVEL` `SHOPPING`

NOUN A **trolley** is a small cart on wheels that you use to carry things such as shopping or luggage. [BRIT; in AM, use **cart**] ○ *She was pushing three heavy suitcases on a trolley.* ○ *supermarket trolleys*

▶ **COLLOCATIONS:**
a **supermarket/airport** trolley
a **luggage/shopping** trolley

trou|sers /ˈtraʊzəz/ `CLOTHES & APPEARANCE`

PLURAL NOUN **Trousers** are a piece of clothing that you wear over your body from the waist downwards, and that cover each leg separately. [mainly BRIT; in AM, usually use **pants**] ○ *He wore a blue shirt and white trousers.* ○ *I bought a pair of trousers.* ○ *He put the key in his trouser pocket.*

▶ **COLLOCATIONS:**
wear/have on trousers
a pair of trousers
trouser **legs/pockets**

try on /traɪ ˈɒn/ (tries on, trying on, tried on) `SHOPPING`

PHRASAL VERB If you **try on** clothing, you put it on to see if it fits you or if it looks nice. ○ *I tried on the shoes but they were too tight.* ○ *That's a pretty top – why don't you try it on?*

→ see note at **wear**

T-shirt /'tiːʃɜːt/ (T-shirts) also **tee-shirt**   `CLOTHES & APPEARANCE`

NOUN A **T-shirt** is a cotton shirt with no collar or buttons and usually with short sleeves. ○ *He wore jeans and a white T-shirt.* ○ *They bought T-shirts that said 'I love New York'.*

> ▶ COLLOCATIONS:
> **wear/have on** a T-shirt
> a **plain/striped/bright** T-shirt
> a **baggy/tight** T-shirt

---

tune /tjuːn, ᴀᴍ tuːn/ (tunes)   `MEDIA & CULTURE`

NOUN A **tune** is a series of musical notes that is pleasant and easy to remember. ○ *She was humming a tune.* ○ *[+ of] They sang the words to the tune of 'Happy Birthday'.*

> ▶ COLLOCATIONS:
> the tune **of** something
> **hum/sing/whistle/play** a tune

> ▶ SYNONYM: melody

---

turn out /tɜːn 'aʊt/ (turns out, turning out, turned out)

1 PHRASAL VERB If something **turns out** a particular way, it happens in that way or has the result described. ○ *Sometimes things don't turn out the way we expect them to.* ○ *I was sure that everything was going to turn out fine.*

> ▶ SYNONYM: work out

2 PHRASAL VERB If something **turns out to** be a particular thing, it is discovered to be that thing. ○ *[+ to-inf] My prediction turned out to be wrong.* ○ *It turned out that I knew the woman who was mentioned in the news report.*

---

turn up /tɜːn 'ʌp/ (turns up, turning up, turned up)

PHRASAL VERB If you say that someone or something **turns up**, you mean that they arrive, often unexpectedly or after you have been waiting for a long time. ○ *We waited for nearly an hour, but the bus never turned up.* ○ *Near the end of the party, Richard turned up with his friend, Tony.*

> ▶ SYNONYMS: show up, arrive

---

tu|tor /'tjuːtə, ᴀᴍ 'tuːt-/ (tutors)   `EDUCATION`

1 **NOUN** A **tutor** is a teacher at a British university or college. ○ *[+ in] James is course tutor in archaeology at the University of Southampton.* ○ *Liam surprised his tutors by failing his second year exams.*

> ▶ COLLOCATION: a **course/university/college** tutor

> ▶ SYNONYM: lecturer

2 **NOUN** A **tutor** is a person who gives private lessons to one pupil or a very small group of pupils. ○ *After I failed my maths exam, my parents paid for me to have a private tutor.*

▶ **COLLOCATIONS:**
hire/find/need/have a tutor
a **personal/private** tutor
a **maths/English/Spanish**, etc. tutor

▶ **SYNONYM:** teacher

tu|to|rial /tjuːˈtɔːriəl, AM ˈtuːt-/ **(tutorials)**

1 NOUN In a university or college, a **tutorial** is a regular meeting between a tutor and one or several students, for discussion of a subject that is being studied. ○ *We learn through lectures, tutorials and practical sessions.* ○ *We usually read a text and then discuss it in small tutorial groups.*

▶ **COLLOCATION:** a **one-to-one/individual** tutorial

2 NOUN A **tutorial** is a computer program or website that gives instructions on how to do something. ○ *There are some good online tutorials for creating a basic website.*

▶ **COLLOCATION:** a **video/interative/online** tutorial

TV /ˌtiː ˈviː/

`MEDIA & CULTURE`

UNCOUNTABLE NOUN **TV**, or **television**, refers to a system of broadcasting pictures and sounds, or all the programmes you can watch. ○ *I don't watch much TV these days.* ○ *Lee appeared on TV shows such as ER.* ○ *What's your favourite TV commercial?* ○ *press and television coverage of the incident*

▶ **COLLOCATIONS:**
on TV
watch TV
see/watch *something* **on** TV
be on/appear on/go on TV
a TV **show/programme/series**
TV **news**
a TV **presenter/star**
a TV **station/channel/network**
digital/cable/satellite TV
live/national/daytime TV

twin /twɪn/ **(twins)**

`PEOPLE`

NOUN If two people are **twins**, they have the same mother and were born on the same day. ○ *Mary and I are identical twins.* ○ *I have a twin brother and an older sister.*

typi|cal /ˈtɪpɪkəl/

1 ADJECTIVE You use **typical** to describe someone or something that shows the most usual characteristics of a particular type of person or thing, and is therefore a good example of that type. ○ *Describe a typical day in your life.* ○ *She's a typical British teenager – interested in fashion, social media and music.*

▶ **COLLOCATIONS:**
a typical **day**
a typical **family/home/house/school**
a typical **customer/man/woman/teenager**

▶ **SYNONYMS:** average, normal

2 **ADJECTIVE** If a particular action or feature is **typical of** someone or something, it shows their usual qualities or characteristics. ○ [+ of] *This report is typical of the way that some journalists depict immigrants.* ○ *He threw himself into the project with typical energy and enthusiasm.*

▶ **COLLOCATIONS:**
typical **of** someone/something
typical of a **way/approach**
typical of a **kind of/sort of** person/thing

▶ **SYNONYM:** characteristic

typi|cal|ly /ˈtɪpɪkəli/

1 **ADVERB** You use **typically** to say that something usually happens in the way that you are describing. ○ *The journey typically takes about two hours.* ○ *Typically, a student applies to three or four universities in the first instance.*

▶ **SYNONYMS:** normally, usually

2 **ADVERB** You use **typically** to say that something shows all the most usual characteristics of a particular type of person or thing. ○ *The menu was typically Swiss.* ○ *Irene was a typically shy first-year student.*

▶ **COLLOCATIONS:**
typically **British/English/American/French**, etc.
typically **small/strong/high/low**
typically **aggressive/honest/modest**

▶ **SYNONYM:** characteristically

WORD FAMILY		
typical	ADJECTIVE	○ *'The Browns' are supposed to represent a typical British family.*
typically	ADVERB	○ *People typically eat turkey at Thanksgiving.* ○ *a typically French village*
typify	VERB	○ *Allan typifies the spirit of the team.*

t

Uu

um|brel|la /ʌmˈbrelə/ (umbrellas)

TRANSPORT & TRAVEL

NOUN An **umbrella** is an object that you use to protect yourself from the rain or hot sun. It consists of a long stick with a folding frame covered in cloth. ○ *Fortunately, I had brought an umbrella.* ○ *After lunch, we relaxed under a beach umbrella.*

▶ **COLLOCATIONS:**
   under an umbrella
   a **beach/golf/sun** umbrella

under|gradu|ate /ˌʌndəˈɡrædʒuət/ (undergraduates)

EDUCATION

NOUN An **undergraduate** is a student at a university or college who is studying for his or her first degree. ○ *Linda is a final-year engineering undergraduate.* ○ *an undergraduate degree programme.*

→ see also **graduate, postgraduate**

▶ **COLLOCATION:** an undergraduate **student/course/degree**

under|ground /ˈʌndəɡraʊnd/

TRANSPORT & TRAVEL

NOUN The **underground** in a city is the railway system in which electric trains travel below the ground in tunnels. [BRIT; in AM, use **subway**] ○ *It's usually quicker to go by underground.* ○ *The London underground carries 3 million passengers a day.*

▶ **COLLOCATION:** an underground **train/station/map**

WHICH WORD: underground, tube, or metro?

You use **the underground** to talk about the railway system that runs under the ground in any city. ○ *Which is your nearest underground station?*

The tube is an informal name for the London underground. ○ *I took the tube from Victoria to Piccadilly Circus.*

The metro is the name of the underground railway system in some cities, for example, Paris. ○ *The best way to get around Barcelona is by metro.*

---

un|em|ployed /ˌʌnɪmˈplɔɪd/ WORK

ADJECTIVE Someone who is **unemployed** does not have a job. ○ *Millions of people are unemployed.* ○ *This workshop helps young unemployed people.* ○ *Have you been unemployed for over six months?*

→ see note at **employ**

▶ **SYNONYM:** out of work

▶ **ANTONYMS:** employed, working

---

uni|form /ˈjuːnɪfɔːm/ **(uniforms)** EDUCATION

NOUN A **uniform** is a special set of clothes which some people, for example soldiers or the police, wear to work in and which some children wear at school. ○ *Our school uniform is black.* ○ *The police wear dark blue uniforms.* ○ *You look very smart in your uniform.*

▶ **COLLOCATIONS:**
  in a uniform
  wear/have a uniform
  school/police/army uniform
  a **nurse's/security guard's** uniform

---

unique /juːˈniːk/

1 **ADJECTIVE** Something that is **unique** is the only one of its kind. ○ *Each person's signature is unique.* ○ *The area has its own unique language, Catalan.*

2 **ADJECTIVE** You can use **unique** to describe things that you admire because they are very unusual and special. ○ *His singing style is quite unique.* ○ *The trip was a really unique experience.*

▶ **SYNONYMS:** special, unusual

▶ **ANTONYMS:** common, everyday

WORD FAMILY		
unique	**ADJECTIVE**	○ *She is a woman of unique talent.*
uniquely	**ADVERB**	○ *The Antarctic is a uniquely fragile environment.*

---

up|set /ʌpˈset/

ADJECTIVE If you are **upset**, you are unhappy or disappointed because something unpleasant has happened. ○ *After she left I felt very upset.* ○ *You sound upset – what's wrong?* ○ [+ by/about] *They are terribly upset by the break-up of their parents' marriage.*

▶ **COLLOCATIONS:**
  upset **by/about** *something*
  look/sound/seem/feel upset
  get/become upset
  very/really/terribly/deeply/so upset

> **WORD FAMILY**
>
> | | | |
> |---|---|---|
> | upset | **ADJECTIVE** | ○ *He was getting really upset about it.* |
> | upset | **VERB** | ○ *The disagreement had upset the entire family.* |
> | upsetting | **ADJECTIVE** | ○ *It was very upsetting.* ○ *an upsetting situation* |

---

up-to-date /ˌʌptəˈdeɪt/ also **up to date**

ADJECTIVE If something is **up-to-date**, it is the newest or most recent thing of its kind. ○ *Make sure you use the most up-to-date version of the file.* ○ *The new system will give passengers up-to-date information.*

▶ **COLLOCATIONS:**
   up-to-date **information/news/figures**
   up-to-date **technology/equipment/software**

▶ **ANTONYMS:** out of date, old, old-fashioned

---

ur|ban /ˈɜːbən/

PLACES

ADJECTIVE **Urban** means belonging to, or relating to, a town or city. ○ *Younger people tend to live in urban areas.* ○ *Britain has a mostly urban population.* ○ *the pressures of urban life*

→ see also **rural**

▶ **COLLOCATIONS:**
   an urban **area/centre/landscape**
   urban **life/living**
   an urban **population**
   urban **problems**

u

Vv

va|can|cy /ˈveɪkənsi/ (vacancies)

WORK

NOUN A **vacancy** is a job or position which has not been filled. ○ [+ for] *We have a part-time vacancy for an office assistant.* ○ *There are not many job vacancies at the moment.*

▶ **COLLOCATIONS:**
   a vacancy **for** someone
   a **part-time/full-time/short-term** vacancy
   a **job** vacancy
   have/create a vacancy
   fill a vacancy

val|ley /ˈvæli/ (valleys)

SCIENCE & NATURE

NOUN A **valley** is a low area of land between hills, especially one with a river flowing through it. ○ *The village is on a hill overlooking a deep valley.* ○ *towns along the Yangtze valley* ○ *the Loire valley*

▶ **COLLOCATIONS:**
   a **deep/narrow/wooded** valley
   a **river/mountain** valley

van|dal|ism /ˈvændəlɪzəm/

CRIME

UNCOUNTABLE NOUN **Vandalism** is the deliberate damaging of things, especially public property. ○ [+ to] *The boy was guilty of vandalism to a bus shelter.* ○ *acts of vandalism*

van|dal /ˈvændəl/ (vandals)

NOUN A **vandal** is someone who deliberately damages things, especially public property. ○ *Vandals destroyed the information boards at the station.*

WORD FAMILY		
vandalize	**VERB**	○ *The walls had been vandalized with spray paint.*
vandalism	**UNCOUNT**	○ *Is graffiti art, or just vandalism?*
vandal	**NOUN**	○ *The windows had been broken by vandals.*

V

vary /ˈveəri/ (varies, varying, varied)

VERB If things **vary**, they are different from each other. ○ *Prices vary enormously, so shop around.* ○ [+ from] *The amount of sleep we need varies from person to person.* ○ [+ in] *The exercises vary greatly in difficulty.*

▶ COLLOCATIONS:
vary **from** something **to** something
vary **in** something
vary **considerably/greatly/widely/enormously**
vary **slightly**

▶ SYNONYM: differ

va|ri|ety /vəˈraɪti/

NOUN A **variety of** things is a number of different kinds or examples of the same thing. ○ [+ of] *A huge variety of products is available online.* ○ [+ of] *The island offers a wide variety of scenery and wildlife.* ○ [+ of] *People change their mind for a variety of reasons.*

▶ COLLOCATIONS:
a variety **of** things
a **wide/great/huge** variety
have/offer/provide a variety
a variety of **reasons/ways/sources**
a variety of **activities/foods/products**

WORD FAMILY		
vary	**VERB**	○ As the necklaces are handmade, each one varies slightly.
variety	**NOUN**	○ We offer a variety of activities to suit everyone.
varied	**ADJECTIVE**	○ My job is interesting because it is very varied.
variation	**UNCOUNT**	○ There is a lot of variation in style among the poems.

vast /vɑːst, væst/ (vaster, vastest) `PLACES`

ADJECTIVE Something that is **vast** is extremely large. ○ *vast areas of land* ○ *vast sums of money* ○ *The vast majority of young people know how to use the Internet.*

▶ COLLOCATIONS:
a vast **area/expanse/stretch**
a vast **range/quantity/number**
vast **sums/amounts**
the vast **majority**

▶ SYNONYMS: huge, enormous, massive

veg|eta|ble /ˈvedʒtəbəl/ (vegetables) `FOOD & DRINK`

NOUN **Vegetables** are plants such as cabbages, potatoes, and onions which you can cook and eat. ○ *Your diet should include plenty of fresh vegetables.* ○ *They grow fruit and vegetables.* ○ *vegetable soup*

▸ **COLLOCATIONS:**
 fresh/raw/green vegetables
 fruit and vegetables
 vegetable **soup/curry/stew**

---

veg|etar|ian /ˌvedʒɪˈteəriən/ (vegetarians) `FOOD & DRINK`

1 **NOUN** A **vegetarian** is someone who never eats meat or fish. ○ *I have been a vegetarian since I was 10.* ○ *There are over 1.5 million vegetarians in Britain.*

2 **ADJECTIVE** **Vegetarian** food does not contain any meat or fish. ○ *The food we serve is mainly vegetarian.* ○ *a vegetarian diet* ○ *a vegetarian meal* ○ *vegetarian lasagne*

▸ **COLLOCATIONS:**
 a vegetarian **diet**
 vegetarian **food/cooking**
 a vegetarian **meal/menu/alternative/choice**
 vegetarian **lasagne/burgers/pizza**

---

venue /ˈvenjuː/ (venues) `PLACES` `MEDIA & CULTURE`

NOUN The **venue** for an event or activity is the place where it happens. ○ [+ *for*] *The Centre is the venue for a three-day arts festival.* ○ *The old church is now used as a concert venue.*

▸ **COLLOCATIONS:**
 the venue **for** *something*
 a **concert/music/entertainment** venue
 a **sports/conference/wedding** venue
 find/choose a venue

---

vio|lent /ˈvaɪələnt/

ADJECTIVE If someone is **violent**, or if they do something which is **violent**, they use physical force or weapons to hurt or kill other people. ○ *Violent crime is on the increase.* ○ *Two players were sent off for violent behaviour.* ○ *The protests are turning increasingly violent.* ○ [+ *towards*] *She left her husband because he was violent towards her.*

▸ **COLLOCATIONS:**
 violent **towards** *someone*
 violent **crime**
 violent **behaviour/conduct**
 violent **protests/demonstrations/clashes**
 a violent **incident/attack**
 a violent **husband/partner/father**
 turn/get/become violent
 extremely/increasingly violent

V

vir|tual /ˈvɜːtʃuəl/ SCIENCE & NATURE

ADJECTIVE **Virtual** objects and activities are generated by a computer to simulate real objects and activities. ○ Players compete in a virtual world of role playing. ○ virtual reality ○ a virtual shopping centre

▶ **COLLOCATIONS:**
virtual **reality**
a virtual **world/environment**

vita|min /ˈvɪtəmɪn, AM ˈvaɪt-/ **(vitamins)** HEALTH

NOUN **Vitamins** are organic substances in food that you need in order to remain healthy. ○ Butter and oily fish are good sources of vitamin D. ○ Healthy people do not need vitamin supplements.

▶ **COLLOCATIONS:**
vitamin **A/B/C/D**
a **source** of vitamins
essential vitamins
take/get vitamins
contain/provide vitamins
a vitamin **supplement/pill/tablet**
a vitamin **deficiency**

vo|ca|tion|al /vəʊˈkeɪʃənəl/ EDUCATION

ADJECTIVE **Vocational** training and skills are the training and skills needed for a particular job or profession. ○ Newer universities tend to offer more vocational courses. ○ vocational training in engineering

▶ **COLLOCATION:** vocational **training/courses/education/qualifications**

volley|ball /ˈvɒlibɔːl/ SPORT & ACTIVITY

UNCOUNTABLE NOUN **Volleyball** is a sport in which two teams use their hands to hit a large ball over a high net. ○ We play volleyball on the beach. ○ members of the volleyball team

▶ COLLOCATIONS:
play volleyball
a volleyball **player/team**
a volleyball **match/tournament/championship**

---

vol|un|teer /ˌvɒlənˈtɪə/   WORK   FREE TIME
(volunteers, volunteering, volunteered)

1 **NOUN** A **volunteer** is someone who does work without being paid for it, because they want to do it. ○ *She helps in a local school as a volunteer.* ○ *I do volunteer work at a children's hospital.*

▶ COLLOCATIONS:
volunteer **work**
a volunteer **worker**
a volunteer **organization/programme**
be/become a volunteer
look for/recruit volunteers

2 **NOUN** A **volunteer** is someone who offers to do a particular task or job without being forced to do it. ○ *I need two volunteers to come down to the front.* ○ [+ for] *There were no volunteers for the job.*

▶ COLLOCATIONS:
a volunteer **for** something
need/ask for a volunteer

3 **VERB** If you **volunteer to** do something, you offer to do it without being forced to do it. ○ [+ to-inf] *Mary volunteered to clean up the kitchen.* ○ [+ for] *He volunteered for the army in 1939.* ○ [+ as] *She volunteered as a nurse.* ○ *He volunteered his help.*

▶ COLLOCATIONS:
volunteer **for** something
volunteer **as** something
volunteer **at** a place
volunteer **to help/work**

WORD FAMILY		
volunteer	NOUN	○ *Our staff are all unpaid volunteers.*
volunteer	VERB	○ *He volunteers at a homeless shelter.*
volunteering	UNCOUNT	○ *Volunteering is about helping yourself by helping others.*
voluntary	ADJECTIVE	○ *She does voluntary work for a charity.*
voluntarily	ADVERB	○ *He voluntarily gave up a well-paid job to become an aid worker.*

V

Ww

---

wage /weɪdʒ/ **(wages)** `WORK` `MONEY`

NOUN Someone's **wages** are the amount of money that is regularly paid to them for the work that they do. ○ *His wages have gone up.* ○ *They are offering an hourly wage of £10.80.*

→ see note at **salary**

▶ COLLOCATIONS:
an **average/high/low** wage
an **hourly** wage
wages **go up/go down**
earn/work for a wage
offer/pay a wage
raise/cut wages
a wage **cut/increase**

▶ SYNONYMS: earnings, pay, salary

---

walk /wɔːk/ **(walks, walking, walked)** `SPORT & ACTIVITY` `FREE TIME`

1 VERB When you **walk**, you move forwards by putting one foot in front of the other on the ground. ○ *They walked together.* ○ [+ to] *When I was your age I walked to school.* ○ [+ into] *She walked into the restaurant.* ○ [+ away] *She turned and walked away.* ○ *They stopped the car and walked a few steps.*

▶ COLLOCATIONS:
walk **to** a place
walk **along** a street
walk **into** a room
walk **in** the park
walk **away/back**
walk **home**
walk 5/10 **miles/steps**

2 NOUN A **walk** is a short journey that you make by walking. ○ *I went for a walk.* ○ *He often took long walks in the hills.* ○ [+ to, + from] *It was a three-mile walk to town from the hotel.*

▶ COLLOCATIONS:
a walk **to/from** a place
go for/take a walk
a **long/short** walk

▶ SYNONYMS: hike, stroll

`W`

walk|ing /'wɔːkɪŋ/

UNCOUNTABLE NOUN Walking is the activity of going for walks. ○ *I do a lot of walking and cycling.* ○ *a walking holiday*

▶ COLLOCATIONS:
like/love/enjoy walking
a walking **route/trail/holiday**

WORD FAMILY		
walk	VERB	○ *I walked home from the library.*
walk	NOUN	○ *The shops are a short walk away.*
walking	UNCOUNT	○ *Walking is good exercise.*
walker	NOUN	○ *You see a lot of walkers on the hills in summer.*

wan|der /'wɒndə/ (wanders, wandering, wandered)

VERB If you **wander** somewhere, you walk without intending to go anywhere in particular. ○ [+ around] *We wandered around the town, looking at the shops.* ○ [+ off] *He wandered off and we couldn't find him.* ○ *They wander the streets with nowhere to go.*

▶ COLLOCATIONS:
wander **around** *a place*
wander **off/away**
wander the **streets**

▶ SYNONYM: stroll

warm /wɔːm/ (warmer, warmest)   `SCIENCE & NATURE`

ADJECTIVE Something that is **warm** has some heat but not enough to be hot. ○ *It is usually warm during the day, but the nights are cold.* ○ *Dissolve the salt in the warm water.* ○ *They have no food or warm clothing.*

→ see note at **mild**

▶ COLLOCATIONS:
it is warm
warm and **sunny/dry**
warm **weather/water**
a warm **summer/day**
a warm **house/room**
warm **clothes/clothing**

▶ ANTONYM: cool

WORD FAMILY		
warm	ADJECTIVE	○ *The next day it was warm and sunny.*
warmth	UNCOUNT	○ *the warmth of the fire*

w

warn /wɔːn/ (warns, warning, warned) BELIEFS & OPINIONS

VERB If you **warn** someone about a possible danger or problem, you tell them about it. ○ [+ that] *My parents warned me that I would fail my exams if I didn't work harder.* ○ [+ of/about] *They warned us of the dangers of travelling alone.* ○ [+ that] *The report warns that unemployment could soon reach 3 million.* ○ [+ to-inf] *We were warned to keep our valuables in the hotel safe.* ○ [+ against] *People warned me against announcing the party online.*

▶ **COLLOCATIONS:**
warn *someone* **about/of** *something*
warn *someone* **against** *something*
experts/doctors/scientists warn about/of/against *something*
the police/the government warn about/of/against *something*

▶ **SYNONYMS:** alert, caution

WORD FAMILY		
warn	**VERB**	○ *Doctors warn us about the risks of smoking.*
warning	**NOUN**	○ *You may receive a warning that an attachment has a virus.*

waste /weɪst/ (wastes, wasting, wasted) SCIENCE & NATURE

1 VERB If you **waste** something, you use too much of it doing something that is not important, necessary, or successful. ○ *I didn't want to waste time looking at old cars.* ○ [+ on] *I decided not to waste money on a luxury hotel.*

▶ **COLLOCATIONS:**
waste *something* **on** *something*
waste **time**
waste **money/water/fuel/energy**

2 NOUN A **waste** of something is a situation when you use too much of it doing something that is not important, necessary, or successful. ○ [+ of] *It's a waste of time going to the doctor with a cold.* ○ [+ of] *That was a complete waste of money.*

▶ **COLLOCATION:** a waste **of** *something*

3 UNCOUNTABLE NOUN **Waste** is the use of money or other resources on things that do not need it. ○ *The food portions are measured to reduce waste.* ○ *I hate waste.*

▶ **COLLOCATION:** **reduce/eliminate** waste

4 UNCOUNTABLE NOUN **Waste** is material that has been used and is no longer wanted. ○ *We should try to recycle more household waste.* ○ *the safe disposal of toxic waste*

▶ **COLLOCATIONS:**
recycle/dispose of/dump waste
hazardous/toxic/nuclear waste
household/industrial waste

W

waste|ful /ˈweɪstfʊl/

ADJECTIVE Action that is **wasteful** uses too much of something valuable such as time, money, or energy. ○ [+ of] *This method is less wasteful of resources.* ○ *attempts to reduce wasteful spending*

WORD FAMILY		
waste	VERB	○ *Try not to waste water.*
waste	NOUN	○ *They dump nuclear waste into the sea.*
wasteful	ADJECTIVE	○ *the wasteful use of resources.*
wastefully	ADVERB	○ *companies that use energy wastefully*

water|fall /ˈwɔːtəfɔːl/ (waterfalls)   SCIENCE & NATURE

NOUN A **waterfall** is a place where water flows over the edge of a steep cliff or rocks and falls into a pool below. ○ *Angel Falls, the world's highest waterfall*

wear /weə/ (wears, wearing, wore, worn)   CLOTHES & APPEARANCE

VERB When you **wear** clothes, shoes, or jewellery, you have them on your body. ○ *Do you have to wear school uniform?* ○ *I sometimes wear contact lenses.*

▶ **COLLOCATIONS:**
wear a **suit/dress/shirt/hat/T-shirt/jacket/coat**
wear **shorts/jeans/shoes/gloves**
wear a **uniform**
wear **glasses/make-up**
wear **black/red/blue**

> **WHICH WORD: wear, put on, or try on?**
>
> You use **wear** to say what clothes someone has on their body. ○ *She wore jeans and a pink top.*
>
> When you **put on** clothes, you put them onto your body, for example in the morning after getting up. ○ *I put on my coat and left.*
>
> When you **try on** clothes, you put them on to see whether they fit or look nice, for example before buying them. ○ *She tried on several dresses.*

weath|er fore|cast /ˈweðə fɔːkɑːst, -kæst/
(weather forecasts)   SCIENCE & NATURE

NOUN The **weather forecast** is a statement saying what the weather will be like the next day or for the next few days. ○ *The weather forecast said it would rain.* ○ *Have you heard the weather forecast?*

web|site /ˈwebsaɪt/ **(websites)**
also **Web site** or **web site**

COMMUNICATIONS

NOUN A **website** is a page or set of pages on the Internet with information about a particular subject. ○ *To find out more, visit our website.* ○ *They post the results on the school website.*

▶ **COLLOCATIONS:**
   on a website
   visit/go to/check a website
   have a website
   create/design/build/develop a website
   a **school/company/official** website

weigh /weɪ/
(weighs, weighing, weighed)

TRANSPORT & TRAVEL   HEALTH

1 VERB If someone or something **weighs** a particular amount, that amount is how heavy they are. ○ *He weighs around 11 stone.* ○ *Your bag must not weigh more than 15 kilos.*

▶ **COLLOCATIONS:**
   weigh *x* **kilos/pounds/stone/grams**
   weigh **less/more**

2 VERB If you **weigh** something or someone, you measure how heavy they are. ○ *The scales are used for weighing fruit and vegetables.*

WORD FAMILY		
weigh	**VERB**	○ *How much do you weigh?*
weight	**UNCOUNT**	○ *What is your height and weight?*

weird /wɪəd/ **(weirder, weirdest)**

ADJECTIVE **Weird** means strange. [INFORMAL] ○ *It must be weird to suddenly become rich.* ○ *He's different. He's weird.* ○ *a weird coincidence*

▶ **COLLOCATIONS:**
   a weird **feeling/sense/experience/dream**
   a weird **person/guy**

▶ **SYNONYM:** strange

west|ern /ˈwestən/ also **Western**

MEDIA & CULTURE

W

ADJECTIVE **Western** means coming from or associated with North America, Australia, or Europe. ○ *If you grow up in the western world, there is pressure to be slim.* ○ *He brought Buddhist ideas into Western culture.*

WORD FAMILY

western	ADJECTIVE	○ *Many of them wore western dress.*
westernize	VERB	○ *The Emperor wanted to westernize his country.*
westernized	ADJECTIVE	○ *They worry that young people are becoming too westernized.*

---

wet /wet/ (wetter, wettest) `SCIENCE & NATURE`

1 ADJECTIVE If something is **wet**, it is covered in water or another liquid. ○ *He rubbed his wet hair with a towel.* ○ *I got my feet wet.* ○ *My clothes were soaking wet.*

▸ **COLLOCATIONS:**
wet **with** something
get wet
soaking/dripping wet
wet **clothes/hair/feet**

▸ **ANTONYM:** dry

2 ADJECTIVE If the weather is **wet**, it is raining. ○ *If the weather is wet, choose an indoor activity.* ○ *It was a miserable wet day.*

▸ **COLLOCATIONS:**
wet **weather/conditions**
a wet **day/weekend/summer**

▸ **SYNONYM:** rainy

▸ **ANTONYM:** dry

---

wheel|chair /'wiːltʃeə/ (wheelchairs) `HEALTH`

NOUN A **wheelchair** is a chair with wheels that you use to move about if you cannot walk, for example because you are disabled or sick. ○ *My mother uses a wheelchair.* ○ *a boy in a wheelchair* ○ *access for wheelchair users*

▸ **COLLOCATIONS:**
in a wheelchair
use/need a wheelchair
a wheelchair **user**
wheelchair **access**
wheelchair **basketball/rugby/tennis**
a wheelchair **race**
a wheelchair **athlete/racer/player**

---

whis|tle /'wɪsəl/ (whistles, whistling, whistled)

1 VERB When you **whistle**, you make a sound by forcing your breath out between your lips or teeth. ○ *As he walked he whistled a tune.* ○ *He whistled in surprise when he saw the car.*

▸ **COLLOCATIONS:**
whistle **at** someone
whistle a **tune**

2 NOUN A **whistle** is a sound that you make by forcing breath out between your lips or teeth. ○ *Jack gave a low whistle.*

▶ COLLOCATION: **give** a whistle

---

wide /waɪd/ (wider, widest)   MEDIA & CULTURE   COMMUNICATIONS

1 ADJECTIVE You use **wide** to describe something that includes a large number of different things or people. ○ *a wide choice of hotels* ○ *WIth the internet you can reach a wide audience.* ○ *a wide difference in tastes*

▶ COLLOCATIONS:
   a wide **choice/range/variety/selection**
   a wide **audience**
   a wide **variation/difference**

▶ SYNONYMS: broad, large

▶ ANTONYM: narrow

2 ADJECTIVE You use **wide** to say that something is done or believed by many people. ○ *The film has attracted wide publicity.* ○ *There is wide support for the plan.*

▶ COLLOCATION: wide **publicity/support**

▶ SYNONYMS: extensive, general

wide|ly /ˈwaɪdli/

1 ADVERB You use **widely** to refer to an action that includes a large number of different things or people. ○ *The treatment can vary widely from person to person.* ○ *He was widely travelled.*

▶ COLLOCATIONS:
   vary/differ widely
   read/publish widely
   widely **travelled/read**

2 ADVERB You use **widely** to say that something is done or believed by many people. ○ *It is widely regarded as one of the best restaurants in the country.* ○ *He was famous and widely respected.*

▶ COLLOCATIONS:
   widely **regarded/known/believed/expected/accepted**
   widely **respected/criticized/praised/publicized**

▶ SYNONYM: generally

WORD FAMILY		
wide	ADJECTIVE	○ *a wide range of topics*
widely	ADVERB	○ *She published widely in scientific journals.*

W

---

wid|ow /ˈwɪdəʊ/ (widows)   PEOPLE

NOUN A **widow** is a woman whose husband has died. ○ *He died, leaving a widow and five children.*

WORD FAMILY

widow	**NOUN**	○ *At 35 she was already a widow.*
widowed	**ADJECTIVE**	○ *She lived with her widowed mother.*
widower	**NOUN**	○ *He is a widower who lives alone.*

wild /waɪld/ (wilds, wilder, wildest) `SCIENCE & NATURE`

1 ADJECTIVE **Wild** animals or plants live or grow in natural surroundings and are not looked after by people. ○ *There are dangerous wild animals in the mountains.* ○ *They shoot wild birds for food.* ○ *The field was full of wild flowers.*

▶ **COLLOCATIONS:**
a wild **animal/bird/cat/dog/horse/pig**
a wild **flower/plant/mushroom/strawberry**

▶ **ANTONYMS:** domestic; tame

2 ADJECTIVE An area of land that is **wild** is natural and is not used by people. ○ *There are not many wild places left in Britain.* ○ *Most of the island is wild and uninhabited.*

→ see Useful Phrases **in the wild**

▶ **COLLOCATIONS:**
a wild **place/area**
wild **land/country**

wild|life /ˈwaɪldlaɪf/ `SCIENCE & NATURE`

UNCOUNTABLE NOUN You use **wildlife** to refer to animals and other living things that live in the wild. ○ *Pesticides can be harmful to wildlife.* ○ *efforts to protect wildlife*

→ see note at **nature**

▶ **COLLOCATIONS:**
protect/preserve/conserve wildlife
harm/threaten wildlife
a wildlife **refuge/park/sanctuary/reserve/centre**

will|ing /ˈwɪlɪŋ/ `PERSONALITY`

ADJECTIVE If someone is **willing to** do something, they are happy to do it or have no objection to doing it. ○ *I am quite willing to answer questions about my work.* ○ *It depends how much you are willing to pay.*

▶ **COLLOCATIONS:**
willing **to help/answer/pay**
perfectly/quite willing

▶ **SYNONYM:** prepared

▶ **ANTONYM:** unwilling

WORD FAMILY		
willing	**ADJECTIVE**	○ You have to be willing to make an effort.
willingly	**ADVERB**	○ People will willingly pay more for good service.
willingness	**UNCOUNT**	○ I had to prove my willingness to work hard.
unwilling	**ADJECTIVE**	○ He was unwilling to tell me what happened.

---

win /wɪn/ (wins, winning, won)   `SPORT & ACTIVITY`

VERB If you **win** a competition, battle, or argument, you defeat your opponent, or you do better than everyone else involved. ○ I don't think they'll win the match. ○ Our team won. ○ Andy Murray won 6-2, 6-4, 6-3.

→ see note at **earn**

▶ **COLLOCATIONS:**
   a **team/side** wins
   win a **race/game/match**
   win a **tournament/championship/competition**
   win an **election**
   win a **battle/war**

▶ **ANTONYM:** lose

win|ner /'wɪnə/ (winners)

NOUN The **winner** of a prize, race, or competition is the person, animal, or thing that wins it. ○ All the prize winners received a certificate. ○ The winner of the game goes through to the next round.

▶ **COLLOCATIONS:**
   the winner **of** something
   the **prize/award/medal** winner

▶ **ANTONYM:** loser

WORD FAMILY		
win	**VERB**	○ Bolt won the 100 metres.
winner	**NOUN**	○ The winner gets a gold medal.

---

wind /wɪnd/ (winds)   `SCIENCE & NATURE`

W

NOUN A **wind** is a current of air moving across the earth's surface. ○ There was a strong wind blowing. ○ A gust of wind had blown the pot over. ○ The leaves rustled in the wind.

▶ **COLLOCATIONS:**
   in the wind
   a wind **blows**

a **strong** wind
a **cold/chilly/icy/warm** wind
a **gust of** wind
wind **power/energy**

WORD FAMILY		
wind	NOUN	○ We shivered in the cold wind.
windy	ADJECTIVE	○ It was windy and my hat blew off.

---

wit|ness /'wɪtnəs/ (witnesses, witnessing, witnessed)

1 NOUN A **witness to** an event such as an accident or crime is a person who saw it. ○ [+ to] *Witnesses to the crash say they saw an explosion.* ○ *No witnesses have come forward.*

▶ COLLOCATIONS:
a witness **to** something
a witness **says/reports** something
a witness **tells** someone something

▶ SYNONYM: eye-witness

2 VERB If you **witness** something, you see it happen. ○ *Anyone who witnessed the accident should call the police.*

▶ COLLOCATION: witness an **incident/accident/crash**

▶ SYNONYM: see

3 NOUN A **witness** is someone who appears in a court of law to say what they know about a crime or other event. ○ *Eleven witnesses will be called to testify.* ○ [+ for] *a witness for the prosecution*

▶ COLLOCATIONS:
a witness **for** someone/something
call a witness
a witness **tells/says/testifies**
a **defence/prosecution** witness
a **key/expert/star** witness

---

wood /wʊd/ (woods)　　SCIENCE & NATURE

1 UNCOUNTABLE NOUN **Wood** is the material that forms the trunks and branches of trees. ○ *Their dishes were made of wood.* ○ *a short piece of wood*

▶ COLLOCATIONS:
made of wood
a **piece/lump** of wood
chop/cut/collect wood

2 NOUN A **wood** is a large area of trees growing near each other. You can refer to one or several of these areas as **woods**. ○ *a walk in the woods* ○ *a cottage on the edge of a wood*

▶ COLLOCATION: **in** the wood(s)

w

wood|en /'wʊdən/

HOME

ADJECTIVE Wooden objects are made of wood. ○ *The room had a wooden floor.*

▶ **COLLOCATION:** a wooden **floor/box/table/spoon**

WORD FAMILY		
wood	**NOUN**	○ *He chopped some wood for the fire.* ○ *a clearing in the woods*
woodland	**NOUN**	○ *an area of dense woodland*
wooden	**ADJECTIVE**	○ *a wooden box* ○ *a wooden spoon*

wool /wʊl/

CLOTHES & APPEARANCE

UNCOUNTABLE NOUN Wool is a material made from the hair of sheep or similar animals, used to make clothes, blankets, and carpets. ○ *The covers are made of wool and cotton.* ○ *warm wool socks* ○ *a 100% wool coat*

▶ **COLLOCATIONS:**
made of wool
a wool **blanket/coat/sock/skirt/cardigan**

WORD FAMILY		
wool	**UNCOUNT**	○ *carpets made of pure wool*
woollen	**ADJECTIVE**	○ *a thick woollen sweater*
woolly	**ADJECTIVE**	○ *a warm woolly scarf*

work /wɜːk/

WORK

UNCOUNTABLE NOUN People who have **work** or who are **in work** have a job, usually one that they are paid to do. ○ *Her dad was out of work.* ○ *Very few people are in work around here.* ○ *I'm looking for part-time work for the summer vacation.* ○ *What kind of work do you do?*

→ see note at **job**

▶ **COLLOCATIONS:**
in work
out of work
look for/seek/find/get work
do/have work
part-time/full-time work

▶ **SYNONYM:** job

W

work|shop /'wɜːkʃɒp/ (workshops)

EDUCATION

NOUN A **workshop** is a period of discussion or practical work on a particular subject in which a group of people share their knowledge or experience.
○ [+ for] *He ran a jazz workshop for young musicians.* ○ *I attended a poetry workshop.*

▶ **COLLOCATIONS:**
a workshop **for** *someone*
run/hold/arrange/organize a workshop
go to/attend a workshop
a **writers'/poetry/team-building** workshop

---

wor|ried /ˈwʌrid, AM ˈwɜːrɪd/

ADJECTIVE When you are **worried**, you are unhappy because you keep thinking about a problem or something unpleasant that might happen. ○ [+ *about*] *His parents are very worried about him.* ○ *She is worried that she won't get a place at university.* ○ *a worried frown*

▶ **COLLOCATIONS:**
worried **about** *someone/something*
very/deeply/extremely/seriously worried
look/sound/seem worried
a worried **frown/glance/expression/look**

▶ **SYNONYMS:** anxious, concerned

wor|ry|ing /ˈwʌriɪŋ, AM ˈwɜːriɪŋ/

ADJECTIVE If something is **worrying**, it causes people to worry. [mainly BRIT; in AM, usually use **worrisome**] ○ *It's worrying that they don't have the right training.*

▶ **COLLOCATIONS:**
it is worrying
very/extremely worrying

▶ **SYNONYM:** concerning

WORD FAMILY		
worry	**VERB**	○ *We worry about the future.*
worry	**NOUN**	○ *Their main worry is the high cost of housing.*
worried	**ADJECTIVE**	○ *She looked extremely worried.*
worriedly	**ADVERB**	○ *'You'll come back, won't you?' he said worriedly.*
worrying	**ADJECTIVE**	○ *a very worrying report about drugs*
worryingly	**ADVERB**	○ *Youth unemployment is worryingly high.*

Xx

X-ray /ˈeksreɪ/ **(X-rays, X-raying, X-rayed)** also **x-ray**   `HEALTH`

1 **NOUN** An **X-ray** is a picture made by sending radiation through something, usually someone's body. ○ *They did an X-ray of her arm.* ○ *He had to have a chest X-ray.*

▶ **COLLOCATIONS:**
   an X-ray **of** something
   have/do/order an X-ray
   an X-ray **shows/reveals/confirms** something
   an X-ray **machine**

2 **VERB** If someone or something **is X-rayed**, an X-ray picture is taken of them. ○ *All baggage is x-rayed at the airport.* ○ *They X-rayed my jaw.*

Yy

---

yawn /jɔːn/ (yawns, yawning, yawned)

1 **VERB** If you **yawn**, you open your mouth wide and breathe in more air than usual, often when you are tired. ○ *She yawned and looked at her watch.* ○ *Luke yawned and stretched lazily.*

  ▶ COLLOCATION: yawn and **stretch**

2 **NOUN** A **yawn** is an act of yawning ○ *She gave a huge yawn.*

  ▶ COLLOCATIONS:
  give/stifle a yawn
  a **huge/big** yawn

---

yoga /ˈjəʊɡə/   `SPORT & ACTIVITY`

UNCOUNTABLE NOUN **Yoga** is a type of exercise in which you move your body into various positions in order to become more fit or flexible, to improve your breathing, and to relax your mind. ○ *She does yoga every day.* ○ *We have a yoga class on Mondays.*

  ▶ COLLOCATIONS:
  do yoga
  a yoga **class/teacher**

Useful
phrases

USEFUL PHRASES

Many ideas in English are commonly expressed using several words, a **phrase**, instead of a single word. Recognizing common phrases will help you when you are reading and using them in your writing will help you to sound more natural.

In this section, you will find some useful phrases used to talk about popular topics from *Cambridge English: First* and *First for Schools*, e.g. friendship – *get to know someone, have something in common, make friends*, or to complete the writing tasks in the exam, e.g. writing letters and emails – *Best wishes, Yours faithfully, Yours sincerely*.

You will also find these phrases organized by topic in the word lists at the back of the book.

---

above all

You say **above all** to indicate that the thing you are mentioning is the most important point. ○ *Above all, chairs should be comfortable.* ○ *The programme is designed to be positive and enjoyable, and above all to make children laugh.*

---

aimed at someone   `MEDIA & CULTURE`

If something is **aimed at** a particular person or group, you intend that the person or group should notice it and be influenced by it. ○ *His first novel for children is aimed at young teens.* ○ *Advertising aimed at children should be curbed.*

---

all of a sudden

If something happens **all of a sudden**, it happens quickly and unexpectedly. ○ *We were dancing, and all of a sudden, we heard gunshots.* ○ *All of a sudden she didn't look sleepy any more.*

---

at first

You use **at first** when you are talking about what happens in the early stages of an event or experience, or just after something else has happened, in contrast to what happens later. ○ *At first, he seemed surprised by my questions.* ○ *I felt a little uneasy at first, but not any more.*

▶ SYNONYM: initially

at last

If you say that something has happened **at last**, you mean it has happened after you have been hoping for it for a long time. ○ *I'm so glad that we've found you at last!* ○ *At last the train arrived in the station.*

▶ SYNONYM: finally

at once

1 If you do something **at once**, you do it immediately. ○ *Stop it, at once!* ○ *She telephoned the police at once.* ○ *Remove from the heat, add the parsley and serve at once.*

▶ SYNONYMS: immediately, straight away

2 If a number of different things happen **at once** or **all at once**, they all happen at the same time. ○ *You can't be doing two things at once.* ○ *People were talking all at once.*

▶ SYNONYMS: at the same time, together

at the last moment/minute

If someone does something **at the last moment**, or **at the last minute**, they do it at the latest time possible. ○ *They changed their minds at the last moment.* ○ *The classes were cancelled at the last minute.*

at the moment

You use **at the moment** to indicate that something exists or is happening at the time when you are speaking. ○ *At the moment, no one is talking to me.* ○ *Have you got a girlfriend at the moment?*

▶ SYNONYMS: now, currently

bear something in mind

If you tell someone to **bear** something **in mind**, you are reminding or warning them about something important which they should remember. ○ *Which player would you choose, bearing in mind age and experience?* ○ [+ that] *Bear in mind that petrol stations are scarce in the more remote areas.*

beat someone to it

If you intend to do something but someone **beats** you **to it**, they do it before you do. ○ *Don't be too long about it or you'll find someone has beaten you to it.* ○ *I was planning to use the title for my first novel, but they've beaten me to it.*

Best wishes

You use **Best wishes** or **With best wishes** at the end of a letter or an email which is polite but friendly, before you sign your name. ○ *I look forward to hearing from you. Best wishes, Jane.*

beyond belief

You use **beyond belief** to emphasize that something is true to a very great degree or that it happened to a very great degree. ○ *We are devastated, shocked beyond belief.* ○ *It has changed almost beyond belief.*

bound to

If you say that something **is bound to** happen or be true, you are sure it will happen or be true. ○ *I'll show it to Benjamin. He's bound to know.* ○ *When there's a toddler around accidents are bound to happen.* ○ *With so many new voters, there are bound to be problems.*

▶ **SYNONYM:** be certain to

bring something to life

If you **bring** something **to life**, especially in a book or a film, it becomes real, interesting, or exciting. ○ *He uses letters and diaries by ordinary soldiers to bring to life the experience of war.* ○ *You then walk through an exhibition which brings the tales to life.*

burst into tears

If you **burst into tears**, you suddenly begin to cry. ○ *She burst into tears and ran from the kitchen.*

by accident

If something happens **by accident**, it happens completely by chance. ○ *She discovered the problem by accident.* ○ *The brothers got into the food business almost by accident.*

▶ **SYNONYM:** by chance

▶ **ANTONYMS:** on purpose, deliberately

do someone a favour

If you **do** someone **a favour**, you do something for them even though you do not have to. [in AM, use **do someone a favor**] ○ *Could you do me a favour? Don't tell Miss Conway that I was here.* ○ *My boss asked if I could do him a favour.*

expecting a baby

If you say that a woman **is expecting a baby**, or that she **is expecting**, you mean that she is pregnant. ○ *She was expecting another baby.* ○ *I hear Dawn's expecting again.*

▶ **SYNONYM:** pregnant

fail a test/exam/course

If someone **fails a test**, **exam**, or **course**, they perform badly in it and do not reach the standard that is required. ○ *I'd failed the first year exam in the History of Art.* ○ *The penalty for cheating is to fail the course.*

→ see also **take a test/exam**

▶ **ANTONYM:** pass a test/exam

fall asleep

When you **fall asleep**, you start sleeping. ○ *Sam snuggled down in his pillow and fell asleep.* ○ *I fell asleep in front of the television.*

fall in love

If you **fall in love with** someone, you start to be in love with them. ○ [+ with] *He was working at a hospital, when he fell in love with Iris, a nurse.* ○ *We fell madly in love.*

feel sorry for someone

1 If you **feel sorry for** someone who is unhappy or in an unpleasant situation, you feel sympathy and sadness for them. ○ *I felt really sorry for Micky.*

2 You say that someone is **feeling sorry for themselves** when you disapprove of the fact that they keep thinking unhappily about their problems, rather than trying to be cheerful and positive. ○ *What he must not do is to sit around at home feeling sorry for himself.*

follow in someone's footsteps

If you **follow in** someone's **footsteps**, you do the same things as they did earlier. ○ *My father is extremely proud that I followed in his footsteps and became a doctor.*

for example

You use **for example** to introduce an example of something. ○ *Note down the owner's details, for example a name and address.* ○ *If a minor financial emergency happened, for example, your fridge broke down, you would not be able to afford to fix it.* ○ *Take, for example, the simple sentence: 'The man climbed up the hill'.*

▶ **SYNONYM:** for instance

for sale
SHOPPING

If something is **for sale**, it is being offered to people to buy. ○ *The boat wasn't for sale.* ○ *All the pictures are for sale.* ○ [+ at/for] *His former home is for sale at £495,000.*

get/be divorced
SOCIAL LIFE

When someone **gets divorced** from their former husband or wife, they separate from them, so they are no longer legally married to them. ○ *My parents got divorced.* ○ [+ from] *She is now divorced from her husband.* ○ *He is divorced, with a young son.*

get/be engaged
SOCIAL LIFE

When two people **get engaged**, they agree to marry each other. ○ *We got engaged on my eighteenth birthday.* ○ [+ to] *He was engaged to Miss Julia Maria Boardman.*

get/be married
SOCIAL LIFE

When two people **get married**, they become each other's husband and wife during a special ceremony. ○ *They made plans to get married.* ○ *We have been married for 14 years.* ○ [+ to] *She is married to an Englishman.*

get rid of something

When you **get rid of** something that you do not want or do not like, you take action so that you no longer have it or suffer from it. ○ *The owner needs to get rid of the car for financial reasons.* ○ *There's corruption, and we're going to get rid of it.*

get to know someone
SOCIAL LIFE

If you **get to know** someone, you find out what they are like by spending time with them. ○ *The 75 students formed small groups to get to know each other.* ○ *I'd really like to see you again and get to know you better.*

give/lend someone a hand

If you **give** or **lend** someone **a hand**, you help them with what they are doing. ○ *Come and give me a hand in the garden.* ○ [+ with] *She just needed someone to give her a hand with a few jobs.* ○ *Can I lend a hand, Maddy?*

go for a drink/coffee
SOCIAL LIFE

If you **go for a drink** or **a coffee** with someone, you go to a bar, cafe, etc. with them to talk and socialize. ○ *Would you like to go for a drink some time?* ○ [+ with] *He said he was going for a drink with some friends.* ○ *The three of us went for a coffee.*

have no/every intention

If you say that you **have no intention of** doing something, you are emphasizing that you are not going to do it. If you say that you **have every intention of** doing something, you are emphasizing that you intend to do it. ○ *We have no intention of selling our concert tickets.* ○ *He has every intention of staying in his current job.*

→ see also **intention**

have something in common SOCIAL LIFE

If two or more people **have** something **in common**, they share the same interests or experiences. ○ *I think you two might have a lot in common.* ○ [+ with] *He had very little in common with his sister.*

in charge WORK

If you are **in charge** of someone or something, you have responsibility for them. ○ *Who's in charge here?* ○ [+ of] *You will be in charge of the smaller children*

in fact

1 You use **in fact** before you give more detailed information about what you have just said. ○ *He didn't go to university. In fact he left school at 16.* ○ *Keeping busy is not the problem – in fact, he is busier than he has ever been.*

2 You use **in fact** to introduce an idea that contrasts with a previous statement. ○ *That sounds rather simple, but in fact it's very difficult.*

▶ **SYNONYM:** actually

in favour of

If you are **in favour of** something, you support it and think that it is a good thing. [in AM, use **in favor of**] ○ *the strongest argument in favour of GM crops* ○ *I wouldn't be in favour of income tax cuts.*

in public MEDIA & CULTURE

If you say or do something **in public**, you say or do it when a group of people are present. ○ *I'd rather not discuss it in public.* ○ *She was reluctant to hold Nick's hand in public.*

in stock SHOPPING

If goods are **in stock**, a shop has them available to sell. If they are **out of stock**, it does not. ○ *Check that your size is in stock.* ○ *Lemon and lime juice were both temporarily out of stock.*

in the end

You say **in the end** when you are saying what is the final result of a series of events, or what is your final conclusion after considering all the relevant facts. ○ *I had to think long and hard about what to do, but in the end I opted to continue.* ○ *I could tell he wasn't impressed with my answers, and in the end I didn't get the job.*

in theory

You use **in theory** to say that although something is supposed to be true or to happen in the way stated, it may not in fact be true or happen in that way. ○ *It was a good idea in theory, but it didn't work.* ○ *The system, at least in theory, might work this way.*

▶ **SYNONYM:** theoretically

▶ **ANTONYM:** in practice

in the wild

SCIENCE & NATURE

Animals that live **in the wild** live in a free and natural state and are not looked after by people. ○ *Fewer than a thousand giant pandas still live in the wild.*

▶ **ANTONYM:** in captivity

in touch

COMMUNICATIONS **SOCIAL LIFE**

If you **get in touch with** someone, you contact them by writing to them or telephoning them. If you **are**, **keep**, or **stay in touch with** them, you write, phone, or visit each other regularly. ○ [+ with] *I'll get in touch with Wendy. She might know something.* ○ *Thanks for getting in touch.* ○ *I'll be in touch as soon as I know anything.* ○ *We didn't keep in touch after they left here.*

→ see also **lose touch**

▶ **SYNONYM:** in contact

keep a secret

If you say that someone can **keep a secret**, you mean that they can be trusted not to tell other people a secret that you have told them. ○ *I can tell you guys because I know you can keep a secret.*

keep someone awake

If something **keeps** you **awake**, it stops you from sleeping. ○ *Did the noise keep you awake?*

let someone know
COMMUNICATIONS

If you **let** someone **know** something, you tell them about it or make sure that they know about it. ○ *If you do want to go, please let me know.* ○ *If I hear anything I'll let you know.* ○ [+ *how*] *Keep in touch and let me know how you get on.* ○ [+ *what*] *Let me know what you decide on Monday, okay?*

look like
CLOTHES & APPEARANCE

If one person or thing **looks like** another, they have a similar appearance. ○ *He's going to look just like his father.* ○ *The okapi looks like a cross between a giraffe and a zebra.*

lose touch
COMMUNICATIONS   SOCIAL LIFE

If you **lose touch with** someone, you gradually stop writing, telephoning, or visiting them. ○ [+ *with*] *She'd lost touch with Jane since college.* ○ *We lost touch after that.*

→ see also **in touch**

make friends
SOCIAL LIFE

If you **make friends with** someone, you begin a friendship with them. You can also say that two people **make friends**. ○ [+ *with*] *He has made friends with the kids on the street.* ○ *Ann hadn't found it easy to make friends in her new school.*

make fun of someone/something

If you **make fun of** someone or something, you laugh at them, tease them, or make jokes about them. ○ *Don't make fun of me.* ○ *They all made fun of my plan.*

▶ **SYNONYMS:** laugh at, tease, mock

make money
MONEY   WORK

If you **make money**, you get money by earning it or by making a profit from a business. ○ *He is trying to make enough money to support his family.* ○ [+ *by*] *The website makes money by selling advertising.* ○ [+ *from/out of*] *The United States makes the most money from foreign visitors.*

make sure

1 If you **make sure that** something is done, you take action so that it is done. ○ *Make sure that you follow the instructions carefully.*

2 If you **make sure that** something is the way that you want or expect it to be, you check that it is that way. ○ *He looked in the bathroom to make sure that he was alone.*

▶ **SYNONYM:** check

make your mind up

If you **make up** your **mind** or **make** your **mind up**, you decide which of a number of possible things you will have or do. ○ *He simply can't make his mind up.* ○ [+ to-inf] *That was when I made my mind up to go.* ○ [+ about] *He says he has not made up his mind about the election date.*

▶ SYNONYM: decide

only child   PEOPLE

An **only child** is a child who has no brothers or sisters. ○ *Perhaps because I was an only child I've always been able to amuse myself.*

on purpose

If you do something **on purpose**, you do it deliberately. ○ *Was it an accident or did David do it on purpose?*

▶ SYNONYMS: deliberately, intentionally

▶ ANTONYMS: by mistake, by accident

on sale   SHOPPING

Products that are **on sale** can be bought. ○ *Tickets go on sale this Friday.* ○ *English textbooks and dictionaries are on sale everywhere.*

out of order

A machine or device that is **out of order** is broken and does not work. ○ *Their phone's out of order.* ○ *The lift was out of order so she took the stairs.*

pass a test/exam   EDUCATION

If someone **passes a test** or **an exam**, they achieve an acceptable standard. ○ *I managed to pass the entrance exam.* ○ *Kevin has just passed his driving test.*

→ see also **take a test/exam**

▶ ANTONYM: fail a test/exam

run in the family   PEOPLE

If a characteristic **runs in** someone's **family**, it often occurs in members of that family, in different generations. ○ *Musical talent obviously runs in the family.* ○ *Coronary heart disease tends to run in families.*

take account of something

If you **take account of** something or you **take** something **into account**, you consider it when you are thinking about a situation or deciding what to do. ○ *We have always taken into account the needs of our disabled customers.* ○ *We refresh the images every year to take account of changes in hairstyles and fashions.*

▶ SYNONYM: consider

take a course/subject ⟨EDUCATION⟩

If you **take a course** or **a subject** at school or university, you choose to study it. ○ *I took a course in journalism at college.* ○ *Girls should be encouraged to take mathematics and science subjects.*

take advantage of something

If you **take advantage of** something, you make good use of it while you can. ○ *We should take advantage of this lovely weather.* ○ *I intend to take full advantage of this trip to buy the things we need.*

take a test/exam ⟨EDUCATION⟩

If you **take a test** or **an exam**, you do it in order to obtain a qualification. ○ *Candidates can take the exam at any time of the year.* ○ *She took her driving test in Greenford.*

→ see also **pass a test/exam, fail a test/exam/course**

▶ SYNONYM: sit a test/exam

take it easy ⟨FREE TIME⟩

If someone tells you to **take it easy** or **take things easy**, they mean that you should relax and not do very much at all. [INFORMAL] ○ *I took it easy for a while.* ○ *The doctor says I'm to take things easy for a few weeks.*

▶ SYNONYM: relax

take part ⟨SPORT & ACTIVITY⟩ ⟨FREE TIME⟩

If you **take part in** an activity, you do it together with other people. ○ [+ in] *They were taking part in a gap-year diving expedition.* ○ *Thousands of students have taken part in demonstrations.* ○ *Runners of every standard are invited to take part.*

▶ SYNONYM: participate

USEFUL PHRASES

take place

When something **takes place**, it happens, especially in a controlled or organized way. ○ *The courses normally take place at the training centre.* ○ *Elections will now take place on November the twenty-fifth.*

take something for granted

If you **take** something **for granted**, you believe that it is true or accept it as normal without thinking about it. ○ *We miss home cooking. Things we took for granted back home.* ○ *The experience has taught him not to take anything for granted and to make the most of every day.*

▶ **SYNONYM:** expect

take time

If something **takes** a certain amount of time, that amount of time is needed in order to do it. ○ *Since the roads are very bad, the journey took us a long time.* ○ *Training takes four years full-time.* ○ *[+ to-inf] The sauce takes 25 minutes to prepare and cook.*

take turns

If two or more people **take turns** to do something, they do it one after the other several times, rather than doing it together. ○ *[+ to-inf] We took turns to drive the car.* ○ *[+ v-ing] Different riders take turns cycling in front to block the wind from other teammates.*

to start with

You use **to start with** to introduce the first of a number of things or reasons that you want to mention. ○ *Cut down on tea and coffee to start with, but also boost levels of oxygen by taking some exercise.*

Yours faithfully   `COMMUNICATIONS`

When you start a formal or business letter with 'Dear Sir' or 'Dear Madam', you write **Yours faithfully** before your signature at the end. [BRIT; in AM, use **Sincerely yours**] ○ *Yours faithfully, Alison Smith.*

Yours sincerely   `COMMUNICATIONS`

When you start a formal or business letter with a person's name, you write **Yours sincerely** before your signature at the end. [BRIT; in AM, use **Sincerely yours**] ○ *Yours sincerely, James Brown.*

Word lists

People

Individuals & groups
female (adj)
human (adj)
human being (noun)
individual (adj, noun)
male (adj)

flatmate (noun)
inhabitant (noun)
neighbour (noun)
resident (noun)

candidate (noun)
classmate (noun)
colleague (noun)
employee (noun)
pupil (noun)
volunteer (noun, verb)

celebrity (noun)
consumer (noun)
guest (noun)
motorist (noun)
patient (noun, adj)
pedestrian (noun)
tourist (noun)
witness (noun, verb)

audience (noun)
community (uncount)
crowd (noun)
population (noun)
society (uncount)
staff (uncount)
tribe (noun)

Family
couple (noun)
cousin (noun)
fiancé (noun)
in-law (comb)
nephew (noun)
niece (noun)
relative (noun)
step- (comb)
twin (noun)
widow (noun)

ancestor (noun)
background (noun)
bring up (ph verb)
expecting a baby (phrase)
follow in someone's footsteps (phrase)
only child (phrase)
pregnant (adj)
relationship (noun)
run in the family (phrase)
take after (ph verb)

Age
adolescent (adj)
adult (noun)
childish (adj)
elderly (adj)
generation (noun)
grown-up (noun, adj)
middle-aged (adj)
teenager (noun)
teens (plural)
toddler (noun)

Clothes & appearance

Appearance
alike (adj)
appearance (noun, uncount)
casual (adj)
cool (adj)
feminine (adj)
look like (phrase)
similar (adj)
smart (adj)

bald (adj)
bare (adj)
curly (adj)
dark (adj)
fair (adj)
grey (adj)
slim (adj)
straight (adj)
thin (adj)

Clothes
costume (noun)
fashion (uncount)
outfit (noun)
uniform (noun)

coat (noun)
hoodie (noun)
jacket (noun)
jeans (plural)
jumper (noun)
pyjamas (plural)
shorts (plural)
skirt (noun)
suit (noun, verb)
sweatshirt (noun)
trousers (plural)
T-shirt (noun)

accessories (noun)
belt (noun)
bracelet (noun)
cap (noun)
earrings (plural)
glasses (plural)
gloves (plural)
jewellery (uncount)
make-up (uncount)
necklace (noun)
ring (noun)
scarf (noun)
tie (noun)

boots (plural)
sandals (plural)
shoes (plural)
slippers (plural)
socks (plural)
trainers (plural)

checked (adj)
cotton (uncount)
denim (uncount)
leather (uncount)
light (noun, adj)
pale (adj)
plain (adj)
silk (uncount)
striped (adj)
wool (uncount)

button (noun)
heel (noun)
hood (noun)
pocket (noun)
sleeves (plural)

change (verb)
dress (noun, verb)
dressed (adj)

fit (verb, adj)
grow into/out of (ph verb)
hang up (ph verb)
match (verb, noun)
put on (ph verb)
take off (ph verb)
try on (ph verb)
wear (verb)

Personality

characteristic (noun)
personality (uncount, noun)

attractive (adj)
cheerful (adj)
considerate (adj)
creative (adj)
dynamic (adj)
easy-going (adj)
energetic (adj)
enthusiastic (adj)
friendly (adj)
funny (adj)
generous (adj)
gentle (adj)
honest (adj)
imaginative (adj)
intelligent (adj)
    intelligence (uncount)
kind (adj)
lively (adj)
loyal (adj)
modest (adj)
outgoing (adj)
patient (noun, adj)
polite (adj)
popular (adj)
promising (adj)
reliable (adj)

sensible (adj)
sensitive (adj)
smart (adj)
sociable (adj)
sympathetic (adj)
talent (noun)
thoughtful (adj)
willing (adj)

ability (noun)
ambitious (adj)
capable (adj)
communication skills (plural)
discipline (uncount)
organized (adj)
rely on (verb)
responsible (adj)

competitive (adj)
serious (adj)
shy (adj)

aggressive (adj)
lazy (adj)
mean (adj)
moody (adj)
rude (adj)
selfish (adj)

Feelings

emotion (noun)
mood (noun)

Positive feelings
admire (verb)
amazed (adj)
    amazing (adj)
calm down (ph verb)
cheer up (ph verb)

confident (adj)
content (adj)
cope with (verb)
curious (adj)
delighted (adj)
encourage (verb)
excited (adj)
  exciting (adj)
fun (adj)
glad (adj)
inspire (verb)
keen (adj)
look forward to (ph verb)
pleased (adj)
pleasure (uncount)
proud (adj)
  pride (uncount)
relax (verb)
  relaxed (adj)
  relaxing (adj)
relieved (adj)
satisfied (adj)
surprised (adj)
  surprising (adj)
thrilled (adj)

Negative feelings
afraid (adj)
anger (uncount)
  angry (adj)
annoy (verb)
  annoyed (adj)
  annoying (adj)
anxiety (uncount)
  anxious (adj)
ashamed (adj)
bored (adj)
  boring (adj)
burst into tears (phrase)
concerned (adj)
cross (adj)

depressed (adj)
  depressing (adj)
  depression (uncount)
disappointed (adj)
  disappointing (adj)
discourage (verb)
embarrassed (adj)
  embarrassing (adj)
fear (uncount)
fed up (adj)
feel sorry for someone (phrase)
frighten (verb)
  frightened (adj)
  frightening (adj)
furious (adj)
guilty (adj)
homesick (adj)
jealous (adj)
miserable (adj)
put up with (ph verb)
regret (verb)
scared (adj)
stress (uncount)
tense (adj)
terrified (adj)
  terrifying (adj)
upset (adj)
worried (adj)
  worrying (adj)

Beliefs & opinions

belief (noun, plural)
  believe (verb)
philosophy (uncount)
politics (uncount)
  political (adj)
  politician (noun)
religion (uncount, noun)

WORD LISTS

church (noun)
mosque (noun)
priest (noun)
temple (noun)

bound to (phrase)
conservative (adj)
have no/every intention (phrase)
in favour of (phrase)
intention (noun)
in theory (phrase)
make your mind up (phrase)
opinion (noun)
oppose (verb)
radical (adj)
support (verb, uncount)
take something for granted
   (phrase)

blame (verb)
critical (adj)
deny (verb)
disapprove (verb)
pessimistic (adj)
warn (verb)

advantage (noun)
approve (verb)
optimistic (adj)

accuse (verb)
argument (noun)
claim (verb)
declare (verb)
demand (verb)
emphasize (verb)
insist (verb)

Speech

advice (uncount)
   advise (verb)
announce (verb)
appeal (verb)
declare (verb)
describe (verb)
express (verb)
instruction (noun, plural)

approve (verb)
claim (verb)
prefer (verb)

emphasize (verb)
insist (verb)

expect (verb)
predict (verb)
promise (verb)
propose (verb)

accuse (verb)
admit (verb)
apologize (verb)
   apology (noun)
blame (verb)
complain (verb)
   complaint (noun)
demand (verb)
deny (verb)
ignore (verb)
make fun of someone/
   something (phrase)
refuse (verb)
warn (verb)

above all (phrase)
for example (phrase)
in fact (phrase)

Academic subjects

archaeology (uncount)
architecture (uncount)
    architect (noun)
geography (uncount)
history (uncount)
    historic (adj)
    historical (adj)
law (uncount, noun)
    legal (adj)
linguistics (uncount)
literature (uncount)

astronomy (uncount)
biology (uncount)
chemistry (uncount)
ecology (uncount)
engineering (uncount)
    engineer (noun)
geology (uncount)
mathematics (uncount)
medicine (uncount, noun)
psychology (uncount)
science (uncount, noun)
    scientific (adj)
statistics (plural, uncount)

Education

academic (adj)
education (noun, uncount)

classmate (noun)
graduate (noun, verb)
head teacher (noun)
lecture (noun)
    lecturer (noun)
postgraduate (noun, adj)
professor (noun)

pupil (noun)
staff (uncount)
tutor (noun)
    tutorial (noun)
undergraduate (noun)

absent (adj)
assignment (noun)
compulsory (adj)
course (noun)
deadline (noun)
dissertation (noun)
level (noun)
marks (plural)
project (noun)
results (noun)
seminar (noun)
skill (noun)
term (noun)
timetable (noun)
workshop (noun)

attend (verb)
fail a test/exam/course (phrase)
hand in (ph verb)
pass a test/exam (phrase)
revise (verb)
take a course/subject (phrase)
take a test/exam (phrase)

kindergarten (noun)
nursery school (noun)
playground (noun)
primary school (noun)
secondary school (noun)
uniform (noun)

campus (noun)
degree (noun)
department (noun)
discipline (uncount)

faculty (noun)
gap year (noun)
higher education (uncount)
library (noun)
prospectus (noun)
vocational (adj)

Social life

lifestyle (noun)

call for (ph verb)
fall in love (phrase)
fall out (with someone) (ph verb)
friend (noun)
   friendly (adj)
get/be divorced (phrase)
get on (ph verb)
get together (with) (ph verb)
get to know someone (phrase)
have something in common
   (phrase)
in touch (phrase)
lose touch (phrase)
make friends (phrase)
social (adj)
   sociable (adj)

bride (noun)
ceremony (noun)
civil (adj)
congratulate (verb)
   congratulations (plural)
get/be engaged (phrase)
get/be married (phrase)
gift (noun)
groom (noun)
guest (noun)
outdoors (adv)
party (noun)

present (noun)
priest (noun)
reception (uncount, noun)
tradition (noun)
   traditional (adj)

club (noun)
   clubbing (uncount)
festival (noun)
reserve (verb)

barbecue (noun)
go for a drink/coffee (phrase)
restaurant (noun)

Home

cost of living (noun)
homesick (adj)
home town (noun)
household (noun, uncount)
standard of living (noun)

apartment (noun)
cottage (noun)
floor (noun)
storey (noun)

bedroom (noun)
dining room (noun)
kitchen (noun)
living room (noun)

air conditioning (uncount)
basin (noun)
freezer (noun)
light (noun, adj)
shutters (plural)
sink (noun)
tap (noun)

messy (adj)
modern (adj)
wooden (adj)

drive (noun)
fence (noun)
garage (noun)
gate (noun)
hedge (noun)
outdoors (adv)

chores (plural)
decorate (verb)
  decoration (uncount, noun)
do up (ph verb)
housework (uncount)

Places

area (noun)
city (noun)
countryside (uncount)
district (noun)
home town (noun)
in public (phrase)
landscape (uncount, noun)
local (adj)
location (noun)
out-of-town (adj)
outskirts (plural)
region (noun)
rural (adj)
seaside (uncount)
site (noun)
suburb (noun, plural)
town (noun)
urban (adj)

inhabitant (noun)
resident (noun)

attraction (noun)
car park (noun)
crossroads (noun)
harbour (noun)
lane (noun)
market (noun)
square (noun)
traffic lights (plural)

architecture (uncount)
block (noun)
church (noun)
cinema (noun)
facilities (plural)
gallery (noun)
mosque (noun)
prison (noun)
shopping centre (noun)
stadium (noun)
temple (noun)
venue (noun)

atmosphere (uncount)
crowd (noun)
  crowded (adj)
developed (adj)
  developing (adj)
domestic (adj)
famous (adj)
narrow (adj)
picturesque (adj)
ruined (adj)
run-down (adj)
vast (adj)

congestion (uncount)
graffiti (uncount)
litter (uncount)
traffic (uncount)
  traffic jam (noun)

Transport & travel

Transport
bus (noun)
carriage (noun)
commute (verb)
fare (noun)
ferry (noun)
link (noun)
meter (noun)
platform (noun)
public transport (uncount)
route (noun)
service (noun)
timetable (noun)
underground (noun)

break down (ph verb)
congestion (uncount)
driver (noun)
fuel (uncount)
motorist (noun)
pedestrian (noun)
petrol (uncount)
roundabout (noun)
rush hour (uncount)
seat belt (noun)
traffic (uncount)
   traffic jam (noun)
traffic lights (plural)

overtake (verb)
pick up (ph verb)
queue (noun, verb)
set out (ph verb)
slow down (ph verb)

Travel & holidays
arrivals (uncount)
board (verb)
boarding card (noun)

departures (plural)
destination (noun)
distance (noun)
gate (noun)
hand luggage (uncount)
harbour (noun)
jet lag (uncount)
journey (noun)
land (uncount, verb)
luggage (uncount)
passport (noun)
passport control (uncount)
security (uncount)
suitcase (noun)
take off (ph verb)
travel (verb, uncount)
trip (noun)
trolley (noun)

accommodation (uncount)
backpacking (uncount)
beach (noun)
book (verb)
book in/into (ph verb)
camping (uncount)
campsite (noun)
check in (ph verb)
check out (ph verb)
get away (ph verb)
guidebook (noun)
hostel (noun)
hotel (noun)
pack (verb)
reception (uncount, noun)
   receptionist (noun)
refreshments (plural)
relax (verb)
   relaxed (adj)
   relaxing (adj)
seaside (uncount)
sightseeing (uncount)

sunbathe (verb)
tour (noun)
tour guide (noun)
tourist (noun)

Food & drink

savoury (adj)
sweet (adj, noun)
taste (verb)
   tasty (adj)

cake (noun)
crisps (plural)
fruit (uncount)
juice (uncount)
milk (uncount)
noodles (plural)
salad (noun)
sauce (noun)
snack (noun)
vegetable (noun)

bacon (uncount)
beef (uncount)
burger (noun)
ham (uncount)
lamb (uncount)
meat (uncount)
pork (uncount)
sausage (noun)
steak (noun)

butter (uncount)
cream (uncount)
egg (noun)
flour (uncount)
salt (uncount)
sugar (uncount)

frying pan (noun)
ingredients (plural)
oven (noun)
recipe (noun)
saucepan (noun)

bake (verb)
boil (verb)
chop (verb, noun)
cook (verb, noun)
   cooker (noun)
fry (verb)
grate (verb)
grill (noun, verb)
mix (verb)
peel (verb)
pour (verb)
roast (verb, adj)
serve (verb)
slice (noun, verb)
stir (verb)

barbecue (noun)
chef (noun)
go for a drink/coffee (phrase)
refreshments (plural)
restaurant (noun)

calorie (noun)
diet (noun, verb)
fast food (uncount)
fat (uncount)
   fattening (adj)
junk food (uncount)
organic (adj)
processed (adj)
vegetarian (noun, adj)

Health

dentist (noun)
health (uncount)
 healthy (adj)
health care (uncount)
optician (noun)
patient (noun, adj)

harm (verb, uncount)
 harmful (adj)
sleep (uncount, verb)
smoking (uncount)
sunbathe (verb)
symptom (noun)

exercise (verb, uncount)
fit (verb, adj)
gym (noun)

alcohol (uncount)
calorie (noun)
cut down (on) (ph verb)
cut out (ph verb)
diet (noun, verb)
fast food (uncount)
fat (uncount)
 fattening (adj)
high (adj)
junk food (uncount)
low (adj)
processed (adj)
put on (ph verb)
salt (uncount)
scales (plural)
sugar (uncount)
vitamin (noun)
weigh (verb)

expecting a baby (phrase)

cold (noun)
depression (uncount)
flu (uncount)
headache (noun)
infection (noun)
jet lag (uncount)
run-down (adj)
sniff (verb)
sore throat (noun)
stress (uncount)
sunburnt (adj)

accident (noun)
 accidental (adj)
ache (verb)
blister (noun)
injury (noun)
 injured (adj)
scar (noun)

antibiotic (noun)
drug (noun)
injection (noun)
medicine (uncount, noun)
plaster (noun, uncount)
prescription (noun)
stitch (noun)
surgery (uncount)
thermometer (noun)
wheelchair (noun)
X-ray (noun, verb)

Sport & activity

athlete (noun)
 athletics (uncount)
badminton (uncount)
baseball (uncount)
basketball (uncount)

football (uncount)
golf (uncount)
gymnast (noun)
gymnastics (uncount)
hockey (uncount)
ice hockey (uncount)
judo (uncount)
martial arts (plural)
rugby (uncount)
run (verb, noun)
   runner (noun)
   running (uncount)
squash (uncount)
swimming (uncount)
table tennis (uncount)
volleyball (uncount)

climbing (uncount)
cycle (verb)
diving (uncount)
hiking (uncount)
sailing (uncount)
skateboard (noun)
ski (noun, verb)
   skiing (uncount)
snowboarding (uncount)
surfing (uncount)
walk (verb, noun)
   walking (uncount)

club (noun)
competition (noun)
fan (noun)
match (verb, noun)
stadium (noun)
take part (phrase)
tournament (noun)
win (verb)
   winner (noun)

bat (noun)
boots (plural)
racket (noun)

energy (uncount)
exercise (verb, uncount)
fit (verb, adj)
gym (noun)
jogging (uncount)
physical (adj)
sprint (noun, verb)
yoga (uncount)

Free time

day off (noun)
interest (uncount, noun)
pet (noun)
take it easy (phrase)
take part (phrase)
volunteer (noun, verb)

cards (plural)
chess (uncount)
crossword (noun)
DVD (noun)
jigsaw (noun)

drive (noun)
hiking (uncount)
playground (noun)
walk (verb, noun)
   walking (uncount)

Actions

behave (verb)
  behaviour (uncount)
carry out (ph verb)
combine (verb)
create (verb)
task (noun)
technique (noun)

breathe (verb)
fall asleep (phrase)
hang up (ph verb)
keep someone awake (phrase)
smell (verb)
sniff (verb)
stir (verb)
stroke (verb)
whistle (verb, noun)
yawn (verb, noun)

attention (uncount)
aware of (adj)
gaze (verb)
glance (verb)
notice (verb)
observe (verb)
  observation (uncount, noun)
spot (verb)
stare (verb)

bang (noun, verb)
crash (verb, noun)
hum (verb, uncount)
splash (verb, noun)

crawl (verb)
keep up (ph verb)
run (verb, noun)
  runner (noun)
  running (uncount)

rush (verb)
slow down (ph verb)
sprint (noun, verb)
stroll (verb)
turn up (ph verb)
walk (verb, noun)
  walking (uncount)
wander (verb)

achieve (verb)
  achievement (noun)
develop (verb)
  developed (adj)
  developing (adj)
  development (uncount)
exist (verb)
  existence (uncount)
progress (uncount)
rehearse (verb)
  rehearsal (noun)
require (verb)
run through (ph verb)
take place (phrase)

abolish (verb)
call off (ph verb)
come across (ph verb)
get rid of something (phrase)
give up (ph verb)
introduce (verb)
set out (ph verb)
set up (ph verb)
sign in (ph verb)
take over (ph verb)
take up (ph verb)

beat someone to it (phrase)
do someone a favour (phrase)
give away (ph verb)
give back (ph verb)

give/lend someone a hand
(phrase)
keep a secret (phrase)
let down (ph verb)
look after (ph verb)
react (verb)
reaction (noun)
take turns (phrase)

bear something in mind (phrase)
come up with (ph verb)
concentrate (verb)
make sure (phrase)
solve (verb)
solution (noun)
take account of something
(phrase)
take advantage of something
(phrase)

attack (verb)
by accident (phrase)
challenge (noun)
damage (verb, uncount)
destroy (verb)
dominate (verb)
on purpose (phrase)
protect (verb)
rescue (verb)
run up against (ph verb)
struggle (verb)
violent (adj)

Work

Jobs & careers
administration (uncount)
agency (noun)
call centre (noun)
catering (uncount)

construction (uncount)
education (noun, uncount)
emergency services (plural)
engineering (uncount)
finance (uncount)
health care (uncount)
information technology
(uncount)
journalism (uncount)
market (noun)
media (uncount)
reception (uncount, noun)
sales (plural, noun)

accountant (noun)
architect (noun)
builder (noun)
chef (noun)
cleaner (noun)
cook (verb, noun)
dentist (noun)
editor (noun)
electrician (noun)
engineer (noun)
firefighter (noun)
head teacher (noun)
journalist (noun)
lawyer (noun)
lecturer (noun)
mechanic (noun)
optician (noun)
plumber (noun)
police officer (noun)
priest (noun)
professor (noun)
receptionist (noun)
reporter (noun)
software engineer (noun)
solicitor (noun)
tour guide (noun)

assistant (noun)
career (noun)
in charge (phrase)
job (noun)
manager (noun)
occupation (noun)
permanent (adj)
position (noun)
professional (adj, noun)
promote (verb)
  promotion (uncount)
staff (uncount)
supervise (verb)
  supervisor (verb)
temporary (adj)

Working life

commercial (adj)
commute (verb)
conference (noun)
department (noun)
employ (verb)
  employee (noun)
flexible (adj)
overtime (uncount)
produce (verb)
shift (noun)
task (noun)
volunteer (noun, verb)
work (uncount)

application (noun)
  apply (verb)
candidate (noun)
interview (noun, verb)
opportunity (noun)
training (uncount)
vacancy (noun)

absent (adj)
day off (noun)
leisure (uncount)
redundant (adj)
resign (verb)
retire (verb)
unemployed (adj)

earn (verb)
income (noun)
living (noun)
pension (noun)
salary (noun)
wage (noun)

ambitious (adj)
communication skills (plural)
creative (adj)
efficient (adj)
experience (uncount)
qualifications (plural)
reliable (adj)
responsible (adj)
skill (noun)

Money

budget (noun)
cash (uncount)
charity (noun, uncount)
cost of living (noun)
credit card (noun)
debt (noun, uncount)
economic (adj)
  economical (adj)
  economy (noun)
fare (noun)
finance (uncount)
  financial (adj)

fortune (noun)
refund (noun, verb)
tip (verb, noun)

afford (verb)
cost (verb)
donate (verb)
do without (ph verb)
make money (phrase)
owe (verb)
pay (verb)
save (verb)
spend (verb)

earn (verb)
income (noun)
salary (noun)
wage (noun)

Shopping

for sale (phrase)
on sale (phrase)
sale (plural, noun)
shopping (uncount)

available (adj)
brand (noun)
brand-new (adj)
goods (plural)
guarantee (noun, verb)
in stock (phrase)
label (noun)
limited (adj)
packaging (uncount)
second-hand (adj)
size (noun)
unique (adj)

basket (noun)
catalogue (noun)
checkout (noun)
consumer (noun)
convenient (adj)
out-of-town (adj)
queue (noun, verb)
shopping centre (noun)
stall (noun)
take back (ph verb)
trolley (noun)
try on (ph verb)

advertisement (noun)
poster (noun)
publicity (uncount)
slogan (noun)

afford (verb)
bargain (noun)
cash (uncount)
discount (noun)
offer (verb, noun)
receipt (noun)
refund (noun, verb)

browse (verb)
click (verb)
enter (verb)
home page (noun)
keyword (noun)
online (adj, adv)
password (noun)
secure (adj)
sign in (ph verb)
support (verb, uncount)

Communications

fluent (adj)
in touch (phrase)
let someone know (phrase)
lose touch (phrase)

best wishes (phrase)
look forward to (ph verb)
Yours faithfully (phrase)
Yours sincerely (phrase)

call back (ph verb)
call centre (noun)
cut off (ph verb)
get through (ph verb)
hang up (ph verb)
mobile (phone) (noun)
phone call (noun)
pick up (ph verb)
ring (verb)
smart phone (noun)
telephone (verb)
text (noun, verb)

laptop (noun)
menu (noun)
tablet (noun)

application (noun)
browse (verb)
click (verb)
enter (verb)
home page (noun)
keyword (noun)
link (noun)
online (adj, adv)
password (noun)
sign in (ph verb)
support (verb, uncount)
website (noun)

Media & culture

advertisement (noun)
  advertising (uncount)
culture (uncount, noun)
entertain (verb)
event (noun)
venue (noun)

action (film/movie) (noun)
cartoon (noun)
comedy (uncount, noun)
current affairs (plural)
documentary (noun)
drama (noun)
factual (adj)
humorous (adj)
style (noun)
thriller (noun)
western (adj)

actor (noun)
appearance (noun, uncount)
audience (noun)
cast (noun)
celebrity (noun)
director (noun)
famous (adj)
fan (noun)
interview (noun, verb)
public (uncount, adj)

TV & films

channel (noun)
episode (noun)
highlights (plural)
programme (noun)
reality TV (uncount)
remote control (noun)
repeat (noun)
series (noun)

soap opera (noun)
station (noun)
TV (uncount)

cinema (noun)
costume (noun)
dressing room (noun)
DVD (noun)
play (noun)
rehearse (verb)
    rehearsal (noun)
run through (ph verb)
screen (noun)
script (noun)
show (noun)
soundtrack (noun)
special effect (noun)
stage (noun, uncount)
studio (noun)
subtitles (plural)
theatre (noun)
trailer (noun)

The press
article (noun)
editor (noun)
fashion (uncount)
gossip (uncount)
headline (noun)
image (noun)
issue (noun)
journalism (uncount)
    journalist (noun)
magazine (noun)
media (uncount)
newspaper (noun)
photograph (noun)
press (uncount)
publish (verb)
report (verb, noun)
    reporter (noun)
tabloid (noun)

aimed at someone (phrase)
announce (verb)
appeal (verb)
describe (verb)
expect (verb)
express (verb)
threaten (verb)

Visual arts
abstract (adj)
artist (noun)
    artistic (adj)
background (noun)
collection (noun)
display (verb, noun)
draw (verb)
    drawing (noun)
exhibition (noun)
gallery (noun)
landscape (uncount, noun)
paint (verb)
portrait (noun)
sculpture (noun, uncount)

Literature
author (noun)
biography (noun)
character (noun)
diary (noun)
fiction (uncount)
hero (noun)
literature (uncount)
novel (noun)
novelist (noun)
plot (noun)
poem (noun)
    poetry (uncount)
reference (adj)
science fiction (uncount)
textbook (noun)

Music

classical (adj)
folk (adj)
jazz (uncount)
musical (adj, noun)
pop (music) (uncount)
rock (music) (uncount)

band (noun)
choir (noun)
composer (noun)
orchestra (noun)

concert (noun)
festival (noun)
gig (noun)
live (adj)
performance (noun)
tour (noun)

album (noun)
chart (noun)
guitar (noun)
hit (noun)
instrument (noun)
lyrics (plural)
piano (noun)
single (noun)
solo (noun)
track (noun)
tune (noun)

Reviews

award (noun)
bring something to life (phrase)
critic (noun)
distinctive (adj)
ending (noun)
entertaining (adj)
   entertainment (uncount)
original (adj)

realistic (adj)
review (noun)
set (adj)
wide (adj)
   widely (adv)

History

archaeology (uncount)
discovery (noun)
evidence (uncount)
history (uncount)
   historic (adj)
   historical (adj)
record (noun)
site (noun)

ancient (adj)
antique (noun)
century (noun)
original (adj)

ancestor (noun)
civilization (noun)

dinosaur (noun)
hunt (verb)
tribe (noun)

abolish (verb)
attack (verb)
battle (noun)
introduce (verb)
invade (verb)
   invasion (noun)
invent (verb)
   invention (noun)
settle (verb)
survive (verb)

Science & nature

Science

astronomy (uncount)
biology (uncount)
chemistry (uncount)
ecology (uncount)
engineer (noun)
   engineering (uncount)
geography (uncount)
geology (uncount)
mathematics (uncount)
physics (uncount)
psychology (uncount)
science (uncount, noun)
   scientific (adj)
statistics (plural, uncount)

technical (adj)
technology (noun)
virtual (adj)

data (uncount)
discovery (noun)
effect (noun)
equipment (uncount)
experiment (noun)
expert (noun)
findings (plural)
instrument (noun)
investigate (verb)
research (uncount, verb)
software (uncount)
theory (noun)
   theoretical (adj)

The natural world

beach (noun)
cliff (noun)
coast (noun)
countryside (uncount)

desert (noun)
earth (noun)
flow (verb)
forest (noun)
global (adj)
ground (uncount)
hill (noun)
lake (noun)
land (uncount, verb)
mountain (noun)
ocean (noun)
path (noun)
peak (noun)
river (noun)
sea (uncount, noun)
shallow (adj)
shore (noun)
slope (noun)
space (uncount)
steep (adj)
stream (noun)
valley (noun)
waterfall (noun)

dust (uncount)
mud (uncount)
sand (uncount)
soil (uncount)
stone (uncount, noun)

absorb (verb)
straight (adj)

flower (noun)
grow (verb)
in the wild (phrase)
nature (uncount)
   natural (adj)
rainforest (noun)
species (noun)
wild (adj)

wildlife (uncount)
wood (uncount, noun)

The weather
cloudy (adj)
fog (uncount)
frost (uncount)
heat (verb, uncount)
ice (uncount)
monsoon (noun).
rain (uncount, verb)
shower (noun)
snow (uncount, verb)
storm (noun)
sun (uncount)
thunderstorm (noun)
weather forecast (noun)
wind (noun)

cool (adj)
drop (verb)
frozen (adj)
high (adj)
low (adj)
mild (adj)
rise (verb)
temperature (uncount)
thermometer (noun)
warm (adj)

blow (verb)
breeze (noun)
climate (noun)
dry (adj)
gentle (adj)
heavy (adj)
pour (verb)
season (noun)
shade (uncount)
slippery (adj)
wet (adj)

drought (noun)
earthquake (noun)
flood (noun, verb)
    flooding (uncount)
hurricane (noun)

Environmental issues
climate change (uncount)
conservation (uncount)
disposable (adj)
    dispose of (ph verb)
emissions (plural)
endangered (adj)
energy (uncount)
environment (uncount)
    environmental (adj)
    environmentally friendly (adj)
fossil fuel (noun)
fuel (uncount)
global warming (uncount)
green (adj)
impact (noun)
organic (adj)
pollute (verb)
    pollution (uncount)
recycle (verb)
resources (plural)
rubbish (uncount)
solar panel (noun)
sustainable (adj)
waste (verb, noun, uncount)
    wasteful (adj)

Technology

automatic (adj)
engineer (noun)
technical (adj)
technology (noun)
application (noun)

browse (verb)
click (verb)
enter (verb)
home page (noun)
keyword (noun)
laptop (noun)
link (noun)
menu (noun)
online (adj, adv)
password (noun)
sign in (ph verb)
software (uncount)
support (verb, uncount)
tablet (noun)
virtual (adj)
website (noun)

equipment (uncount)
instrument (noun)
machine (noun)
out of order (phrase)
tool (noun)

detective (noun)
investigate (verb)
police officer (noun)

evidence (uncount)
fine (noun, verb)
guilty (adj)
innocent (adj)
law (uncount, noun)
  legal (adj)
  lawyer (noun)
  illegal (adj)
prison (noun)
proof (uncount)
punish (verb)
  punishment (uncount, noun)
solicitor (noun)
witness (noun, verb)

Crime

burglar (noun)
  burglary (noun)
crime (noun)
  criminal (noun)
murder (uncount, verb)
rob (verb)
  robbery (noun)
steal (verb)
theft (uncount)
thief (noun)
vandalism (uncount)
  vandal (noun)
violent (adj)

arrest (verb)

Describing things

combination (noun)
consist of (ph verb)
factor (noun)
involve (verb)
  involved in (adj)
make up (ph verb)
section (noun)

accurate (adj)
approximate (adj)
  approximately (adv)
major (adj)
  majority (uncount)
minor (adj)
  minority (uncount)
per cent (noun)

above all (phrase)
beyond belief (phrase)
significant (adj)
standard (noun)
typically (adv)

alternative (noun, adj)
optional (adj)
particular (adj)
vary (verb)
  variety (noun)

challenging (adj)
demanding (adj)
fact (noun)

Positive qualities

appropriate (adj)
benefit (noun)
convenient (adj)
distinctive (adj)
effective (adj)
efficient (adj)
innovative (adj)
luxury (noun, adj)
peaceful (adj)
positive (adj)
realistic (adj)
relevant (adj)
suitable (adj)
unique (adj)
up-to-date (adj)

amazing (adj)
brilliant (adj)
colourful (adj)
entertaining (adj)
extraordinary (adj)
fantastic (adj)
fascinating (adj)

fortunate (adj)
funny (adj)
genuine (adj)
impressive (adj)
outstanding (adj)
pleasant (adj)
remarkable (adj)
stunning (adj)

Negative qualities

critical (adj)
disapprove (verb)
error (noun)
harmful (adj)
negative (adj)
outrageous (adj)
tricky (adj)
wasteful (adj)
weird (adj)

Time

annual (adj)
daily (adj, adv)
monthly (adj)
regular (adj)
repeat (noun)
routine (noun)
permanent (adj)
temporary (adj)

century (noun)
decade (noun)
fortnight (noun)
gap year (noun)
term (noun)

deadline (noun)
diary (noun)

overtime (uncount)
timetable (noun)

ancient (adj)
current (adj)
historic (adj)
modern (adj)
up-to-date (adj)

all of a sudden (phrase)
at first (phrase)
at last (phrase)
at once (phrase)
at the moment (phrase)

at the last moment/minute
  (phrase)
in the end (phrase)
to start with (phrase)

end up (ph verb)
go on (ph verb)
keep up (ph verb)
last (verb)
pass (verb)
rush (verb)
spend (verb)
take time (phrase)
turn out (ph verb)

Key to grammatical labels in word lists

adj	adjective
adv	adverb
comb	combining form
noun	noun
phrase	phrase
ph verb	phrasal verb
plural	plural noun
uncount	uncountable noun
verb	verb

 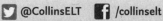

 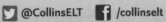